D0915408

German Peasants and
Agrarian Politics, 1914–1924

German Peasants and Agrarian Politics, 1914–1924

The Rhineland and Westphalia

Robert G. Moeller

The University of North Carolina Press

Chapel Hill and London

Library of Congress Cataloging-in-Publication Data

Moeller, Robert G.
    German peasants and agrarian politics, 1914–1924.

    Bibliography: p.
    Includes index.
    1. Peasantry—Germany—Political activity—History—
20th century.   2. Agriculture and state—Germany—
History—20th century.   3. Germany—Politics and govern-
ment—20th century.   4. Germany—History—20th century.
I. Title.
HD1536.G3M64   1986   322.4′4′0943   85-14120
ISBN 0-8078-1676-0

For my parents,

Marian S. and H. G. Moeller

Contents

Illustrations

Tables

Acknowledgments

Why German peasants? Like many other students of modern German history, I came to my subject because of a fascination with the collapse of the Weimar Republic and the triumph of National Socialism. In most accounts of these events peasants were typically presented as particularly zealous opponents of Weimar, but their antagonism toward democratic institutions was more often asserted than explained. I was interested in the political behavior of groups in the middle—between capital and labor—in a period of sustained crisis, and a study of the peasantry in Weimar seemed an excellent way to explore this topic.

In the years that have passed since the inception of this project, I have accumulated many, many debts. The late Geoffrey Barraclough, then at Brandeis University, convinced me of the potential significance of systematic work on the German peasantry. At the University of California, Berkeley, Hans Rosenberg, then emeritus, generously gave of his time and counsel in the early stages of my dissertation research. That work was supervised by Gerald Feldman, who has remained an excellent critic and colleague, and whose influence on this book will be immediately apparent to those who know his important studies of the First World War and Weimar. Jan deVries also provided excellent advice and made me aware of the ways in which historians can learn from economists. During fifteen months of research in Germany, Hans-Jürgen Puhle saved me from the potential isolation of archival work, and he has commented on more than one version of the manuscript since.

Funding for my research was provided in the earliest stages by the German Academic Exchange Service and the Council for European Studies, and later by the Social Science Research Council, the Stiftung Volkswagenwerk, and, most recently, by the Columbia University Council for Research in the Social Sciences. The generous support of these institutions was invaluable. Ann Keisling, who spent a long year with the German peasantry, was an excellent research assistant. She and Alexander Wells helped with the final stages of manuscript preparation. Special thanks are due the archivists in the Federal Republic of Germany and the German Democratic Republic who helped to lead me through the documents. Martin Schumacher made me aware of the extensive resources of the Landwirtschaftskammer Rheinland, whose officials graciously granted me access to it and to materials now in the Nordrhein-Westfälisches Hauptstaatsarchiv in Düsseldorf. The librarians of the Landwirtschaftskammer Westfalen-Lippe similarly allowed me to work in their invaluable collection of rare, published sources. Crucial for my work as well were the personal papers of Engelbert Freiherr Kerckerinck zu Borg; my thanks to his son, Max Freiherr Kerckerinck zu Borg, who granted me permission to use this collection, and to Max Freiherr von Twickel, formerly of the Landschaftsverband Westfalen-Lippe, who first informed me of this rich source.

The progression from dissertation to book was greatly facilitated by my participation in a multi-year project, funded by the Stiftung Volkswagenwerk, that investigated "Inflation and Reconstruction in Europe, 1914–24." The opportunity to meet regularly over a five-year period with German, American, and British colleagues offered me many occasions to discuss my work and to learn from the criticisms and ongoing research of the other members in the project. In particular, I am grateful for the insights offered by Jens Flemming, Carl-Ludwig Holtfrerich, Claus-Dieter Krohn, Andreas Kunz, Jonathan Osmond, and Peter-Christian Witt. In addition, I learned much from discussions of my work at Princeton University's Shelby Cullom Davis Center, Columbia University's Seminar in Economic History, and the New York University Seminar in European Social History.

I also benefited enormously from the critical comments of friends and colleagues who took time from their own work to respond to mine. David Abraham, David Blackbourn, Shearer Davis Bowman, Jane Caplan, James Cronin, David Ringrose, Ronald Ross, Reinhard Rürup, Hanna Schissler, and Reginald Zelnik have commented on parts of the manuscript. Renate Bridenthal, Robert Edelman, Geoff Eley, William Mathews, and Mary Nolan all read through the dissertation or early versions of this manuscript, offered a range of critical perspectives that forced me to define my own more carefully, and lent me the encouragement and support that helped me through the final stages of completing the manuscript. I first met Thomas Childers and Larry Jones in the "Inflation and Reconstruction" research group; both offered valuable suggestions for my work in that project, and both undertook a close critical reading of an earlier version of this manuscript as well. Their constructive comments were extremely useful, and they unselfishly shared with me their own considerable knowledge of Weimar. Both have contributed much to making this a better book. Lewis Bateman, my editor, provided consistently sound advice as well.

Thanks are also due to the editors of the following journals for permission to use parts of materials that they first published: to *Agricultural History* for "Peasants and Tariffs in the *Kaiserreich*: How Backward Were the *Bauern*?"; and to *Central European History* for "Dimensions of Social Conflict in the Great War: The View from the German Countryside." The editors of *Die deutsche Inflation: Eine Zwischenbilanz* (Berlin, 1982) also granted permission to use parts of "Winners as Losers in the German Inflation: Peasant Protest over the Controlled Economy 1920–1923," which first appeared there.

The assistance offered by Heidrun Homburg and Josef Mooser deserves special note: not only have they given me intellectual support throughout the entire project, they have also repeatedly offered hospitality and friendship to sustain me through numerous research trips to Germany. In this country, my intellectual and emotional life has been vastly improved by Lynn Mally, who took time from her own studies of Russian workers and proletarian culture to learn far more about Rhenish and Westphalian peasants than she had ever hoped or wanted to.

Finally, my parents, H. G. and Marian S. Moeller, to whom this book is dedicated, raised me to make my own decisions, even when they did not totally comprehend them. I'm not sure they have always understood why I wanted to write this book, but without their support it never would have been written.

German Peasants and
Agrarian Politics, 1914–1924

Introduction

Peasants were not among the supporters of the Weimar Republic. Any student of Weimar's collapse knows that the 30 percent of all Germans who still earned their living from agriculture in the 1920s were overrepresented among those most ready to back the right-wing causes that wished nothing more than an end to parliamentary, democratic government in Germany. However, despite the generally acknowledged significance of the peasantry in shaping the electoral fortunes of the Nazis and in contributing to the demise of parliamentary politics in the 1920s, there are surprisingly few investigations that analyze the sources of peasant antagonism toward Weimar democracy.[1] Most works that do examine this phenomenon concentrate largely on the late 1920s and the Nazis' turn to rural voters, and these studies tend to trace the political radicalization of the countryside to the agrarian crisis of Weimar's later years.[2]

Another established framework of analysis identifies the origins of the peasants' antagonism toward Weimar and their support for right-wing political solutions not in the Great Depression of the 1920s but in the "Great Depression" of the last quarter of the nineteenth century. From this perspective, peasant acceptance of National Socialism is the final step along a straight path that originates with peasant rejection of industrial society in the late nineteenth century. Antidemocratic, antisocialist, antiparliamentary, anticapitalist attitudes, entrenched in the German countryside long before the 1920s, survive with little difficulty into Weimar and find their culmination in the triumph of the Nazis.[3]

At key points, the long- and short-term explanations of peasant antagonism toward Weimar converge. Common to both is an emphasis on the peasantry's willingness to follow the lead of others—whether traditional, aristocratic, conservative elites, or those espousing a populist rhetoric of *Blut und Boden*. Not only were peasants unable to articulate their own interests; with apparent ease, they were manipulated by outsiders to support policies and programs that often contradicted those interests.

This book rejects both of these alternatives and locates the sources of agrarian antagonism toward Weimar in a different context. It focuses on the First World War and the early years of Weimar democracy and argues that an explanation of the peasantry's hostility toward parliamentary politics must be found there. This study questions those analyses that concentrate only on the years immediately preceding Weimar's collapse as well as those that stress the continuities in rural political attitudes from the late nineteenth century to the 1920s. Instead, it

3

stresses the significance of a period of radical discontinuity in the rocky transition from Kaiserreich to Weimar: the decade of war and inflation, 1914–23. From the perspective of the German peasantry, these years of military defeat, revolution, and dramatic political change were unified by the suspension of a normally functioning market and by sustained state intervention into the agricultural sector. This book seeks to establish that peasant rejection of parliamentary institutions was firmly grounded in the immediate circumstances of the war economy and the uneven process of postwar recovery. It emphasizes that conservative agrarian ideology was carefully formulated in response to the specific peasant grievances that originated in this period of ongoing economic and political crisis.[4]

The findings of this study are based on a regional examination of the northern Rhineland and the province of Westphalia, the present-day state of North-Rhine Westphalia (Nordrheinwestfalen), divided in the late nineteenth century and in Weimar into two Prussian provinces.[5] This regional focus marks an intentional move away from the historiographical fascination with the Junkers, grain-growing estate owners east of the Elbe; their political arm, the Agrarian League (Bund der Landwirte); and its successor in Weimar, the Rural League (Reichslandbund).[6] Perhaps because of their obvious political significance, these actors have dominated the literature of modern German agrarian history with the consequence that their experience has often been read as the experience of *all* German agrarians. Recent discussions of modern German social history have emphasized the potentially distorting "Prussocentric" bias that characterizes much of the research on the Kaiserreich and Weimar.[7] This book stresses that there were great differences *within* Prussia as well. The Rhineland and Westphalia, unlike the east Elbian home of the Junkers, were areas of peasant farms seldom exceeding fifty hectares, not large estates. The principal source of agricultural labor was not large teams of migrant Polish seasonal laborers, but the peasant family. Peasant production decisions were influenced less by the foreign export markets where Junkers sold their grains than by nearby urban markets for dairy and livestock products. In short, in the Rhineland and Westphalia the patterns of production and the structure of rural social relations differed significantly from those in the eastern and northern parts of Prussia.[8]

More than social structure and crop rotations distinguished east Elbian Junkers from peasant farmers in the Rhineland and Westphalia: confession divided them as well. Rhenish and Westphalian peasants were overwhelmingly Catholic in a predominantly Protestant Prussia, and their religion shaped their electoral behavior. They found their political home not with the Junkers in the Conservative party during the Kaiserreich, nor in the German National People's Party (DNVP, Deutschnationale Volkspartei) in Weimar, but rather in the Center party, a confessionally-based political organization that drew on a socially heterogeneous constituency. Catholic peasant electoral behavior throughout the period covered by this study reveals a constancy that testifies to the strength of confessional bonds. It also makes this region of particular interest as a case study of conservative agrarian influence within the Center, and of that party's difficulties in balancing the conflicting interests of its diverse constituency.[9]

This book's provincial lens provides a magnified look at many aspects of peasant economy and politics that remain blurred or unnoticed in studies focused on the national level.[10] It does not fully capture others. When the local level and the village emerge in the provincial archival record, their voices are heard in this study as well; at other times, however, they are silent. This decision to pay more attention to elite, interest-group politics than to the cultural, religious, and associational life of the village is not meant to dismiss the impact of local events on peasant political attitudes. As a student of Rhenish rural society in the 1920s observed, "a drinking circle or a bowling club can absorb its members more than a [political] party."[11] Formal and informal institutions at the local level can shape what Rudy Koshar has recently labeled "apolitical politics," essential to the "maintenance of social hegemony" through ostensibly nonpolitical structures.[12] The present work, however, offers an analysis of neither the village nor the German agricultural sector as a whole, neither the parish pump nor the nation; like the provincial level on which it focuses, it lies in between. From this perspective, it offers an analysis of conservative agrarian politics in Weimar, and outlines a full range of questions to be asked and hypotheses to be tested at other levels.

Where this study does capture peasants most completely is in their lives as economic actors, and it is in this area that its conclusions can most readily be generalized. For peasant farmers in advanced capitalist societies, no other aspect of their existence has so profound an impact on the demands that they place on their political leaders and interest-group organizations. For a number of reasons, economic concerns are at the center of the peasant's life. The borders between the structure of economic enterprise and the family are unclear when family members constitute the farm's labor force and when co-workers, related by blood, share a common table and residence. The family farm is at once the site of production and of consumption, both workplace and home. The economic decision to expand livestock herds or to introduce a new crop rotation, for example, has an immediate impact on familial relations; new patterns of production mean a renegotiated division of labor within the family. Peasants seldom leave their place of work, and their lives are in large part determined by the annual cycles inherent in production. The demands of production also determine the application of the peasant's various skills as entrepreneur, salesperson, agronomist, veterinarian, and laborer.

Peasant associational life often concentrates on shared occupational concerns. Interest-group organizations that become a locus for peasant politics are frequently formed initially to pursue specific economic objectives. Even peasant social events are occasioned by economic ones—markets, hiring fairs, livestock auctions. Religious events are no exception: a wedding can reflect a property merger, and "love" is equated with "calculation." A blessing of the fields and prayers for a good harvest are no idle rituals, even if individual producers know that they ultimately can blame no one but themselves for their production decisions. Understandably, those decisions preoccupy them more than the decisions of an industrial entrepreneur preoccupy the workers and white-collar employees who execute orders that they themselves have not determined.[13]

It is this quality of control and independence that unifies peasant producers with one another and with other small-scale business concerns in which individuals own their own shops and tools.[14] Like that of the other groups of small-scale producers in a capitalist economy, the attention of peasants is riveted on the market. Their ability to plan production, to read relative prices, to decide what to market when, and to schedule the purchase of machinery and other production goods immediately affects their economic welfare and, in the long term, their ability to pass on their farm to their heirs. Even if they have little control over its workings, they confront the market directly.

To list these aspects of peasant farming is not to romanticize the independent producer, but rather to suggest the ways in which economic concerns assume a greater significance for the peasantry than for many other occupational groups. It also explains why an analysis of the peasantry's economic welfare looms so large in this study and in the political programs and rhetoric of those who seek to represent peasant interests.

Still, the argument of this book is not that peasant political attitudes can be explained entirely in terms of economic interests or of the influence of the organizations that seek to represent those interests. On the contrary, this study devotes considerable attention to the determination of electoral behavior and political loyalties by a distinctly noneconomic element—religious confession. Suzanne Berger, writing of French peasants in the twentieth century, argues that "politicization" takes place when "individuals or communities perceive the links between local events and the problems of private life, on the one hand, and national political events and structures on the other. Where social and economic well-being are understood to be the product of purely local forces and decisions, where the events of private life are interpreted as the result of personal qualities or failings, there are no national politics."[15] This book confirms Berger's insight, and concentrates on a period in which direct state intervention into the market for agricultural products made the relationship between "national political events" and the "problems of private life" immediately apparent. However, the forms of peasant political response to state intervention during the First World War and the postwar inflation must be seen against the background of another instance of forceful government intervention into the Rhenish and Westphalian countryside. In the 1870s, Bismarck's attack on German Catholicism—the *Kulturkampf*—was a clear example of the intervention of the national government into the lives of its Catholic citizenry, and its lasting political impact was undeniable; it stigmatized a

Catholic minority within a Protestant Prussia, and in the process it firmly tied Rhenish and Westphalian peasants to the Center party.[16]

The legacy of the *Kulturkampf* in the Rhenish and Westphalian countryside fully supports Berger's observation that the political forms adopted by peasants are dependent on the way they "were organized when the impact of national decisions on the substance of peasant life began to be felt by important sectors of the rural community."[17] Once pledged to the Center party, Catholic peasants remained there, as did the Catholic aristocrats who assumed leading roles in agricultural interest groups and within provincial and national party hierarchies. The *Kulturkampf* also permanently placed confessional concerns on the party's political agenda.

State intervention into peasants' lives in the years 1914–23 was no less profound in its impact, but it was of a very different sort: at issue was peasant economic well-being, rather than confessional concerns. Under the controlled economy (*Zwangswirtschaft*), instituted in the fall of 1914 and maintained in direct and indirect forms until the fall of 1923, the effect of official policy on peasant economic welfare was direct and immediately perceptible. This book argues that state intervention into the market was the central dimension of peasant experience in the war and in the period of postwar reconstruction. The controlled economy defined an element of continuity that survived the radical changes in political forms after 1918–19 and created a solid basis for the conservative organization of the agricultural sector. The ongoing conflict over economic controls exacerbated the tensions between peasant producers and urban consumers both within the nation and within the Catholic Center. This study investigates the nature of these conflicts and their political implications for the early history of Weimar.

These are the broad outlines that frame this book. The narrative that fills them proceeds in a straightforward, chronological fashion. The first two chapters set the scene, define the region, describe the nature of peasant social structure and production patterns, and introduce the agricultural interest groups that organized peasants in the late nineteenth century; assessing the impact of the decade of war and inflation is possible only against this background. The following two chapters concentrate on the peasantry's experience under the state-imposed controls of the First World War, and on the political response of agricultural interest groups to government intervention and the postwar revolution of 1918–19. State intervention into the agricultural sector was maintained in the early years of the Weimar Republic, and peasant resistance to controls survived as well; these topics occupy Chapter 5, which also touches on the problems confronted by the national government in formulating agricultural policy during the postwar inflation. Chapter 6 again focuses on interest-group leaders in their attempts to define a political response to the crisis of the early postwar years. Chapter 7 outlines an economic and political balance sheet for the agricultural sector during the decade of war and inflation. Of course, the implications of this story extend beyond the end of the inflation in the fall of 1923; thus, Chapter 7 also briefly suggests the significance of this ten-year period for the political behavior of the peasantry in the later years of the Weimar Republic, and for the ultimate acceptance, even by a peasantry politically immunized by its religion, of the alternative offered by National Socialism.[18]

ONE

Learning to "Complain without Suffering": Peasant Farming in the Kaiserreich

When the citizens of the newly unified Reich were officially counted in the first nation-wide occupational census in 1882, 41.6 percent of all Germans still earned their livelihood in the agricultural sector. It was only in the next two decades that Germany became an industrial nation, undergoing the irreversible transformation from *Agrar-* to *Industriestaat*. In no regions was this transformation more pronounced and dramatic than in the northern Rhineland and the western part of Westphalia. Before the middle of the nineteenth century, this part of western Germany already constituted a major center of early industrialization, particularly for metal-working and textile production—but the development in the last decades of the century was of a different scale, characterized by the rapid expansion of heavy industry, particularly mining and the production of iron and steel. Industrial expansion meant the creation of entirely new cities, each of which was virtually dominated by a single concern. Established cities expanded as well, and the Ruhr emerged as the urban heartland of an industrial Germany.[1]

Not surprisingly, these developments made the Rhineland and Westphalia far better known for their mines and factories than for their farms.[2] However, industrial growth in the Ruhr did not mean that Rhenish and Westphalian peasants disappeared from the landscape in the late nineteenth century. Outside of the Ruhr—which lies between the Ruhr and Lippe rivers, extending westward across the Rhine to Krefeld and southward to include Düsseldorf and Hagen[3]—agriculture remained a major employer (see Appendix Table 1). Indeed, total employment in agriculture remained fairly constant throughout the period of most rapid industrialization, and even relative figures do not indicate the complete disappearance of the agricultural sector. By 1907 agriculture's share in total employment had fallen, but in many counties it still remained well above 30 percent (see map and Appendix Table 2).

In fact, the process of advanced industrialization in western Germany was paralleled by a process of "agriculturalization" in the surrounding countryside. The concentration of industry in urban centers and the decline of rural industry made for a greater occupational homogeneity among those who remained outside the cities.[4] Homogeneity also characterized the social origins of the rural popula-

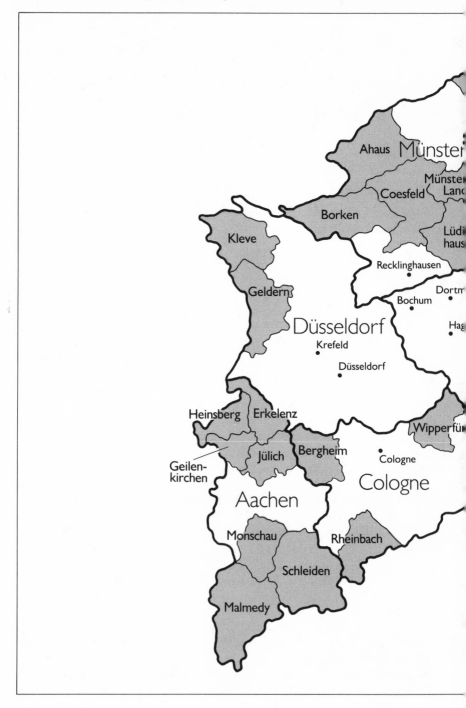

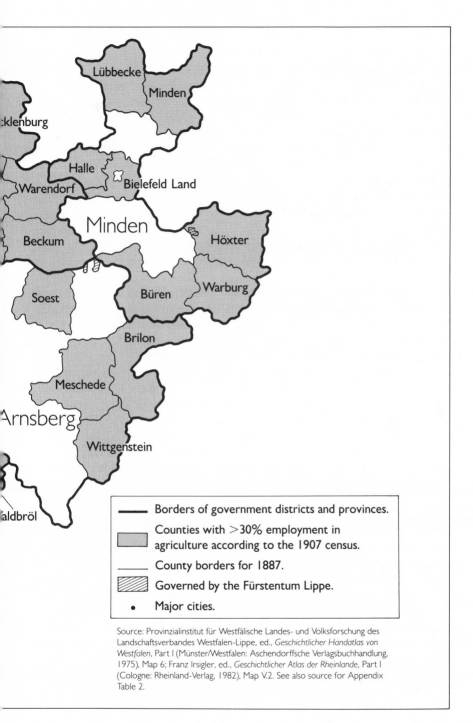

Lübbecke

Minden

:klenburg

Halle

Warendorf

Bielefeld Land

Minden

Beckum

Höxter

Soest

Büren

Warburg

Brilon

Meschede

Arnsberg

Wittgenstein

aldbröl

—— Borders of government districts and provinces.

☐ Counties with >30% employment in
    agriculture according to the 1907 census.

___ County borders for 1887.

▨ Governed by the Fürstentum Lippe.

• Major cities.

Source: Provinzialinstitut für Westfälische Landes- und Volksforschung des
Landschaftsverbandes Westfalen-Lippe, ed., *Geschichtlicher Handatlas von
Westfalen*, Part I (Münster/Westfalen: Aschendorffsche Verlagsbuchhandlung,
1975), Map 6; Franz Irsigler, ed., *Geschichtlicher Atlas der Rheinlande*, Part I
(Cologne: Rheinland-Verlag, 1982), Map V.2. See also source for Appendix
Table 2.

tion: after 1890 an expanding industrial labor force came from outside the Rhineland and Westphalia, particularly from east of the Elbe, and by 1905 as much as 20 percent of the population in some Ruhr cities was Polish-speaking;[5] in contrast, the overwhelming majority of those employed in the agricultural sector had never lived beyond the borders of their home counties, and almost none came from outside the province of their birth (see Appendix Table 3).[6] To rural inhabitants, the city and its occupants became increasingly foreign. The split between town and country that was emphasized in romantic, agrarian rhetoric had a firm basis in reality.[7]

Rural society was increasingly distinct from urban life in other important respects. Beyond the obvious differences in the nature of agricultural and industrial production, a comparison of labor relations in the two contexts reveals significant contrasts. In the cities, large numbers of wage-earning workers confronted a handful of employers, and most of these workers were men; particularly in the Ruhr, heavy industry provided few factory jobs for women. In contrast, the farming communities of the Rhineland and Westphalia were characterized by holdings worked by peasant families, and women were employed alongside men (see Appendix Tables 1, 4, and 5).[8] Labor relations approximating those in large-scale industries did exist on big estates like those that dominated the countryside in many regions east of the Elbe, but in the Rhineland and Westphalia such estates were few in number, and they were often rented out to peasant tenant farmers. An agricultural proletariat did not confront a class of large landowning employers.

Rural social stratification in the Rhineland and Westphalia was not characterized by tremendous extremes among peasant farmers (see Appendix Tables 6 and 7). "Dwarf" peasant holdings like those in southwest Germany were not as rare as large estates,[9] but marginal producers—farming less than two hectares—were most often only part-time peasants, employed primarily in industrial jobs.[10] The dominant custom of primogeniture prevented farms from being divided anew with every generation, and even in those exceptional areas of partible inheritance, efforts were made to maintain large farms intact.[11]

It was such characteristics that led late nineteenth- and early twentieth-century observers to see these regions as "classic peasant country," home of the "true" peasantry.[12] This "true" peasantry, according to contemporary usage, was comprised of those who farmed land extensive enough to support and employ the farm family and to necessitate a draft team of horses or oxen. In the Rhineland and Westphalia, this included few holdings of less than five hectares and few greater than fifty hectares.[13] The Reich's first occupational census of 1882 revealed clearly that farms between these limits encompassed most of the arable land in these regions, and rural social stratification changed very little before 1914 (see Appendix Tables 6 and 7). When contemporaries referred to peasants, it was these family farmers they meant, and it is such peasant farmers who are at the center of this study.[14]

Patterns of Peasant Production: Bases for Accommodation and Change

Not only a relatively homogeneous social structure distinguished western Germany from the southwest and from the regions east of the Elbe; so too did the market structures confronting Rhenish and Westphalian agricultural producers. These were not subsistence farmers covering only their own consumption and holding the market at arm's length,[15] nor were they oriented toward the export markets where east Elbian Junkers had sold their grain since the sixteenth century.[16] Agricultural products from farms in the Rhineland and Westphalia traveled short distances to consumers in nearby cities, and the shifting demand patterns generated by these consumers—not fluctuating grain prices on the world market—were the principal determinants of the production decisions of peasant farmers. Tremendous improvements in the transportation system in the late nineteenth century meant that the cities became even more reliable markets, and the expanding urban areas consumed virtually everything that the surrounding countryside could produce.[17]

It is worth emphasizing the structural differences between the agricultural markets east and west of the Elbe because descriptions of German agriculture's fate in the late nineteenth century often blur these important distinctions. German agricultural producers are frequently portrayed as universally entering into an irreversible downturn beginning with the onset of the "Great Depression" in the 1870s—yet the fall of agricultural prices after 1873 had very different consequences in different parts of Germany. East Elbian grain producers had once competed effectively in, and depended on, world markets, but after 1870 an improved international shipping network brought inexpensive grain from Argentina, Australia, and the Great Plains of the United States onto the world market and into Germany as well. The flood of cheap grain coincided with a general price deflation. Exacerbating the east Elbian crisis further were rapidly rising labor costs, due to the emigration of wage laborers abroad and to west German industry.[18]

Rhenish and Westphalian peasants producing for nearby markets and facing low transport costs also suffered from declining grain prices, but not with the same severity. Competition with industry for labor presented a challenge, but the primary reliance on the labor of the farm family made this threat less serious. Losses in income from grains were countered, at least in part, by relatively less dramatic declines in meat prices, and falling prices did not halt continued gains in output and productivity achieved during the "Great Depression."[19]

Moreover, agricultural producers in western Germany proved far more flexible than their counterparts east of the Elbe in adjusting their patterns of production to shifts in relative prices for their goods. A close look at production patterns in the Rhineland and Westphalia reveals that while east Elbian grain producers were reeling from the blow of price declines, revived only by the assurance of tariff protection after 1879, peasant farmers west of the Elbe were discovering alternative survival strategies. Shifts in the structure of production permitted them to adjust to the decline in agricultural prices and reflected an aggressive response to altered market structures that did not conform with popular conceptions of peasant resistance to change.[20]

It was the peasant support of tariffs in 1878–79 that prompted charges of rural economic backwardness.[21] For liberal critics of tariff protection in the late nineteenth century—and for many liberal historians since—a continued commitment to the production of grains in the face of declining prices and competition from lower-cost production areas was an irrefutable index of peasant unwillingness to confront increased market competition.[22] Tariffs, these critics argued, did not benefit most peasants. In fact, by increasing bread prices, tariffs decreased the disposable income of consumers that could have been used to buy the high-quality dairy and livestock goods produced on peasant farms. According to this argument, peasants accepted the economically irrational proposition that measures in the best interests of grain-growing Junkers were measures in the best interests of all agricultural producers. The alternative scenario most often proposed by critics was for peasants to end grain production and commit all their resources to dairy farming, relying exclusively on purchased feed. The suggestion of concrete alternatives usually extended no further than references to the Danish and Dutch examples, where presumably a much more efficient and rational adjustment to changed market conditions was possible in the absence of agricultural protection, and cheap imported feeds replaced those grown on the farm.[23]

There is certainly no question that Rhenish and Westphalian peasants continued to devote their energies to the production of bread grains throughout the Kaiserreich (see Appendix Table 9). That such practices represented an irrational retreat behind tariff walls is, however, less unambiguous. On one level, a system of price supports borne ultimately by the consumer need not necessarily represent a retreat from the realities of the market. Indeed, German iron and steel producers also sought protection from foreign competition, at least until the late 1880s—but they have not been charged with economic backwardness. Moreover, tariffs on bread grains were part of a package that included a comprehensive set of veterinary restrictions inhibiting imports of foreign meat, and lower tariff levels on those grains actually used for livestock feeds.[24] Peasants might also market some grains, and the evidence from the Rhineland and Westphalia indicates that even the smallest farm typically received at least 10 to 20 percent of its income from this source.[25]

In addition, the ex post facto options of producing *either* grains *or* dairy and livestock products were not among those carefully considered by most Rhenish and Westphalian agricultural producers, nor were they recommended by contemporary agricultural economists. Rather, established practice and scientific counsel emphasized the merits of a diversified system of production. Exclusive concentration on a single product was seen as excessively risky. Far preferable was the form of mixed farming—livestock production, particularly cattle, alongside grains and root crops—that had long prevailed in the Rhineland and Westphalia. In its many permutations, it was an outgrowth of the improved three-field crop rotation that was in use throughout western Europe by the end of the eighteenth century. Grains, hay, and root crops provided the basic winter feed supply; stall-feeding in winter allowed easier collection of manure; greater supplies of manure permitted better fertilization and reduction of the fallow, and in turn stimulated higher yields of grains and root crops. Rising urban demand for livestock products in the second half of the nineteenth century simply meant that the function of livestock changed: cattle no longer served solely as producers of manure, but became important sources of marketable meat and dairy products as well. As agricultural economists put it, cattle ceased to be means to an end and became ends in themselves.[26]

Contemporary agricultural economists warned against covering feed needs with purchased feeds, and self-sufficiency in basic feed production was praised as a virtue. Many grains thus were used as feeds and reached the market only indirectly.[27] What grains were sold, particularly under protected prices, provided a steady and reliable source of income to cover the costs of tariff-free imported feed supplements or high-quality basic feeds such as corn or barley, which were excellent for pig-fattening and on which tariffs were relatively low.[28]

Since basic feeds were produced on the farm, arable output had to expand with expanded livestock holdings.[29] Precisely the organic relation between livestock and arable farming made this possible. More cattle receiving better feed, particularly during winter stall-feeding, produced more and higher quality manure. Since manure had a very low market value, it was almost always used on the farm. Better fertilization further increased yields, which in turn increased the feed supply and the size of the livestock herd that the feed supply could support.

Within this organic system, there was much room for adjustment to shifting relative prices. Bumper crops and declining prices for rye could be countered by the expansion of pig holdings. Under normal circumstances, peasants might well fatten pigs only for their own consumption,[30] but when grain prices fell, pigs could be purchased for fattening. Prices for all grains tended to move in the same direction, with the result that barley, the most important grain for pig-fattening, was typically cheap in the same years that rye prices were down. Using rye as pig feed was an easier adjustment than curtailing rye production and purchasing barley in the short term.[31] The expansion of pig-fattening when grain and potato prices were low is only one example of the system's flexibility. Milk cows could be bought or bred. Calves could be butchered when still young, sold for fattening, or fattened on the farm. Milk could be sold as fresh milk or made into butter, leaving the skim milk as feed for calves and piglets.[32]

Of course, some shifts in the organization and nature of production could not be made so easily. If livestock herds were greatly expanded, costly new stalls had to be built. High costs were also associated with the process of bringing land under cultivation by drainage or of transforming arable land into pasture. Such changes represented long-term investments. In addition, the production time for many agricultural products placed restrictions on the peasant's ability to adjust to shifting prices.[33] Moreover, not all peasant producers benefited uniformly from the increases in output. The expansion of livestock holdings, for example, was not equally distributed across all farms, and those farming more than ten hectares shared disproportionately in the increases in holdings of cattle (see Appendix Table 10). Bigger farms often had more pasture land—an advantage for dairy farming, which depended heavily on grazing—and larger herds of cattle permitted better breeding. Peasants with large holdings were also in a better position to sell off small plots of land to finance capital improvements.[34] Often the peasants on smaller farms devoted more attention to pig-fattening and planted more of their arable land in rye and potatoes to cover their feed needs (see Appendix Table 11). In other cases, small farms in the immediate proximity of urban markets might concentrate particularly on pig production or on labor-intensive production of vegetables and fruits.[35] But for most peasants the mixed-farming system was quite flexible, within certain constraints, and it assured them a regular income that was not dependent on the sales of any single product.

The diversified system practiced by most west German peasants thus resembled a vertically concentrated industry, encompassing all stages of production from raw materials to the finished product. The decision of what to market and what to use in the production process was a highly complex one, reached by individual peasants using their knowledge of their fields, their livestock, and their labor force as well as of the long-term relative price trends. Decisions about the production of livestock were never made independently of decisions about the use of arable land.[36] For agricultural producers in the Rhineland and Westphalia, the support for tariffs was thus in no way inconsistent with other less defensive forms of response to changing market conditions. Perhaps alternative forms of adjustment existed,[37] but they seldom appeared in the theories of agricultural economists or in the practice of Rhenish and Westphalian agricultural producers.

Labor Relations in the Countryside

One additional consideration explained the continued commitment of Rhenish and Westphalian peasants to a diversified system of mixed farming: it provided excellent opportunities for fully employing the entire farm family. Farms that concentrated on grain production required large numbers of temporary agricultural wage-laborers at certain restricted periods during the year, for harvesting and planting. But the greater the emphasis on livestock and dairy farming, the easier it was to employ family members in a production process that spread the demand for labor fairly evenly over the year. Moreover, as wage-laborers became less readily available in areas near urban industrial centers, the labor of the farm family became increasingly vital to the farm. The shift in production toward a labor-intensive organic system increased the viability of the family farm and made it an extremely efficient production unit,[38] particularly at a time when complaints about the scarcity of agricultural wage labor were chronic. Indeed, it was those labor shortages and the related problem of an increasing agricultural wage bill that upset west Elbian peasants far more than competition from foreign grain producers.[39]

Still, farms of more than twenty hectares continued to employ small numbers of wage-earners (see Appendix Tables 4 and 5). Although seldom exceeding the number of family members employed on the farm, these workers were essential, and their escalating wage demands provided another indication of the impact of nearby cities on peasant production. Industry offered not only higher wages, but also shorter work hours and more regular employment. Rural employers could remain competitive with industrial employers only by meeting their workers' demands for wage increases.[40] Among those agricultural workers first to leave the countryside were casually employed day-laborers (*Tagelöhner*), who easily found alternative employment when industry's demand for unskilled labor increased. Women workers were often in even shorter supply than men, and particularly in the eastern part of Westphalia they turned away from agriculture to employment in the textile industry.[41]

Another source of labor also proved increasingly unreliable. Until the late nineteenth century in much of Westphalia, particularly in the northern part of the district of Münster and in the eastern part of the province (the Minden-Ravensberg area), a large part of the labor force had consisted of *Heuerlinge*. These were agricultural workers who were given a small plot of land at a significantly reduced rent with a long-term lease, usually anywhere from three to twelve years. In addition, the landlord provided a draft team for plowing and wagons at harvest time. *Heuerlinge* received the major share of their cash income from livestock sales and held two to three cows at most. They needed a steady cash income to cover their feed requirements, since their arable land was typically not large enough to produce feed to cover these needs. In return for his reduced rent and other services from his landlord, the *Heuerling* was obliged to work on the landlord's farm a set number of days annually, usually for wages below the market rate. Although called by different names, similar labor arrangements had long existed in other parts of the Rhineland and Westphalia.[42]

This labor system originated partly in response to the pattern of isolated single-family farm settlement in these areas.[43] The absence of village settlement meant that a labor supply could be guaranteed only by renting workers small plots of land, thus tying them to peasant farms. The origins of the system lay also in the widespread practice of primogeniture: for peasant sons and daughters who did not inherit a substantial holding, a *Heuerstelle*, the small plot of land that a *Heuerling* farmed, provided an opportunity to accumulate some capital and ultimately to rent or purchase an independent holding.

This system of labor relations was highly regarded as a means of maintaining an adequate rural labor force in the countryside while providing an avenue for the upward mobility of agricultural workers. However, by the end of the nineteenth century, this optimistic assessment conformed less and less with the realities of rural labor relations. Except for their contractual obligation to provide their landlord with labor services, many of these renter-workers closely approximated other smallholding peasants who owned or rented their land. Over time, rents increased as labor services diminished, and many tenants had one foot firmly planted in the industrial sector and received a large part of their income from industrial employment.[44]

Certainly by the end of the nineteenth century, peasant-*Heuerling* relations had lost all paternalistic vestiges. As one investigator of rural labor observed in 1910, "We are dealing with the ruins of an old labor system."[45] Students of the system as a possible model for maintaining a reliable work force east of the Elbe concluded that, as a means to provide employers with a steady labor supply and workers with a springboard for upward social mobility, "the *Heuerlinge* exist only in the minds of the professors."[46] Indeed, one critical student of rural labor relations, a young Max Weber, charged that the myth of upward mobility could not accord with reality: industrial development not only drove up wages, drawing the *Heuerlinge* into industrial employment, but also drove up land prices, making it increasingly difficult to expand landholdings through purchase.[47] Children of smallholding peasants who faced impediments to upward social mobility in the countryside chose the alternative of mobility into industrial employment. The distinction between those *Heuerlinge* who remained in the agricultural sector and agricultural laborers with a smallholding became less and less clear.[48]

The decline of the institution of the *Heuerling*, coupled with the departure of casual agricultural workers for jobs in industry, forced employers to search for other ways to meet their labor needs. Their solution to this chronic problem of labor scarcity was not that frequently adopted east of the Elbe—importing foreign workers from Prussian Poland and Galicia.[49] Seasonal workers from east of the Elbe often worked in teams too large to be used efficiently on the smaller west Elbian farms. Moreover, employers confronted the possibility that seasonal workers who were brought long distances at great expense would break their contracts and flee to employment in industry at the earliest possible opportunity.[50]

The solutions to problems of labor shortages more commonly took other forms. In addition to increased reliance on family labor, many peasants farming more than twenty hectares expanded their use of machinery, particularly for threshing; those who could not afford a large machine often owned one collectively with neighbors (see Appendix Tables 12 and 13).[51] Employers also turned to contractually bound workers employed for a year at a time (*Gesinde*). These hired hands had specifically defined skills and responsibilities, and their salaries varied accordingly. Like the demand for family labor, the demand for these full-time salaried workers was also stimulated by the shifts in emphasis of production outlined above.[52]

Some contemporary writers tried to minimize the social distance between these workers and their employers. *Knechte* (servants) and *Mägde* (maids), they argued, were more like family members than hired help: they were recruited from the families of smallholders or *Heuerlinge* and came from the same sociocultural milieu as their peasant employers; they shared their meals with their employers and slept under the same roof. This romanticized vision undoubtedly never had too firm a basis in reality, and by the late nineteenth and early twentieth century it had little to do with the conditions of rural wage labor. Rather, relations between contractually bound workers and their employers became increasingly formal and clearly defined.

When contractual workers could not be recruited locally, they were most often brought by hiring agencies from the neighboring province of Hanover or across the western border from Holland. These workers, even if they were German, often spoke different dialects and came from cultural backgrounds different from those of their employers. The ideal of the trusted worker who stayed on with one employer for years contrasted sharply with the reality that workers often remained no longer than two or three years with one employer. And in areas closer to urban centers, workers sometimes simply broke their contracts to leave for industrial employment. For those who stayed, wages included fewer payments in kind and were reckoned strictly in monetary terms. In addition, the social distance between workers and employers became more pronounced.

Nonetheless, the increasingly formal relations between employers and employees did not lead to labor conflict or to widespread attempts at unionization. Although many Rhenish and Westphalian peasants hired some outside help, even on a farm of fifty hectares the total work force was never very large. The problems confronting those who tried to organize agricultural wage-earners on large estates east of the Elbe were only exaggerated in this context. Moreover, agricultural laborers enjoyed no legal rights to strike and organize: in Prussia throughout the Wilhelmine period, the status of agricultural workers was narrowly prescribed by legislation that dated back to the early part of the nineteenth century. The most effective form of agricultural labor protest was not a vain struggle against repressive employers and a legal system that virtually forbade organization, but the departure from the countryside for employment in industry.[53]

Agricultural Prosperity in the Age of Kaiser Wilhelm

By now, it should be clear that any picture of an economically backward peasantry, unwilling or unable to adjust to changed circumstances, accorded more with the popular imagination of urban agrarian ideologues than it did with the structure of the peasant economy in the Rhenish and Westphalian countryside. Both the forms of adjustment to changing patterns of demand and the shifting contours of rural labor relations provide ample evidence that Rhenish and Westphalian agricultural producers squarely confronted and successfully mastered the problems posed by the market in an advanced industrial economy. Their dynamic responses to declining grain prices and labor shortages were far more effective than the loud cries of east Elbian estate owners for ever-higher tariffs or heavily subsidized export advantages.[54]

Changed production patterns and responses to the increased cost and reduced supply of agricultural wage-labor provided the means to dampen the impact of price declines before the middle of the 1890s. There was certainly little incentive to abandon these practices thereafter as prices for both grains and livestock began to rise steadily.[55] With minor exceptions, these trends were not reversed before 1914. The continued expansion of urban centers meant that, as one student of agricultural development in these regions put it, "until 1914, the market demand for agricultural products increased daily."[56] As a consequence, agricultural producers concentrated on increasing output and paid less attention to the standardization of production and to streamlining marketing techniques.[57] Their success is suggested by their ability to increase the output of arable crops while greatly expanding livestock holdings, all within the organic cycle of the mixed-farming system. Improved breeding and feeding techniques further meant that livestock was heavier and that cows gave more and richer milk.[58] Continuously rising land prices provided an additional indication of the prewar prosperity of west German agriculture.[59] Moreover, while land and product prices rose, the prices paid for purchased inputs—particularly fertilizer—remained constant or, as in the case of agricultural machinery, showed a downward tendency.[60]

Evidence of structural instability or an unhealthy agricultural sector is certainly not to be found in the data on indebtedness. A survey conducted in 1902, the most comprehensive of its kind before the First World War, revealed clearly that west German agriculture defied any textbook generalizations about the overindebtedness of farms in the empire (see Appendix Table 14). Mortgage indebtedness increased in the years before the war, but only gradually. The interest on mortgage debt, set at stable, fixed rates, could be carefully calculated, and increased borrowing more likely reflected investments for the intensification of production in response to expanding markets than a reaction to crisis and decline.[61]

In terms of the organization and nature of their production, peasant farmers in these west Elbian areas entered the twentieth century producing efficiently with a clear sense of the market structures confronting them. As successfully as any agricultural producers in the Kaiserreich, Rhenish and Westphalian peasants had learned to live with the realities of an advanced industrial economy and offered the "ideal picture of a capitalist peasantry."[62] There was good reason to see the two prewar decades as the best in the history of German agriculture, comparable in this respect with the period of booming expansion, 1850–70.[63] By 1914, memories of the "Great Depression" might still be invoked to deliver rhetorical justification for tariff increases, but they had otherwise been submerged beneath an extended period of prosperity and stability. Admittedly, for agricultural producers, even if things are good they can always be better, and peasant farmers are chronic complainers. At least in the last two prewar decades, however, there was substantial evidence in the Rhineland and Westphalia to confirm the judgment of left-liberal Progressive party politician Eugen Richter that German agricultural producers had "learn[ed] to complain without suffering."[64]

TWO

Defining the Agrarian Interest in the Wilhelmine Age

The reign of Kaiser Wilhelm II was an age of the organization and articulation of economic interests. The limits set on parliament's powers by Bismarck's constitution, the absence of ministerial responsibility to the popularly elected legislature, and the entrenched influence of a career civil service accorded economic interest groups—"the heirs of Bismarck," in Dirk Stegmann's telling phrase—a central role in shaping public policy.[1] Along with other economic and occupational groups, German agrarians organized as well. Indeed, the Agrarian League, founded in 1893, emerged as one of the most powerful and influential of Bismarck's heirs. This highly effective pressure group with its close ties to the civil service and the military not only commanded the attention of the Kaiser and his ministers but also profoundly shaped the Conservative party, transforming it from an exclusively Prussian, elitist institution into a demagogic mass organization. Although the league's major electoral base remained in rural areas, it aided the Conservative party in extending its appeal to a broad middle-class constituency, particularly among the old *Mittelstand* of artisanal producers and small-scale retailers.[2]

The outlines of the Agrarian League's history are too familiar to require further elaboration. Because of its tremendous political importance, it has exercised a near monopoly on studies of agrarian organization in the Kaiserreich. Just as the history of the agricultural crisis east of the Elbe in the late nineteenth century has been read as the history of German agriculture in general, so has the history of the east Elbian-dominated pressure group overshadowed the significance of other forms of rural organization. The peasants in western Germany who were not organized in the Agrarian League are pictured essentially as following the east Elbian lead and as showing little originality in defining a program to meet the needs of their constituents. In many accounts, peasant followers fell in behind the Junkers even before the formal creation of the Agrarian League. This dominance of east Elbian Junkers as representatives of all German agrarians is traced to the achievement of protection for agriculture in 1878–79. According to one standard interpretation, politics and economics are closely linked: as peasants hid behind tariff walls, unable and unwilling to adjust their production decisions to the realities of a capitalist market, so too did they retreat behind the conservative political leadership of the Junkers.[3]

This general scenario fits developments in the Rhineland and Westphalia very poorly. It ignores the success of peasants in these areas at responding to altered market conditions by means other than tariffs, just as it misrepresents the forms of their interest groups. In both provinces the organization of agrarian interests predated the creation of the Agrarian League, in the Rhineland by a decade and in Westphalia by three decades. In both cases, the emergence of the competitor controlled by east Elbian interests and its westward expansion in the 1890s had an impact on the activities and rhetoric of interest-group leaders, but they continued to perceive themselves as independent of, and free from any control by, the Junker-dominated Agrarian League. Peasants and Junkers might "*strike to-gether*," in the words of one Peasant Association (Bauernverein) official, when their interests ran parallel, but they would frequently "*march separately*," often to the beat of different drummers.[4]

It was not only the Elbe that separated the Junkers from west Elbian peasant organizations, and the differences dividing them were ultimately as significant as their similarities. Most importantly, the members and leaders of the Peasant Associations were predominantly Catholic. Since the *Kulturkampf* of the 1870s, heavily rural Catholic districts had consistently backed the defender of the Catholic church and the confessional school, the Center party. In fact, few regions were more crucial to the national electoral success of the confessionally-defined Center party than the Rhineland and Westphalia, where heavily Catholic rural areas were among those known as the Center's "Riviera" districts—areas so solidly Catholic and politically reliable that candidates might just as well vacation during election campaigns (see Appendix Tables 15 and 16).[5] There were important exceptions; in Minden-Ravensberg, Westphalia's eastern flank, and in the southernmost tip of the province, the rural district of Wittgenstein, the countryside was as uniformly Protestant as other areas were overwhelmingly Catholic. But while lending truth to interest-group claims of an interconfessional membership, these exceptions did not loosen the close ties between Peasant Associations and the Center party. Undoubtedly, as one student of Wilhelmine politics put it, "if they were not Catholic, Catholic agrarians would be Conservative."[6] Their confession, however, was immutable, and it fundamentally shaped their political affiliation.

The defining characteristic of the Center was its claim to represent all those united by a common confession, from Catholic mine-owners to Catholic miners, from Catholic estate-owners to Catholic agricultural wage-laborers, and to offer all within the "Center Fortress" a "balanced justice." Of course, conflicts of economic interests could easily throw theoretical harmony off key—but in many parts of Germany the cacophony was barely audible and readily silenced, particularly where confessional divisions paralleled those defined by occupation. Thus, in the south German state of Württemberg the party could appeal directly to the "middling" classes of small businessmen, peasant farmers, and small-scale retailers and artisans integrally tied into the rural economy, while paying far less attention to the interests of largely Protestant industrial workers and entrepreneurs in the cities. In Bavaria and Silesia, other Center strongholds, limited industrialization allowed the party to identify more exclusively with agrarian interests.[7]

In the Rhineland and Westphalia, cities filled with Catholic workers dotted a countryside filled with Catholic peasants. A Catholic landed aristocracy saw its position of social and political prominence directly challenged by Catholic professional groups and entrepreneurs, on the one hand, and by organized Catholic workers on the other. Occupational splits by no means paralleled confessional ones (see Appendix Table 17).[8] Heavily agricultural areas were often more solidly Catholic than the nearby cities, but even in urban areas the concentration of Catholics surpassed the Reich and Prussian averages. The consequence of this social diversity for the nature of Center politics in these provinces can hardly be overstated. In other parts of the Reich, the polemical claim of one agrarian leader that "the Center will be agrarian or it will not exist"[9] might come close to a description of political reality. In the Rhineland and Westphalia, this could not be the case; there, perhaps more than anywhere else in the Reich, it was more likely, as a Center representative described it, that "all the problems that the German nation has on a large scale, we see beforehand on a small scale within our party."[10]

In the Wilhelmine period, among the most difficult problems facing the German nation stemmed from the conflicts between industrial and agrarian interests, particularly over taxation and tariff protection. In addition, by 1914 political demands for the democratic reform of Bismarck's constitution, the increased representation of organized workers, and the expansion of parliament's powers came not only from Social Democrats but from a broad spectrum of progressive liberals and Catholic workers, organized outside the socialist "Free Trade Unions."[11] These problems loomed large for the Center party in the Rhineland and Westphalia as well. It is the role of the Peasant Associations in these developments, their ability to articulate and defend agrarian interests, and their political relationship with the Center party that are the focus of this chapter.

Forms of Agrarian Organization

In neither the Rhineland nor Westphalia were the Peasant Associations the earliest forms of agrarian organization: they were preceded by semi-official, state-subsidized Agricultural Associations (in Westphalia, Landwirtschaftliche Vereine, and in the Rhineland, Landwirtschaftliche Casinos or Lokalabteilungen) that dated back to the first half of the nineteenth century. From the start, the Agricultural Associations had close ties to government officials, and many were founded and led by the local Prussian district administrator (Landrat). They also received direct funding from the state. Members usually came from the upper crust of provincial society—by no means limited to practicing farmers—and included clergy, teachers, government officials, and a healthy dose of aristocratic estate-owners. The exclusive membership of these associations and their semi-official status limited their claims to represent the interests of all agricultural producers and left much room for other forms of organization. Even the creation in the 1890s of Agricultural Chambers (Landwirtschaftskammer), unifying the representatives of local organizations at the provincial level and tying them to a central Prussian organization, did little to alter this situation.[12]

It was the state connection and the restrictive quality of these organizations that had prompted Catholic aristocrats in the Rhineland and Westphalia to seek alternative forms for representing agrarian interests before the 1890s. In both cases, these leaders were active in the work of the Agricultural Associations as well, but they emphasized the need for "free" associations that could defend agrarian interests uncompromised by official connections to the state. In addition, Catholic aristocratic participation in the Peasant Associations represented a means for an indigenous provincial elite to extend and preserve its political influence in a mass society. Protestant nobles east of the Elbe assumed as part of their birthright a position of social and political prominence defined in part by close ties to the Prussian state.[13] In the Rhineland and Westphalia, the Catholic religion barred a landed nobility from automatic political prominence, and confessional differences could also strain ties to the Prussian civil service. Indeed, as a direct result of the *Kulturkampf*, ten of eighteen Catholic district administrators in Westphalia had been removed from office. The relatively small number of Catholic provincial nobles appointed to such posts in these provinces after the 1870s provided one clear index of the maintenance of an important division between a Protestant east and a Catholic west.[14]

Because Catholic nobles were denied a ready-made basis for their authority, their participation in a range of voluntary associations assumed great importance as the means to define and defend their social status. Such organizations were often closely linked to the Catholic church. On the one hand, they included groups restricted to nobles and narrowly circumscribed by confessional concerns, such as the Association of Catholic Nobles (Verein katholischer Edelleute) or the Association for the Honor of the Holy Family (Verein zu Ehren der heiligen Familie). In addition, there were numerous associations that turned outward, serving to integrate Catholic aristocrats into the larger society rather than to isolate them from it. For Catholic nobles in the Rhineland and Westphalia, the very concept of an exclusive court aristocracy, bound to the Prussian king, was anathema. Rather, the nobility should ground itself firmly in the people, the *Volk*, the church, and the Catholic religion. Associational life could translate this theory into practice.[15]

In no case were these general outlines more clearly realized than in the founding of the Westphalian Peasant Association in 1862. This organization grew out of the efforts of Burgfried Freiherr von Schorlemer-Alst, the "Peasant King," to establish a society for the "religious, ethical, material, and social" improvement of the Westphalian peasantry.[16] Schorlemer-Alst explicitly described his project as part of the Catholic church's general response to the "social problem" and the perceived dangers endemic in a "liberal" economic order. The Peasant Association was to be a "corporation based on a religious foundation which . . . can pit a healthy new organism against the poison and despotism of the so-called modern freedom."[17] In the "materialistic" contemporary society, the peasant was burdened with responsibilities—particularly taxes and military services—with no corresponding rights; but as long as peasants failed to organize in defense of their interests, they had no one to blame for their plight but themselves. "Estates" (*Stände*), once legally defined and determined by birth, were now to be occupationally defined, determined by "world-view" and economic interests. Organization along these lines could provide the basis for more effective political mobilization.

The confessional tie of the Westphalian Peasant Association was apparent not only in Schorlemer-Alst's debt to the language of conservative Catholic corporatist social theory: all thirty-seven of the founding members were Catholic, and initially the organization did not attempt to extend its activities into the Protestant districts of Minden-Ravensberg. In addition, Schorlemer-Alst closely coordinated his plans with Wilhelm Emmanuel von Ketteler, a former Westphalian, who as bishop of Mainz had exhorted Schorlemer-Alst to organize agricultural interests along "Christian," "corporatist" lines. Significantly, however, the confessional connection did not mean direct clerical participation, as it did in other areas where an established provincial elite was absent. In Westphalia, and in the northern Rhineland as well, it was not the clergy but rather a firmly established provincial nobility, a "leavening of social superiors," that assumed leadership roles in the Peasant Associations.[18]

Schorlemer-Alst's participation in this facet of provincial associational life was completely consistent with his active role in confessionally-defined politics. Catholic politics, according to him, should ultimately follow corporatist lines, and the peasant "estate" (*Bauernstand*) must organize to represent its interests along with other occupationally defined groups. Such beliefs were behind Schorlemer-Alst's participation, along with other Catholic nobles, in the drafting of the Soest Program in 1870; this document was later claimed by the Center party as its first platform.[19]

The bonds between the Peasant Association and political Catholicism, strong by 1870, became rock solid in the following decade. The history of Bismarck's ill-conceived attempt to win the support of political liberals by attacking political Catholicism is well known.[20] In the Westphalian countryside, it clearly left its traces, mobilizing peasant voters around the confessional standard and engaging Schorlemer-Alst and many other Catholic nobles in the defense of confessional interests. It is impossible to know whether the declining agricultural prices after 1873 or the *Kulturkampf* more forcefully stimulated the organization of Westphalian peasants, but together these developments swelled membership in the Peasant Association from slightly less than 2,000 in 1870 to ten times that number a decade later.[21]

The Rhenish counterpart to the Westphalian organization was founded after Bismarck had turned his attention away from Catholics to other "enemies of the Reich," but it, too, clearly bore the stamp of political Catholicism. Felix Loë-Terporten, like his close friend and "aristocratic brother" Schorlemer-Alst, had been extremely active in church and political affairs within the Catholic fold long before the *Kulturkampf*, and he had even spent six months in comfortable confinement for violation of the restrictive legislation on Catholics imposed under the May Laws.[22] In the early 1880s, strongly influenced by the Westphalian example, Loë-Terporten turned his attention to the creation of an agricultural interest group for the Rhineland. Against the background of the ongoing agricultural crisis, membership increased rapidly, particularly in the northern part of the province: the organization counted 5,000 members at the end of its first year of existence, and had expanded to over 30,000 by 1890.[23]

It is difficult to know with confidence the segments of rural society from which the associations recruited their membership.[24] There is, however, much evidence to suggest that in both provinces, association members were the well-to-do heads of family farms who earned their entire livelihood from their work in the agricultural sector. Like the contemporary understanding of a "true" peasant, the original statute defining membership in the Westphalian association excluded those not fully employed in the agricultural sector as independent producers. A minimum prerequisite for potential recruits was an "independent" holding or a "draft team of two horses."[25] Such a restriction would immediately eliminate part-time farmers, and in fact would include few who farmed a holding of less than ten hectares, the lower bound specified by the association for a "peasant farm" (*Bauernhof*). Schorlemer-Alst might make the polemical claim that the name "peasant" should be borne with dignity by *all* who worked the land, from "Prince to day-laborer,"[26] but in reality, the Peasant Associations in the Rhineland and Westphalia were primarily organizations of and for independent family farmers.[27]

Association leadership outside of the noble upper echelon was recruited from the highest ranks of the well-to-do peasantry. In the steering committees of county-level branches, nobles worked together with the owners of substantial farms (*Gutsbesitzer*), who were essential as well in the network of cooperative economic ventures sponsored by the Peasant Associations (discussed below). The landholdings of the nobles were often no more than two or three times larger than those of these prosperous peasants, and by the late nineteenth century aristocratic holdings were not expanding at the expense of largeholding peasant farmers. Nobles managed their own estates and shared with wealthy peasants a practical interest in the everyday problems of agricultural production. Though divided by the status gap created by an aristocratic title, both nobles and *Gutsbesitzer* shared prominence as rural notables, active in the Peasant Associations and in other aspects of rural associational life and local self-government. The leadership structure of the Peasant Associations thus reflected and reinforced the hierarchical structure of rural society.[28]

In the 1870s, some association leaders in Westphalia had expressed fears that restrictive membership practices and a leadership dominated by nobles and wealthy peasants would leave organized "bourgeois peasants" confronting disgruntled "proletarian peasants." However, proposals to extend membership to agricultural workers received little support. A similar reluctance to extend membership to workers and smallholders in the northern Rhineland created a deep rift between the Rhenish association and a competitor, the Trier Peasant Association, which expanded into the southernmost districts of the province, areas dominated by smaller farms.[29]

Outlines of a Conservative Agrarian Ideology

Loë-Terporten and Schorlemer-Alst offered a conservative corporatist ideology as the best antidote to the growing influence of political liberalism in the last third of the nineteenth century. Never precisely defined, liberalism was identified with all the chief ills of modern society. It was responsible for "Manchesterism," a convenient code word for capitalism, a free market economy, and all other potential threats to the agricultural sector created by industrial development. The downfall of the old order was traced to the French Revolution that had destroyed the social harmony of an estate-based (*ständisch*) society. Liberalism was the creator of a parliamentary order in which there would be "rule by head count," the political tyranny of the propertyless masses, rather than representation by estate. The ultimate benefactor of these developments was political socialism, the outgrowth of liberalism—and socialism sought nothing less than the destruction of the family, the church, the confessional school, and private property. The rhetoric of Loë-Terporten and Schorlemer-Alst was also often peppered with anti-Semitism and loose associations between international finance capital, socialism, and Jews. The alternative to the emerging bourgeois order was a corporatist society in which a "healthy peasant estate" would join other occupationally defined groups in a harmonious exchange.[30]

In many respects, the language of this conservative agrarian ideology was firmly grounded in the experience of Rhenish and Westphalian peasants. Stressing the unity of the "peasant estate" could not erase the reality of a stratified, highly competitive agricultural sector, but it did describe the relative homogeneity of Peasant Association members among whom differences of wealth and social status were not extreme. Praise of the patriarchal family and the sanctity of private property were no mere euphemisms in areas dominated by family farms and increasingly reliant on the labor of family members. Attacks on a liberal economic order had a specific meaning in areas where breach of contract by workers was commonplace. Moreover, in this and other instances, the agrarian critique was not of the capitalist system per se but only of its manifestations considered disadvantageous to agrarian interests, particularly in the commercial sphere.[31] The fear of democratic, parliamentary rule by "head count" was not an abstraction in areas where the working class of nearby cities was organizing politically and threatening agrarian interests in crucial questions like tariff protection and property taxes.

The "psychological and organizational skills" of would-be agrarian leaders are important, as Barrington Moore rightly observes, "but they work only when they are in line with the everyday experience of the peasants whom leaders seek to set in motion."[32] The ideology offered by the conservative leadership of the Peasant Associations fully confirms Moore's judgment; it articulated, ordered, and interpreted the reality of rural society in a fashion plausible to association members. In addition, this conservative world view was not advanced in a vacuum; rather, it was reinforced by the church and the network of informal associations often tied to the church, those other sources of an "apolitical politics" that occupied peasants' lives.[33]

To note the ways in which the ideological formulation of Peasant Association leaders presented a consistent interpretation of the social reality confronting their members is not to suggest that it represented the *only* possible interpretation. To judge it merely as rhetoric, however, would be to understate its resonance in the countryside and to imply an alternative that Rhenish and Westphalian peasants might otherwise have adopted. Such alternatives were not forthcoming from peasants themselves, and from outside the peasantry, they were few. Even after the suspension of the Anti-Socialist Laws in 1890, socialist attempts to offer the peasantry different appeals were limited by the continued commitment of the SPD (Sozialdemokratische Partei Deutschlands) to a Marxist analysis that predicted the demise of peasant holdings as the laws of the concentration of capital proceeded in the agricultural sector. Economic questions like the tariff issue also fundamentally divided the SPD from the peasantry, and in Catholic regions socialists were associated with attacks on the confessional school.[34] Liberal democratic peasant organizations were rare in the Kaiserreich, and they made no attempts to organize in the Rhineland and Westphalia.[35]

The only concerted ideological and organizational challenge to the firmly established position of the Peasant Associations came in the early 1890s from the Agrarian League. From the start, the Peasant Associations greeted the new organization as an ally in defense of common agrarian interests, while stressing that the positive parts of the league's program differed more in rhetoric than in substance from the long-established demands of the Peasant Associations. At the same time, however, Peasant Association leaders consistently stressed the factors that separated the two organizational structures and made any merger impossible.[36] They could "strike together" in the early 1890s against moves to reduce the level of tariff protection, but they "marched separately" when it came to questions of graduated freight rates or a canal to carry east Elbian grain to western markets. Moreover, the anticapitalist tone of the league was inappropriate in regions where ties between industry and agriculture had always been important to both sides.[37]

The highly centralized nature of the Agrarian League further distinguished it from the Peasant Associations. After 1900, regional associations were tied into a national umbrella organization, the Federation of Christian German Peasant Associations (Vereinigung der christlichen deutschen Bauernvereine), which included groups in Bavaria, Hesse, Nassau, Alsace, Silesia, and Baden as well as those in the Rhineland and Westphalia. However, the creation of this organization had little impact on the highly decentralized, regionally confined member associations. Before World War I the national organization had no permanent office in Berlin; instead, a coordinating staff changed its personnel and location periodically, moving from one association to another. The Rhenish and Westphalian organizations were among the most important in the national federation, but regional particularism and the emphasis on autonomy were behind a strong aversion to any national organization that extended beyond a loosely knit confederation.[38]

Unlike the Agrarian League, the Peasant Associations did not seek to organize a mass following. The league's attempt to represent a "healthy *Mittelstand*" distinguished it from the Peasant Associations' self-limitation to an occupationally defined clientele.[39] Indeed, in this respect the Peasant Associations were far more characteristic of interest-group organization in the Wilhelmine period. Like trade unions, industrial organizations, and occupational associations within the *Mittelstand*, they limited their membership and the range of issues that they sought to defend. Beneath a conservative ideological guise, they constituted a form of lobby organization more akin to post-1945 agrarian pressure groups than to the mass electoral organization of the Agrarian League, a hybrid in the peculiar soil of the Wilhelmine political terrain.[40]

Of even greater significance in separating the Peasant Associations from the Agrarian League, charged Peasant Association leaders, was the league's domination by east Elbian interests and its clear connection to the Conservative party. The Peasant Associations, insisted Loë-Terporten and Schorlemer-Alst, were not political or committed to any one party. Of course, in both provinces ties to political Catholicism were as old as the organizations, but in the early 1890s, particularly in Westphalia, more than assertions of independence lay behind the insistence on remaining open to a range of political tendencies. An independent organization in the predominantly Protestant region of Minden-Ravensberg merged with the Westphalian association in 1887, transforming the association's interconfessional composition from rhetorical posturing into a practical reality. Protestant representatives were included in the highest leadership ranks of the expanded organization.[41] Rural districts in Minden-Ravensberg had provided support for Adolf Stoecker's anti-Semitic Christian Social party as long as it was allied with the Conservatives, and they remained Conservative strongholds after Stöcker's break with the party in 1893. Wittgenstein, in the southern part of the province, was another Protestant island in a Catholic sea, and it too remained an important exception to the rule of Catholic homogeneity and Center predominance (see Appendix Table 15).[42] Still, although claims of interconfessionality were more than rhetoric, there is no question that Protestant encroachments did little to dilute a concentrated brew of political Catholicism in the Rhineland and Westphalia. The Peasant Associations remained closely identified with the Center, and, as we will see at the end of this chapter, attempts to alter that situation were consistently unsuccessful.

From Corporatist Ideology to Cooperative Practice

The formulation of a coherent ideology consistent with the realities of peasant life was an important function of the leadership of the Peasant Associations, but they offered their membership much more than this. The network of cooperative services sponsored by the Peasant Associations addressed the peasantry's material conditions directly, and offered a firm underpinning for an ideological emphasis on collective action and "self-help" as effective forms of adjustment to a capitalist society.[43]

Without question, the most important and successful economic institutions supported by the associations in both the Rhineland and Westphalia were credit cooperatives. What had begun as an informal system of classified advertisements linking rural borrowers and lenders in the association newspapers grew by the 1880s into a formal system of credit provision through cooperative savings and loan institutions. The cooperatives were initially intended to protect the peasantry from the allegedly usurious interest rates of urban money lenders. The fact that their membership and the services they provided expanded most significantly in the 1890s suggests that more importantly, they met the need for credit of a peasantry increasingly involved in money transactions in a market economy. The cooperatives were seldom in the business of providing long-term mortgage loans, but they did offer short-term money to cover various production costs—fertilizer, wages, taxes, seed grain, and additions to livestock herds.[44] Interest rates on these loans seldom exceeded 5 percent, varied little from year to year, and typically remained below the Reichsbank discount rate.[45] The credit cooperatives thus could replace other sources of commercial credit and could guarantee stable interest rates. They also maintained current accounts for their members and offered checking services. They did not restrict their membership to those actively involved in agricultural production, and they could thus mobilize the idle capital of rural artisans and even of agricultural workers.[46]

In both provinces, the establishment of central provincial banks facilitated the transfer of funds to cooperatives in need of them. The central banks were also deposit institutions for those member cooperatives with more funds than borrowers. Provincial organizations in turn were linked directly to a national institution, the Prussian Central Cooperative Bank, which integrated the cooperatives into a larger financial network and invested excess capital in long-term securities, usually government bonds. It also served the important function of auditing member banks that were often staffed by volunteer personnel.[47]

Interest-group spokesmen never tired of extolling the virtues of the cooperatives. They stressed the benefits of a savings and loan system tailored to the needs of the individual community, where officers at the local level often had first-hand knowledge of the financial circumstances of cooperative members. Cooperatives were small in size, usually with no more than a few hundred members and servicing a community of only two thousand to three thousand people.[48] The rhetorical emphasis on the success of the cooperatives at shielding their members from the harsh realities of the market should not, however, obscure the extent to which the steady flow of short-term capital at low interest rates facilitated the successful adaptation and integration of peasant producers into a capitalist economy.[49]

The expanding volume of business conducted by the savings and loan associations clearly indicates their increasing importance in the two decades before World War I. In Westphalia, the total turnover (*Gesamtumsatz*) swelled almost sixfold, from 53,135,240 marks in 1895 to 316,884,049 marks in 1910. Similarly, the number of cooperatives, which stood at 256 in 1894, had increased to 432 by the turn of the century, and another 105 had been founded by 1910. Membership grew correspondingly: in 1890, cooperatives counted 20,235 members; by 1895, the number had increased to 34,582; and by 1910, it stood at 88,987.[50] The growth of the cooperative network in the Rhineland was equally impressive. By 1895, 145 savings and loan cooperatives were in existence. By 1906, the number had increased to 514, including 46,700 members, and the total turnover had reached 148,570,000 marks. Savings deposits amounted to 52,474,000 marks, and outstanding loans totaled 41,147,000 marks.[51]

No other branch of the cooperative movement enjoyed the success of the credit network. Marketing and purchasing institutions, as well as a network of dairy cooperatives, confronted well-established commercial competitors that impeded the expansion of the Peasant Associations into these areas. The loyalty of members to their cooperative often ended as soon as a commercial middleman could offer a better deal.[52] Still, some efforts were made in cooperative marketing and purchasing before 1914, and particularly the volume of collective purchases increased steadily.[53]

Cooperatives were complemented by other practical forms of assistance, ranging from group rates for life and personal property insurance to arbitration services designed to resolve grievances between members and to keep internal squabbles out of the courts. Local association offices offered individual advice on tax laws and architectural assistance with building projects, and sponsored a range of experimental endeavors with crop rotations, machines, fertilizers, and breeding schemes. Technical and scientific advice had once been the preserve of the highly exclusive Agricultural Associations, and the Peasant Associations served to increase access to this sort of information. Organization of committees at the local level around specific interests—fruit-tree growers' associations, cattlebreeders' associations, horsebreeders' associations, et cetera—also multiplied the ways in which the association firmly established itself as an agent not only of useful advice but also of rural sociability, by providing members with frequent opportunities to come together around shared concerns. At the local level, district membership meetings complemented annual provincial general assemblies, creating a forum for open discussion of topical political issues, interest-group demands, and the exchange of practical information. Publication of an annual "Peasant Almanac" served as an additional daily reminder of the benefits of association membership.[54]

Membership also included subscription to the associations' newspapers, which captured and expressed the multifaceted nature of the associations' activities. A regular fare of conservative ideological rhetoric appeared alongside information on prices, warnings about unsavory commercial middlemen, advertisements for agricultural production goods and for laborers seeking work, and reports of experiments with machines, fertilizers, and breeding, as well as straightforward explanations of tax laws, and other legislation affecting agricultural producers. It is impossible to know whether association members rushed first to read leadership paeans to an organic "peasant estate," reminders that peasant happiness lay not in great wealth but in religion,[55] the latest word on "Hoof and Mouth Disease and its Prevention,"[56] price reports, or the news that Germany could boast "ca. 19,500 unique types of insects" and the interesting information that the "half-winged sorts" could reproduce "by a fantastic procedure" even when both sexes were not present at the same time![57] However, by addressing the "War Against the Blood Louse"[58] the Peasant Association leaders could improve their chances to transmit their own variety of the war against Social Democracy, parliamentary reform, and legislation believed deleterious to agrarian interests. By taking on a broad range of peasant interests, the associations were able to place themselves at the very center of their members' existence. On this basis, they could legitimately claim the authority to articulate, communicate, and represent a conservative agrarian ideology.[59]

To be sure, the Peasant Associations were not alone in creating or purveying a conservative world view; they coexisted with other institutions that contributed to shaping peasant attitudes toward the political and economic changes taking place around them. No single institution in rural society played as central a role in its members' lives as that played by the "cradle to grave" organizational subculture of Social Democrats in industrial cities.[60] Nor, unlike the institutional framework created by the SPD, did rural forms of voluntary associations bear the imprint of an explicitly political, systematically formulated ideology. But within the network of rural associational life, other institutions more often complemented than challenged the conservative ideology offered by the associations, and no other institution touched on such a range of peasant cultural, social, political, and economic concerns.

The continued growth of the Peasant Associations and the absence of any organizational competitors testified clearly to their success. Membership in the Westphalian organization, at 23,000 in the mid-1890s, had grown to 27,800 a decade later and exceeded 30,000 by 1912.[61] The Rhenish organization, already at 43,347 at the turn of the century, included 54,468 members, organized in 1300 local branches, by 1907.[62] If we accept that these organizations continued to be comprised of peasant family farmers, these numbers are impressive. The membership total for Westphalia exceeded the number of farms of ten hectares or more. In the Rhineland, the degree of organization was even greater: the 1907 membership figure represented more than 100 percent of those farming more than five hectares. The extremely high degree of organization among that group suggests that for independent family farmers, Peasant Association membership was a part of their self-definition. The associations' claims to represent the political and economic interests of organized agriculture in the prewar period were well founded.

From Economic Self-Help to Political Representation

The Peasant Associations' authority as the most important representative of agrarian interests was also based on their ability to defend those interests in the political arena. The political party that the associations could most readily influence was the Center. The relations between conservative Peasant Association leaders and the Center were constantly in the background of the discussion of the associations' founding, and the history of the associations is inseparable from that of the party. Long after the end of the *Kulturkampf*, these provinces, particularly their heavily Catholic rural districts, remained Center strongholds.

Still, the tensions underlying relations between the party and its conservative agrarian wing—in the Rhineland and Westphalia, largely synonymous with the Peasant Association leadership—belied this apparent solidity and constancy. The end of the *Kulturkampf* initiated a period of redefinition within the Center, an ongoing process that had not been completed by 1914. "Residual Catholicism"[63] alone was no sufficient basis for party unity, and Center leaders attempted to provide an alternative political foundation on which it would be possible to resolve the inevitably conflicting interests of a diverse constituency. Those interests, unlike the sacraments, could not be reduced to simple formulae. Defining the "balanced justice" essential to the integrity of the Center became increasingly difficult in the two decades before the First World War.[64]

Open conflicts between national Center leaders and conservative agrarians emerged shortly after Bismarck's fall. From Bavaria came demands that the party pay greater attention to agrarian concerns, and the oppositional tactics of the Agrarian League found a parallel in the activities of the Bavarian Peasant League (Bayerischer Bauernbund) whose anticlericalism and rejection of "priests, nobles, and officials" presented a direct threat to the Center.[65] No equally radical rumblings came from the Rhineland and Westphalia, testimony to the firmly entrenched position of a noble leadership in the Peasant Associations, the ability of established interest groups to unify a membership of noble landowners and peasant producers, and the success of the Peasant Associations at winning credibility for their claims as the most important representative of agrarian interests. Here as well, however, agrarians made no secret of their displeasure with the Center.

Skirmishes broke out in the early 1890s when Peasant Association leaders in both provinces supported Leo von Caprivi's military reform bill, pitting conservative support for a strong army against the party's consistently antimilitarist position.[66] Even more serious was the conflict over Center votes for the tariff reductions proposed by Caprivi. It was Caprivi's action that had sparked the creation of the Agrarian League. Indeed, fears of a negative agrarian response forced the abstention of some Center members in the final votes on the Caprivi tariffs despite the party's majority decision to support the chancellor. Such exceptions, however, were cold comfort for agrarian leaders who saw their interests as totally neglected.[67]

Rhetorical hostility erupted into an open break in Westphalia. At a stormy meeting of provincial party leaders in 1893, Schorlemer-Alst demanded that the Center underline its commitment to agricultural interests by running agrarian candidates in at least four of the nine provincial electoral districts dominated by the party. When the provincial Center leadership roundly rejected Schorlemer-

Alst's demand with the argument that special treatment of one occupational group would lead to similar demands from all others, the "Westphalian Peasant King" defiantly left the meeting and made plans to run independent agrarian candidates in competition with the Center slate. Party leaders acted quickly and decisively against such separatist tactics, and even in agrarian circles Schorlemer-Alst found himself a leader with few followers. His actions met with the opposition of not only the Center party press but also the Catholic clergy. Only days before the election, Schorlemer-Alst could hear prayers from the pulpit "for a member of our community who has become untrue to Catholic interests."[68] Within the Peasant Associations as well, there was limited tolerance for such heterodoxy: if Schorlemer-Alst refused to be "an orderly Center man," some members threatened to leave the association, not the Center. Against these formidable foes, Schorlemer-Alst's initiative had little hope of success, and his agrarian candidates fared poorly.

A chastened Schorlemer-Alst quickly made his peace with the party, stressing that agricultural interests were best represented within the Center. Only once again, in 1898—three years after Schorlemer-Alst's death—did the association break ranks with the Center, again complaining that the party should do more to promote agricultural interests and should listen less to the lawyers who allegedly dominated the party's Reichstag delegation. Again, the Center had little difficulty in soundly defeating the agrarian alternative candidates and laying to rest such renegade tendencies.

Developments in the Rhineland showed striking parallels. There too the stimulus for open agrarian protest against party policy was the Center's support for Caprivi's tariff revisions. The Rhenish Peasant Association charged that by its action, the Center had "sunk to the level of a party of government" and had betrayed the loyalties of its agrarian constituents.[69] Felix von Loë-Terporten, head of the Rhenish association, emphasized his support for the Center party on confessional issues but added that, in his opinion, party discipline should stop there. Outside of this narrow realm, the Center must allow "its members freedom with regard to all other issues."[70]

Loë-Terporten continued to snipe at Center party leaders from other directions. The party's abandonment of agrarian interests was, he charged, symptomatic of its growing commitment to a parliamentary political order that was incompetent to act justly on important economic questions. His alternative extended no further than a vague corporatist vision, and he proposed an estate-based, occupationally defined organization, not a democratically elected parliament, as the forum most capable of determining economic policy.[71]

The party's complete unwillingness to support conservative corporatism or such antiparliamentary diatribes became quite obvious at the 1894 meeting of the General Assembly of German Catholics (Generalversammlung der Katholiken Deutschlands), the Center's ersatz for an official party congress. Even

Schorlemer-Alst, in a conciliatory mood after his failure in the recent Reichstag elections, was unwilling to back his aristocratic colleague from the Rhineland. The assembly adopted a very general resolution supporting state efforts to encourage the creation of cooperative occupational organizations, but this amounted to little more than a condescending nod to Loë-Terporten. The party's official position was and remained that such associations should complement a parliamentary political framework, not usurp its authority.[72]

Although Loë-Terporten's attacks on the party continued until his death in 1896, the consistent rejection of his anti-Center rhetoric and corporatist proposals by the clergy and by the loyal party press in the Rhineland set clear limits to his direct influence on party policy.[73] Attempts to revive an autonomous agrarian opposition in the late 1890s were equally unsuccessful, and heretics insistent on independent agrarian candidacies after the turn of the century found themselves opposed by both the party and the Peasant Association. Grudgingly, Peasant Association leaders conceded that it was their "fundamental principle" to put certain limitations on their own interests in favor of the common good.[74] Such avowals, however disingenuous, reflected a clear admission that, as one Rhenish leader stated in 1898, "Most of us belong to the political party of the Center, and I would have to say that whichever party we belong to, that political affiliation comes to us in the cradle."[75] These birthrights were virtually inviolable.

For conservative agrarians in the Rhineland and Westphalia, the political lesson of the 1890s was that agrarian interests presented in opposition to the Center party had little chance for success. The party controlled too effective and efficient an electoral machine in the form of the Catholic clergy and, particularly in rural areas, the faithful heeded the word from the pulpit at election time.[76] Moreover, for rural voters the most obvious alternative was the Conservative party, which was easily identified with the east Elbian-dominated Agrarian League and associated with the Protestant Prussian ghost of the *Kulturkampf* (such overtones could be heard beneath clerical charges of Schorlemer-Alst's betrayal of "Catholic interests" in the 1893 elections). At least from the 1870s on, the concept of a Catholic "sociocultural milieu" applies well to the rural parts of these provinces, so uniformly Catholic, occupationally homogeneous, and traditionally committed to the Center. Center loyalties were forged in the *Kulturkampf* when Catholics had fully understood their minority position within a predominantly Protestant Prussian state.[77]

In his conflict with the party in the 1890s, Loë-Terporten had predicted that "a political contradiction between spiritual leaders and lay people was unavoidable in the long term if the honored clergy continues as a group to take a specific position in purely political and [party] personnel questions and to fight other opinions so decisively."[78] However, in the years before 1914 this prediction was not fulfilled. The Peasant Associations are often cited as one of several confessionally related organizations that helped to get out the Catholic vote.[79] When they did so in support of the Center, this may have been the case; when they tried to storm the Center Fortress from without, they were ineffective.

Setting limits to agrarian influence and rejecting corporatist political alternatives did not, however, mean Center neglect of agrarian concerns. Indeed, the scales of the Center's "balanced justice" often tipped decidedly in favor of the party's peasant constituents. The Center could not tolerate separatist appeals that threatened to undermine its electoral strength or unequivocal demands from any of its constituencies, but it also realized that socioeconomic strains might burst the bonds of a "sociocultural milieu." As long as agrarian interests remained *within* the Center, the Center supported them; it could ill afford not to, when outdated voting districts and the Prussian three-class voting system guaranteed the overrepresentation of rural areas and a Catholic countryside provided a crucial part of its electoral base.[80]

The protest unleashed by official support for Caprivi's trade treaties was thus quieted not only by stressing confessional ties but also by the Center's active advocacy of economic measures in the interests of west German peasant farmers. Most notable were restrictions on livestock imports, the strict enforcement of veterinary codes, control of margarine production and sales, and the removal of graduated railroad freight rates that served only the interests of estate-owning grain producers and threatened to saturate west Elbian markets with east Elbian products.[81] Any lingering doubts over Center support for its peasant constituents, moreover, were decisively removed by the party's decision to support the reconstruction of the high tariff walls in 1902.

Even in this clear instance of support for agrarian interests, however, the party stopped far short of endorsing a conservative agrarian ideology, nor did it accept the extreme demands of the Rhenish and Westphalian associations. Significantly, the Center's principal agrarian spokesman for the tariff legislation was not a titled leader of a Peasant Association—rather, it was Carl Herold, a Westphalian representative in the Reichstag and the Prussian parliament (Landtag), as loyal to the principles of parliamentary politics and compromise within the Center Fortress as he was to agrarian interests. Herold was firmly rooted in the agrarian associational life of the province, owner of a large farm, a member of the Peasant Association's steering committee, and active in the cooperative network.[82] He had originally been handpicked by Schorlemer-Alst as his successor within the party. It was soon apparent, however, that although Herold assumed the "Peasant King's" role as a major Center advocate of agrarian interests, he diverged from Schorlemer-Alst's antiparliamentary political style and rhetoric. Herold understood clearly that compromise and negotiation were essential to the pursuit of special interests and to the fundamental stability of the Center.

There was certainly no question of Herold's support for agrarian protection, but he was equally forceful in denouncing both the filibustering obstructionism employed by the SPD to block all tariffs and the exaggerated demands of the

Agrarian League, endorsed by his Rhenish and Westphalian colleagues.[83] Herold, confronting charges that the Center had not been sufficiently aggressive in its defense of agrarian interests, reminded his constituents that the party had "done what it could. . . . In the interests of the agricultural sector, the entire population has to bear a certain burden, but on the other hand, this must be limited out of consideration for other occupational estates."[84]

This simple lesson, fundamental to a functioning parliamentary system and essential to the stability of the Center Fortress, was mastered by Herold, insuring him a key position within both the Reichstag delegation and the national party organization. It was a lesson never learned by the conservative leaders of the Peasant Associations, nor could they abide the spirit of parliamentary compromise that it implied. Herold made no secret of his support for agrarian interests, but that support was never combined with vague visions of a corporatist future in which parliament would have no influence over economic questions. Far more than his antiparliamentary counterparts in the Rhenish and Westphalian Peasant Associations, he was a forerunner of a conservative political Catholicism realized in the Christian Democratic Union after 1945—a party that could remain antisocialist and proagrarian while accepting the existence of Social Democrats and supporting working-class social reforms and measures favorable to industrial interests. Herold thus stood on the party's right wing but nonetheless firmly within the party.

Herold's political realism conformed to the changing contours of the Center Fortress. Since Bismarck's fall, the Center had definitely not moved in the direction of a corporatist structure nor, for that matter, in that of the Christian Conservative party, envisioned as another political alternative by Schorlemer-Alst.[85] Though even after the turn of the century the party maintained its progovernmental, pro-Conservative course and did not join a "Gladstonian coalition" reaching leftward to the SPD,[86] it definitely could accommodate elements sympathetic to such an option. Indeed, in the Rhineland and Westphalia, pressure for reform within the party intensified.

Party leaders acknowledged that in areas where the competition with the SPD was immediate, the Center could ultimately hope to maintain its position only by winning votes from large numbers of Catholic workers.[87] The loyalty of Catholic peasants to the party had survived the separatist challenges of the 1890s, but the loyalty of Catholic workers was far less certain. Since the 1890s, the Center had actively attempted to save Catholic workers from the Social Democratic siren, and the Ruhr had become the most important center of Catholic working-class organization. Both the Christian Trade Unions (Christliche Gewerkschaften), Center-affiliated alternatives to the socialist Free Trade Unions, and the People's Association for Catholic Germany (Volksverein für das katholische Deutschland), closely tied to the party, had their greatest successes and their principal headquarters in the Ruhr. The People's Association, initially supported by Loë-

Terporten in 1890 as a narrowly defined confessional organization, quickly lost his favor as it developed into a mass political organization committed to parliamentary politics, democratization, and social reform. Its membership drew on workers and a broad spectrum of the Catholic middle class. Of its 300,000 members in 1902–3, 187,012 came from the Rhineland and Westphalia. As it continued to grow to over 800,000 by 1914, becoming the Center's most significant mass organization, the Ruhr remained its most important center of concentration.[88]

Before 1914, numbers did not automatically translate into strength. Catholic workers and the reform-minded leadership of the People's Association were hamstrung by outdated electoral districts that insured rural overrepresentation, and by an internal party decision-making structure that concentrated considerable power in the hands of the Center parliamentary delegation in Berlin. The democratization of party membership did not translate into the democratization of internal party decision-making.[89] The potential costs of disregarding Catholic working-class interests, however, became increasingly apparent. Despite official support for the reintroduction of tariffs in 1902 by both Christian Trade Unions and the People's Association, the party's identification with the "dear loaf" led to sizable losses in the 1903 Reichstag elections, immediately visible in the gains of the SPD.[90] To be sure, before 1914, when forced to choose between working-class consumers and agricultural producers, the party continued to side with the latter. The "Alliance of Knights and Saints," the "Blue-Black" coalition that united Conservatives and the Center after 1909, clearly favored the interests of conservative agrarians over those of reform-minded workers and Catholic liberals.[91] But the Center's claims in 1910 that it was "the only bourgeois party in the large industrial districts which up to now has victoriously held those constituencies so hard pressed by the Social Democrats"[92] could not be based forever on such alliances. The increasingly vocal demands of Christian Trade Unionists and leaders of the People's Association for parliamentary reform and an end to the plutocratic suffrage in Prussia made that clear, as did the Center's continued losses in urban areas in the 1912 Reichstag elections.[93]

A reform of the Prussian electoral system or the reapportionment of Reichstag districts would obviously cut two ways for the Center: though satisfying many Catholic workers, it would unavoidably reduce party strength in its safe agrarian districts. Even such considerations, however, did not stop Carl Trimborn, a lawyer and middle-class liberal leader of the People's Association, from demanding the democratization of communal self-government and denouncing a "socially reprehensible" Prussian suffrage that, judged by any standard, was a "bad electoral system." Trimborn was powerful in the Rhenish party organization and by 1914 in the Reichstag delegation as well. Like other middle-class party leaders he remained suspicious of direct coalitions with the SPD, but on the other hand he realistically conceded that "we won't eliminate Social Democrats from the world by not allowing them into the Prussian parliament."[94] Trimborn and others like him in the People's Association and the Christian Trade Unions were certainly not as outspoken as were Social Democratic advocates of reform, but on the eve of the war the differences separating them from many socialists on a range of issues were of degree, not kind. Moreover, though cooperation with the SPD remained extremely problematic, the costs of the "Blue-Black" coalition proved to be high, particularly as tariff negotiations recommenced and Conservative agrarian resistance to all meaningful tax reform left the Center little room to maneuver.[95]

If such an uncertain future presented problems for many middle-class Center leaders, it was even more troubling to conservative agrarians in the Rhineland and Westphalia. Those who demanded reforms in the nearby cities of the Ruhr made Catholic agrarians increasingly uncomfortable in the party that had been their political home since the 1870s. Nonetheless, the complete abandonment of the Center Fortress by archconservatives like Clemens von Schorlemer-Lieser, son of the founder of the Westphalian association, was an option that few were willing to take. Schorlemer-Lieser's Conservative leanings might make him acceptable as the first Catholic high president of the Rhineland, and after 1910 as Prussian minister of agriculture, but his move was exceptional in Catholic conservative agrarian circles.[96] Most Peasant Association leaders were still bound to the Center by confessional ties, and on a pragmatic political level the experience of the 1890s suggested that an open break with the party could have grave consequences.

For its part, the Center was able to avoid a head-on collision with Peasant Association leaders by not only backing agrarian concerns and relying on a clerical electoral machine, but also assiduously circumventing the question confronting the party since the 1890s: whether it was to be a religious interest group or a political party.[97] Its claims to be a "People's Party" uniting all "classes and occupational estates" only underlined the dilemma rather than resolving it.[98] As long as the shift toward reform within certain Center constituencies remained incompletely reflected in practice and unarticulated in theory, the party could continue to win the votes of its rural followers without confronting them with a political program that they might well have found unacceptable. In the years before 1914, however, it seemed unlikely that this delicate balance between those backing and those opposing reform could be maintained indefinitely.

In 1912, both the Rhenish and the Westphalian Peasant Associations celebrated anniversaries—for the Rhenish, its thirtieth, and for the Westphalian, its fiftieth. Amidst the self-congratulatory accounts of organizational achievements were to be found ominous references to "the difficult battles that we will not be spared in the future, in which the very bases of the existence of the agricultural sector will be at stake."[99] Tariffs, property taxes, and proposed political reforms would present major challenges for the Peasant Associations, particularly as they confronted "one hundred representatives . . . who have written revolution on their flags."[100] Moreover, socialists were not the only threat, and Clemens von Loë-Bergerhausen, head of the Rhenish organization since 1903, decried the widespread confusion that blurred a proper understanding of the "bourgeois idea of societal and state order."

The prosperity of the prewar years and the continued commitment of the state and the Center party to agrarian economic interests muted the rhetorical ring of such dire predictions, but it was nonetheless clear that the Peasant Associations could not rest comfortably on their laurels. Within the nation and within the Center, conservative agrarians confronted a full agenda of issues immediately affecting their interests. Their opponents, moreover, included not only socialists but also Catholic workers and reform-minded Center liberals who, though hardly ready to write revolution on their flags, also demanded national political reforms and, within the Center, a redefinition of "balanced justice." In areas where Catholic workers outnumbered Catholic peasants, redressing the balance could come only at the expense of the latter. In 1914 the Center Fortress was still far from collapse, but the cracks in its foundations were increasingly difficult to caulk. A common confession was no longer sufficient, and alternatives were not apparent.

THREE

The War at Home: Agrarian Protest and the Controlled Economy

In August 1914, no one in Germany expected a long war, and few had considered the massive demands on the German economy that a protracted conflict would pose. The growing threat of a European war before 1914 had provided German agrarians with a justification for demanding the protective tariffs theoretically capable of promoting domestic self-sufficiency—but these polemical defenses of economic interests were never translated into systematically formulated policies. The general belief in a short war made such planning seem unnecessary.[1] Only gradually did the German state begin to define a system of market regulation to meet the demands of the army at the front and the army of industrial workers essential to the war effort at home.

State intervention in the economy was not unprecedented in Germany. Indeed, the involvement of the state in economic regulation before 1914 is often taken as an index of the relatively early and well-articulated emergence of "organized capitalism" in the German context.[2] But the forms of state interference in the economy after the start of the war were qualitatively different and had few easily identifiable roots. The state's attempt to regulate the production, distribution, and marketing of a broad range of products was tantamount to the suspension of a normally functioning market. Under these circumstances, *economic* decisions had immediately apparent *political* dimensions. The "invisible hand" of the market was replaced by the quite visible hand of the government.[3]

As the structure of the controlled economy emerged, it became clear that the government's highest priority was the armaments industry, to which all other sectors of the economy were to be subordinated. For agricultural producers, this meant subjection to a system of price controls and delivery quotas intended to insure an adequate food supply at prices that would not translate into intolerably high wage demands or increased urban unrest. In setting these priorities, the government signaled its increased reliance on the advice and cooperation of organized industrialists and industrial workers, by implication, a renegotiation of the balance of power among social groups within Germany.

Before 1914, there can be little question that the agricultural sector in Germany enjoyed a position of importance in the minds of politicians and policy-makers that was no accurate measure of its economic significance. Well-established social hierarchies shored up by a plutocratic suffrage in Prussia, a distribution of Reichstag seats that was heavily weighted toward rural areas, and agriculture's close ties to the state administrative arm perpetuated this situation. An attempt to redress this imbalance was clearly on the agenda in the years immediately preceding the war. In the Center party as well, a fair representation of working-class interests could not be postponed indefinitely without permanently estranging Catholic workers from the party. The *Burgfrieden* of August 1914—the agreement to suspend domestic political differences for the duration of the war—at least temporarily postponed reform efforts, but by the spring of 1917 conflicts over the nature of Germany's social and political future reemerged. Under dramatically altered circumstances, a discussion of political reform was resumed within both the Center and the nation.

In the meantime, in the fights over the form and implementation of the controlled economy, the balance of power among societal elites had shifted de facto decisively toward industrial entrepreneurs and industrial workers. By 1917, it required little prescience to realize that these changes would assume formal political dimensions.[4] Unwelcome to agricultural producers under the best of circumstances, this abrupt, forceful, and undeniably irreversible shift in the balance of power in German society met with unequivocal rejection by conservative agrarians. From the perspective of agricultural producers, the controlled economy and the political changes that it reflected presented a program of affirmative action for consumers. Like any group that has long enjoyed a privileged, protected position, peasants did not graciously accept policies that elevated the interests of other groups, particularly of industrial workers, above their own. This chapter analyzes these dimensions of the war at home and their implications for conservative agrarians in the Center party.

The Poorly Controlled Controlled Economy

In the first two war years, the Berlin government's attempts to provide adequately for the army *and* the domestic market were at best disorganized and at worst chaotic. The state confronted a formidable problem: a reduction of food imports caused by the disruption of international trade and the Allied blockade. Before 1914, Germany had consistently been a net importer of agricultural products. By the fall of 1914 it was already obvious that domestic agricultural production would have to compensate for declines in foreign supplies. The panic-buying, hoarding, and rapid price increases in the first months of the war also demanded a response and made it clear that the domestic market, allowed to function on its own, could not be relied on to generate equitable solutions.

Difficulties were obvious; solutions were not. The government responded to shortages and rising prices with a system of price ceilings and rationing that proved to be extremely cumbersome from the start. An administrative network, specifically designed to regulate the pricing and distribution of agricultural products, grew convulsively and followed no comprehensive plan.[5] Price regulation did not exist for all products, and maximum prices were introduced only as they were seen to be necessary—usually when the market price for a product had reached a level considered too high by urban consumers.[6] Before 1916, little attempt was made to guarantee that the relative prices for agricultural goods would realistically reflect the relative costs of their production.

The haphazard application of price controls meant that fixed prices, theoretically intended only to regulate distribution and to maintain tolerable price levels for consumers, inevitably influenced the production of agricultural goods as well. This became obvious with the introduction of the earliest maximum prices. Prices were initially set for bread grains, and in addition, in October 1914, the use of bread grains for livestock feeds was strictly forbidden; but feed prices were left uncontrolled and rose very rapidly, and no maximum prices were set for livestock on the hoof. Producers responded by withholding grains from the market and by using grains illegally for pig-fattening. The government responded by ordering the automatic confiscation of all grain reserves and the butchering of large numbers of pigs, so that the pig would cease to compete with human consumers for scarce food sources. It soon became apparent, however, that such measures could only temporarily eliminate the temptation to use grains illegally as livestock feed.[7]

This course of events characterized the inadequate nature of the government's price-setting policy in the first two years of the war.[8] The earliest experiences with price controls revealed that patriotic appeals to meet delivery quotas did not numb the responsiveness of Rhenish and Westphalian peasants to relative price signals. Their behavior in the spring of 1915 amply demonstrated that if the costs for purchased feeds rose rapidly, then grains and potatoes, otherwise marketed, would be fed directly to livestock.[9] Decisions about price-setting in any single branch of production had an impact on all others. The diversified mixed-farming system that had allowed peasants great flexibility in reducing risks and reacting to shifting relative prices before 1914 provided them with the means to adjust to and circumvent the controlled economy during the war.

Though rapid adjustments could bring the individual producer windfall profits, peasants nonetheless greatly resented the frequent, unpredictable changes in government policies and the resulting shifts in relative prices.[10] Local officials stressed the importance of announcing prices before the planting season to allow peasants to make their production decisions well in advance, but price-setting policy in the first two war years definitely did not achieve this goal. August Skalweit, an expert in agricultural economics and a consultant to the government, articulated this criticism of a system whose "only recognizable rule was that

"Agricultural Producers, Grow Flax!" A peasant son in uniform appeals to his father to adjust his production to meet the needs of the war economy. *Courtesy of Bundesarchiv, Koblenz.*

prices for individual products were higher the later they were introduced. . . . Thus there was a system of relative prices among the individual products that stood in contradiction both to the natural conditions of production and to the demands of the war economy."[11] Uncertainty and unpredictability, shaped by government policy, replaced the stable bases of steadily rising, unfluctuating prices that had determined peasant production decisions before 1914.

The Growing Gap between City and Countryside

By the winter of 1915–16, the problem of securing an adequate food supply involved far more than finding the relative price levels that would stimulate production and prompt deliveries. No system of regulation and price controls could have compensated for the absolute decline in agricultural production caused by reductions in supplies of imported fertilizer and feed supplements, the deterioration of machines that could not be replaced or adequately repaired, and dwindling soil fertility.[12] Reductions in an even more fundamental factor of production—labor—were even graver, and by 1917, in the Rhineland and West-phalia, the estimates of agricultural workers and peasants either drafted or si-phoned off into the war industries ranged from 23 to 50 percent of the available male labor force.[13]

For peasant family farmers, the losses of workers were even more serious than the absolute numbers suggest. As one district administrator commented, "for them it is a question not only of a worker but also of the farm manager."[14] Appeals for exemptions from military service by family farmers were often denied, be-cause their potential contribution to the total food supply was deemed to be less than that of a large estate manager.[15] To be sure, peasant women were no strangers to work on the farm and already constituted a significant part of the agricultural labor force before the war. They assumed an even more crucial role after August 1914. But women, though essential in the fields at harvest and planting time, were usually in charge of the livestock and were less familiar with the total management of the farm. Moreover, in the absence of drafted male relatives, many women who were left to run a farm found assistance only from invalids, children, and neighbors who suffered from labor shortages themselves.[16]

The scarcity of all factors of production translated directly into major declines in agricultural output. These, coupled with producers' reluctance to deliver, prevented many districts from meeting their mandated quotas.[17] The annual reports of harvest yields supplied to government offices (summarized in Appen-dix Table 18) are obviously subject to question, and officials openly conceded the problems created by chronic underreporting,[18] but the downward tendency of these figures provided at least one clear index of the scale of agricultural short-ages and production declines. The figures reflected not only reduced yields, but also the growing unwillingness of peasant farmers to devote acreage to bread grains, the crops most strictly controlled. The longer the war continued, the stricter were the controls on reporting yields and acreage planted, as suggested by the slight increases recorded for harvest yields in 1918—yet even these figures still remained significantly below prewar levels.[19] Holdings of cattle and pigs also declined, and horses were confiscated for use by the military (see Appendix Table 19).[20] Officials at the local level repeatedly called attention to the reductions in slaughter weights of livestock as well;[21] at the same time, deliveries from outside the Rhineland and Westphalia also diminished. The consequence was that to maintain meat rations, more animals had to be slaughtered.[22] This in turn resulted in the confiscation of breeding stock, milk cows, and draft animals.[23]

The problem of establishing ration levels moved in a vicious circle: increasing the bread supply for urban consumers meant decreasing feed supplies for livestock producers; fewer cows resulted in reduced milk and butter supplies, and decimated livestock herds meant that available pasture might not be fully exploited; and reductions in protein and fat supplies from dairy sources necessitated raising meat rations—which directly contradicted the initial objective of increasing bread rations. The dilemma seemed insoluble.[24] As one critical commentator put it, guaranteeing ration levels and determining a "fair price" were by the end of the war "equivalent to squaring the circle."[25]

It was ultimately impossible to assess the relative blame of misguided policies and of real declines in causing the shortages. Easier to measure was the rift between the consumers and producers of agricultural goods that expanded as rapidly as supplies declined.[26] Each side cared little about the hardships confronting the other, and each was convinced that government policy advanced only the other's welfare. From both sides of the divide, criticism was launched at the state for its failure to perform the tasks of economic regulation it had assumed. But common grievances, directed at a common source, in no way unified city and countryside: consumers and producers saved their harshest words for each other. Tensions generated by food shortages quickly became the raw material of diatribes in the Prussian parliament and the Reichstag. In a typical inversion of the future right-wing stab-in-the-back legend, the socialist Adolf Hofer proclaimed in the Prussian parliament, "If the German people starves, then it's German agrarians who are to blame, not the English; it's they who are carrying out the English starvation plan. . . . Thus, gentlemen, our agrarians are in effect the allies of England."[27] The conservative agrarian response matched Hofer's sharp invective, and the consumer-producer conflict became a principal battlefield in the war at home.

It is difficult to overstate the significance of this conflict between the rural producers and urban consumers of agricultural products, particularly in areas like the Rhineland and Westphalia, where rural districts were in such close proximity to large urban centers. By the summer of 1915, it represented one of the greatest single threats to the maintenance of domestic peace.[28]

To be sure, before 1914 agriculture had confronted the hostility of the organized working class when it demanded tariff protection, and workers blamed peasants for the "dear loaf." After 1914, however, the terms of the conflict were dramatically altered; not only the price of food was at issue but also, frequently, whether food would be available at any price. Urban middle-class groups, often the political allies of agriculture before 1914, now echoed and frequently amplified worker protest. Large sectors of the urban middle classes confronted provisioning problems even greater than those facing many workers. Workers in war industries were often entitled to bonuses not available to independent artisans, white-collar workers, and tradespeople, and the wages of other middle-class groups—particularly civil servants—lagged further behind price increases than did those of armaments workers.[29] As government officials warned peasants who circumvented controls, agriculture might write off the opposition of industrial workers, but in its open resistance to regulations it ran the risk of also alienating "the numerous and politically significant circles of civil servants, white-collar workers, and that hardly unimportant number of workers not involved in war industries."[30] The common complaints over food shortages—the single most important and immediately visible index of the declining urban standard of living—provided all city dwellers with a common enemy in the countryside, where supplies were allegedly always abundant, and where the hope for usurious prices encouraged underreporting and delayed deliveries.

Antiurban feeling among peasants ran no less deep. Typical was the report of one district administrator in eastern Westphalia who pointed to the discontent in rural areas and stressed that "the population in agricultural areas has the impression that in questions of the food supply, the interests of consumers are considered exclusively, and that the central offices make their decisions in accord with the wishes of the industrial working class without paying any attention to producers." The explanation offered was straightforward: "The people in my district have the impression that decisions are dictated by the fear of the urban masses. Evidence, they argue, is provided by unequal distribution of food supplies and the much better treatment of industrial areas relative to [rural] areas where it is assumed that the population won't let itself be brought to protest because of its patriotic attitudes."[31]

After 1917, mutual recrimination on both sides of the consumer-producer split increasingly preoccupied all involved in the war at home. The gulf that divided German society into two groups blurred social distinctions in both city and countryside and redefined self-perceptions and the bases for collective action.[32] In a characteristic statement fully a year before the armistice, the government president of Cologne observed that "the continuing and ever-growing difficulties of our economic life increasingly dominate public morale and divert attention and concern from the important events at the front." His rhetorical pledges of widespread faith in the Kaiser and in the General Staff notwithstanding, he conceded that "in the events of everyday life, such patriotic sentiments retreat behind the

This wartime "Appeal to German Agricultural Producers," issued by the German Agricultural Council in 1916, called for greater understanding between peasants and workers. *Courtesy of Bundesarchiv, Koblenz.*

concerns about the home front. . . . The worry about our daily bread and securing the food supply is our primary concern."[33] By 1917, such a candid assessment was no less common currency than the belief in a short war had been in the summer of 1914.

Attempting to "Square the Circle"

Each person should give as he has decided for himself; there should
be no reluctance or compulsion; God loves a cheerful giver. (2 Corinthians 9:7)[34]

By the winter of 1916, there were few "cheerful givers" in the Rhenish and Westphalian countryside. Moral exhortations from the clergy, even when accompanied by such relevant scriptural passages, could not suffice to mitigate the food crisis. Attempts to bridge the consumer-producer gap in the last two years of the war took on other forms and were largely of two sorts: 1) changes in official policies, including the adjustment of relative prices to discourage the sorts of production shifts characteristic of the early war years, along with stricter enforcement of existing controls; and 2) the explosive expansion of an illegal alternative to controls: the black market. The two forms of response to shortages obviously worked at cross-purposes. The greater the amounts that disappeared onto the black market, the more difficult it became to discover, let alone implement, an official policy mix that could promise to generate the increased production of basic food supplies.

In areas like the Rhineland and Westphalia, where farms were easily reached from nearby cities, the black market took on particularly striking proportions. As long as black-market prices remained substantially higher than those set by the government, peasant pledges of patriotic support for the war effort did not preclude the rush for profits.[35] It was extremely difficult to police the illegal trade at its source due to the pattern of individual farm settlement characteristic of these regions,[36] and even in those instances where violators did come to trial, the nominal penalties set by the courts did nothing to deter others.[37] Urban buyers had little incentive to incriminate their suppliers, given what was described by one district administrator as a "war psychosis," the fear that "with a long duration of the war, no one will be able to acquire adequate food supplies."[38]

The widespread and generally accepted nature of participation in the black market guaranteed that moral suasion and patriotic appeals were largely ineffective.[39] When in the course of 1917 and 1918, 300,000 head of cattle and over 1,000,000 pigs could disappear without a trace after being purchased by the official meat distribution agency in the Rhineland, it was obvious that more than one eye was being closed to violations.[40] Military personnel, large industrial concerns, and even the communal governments charged with administering the controlled economy were often among the most serious violators of controls; confronted with such examples, peasants were hardly discouraged from participating as well.[41]

By the end of the war, many consumers were completely dependent on the supplements to rationed supplies obtained from the black market,[42] leading some officials to argue against strict enforcement of controls and in favor of leaving well enough alone.[43] Others, however, maintained that a thoroughgoing prosecution of black-market violators was the only way to guarantee a fair distribution of scarce food supplies.[44] Advocates on both sides of the question acknowledged that the longer the black market existed, the more it would become accepted as an essential supplement to the controlled economy. This in turn contributed to a general resistance to government restrictions and intensified the fundamental doubts of both producers and consumers that the government was capable of regulating the economy in a just fashion. The situation was summarized by the government president in Arnsberg, who reported that "no one cares about maximum prices any more, not the producer, nor the commercial middleman, nor the consumer."[45] The growing mutual dependence of consumers and producers on the black market, moreover, did nothing to improve relations between the two groups. On the one hand, general knowledge of the extent of the black market belied producers' claims to have delivered as much as possible. On the other hand, the fact that buyers for black-market products were always available led peasants to reject consumers' claims that they could not afford price increases for rationed goods.[46]

For peasant producers, the government's credibility was definitely not restored nor were relations with consumers improved by that other response to worsening shortages, the elaboration of the control network after the winter of 1916–17. The growing pressure of socialist and Christian trade unions and the Social Democratic Party to secure an adequate food supply by whatever means necessary culminated in angry protests against the "completely unsatisfactory regulation of the German provisioning system."[47] The official response was the expansion and tightening of controls, not the price increases suggested by many agricultural experts and government officials.[48] By early 1917, the threats of industrial unrest and strikers' demands for an improved food supply prompted far greater government concern than the discontent of peasant producers.[49]

Georg Michaelis, appointed as Prussian food commissar—the coordinator for war agricultural policy—assumed responsibility for expanding the control network. Michaelis, who would later go on to confront even greater problems as chancellor, received an intensive briefing on the war at home as he set out to solve the food crisis. Meeting with worker representatives in Dortmund and Cologne in late March 1917, he was reminded that among industrial workers, notions of equity had taken on a very basic form. Stricter controls on agriculture were essential since "up until now, agricultural producers have not had to starve."[50]

Michaelis's proposed offensive, though falling short of consumer demands for the direct regulation of individual peasant production decisions,[51] included searches for concealed reserves on peasant farms and additional controls for those with records as violators.[52] Searches extended even into living quarters. The structure of farm houses in the Rhineland and Westphalia made this virtually unavoidable since storage rooms, livestock stalls, and the family dwelling were all under one roof,[53] but zealous inspectors went even further, making their way into peasants' bedrooms. Stricter controls often produced more peasant resentment than increased supplies, and the presence of military personnel among search committees evoked tremendous bitterness, particularly when they exploited their position to sell confiscated goods on the black market.[54] Still, any results from the searches only confirmed the widespread belief that peasant producers were continuing their rearguard actions against the war economy, a passive resistance that demanded continued vigilance and strict enforcement of controls.[55]

The representatives of urban workers were not alone in emphasizing the need for intensified scrutiny of peasant producers. The conservative, aristocratic Prince von Ratibor und Corvey, high president of the province of Westphalia, was certainly no enemy of agrarian interests, but he was also responsible for coordinating the provincial provisioning network for the duration of the war. In this capacity, he turned a deaf ear to agrarian protest over the ever-stricter and personally humiliating audits of reserves; rather, he insisted that "as long as the claims of the producer about his harvest and the results of the search of the farm and storage areas provide grounds for doubts," officials had no choice but to continue searches in peasant homes. Though not with the indignation and outrage of working-class representatives in the cities, he conceded that "under the circumstances . . . a strict search and control is absolutely necessary, all the more so since in the course of the war, reliability, honesty, and good faith have disappeared in large measure in agricultural circles as well."[56]

The disappearance of "reliability, honesty, and good faith" among peasant producers is measured with as much difficulty as are the supplies that found their way onto the black market. However, there can be little question that by the end of the war, the controlled economy was far more effective at generating rural resentment than it was at increasing the supplies of grain, milk, and meat. The institution of tighter controls met not with sympathy but with "stubborn resistance."[57] Confrontation with a confusing, largely unsympathetic bureaucratic network became part of the day-to-day experience of the peasantry. Farm-by-farm searches, fixed prices, and delivery quotas were constant reminders of state intervention into the economic affairs of the producer, as were the antagonistic exchanges between individuals and local officials when peasants pursued the formal procedures established for the investigation of alleged inequities and hardships under the control network. Although the record of such encounters is spotty and unsystematic, the sources that do exist provide evidence that the forms of peasant confrontation with state authorities were as unpleasant as they were unprecedented.

Controversy over a fair price between buyers and sellers of livestock on the hoof is as old as livestock trading itself—but under the circumstances of the war economy, such bargaining became a conflict between peasants and state officials. Thus Jacob Imig, a peasant from the lower Rhine valley, felt compelled to inform the Rhenish high president that had officials not mistakenly driven his confiscated cow an additional nine kilometers beyond the nearest collection point, it would have weighed more and brought a higher price when it was finally delivered.[58] An aristocratic Westphalian landowner was astonished that a cow confiscated from his estate could have lost fifty-eight pounds between the farm and the central market, and he demanded compensation from the district administrator.[59] From the same district, a peasant, Anton Potthast, complained that the officials who had come to take away two confiscated pigs had brought no "control lists" and had simply "made a few notes with pencil." He reminded the district official that with such methods "the German nation cannot control deliveries"; it would be easy for "a mistake to slip in . . . because pencil smears so easily. The control official can thus register the confiscation properly only if he has a proper receipt book that is filled out in ink according to regulations." This lengthy, didactic preamble was followed by Potthast's complaint that he had been underpaid by 45 marks for his pigs and the threat that his next appeal would be to the provincial high president who ultimately had "ordered the confiscation for this district."[60]

In other instances, petitioners hoped that a personal visit to local officials would win sympathy for their special appeals and requests for dispensation. In the summer of 1918 Fräulein Marie Homringhausen, who worked a small farm in the southern Westphalian district of Wittgenstein, took a day off from her labors to inform local officials of the economic irrationality of their confiscation policies. She asked that her cow be spared from delivery until later in the year because the animal was essential for the fall plowing. On the recommendation of officials from her local village, the request was denied on the grounds that "her brother has been drafted, and the womenfolk (*Frauenleute*) can hardly take care of their smallholding anyway."[61] From a neighboring town, a similar complaint came from the widow of Friedrich Spies, a fallen soldier: she also claimed to need at least three cows for plowing on her small farm of 8½ hectares. Perhaps the officials approved her request to be spared from delivering one draft animal because she offered still other mitigating circumstances—two small children and a sixty-three-year-old mentally ill aunt who was no help on the farm.[62]

Such tales of individual hardship did not always prompt a sympathetic official response, however. In mid-April 1918, the widow of Rudolf Kasperski journeyed to the office of the local official in Berleburg, a small town in Wittgenstein, seeking not an exemption from upcoming deliveries but rather the requisite official permission to purchase a cow. She argued that she required a source of fresh milk daily for an aging steer that in turn was essential for her draft needs. After interviewing Kasperski, the local official took seriously his charge to evaluate her request. In response to his written inquiry, the council in Kasperski's village advised against allowing her to purchase the milk cow. Armed with this information, he explained, "In my opinion, Frau Kasperski is not in a position to feed and take care of a cow. In all respects, she is very negligent and she seems to be somewhat melancholy." On this basis, he suggested that "she would be well served with the purchase of a couple of goats," a proposal seconded by the local veterinarian and adopted by the district official.[63]

In early 1917 Wilhelm Klein, a fifty-seven-year-old peasant in a Rhenish district near the Westphalian border, was no happier with local officials, and he took his appeal to the provincial high president. Excusing his impertinence in demanding the attention of such a high-ranking authority, Klein explained that " 'Necessity knows no sanctions.' " Klein had recently received notification that he should deliver an ox, confiscated for slaughter; this action, he argued, would leave him unable to meet his draft needs, since only a cow and a steer would remain on his farm. As circumstances complicating his situation, he pointed to a sick wife and a brother, half-owner of the ox, who assisted him only for wages. Investigations by the county district administrator led to a teacher in Klein's village who testified that the petitioner was fully able to deliver the ox and had misrepresented his relation with his brother, who in fact ran his own farm together with Klein. Klein's complaint justified no positive action on his behalf but did prompt a thorough investigation of his brother, who was still subject to conscription.[64]

Another common category of appeals was for exemption from military service or the temporary furlough of agricultural workers and peasant farmers. For peasant farm families, such petitions reflected both personal and economic interests, and their response to the rejection of their requests was undoubtedly colored by both concerns as well.[65] Particular bitterness also accompanied the punishment of nondeliverers, which included suspension of the peasant's control over the grain consumed by the farm family and the substitution of a ration card.[66]

In still other cases, individual complaints over controls reflected perceived inequities relative to other regions. West German peasants often criticized measures that they saw as favoring the interests of east Elbian estate owners,[67] and they also complained about differences in treatment much closer to home. When the news reached one part of eastern Westphalia that grain delivery quotas had been reduced in other areas, demands for equal treatment followed immediately. A local official warned that, confronted with such apparent injustice, peasants "will lose faith in local government officials since they very well know that conditions are not at all different" in neighboring districts; "we can anticipate opposition to the execution of wartime measures and material losses. The loss of faith will destroy attitudes that will not be restored for years to come."[68]

Not only did peasants look suspiciously over the provincial or district border, they also kept a watchful eye on the treatment that their neighbors received. Thus, for example, one Wilhelm Schneider could add to his appeal for postponement of the delivery of a confiscated cow, "The man who lives next to me has more livestock than I do and since delivering one head of cattle last fall, he hasn't delivered a thing." Both of Schneider's sons had been drafted, and one had died in military service. Schneider clearly described these circumstances to underline the legitimacy of his appeal; in contrast, he pointed out, his neighbor "has been free from military service so far." Schneider volunteered the suggestion that "perhaps one could take a couple of animals from him," but he hastened to warn the district administrator that for a reliable report on the neighbor's ability to deliver he should definitely not turn to the local magistrate, because that official "spreads lies about my livestock deliveries."[69]

By themselves, these examples of individual complaints cannot constitute a comprehensive picture of the discontent of peasant producers, and those who made their protest a matter of public record were undoubtedly in the minority.[70] Nor is there any way to determine whether Marie Kasperski was in fact better served with two goats rather than a cow, or whether Schneider could easily have delivered an additional head of cattle despite his claims to the contrary. However, right and wrong are less directly gauged than are the feelings of outrage that underlay peasant appeals. Read together with the evidence of the flourishing black market, the chronic underreporting of yields, and the other examples of "passive resistance" to the war economy found in the reports of local officials, such individual testimonies can richly elaborate the outlines of peasant discontent.[71] They also illuminate a fundamental aspect of the war economy: peasant production decisions were no longer exclusively the responsibility of peasant producers. State officials could determine how much of what should be delivered to whom at what price, and peasant fears of economic decline could easily be attributed to the perceived inequities of guidelines over which they had no control, rather than to individual incompetence or the workings of an anonymous market.

The evidence also suggests that the relationship between state policy and peasant economic welfare was immediately apparent. When peasants had complaints over prices or mandated delivery quotas, they directed their anger not at commercial middlemen or a distant world market—the favored targets before 1914—but rather at the local official responsible for carrying out the measures of the controlled economy. The consequence was, as the Rhenish Agricultural Chamber press noted shortly after the war's end, that "the otherwise so good-natured head of county government and the accessible local mayor became symbols of intolerable police authority and the exercise of arbitrary power"; erstwhile friends of agriculture, now they appeared as an "annoying reminder and executor of the controlled economy."[72] Ascribing responsibility for the controls to industrial workers and Social Democrats—those forcing the Kaiser's hand—rather than to the Kaiser or his local officials, represented one possible resolution of this conflict. By 1918, however, even this tactic could do little to dissipate the bitterness of agricultural producers over wartime measures. The future of those measures was an open question that understandably preoccupied Rhenish and Westphalian peasants.

From Passive Resistance to Political Protest

The protest and passive resistance to the war economy by literally thousands of peasant producers had a profound impact on agricultural interest groups in the Rhineland and Westphalia. These organizations did not fabricate peasant discontent. Peasants needed no assistance in recognizing that the war economy represented an immediate threat to their economic livelihood.[73] Interest-group leaders did, however, offer a coherent interpretation of peasant distress and provided a structure within which protest could begin to move from individual to collective forms.

The cause of peasant discontent might easily vary from case to case—the government official who confiscated a cow, the industrial worker whose welfare seemed of greater concern to the state than that of the peasant, the soldier who aided in the searches for hidden reserves and then abused his authority by becoming a black marketeer, or the government in far-off Berlin that made arbitrary decisions apparently with no real knowledge of conditions in the countryside. Like the peasants described by anthropologist Eric Wolf, agricultural producers in the Rhineland and Westphalia protested the "parochial manifestations of great social dislocations."[74] The inchoate response of individual agricultural producers took shape in the formulations of interest-group leaders. This process cannot be understood either exclusively as the conscious orchestration or manipulation of peasant sentiment from above by conservative elites, or as the radicalization of leaders by an angry rank and file. Interest-group leaders gave peasant discontent a political gloss that the peasants themselves could not provide, but the emphases of leadership response and the forcefulness of their protest directly reflected their constituents' concerns. In this complex process of articulating peasant grievances, the nature and self-perception of interest-group representatives underwent important changes. Charting these changes and describing the move from economic to political protest that they entailed will occupy the remainder of this chapter.

Agrarian interest-group leaders could do little to influence government economic policy directly during the war; for them, there was no parallel to the extensive inclusion of management representatives in the organization and administration of those parts of the controlled economy that directly affected industry. The representatives of organized labor were also integrated into many offices with political influence on economic and domestic policy. Both steps clearly reflected the concessions that these groups could extract from the government for their cooperation in the *Burgfrieden* after August 1914. Despite their conflicts with management and the military over other issues, trade-union leaders shared with them a hard-nosed attitude toward the agricultural sector. Agriculture was excluded from this alliance of army, industry, and labor, and support for ever-tighter controls on agricultural production helped to unify these three otherwise quite diverse groups.[75]

While industrial and labor organizations found their positions strengthened and their influence enhanced, agricultural interest groups could register no similar gains. In fact, the cooperative marketing and purchasing network—painstakingly fostered by the Peasant Associations before 1914—atrophied during the war. Proposals to increase the participation of these institutions in the administration of controls could not even muster support from agriculture's traditional allies.[76] Indeed, many government officials argued that state control would be essential not only for the duration of the war but, in all likelihood, during the transition to a peacetime economy as well.[77]

Although the long-term impact of the war on the network of cooperative savings and loan associations was equally injurious, their problems were of a very different order. Serious reductions in supplies of production goods and limited opportunities for profitable investments meant that the demand for short-term credits fell off significantly while savings deposits expanded dramatically.[78] Money not only went into savings but was also used to pay off prewar debts, both to credit cooperatives and to other creditors (see Appendix Table 20).[79] The increased flow of capital into the credit cooperatives was an obvious target for the protest of urban critics who pointed to the discrepancy between the expanded reserves of the cooperatives and the alleged woes of agricultural producers. But agricultural interest-group leaders were quick to counter that the flush created by increased savings was no healthy glow. It reflected not higher profit margins, but the inability of producers to replenish soil fertility, machinery, farm buildings, and livestock holdings. The expansion of savings was symptomatic of a dangerous development, the forced liquidation of capital.[80]

One outlet for the excess funds of individual cooperative members and provincial banks was investment in paper securities, particularly war bonds. The Peasant Associations untiringly reminded their members that "few investment opportunities offer as much security. The entire German nation with its entire income and wealth is liable for this loan."[81] Such optimistic assurances were perhaps ultimately less compelling than the genuine absence of alternative investment opportunities. Whatever their motivations, by 1918 individual members and the central cooperative banks associated with the Peasant Associations in the Rhineland held 157 million marks in war bonds, a level exceeded in Westphalia a year earlier by 50 million marks. Of course, these amounts also reflected the impact of that other, and ultimately more important, method of war-financing, the printing press.[82] The wartime inflation not only increased the nominal flow of capital into paper securities but also undermined the assurances that "few investment opportunities offer as much security." Indeed, investments in the German state were investments in an increasingly uncertain future.

Thus, unlike the interest-group representatives and organizations of labor and management, agrarian leaders could offer their members only a narrower, not a wider, range of services during the war. Vocal attacks on the war economy were among the few forms of representation that agricultural interest groups could still provide, but these direct appeals provoked little more official reaction than did the impassioned petitions and passive resistance of individual producers. From the beginning of the war, the Peasant Associations, the Agricultural Chambers, and the latter body's local branches, the Agricultural Associations, offered themselves as the appropriate forum for the public discussion of peasant discontent over the war economy and as the advocate most able to defend peasant interests. The Chambers were compromised, however, by their semi-official status that limited their capacity to criticize government policy directly.[83] Far more open and blunt in their broadsides against the war economy were the Peasant Associations.

Unlike the war-aims question, public discussion of the food problem was not totally silenced.[84] Nonetheless, limits were set to agrarian attacks on specific policies by the political and social ties of conservative interest-group leaders to the high-ranking provincial officials who were responsible for administering the measures formulated by a conservative Kaiser's government. Interest-group leaders were caught in an ambiguous position by the war: they realized the need to respond to the growing discontent of their constituents if they were to maintain their authority, and as landowners subject to controls, they shared with them many common complaints about the war economy; at the same time, they reminded their members of their patriotic duty to comply with the restrictions imposed by the war economy. Moreover, patriotism paralleled self-interest, and interest-group spokesmen emphasized that the exacerbation of urban-rural tensions would alienate former friends and undermine agriculture's attempts to reintroduce tariffs or other forms of governmental support after the end of hostilities. By the winter of 1917, however, the extent of the black market and the declines of deliveries indicated that thousands of peasant producers were not convinced that it was the dilatory producer who gave the critics of agriculture their best ammunition. Open attacks by interest-group leaders on the war economy intensified as deliveries declined.[85]

In the interest-group press, the frustration over poorly defined and coordinated price policies was expressed in attacks on the criminal prosecution of those disregarding wartime regulations. Violations, according to agrarian spokesmen, often reflected little more than misinformation or the peasant's unavoidable ignorance of one out of hundreds of rules. An account from the Rhenish Peasant Association press from the fall of 1916 captures the escalating level of peasant discontent and the increasingly aggressive nature of interest-group response:

> From the sentences that have been handed down, many judges would seem to think that the peasant is eager to violate official measures. For example, someone gets a harsh punishment for feeding his pigs with restricted feeds. Well, what should this individual do? He has already done everything in his power to obtain feed, but without results. He can't slaughter the animal without permission, unless it has attained a certain minimum weight. And if he gives up and abandons pig-raising, he has no sympathy or understanding for the Fatherland. In short, whatever he does is wrong. Such cases are quite common in the agricultural sector. And it's precisely such cases that rob the peasant of his desire to produce.[86]

Although government policy deserved vigilant scrutiny, interest-group leaders stressed that those ultimately bearing the responsibility for misguided controls were the trade unionists and Social Democrats who exploited their indispensability to the war effort in order to pursue their own special interests.[87] This assessment, a standard part of the interest-group critique of the war economy, clearly reflected the material reality beneath the consumer-producer divide. It also left the representatives of organized agrarian interests openly at odds with the representatives of the organized working class. Long before 1914 the Peasant Associations had become accustomed to confrontations with the SPD and with socialist-oriented Free Trade Unions. During the war, however, Christian black joined socialist red in attacks on the agricultural sector.[88] Particularly in the Rhineland, home of the central offices of the organized Catholic working class, the Peasant Association engaged in head-on exchanges with the Christian Trade Unions. Confession could not patch up this fundamental split, and Peasant Association leaders responded to attacks in kind, charging that the Christian Trade Unions had poisoned urban-rural relations by leading a self-interested onslaught on all agrarians and thus threatening the domestic peace. Such sharp exchanges outlined the institutional dimensions of the consumer-producer split and did nothing to improve the strained relations between workers and peasants in the Center party.

Framing an Ideological Response

By the end of the war, it was increasingly difficult for interest-group leaders to negotiate a path between the Scylla of peasant discontent and the Charybdis of residual loyalty to governmental authority. Thus in one breath they could encourage their members to buy war bonds, meet delivery quotas, and join the Fatherland party (Vaterlandspartei), and in the next, could sanction nondeliveries as a form of protest against the injustices of the war economy.[89] The way out of this dilemma during the war was increasingly to shift the focus of criticism away from the Kaiser and his officials, to working-class consumers. Added to the disputes over economic policy were debates over war aims and over demands for political reforms. For interest-group leaders, the task was to forge clear links between these various issues—in short, to elucidate the connection between peasants' "parochial concerns" and the "great social dislocations" at the national level.

The reintroduction of proposals for political reform in the spring of 1917 focused the conservative agrarian response. Of course, pressure for electoral reform in Prussia was not new, and as long as reform had been demanded, Rhenish and Westphalian interest-group leaders had opposed it. Temporarily tabled by the *Burgfrieden*, the reform debate reappeared under very different circumstances in the spring and summer of 1917. Industrial unrest and strike activity had concentrated primarily on living conditions and the inadequacies of the provisioning system, but increasingly these strikes came to have a political dimension as demands for political reform and for an end to the war were added to the demands for bread.[90] Promises of the reform of the plutocratic Prussian suffrage were offered as one strategy to quiet worker unrest over deteriorating living conditions. As Wilhelm Groener, one of the more enlightened members of the General Staff, reflected, it was essential "to feed the masses with ballots instead of meat and bread" as long as the provisioning system remained a leaky dam.[91]

Clemens Freiherr von Loë-Bergerhausen and Engelbert Freiherr Kerckerinck zu Borg, the leaders, respectively, of the Rhenish and Westphalian Peasant Associations, wasted no time in launching a frontal assault against the reform proposals outlined in the Kaiser's "Easter Message" of April 1917. Loë-Bergerhausen was one of a long line in his family to assume the position of a conservative Center party spokesman and a leader in the Rhenish association; always on the right of the Center before 1914, he was to show precisely how deep his conservative stripe ran in the debates over Prussian political reform at the end of the war.

Kerckerinck assumed the presidency of the Westphalian organization in 1916.[92] He had studied law and had followed a typical path for a son of the aristocracy, serving a brief legal internship, joining a reserve officer corps, marrying into the well-known von Galen family, and taking over the management of his own family's large estate near Münster. Since 1912, he had served as a Center party delegate in the Reichstag, and there was no question of his adherence to the party's conservative right wing. After 1916 he also headed the umbrella organization that loosely united all Christian Peasant Associations. He moved its offices permanently to Berlin in order better to monitor (and, where possible, to influence) government policy, and he selected a fellow Westphalian, August Crone-Münzebrock, as its general secretary. By the end of the war, Kerckerinck had established himself as a major spokesman for agrarian interests west of the Elbe and within the Center Fortress. Perhaps no leader since Schorlemer-Alst had given the Peasant Association such dynamic, yet profoundly conservative, leadership.[93]

Despite an age difference of many years, Loë-Bergerhausen and the younger Kerckerinck were personal friends and worked closely together. As heads of the two most powerful organizations within the Federation of German Peasant Associations, they could exert a major influence on the national policies of that group as well as within their provincial organizations. In their response to proposals for the reform of the Prussian three-class electoral system, both men drew heavily on the ideological mainstays of the prewar era. "God did not establish the world on the basis of uncontrolled equality," asserted Loë-Bergerhausen, "but rather on the principle of an authoritative division of labor." Economic backwardness, religious intolerance, politics of the marketplace—these were the inevitable consequences of the tyranny of the majority and of rule by "head-count," as embodied in democratically elected parliamentary institutions. Universal suffrage, he claimed, would mean no less than the introduction of an unfair tax system and socialization, the end of the confessional school and normal family life, and the despotic rule of the working class. In no more original a vein, he and Kerckerinck resorted to the contrast between an "organic perspective" and an individualistic "materialist-mechanistic perspective," drawing on the contrast of pre- and post-1789 France to make their point.[94]

These knee-jerk conservative responses harkened back at least to the 1870s, if not to the heritage of Ludwig Haller and Adam Mueller.[95] However, in the summer of 1917 they were deployed in a very different context, that of the war economy and the rift between producers and consumers. "The unrestricted transfer of the national electoral system to Prussia and particularly to the west," Loë-Bergerhausen argued, "would mean the one-sided representation of working-class interests and the virtual exclusion of any consideration of rural needs." He reminded his constituents that "in the Rhineland and Westphalia, a rural population of 2,394,209 faces an urban, predominantly industrial population of 6,553,366." The consequences of electoral reform for the agricultural sector required little imagination: "From everything we know, and most recently after the experience we have had during the war, it seems entirely out of the question that the interests of agriculture will be acknowledged and adequately considered."[96]

Kerckerinck also explicitly stressed this connection between the realities of the war economy and the implications of universal suffrage in Prussia. Building on widely held concerns about a future shaped by "the growing majority of consumer representation in legislative bodies,"[97] he explained in June 1917: "For the most part, political things do not concern us [the Peasant Associations]. . . . But we always have to concern ourselves with political questions that have an impact on our economic interests." Surely no other questions fell more squarely into this category than those raised by the "New Orientation," the proposals for suffrage reform and the extension of parliament's powers. Kerckerinck continued:

> Today the estates that are in a numerical minority, agriculture and the producing *Mittelstand*, can already begin to feel the noose that is being tied for them. Even before the war, the pressure from the other side had taken on unpleasant forms. During the war, at first, it seemed that there was a wave of national enthusiasm, cleansing us from the ashes of class battles and marking a mutual understanding among various groups. The internal developments of the last years appear to have had a different result. Today the worker works for the war effort, the state depends on this work, and socialist leaders exploit this combination of events. To this is added the psychological impact of the Russian revolution, which is flooding over our country as well.

The war in the trenches was thus augmented by "a military campaign against the bearers of the bourgeois order, especially against agriculture and the *Mittelstand*, which has been as consciously organized as England's campaign against the Allied Powers."[98]

Kerckerinck and Loë-Bergerhausen's volatile blend of prewar conservatism and antagonism toward the war economy equated those clamoring for democratization with those demanding tighter controls on agricultural production: those who had exploited their position since 1914 to achieve the latter objective were now exploiting their position to achieve the former. Certainly a robust antisocialism and hymns in praise of the sanctity of private property were no additions to the polemical repertoire of the conservative agrarian elite, but against the background of the war economy they could take on new meanings. The connection between the political power of urban consumers and economic policies that disadvantaged the agricultural sector was hardly remote for agricultural producers who had just endured a police audit of their grain reserves and who, by the winter of 1916–17, seldom met delivery quotas without threats of confiscation. Peasants may have been abstractly concerned that political democratization and the introduction of universal suffrage in Prussia might ultimately mean nothing less than the collapse of western civilization, as conservative agrarian leaders predicted, but a more concrete and far less demagogic basis for opposition to reform proposals was the fear that political reform might result in the extension of state intervention into the economy beyond the end of the war.

The enemy was not only the socialist left, but *all* those pushing for political reform. Significantly, as evidence supporting his fears of a future state-regulated economy Kerckerinck cited not an SPD leader or *Vorwärts*, but rather the statement of the leader of the Catholic Workers' Movement (Christliche Arbeiterbewegung), Joseph Joos of München-Gladbach, that " 'in a new Germany, it will no longer be possible to leave it up to every peasant and estate owner to farm as well or as poorly as he wishes.' " The implication, according to Kerckerinck, was clear: "In short, the state regulation, which already weighs so heavily on our production but which we have to bear as an exceptional condition for the nation, is declared as a permanent condition for the future."[99]

In their attacks on reform proposals, Peasant Association leaders linked economic discontent to a political program; they skillfully translated well-established antisocialist, antiparliamentary tirades into the language of the war at home; they invoked a collective memory of a prosperous, secure past and juxtaposed it to the political and economic uncertainties of the present; and their ominous predictions for the future defined a solid basis for collective action. It is difficult to measure with certainty the impact of these political formulations at the membership level of the Peasant Associations. At the very least, however, we can plausibly speculate that Rhenish and Westphalian peasants had little reason to question this vision. No more than interest-group attacks on economic policy could it remove the sources of their discontent, but it provided a clear political dimension to that discontent and described a connection between the economic crisis and proposals for political reform in the last two years of the war.

The leadership of the Center party in no way endorsed the conservative agrarian rejection of political reform. Although Kerckerinck and Loë-Bergerhausen had powerful allies in the highest echelons of the Catholic church, they confronted the united opposition of organized Catholic workers and the waning tolerance of middle-class party leaders. Many of the latter did not share the demands of the Christian Trade Unions and of the People's Association for Catholic Germany for immediate adoption of the Kaiser's "Easter Message," but they had even less sympathy for the intransigence of the agrarian right.[100]

In internal party discussions of electoral reform the extremes clashed head-on—particularly in the Rhineland, where Loë-Bergerhausen collided with Heinrich Brauns, a key figure in the People's Association, and with leaders of the Christian Trade Unions.[101] The dimensions of the conflict became public when a conference of "Worker-Voters in the Center Party" convened in Bochum in June 1918 to express its unequivocal support for suffrage reform. The delegates unanimously rejected lame attempts by Kerckerinck and others to substitute plural voting schemes for truly meaningful change.[102] The meeting also revealed that connections between political reform and the war economy existed not only in the minds of conservative agrarians: charges that the Center press had been too mild in its treatment of a "greedy" agricultural sector during the war were coupled with the demand that the party "do more for consumer interests."[103] In general, the party would have to modify its pronounced orientation toward agrarian concerns if it hoped to alter the impression that it "subordinated the interests of the industrial and manufacturing population, particularly in western Germany, to those of agriculture."[104] The Center's parliamentary delegation shared the responsibility for not adequately controlling agricultural price increases, and forceful action in this area would be essential in order to insure working-class faith in its elected leaders.[105]

The threatening tone of the meeting was exemplified by the remarks of a union secretary and city council member from Essen who warned that if the party did not remedy the common conception that "it primarily counts on peasant votes . . . , the Catholic workers of the west will not remain within the Center in the long run." The Center was no longer "habitable"; the air within was stuffy, and it was time to "clean, improve, renew . . . strengthen the party and bring young blood into it."[106] The conference concluded that the very future of the Center party was at stake. Greater representation for workers, both within the party in the western industrial areas and at the national level, was the highest priority. Any Center representative who did not support universal suffrage should be denied the votes of Catholic workers.[107]

Within the Center, the divisions over political reform ran parallel to divisions over the question of war aims. Peasant Association leaders rejected any notion of peace without annexations and continued to bank on territorial aggrandizement as the means to compensate all Germans for the sufferings caused by the war.[108] Despite Herold's insistence that no special organization was necessary in order to allow loyal Center party members to assert their confidence in their country,[109] Kerckerinck made no secret of his support for the rabidly nationalistic, annexationist Fatherland party, and Loë-Bergerhausen was a leader of its Rhenish branch.[110] Skirmishes within the Center party over war aims broke into open hostilities with the creation of the Inter-Party Committee in July 1917 and with Matthias Erzberger's emergence as a key Center leader. Center cooperation with Majority Socialists only confirmed the worst fears of conservative agrarians that the party had taken an irreversible turn to the left. Concessions abroad and at home were bound together, and the forces pushing for a "Scheidemann peace" were those pushing for domestic reform. In the opinion of conservative leaders of the Peasant Association, the Center party was lining up on the wrong side on both issues.[111]

By the summer of 1918, the Center was deeply divided over the future structure of the war economy, political reform measures, the nature of the peace, and the very bases of the party. As labor leader Adam Stegerwald reflected, the central position of the party in the Reichstag created the superficial impression that the Center was at the apex of its power. "Internally, however," he quickly added, "a split now exists in the party and has for a while, which is without precedent."[112] On neither side of this division between the party's worker and peasant representatives were there indications of a willingness to compromise. Indeed, on both sides increased organizational activity testified to preparations for a drawn-out conflict. As Kerckerinck realized, the defense of conservative interests in postwar Germany would require not only an ideological framework but also organizational strategies for mobilizing agricultural producers within the Peasant Associations in opposition to political reforms. With a growing sense of immediacy, Kerckerinck and Loë-Bergerhausen emphasized that the key to political power was effective organization in the pursuit of common economic objectives. In the pragmatic analysis offered by the Rhenish association press, "Politics is power, and self-interest typically triumphs over philosophical dreams. If we want to achieve a sound agricultural policy, then we have to protect the countryside from political disenfranchisement."[113]

Emphasizing the essentially economic motivation for the political lobbying of agricultural interest groups allowed agrarian spokesmen to maintain their allegedly nonpartisan, apolitical status. Of course, such disclaimers were meaningless in a context that injected all economic questions with a political content, but they did allow Peasant Association leaders to avoid explicit party political affiliation and thus an open confrontation within the Center. As Kerckerinck candidly explained to Martin Spahn, the conservative son of Center party leader Peter Spahn, "We have to be careful since we cannot afford to be too 'purely political.'" The avoidance of specific party political labels was essential given the political heterogeneity of Peasant Association members, both within the national federation that included some largely Protestant organizations, and in Kerckerinck's native Westphalia, with its southern and eastern Protestant fringe. "To make up for it," Kerckerinck admitted, "we put that much greater an emphasis on *Wirtschaftspolitik*." He concluded that "the question of electoral reform is also a central economic question, given that the protection of the economic interests of the agricultural population is dependent on its just political representation."[114]

More than mere talk of organization was necessary, and Kerckerinck and Loë-Bergerhausen encouraged their members to translate words into action. Looking back in the summer of 1918 on the activities of the Peasant Associations in the previous two years, Kerckerinck stressed the importance of a lobby organization at the national level and called for increased activity at all other levels as well.[115] In villages and administrative districts, meetings should be held more frequently than in the past, and the steering committees of provincial organizations should increase their membership and meet at regular intervals. Of course, the exigencies of the war clearly restricted the possibilities for realizing these proposals;

many interest-group officials had been drafted, and the activities of marketing and purchasing cooperatives had been brought to a standstill. However,
Kerckerinck's reflections indicated his recognition that new forms and increased
organizational activity appropriate to a changed political context would be essential in the transition from war to peace.

Assessing the Impact of the War

Four years of war had a profound impact on the peasantry of the Rhineland and
Westphalia. To be sure, agricultural producers were not the only Germans to make
sacrifices or to chafe under the restrictions of the war economy, and at least—as
urban consumers repeatedly emphasized—in the countryside there was always
something to eat. Nevertheless, by the last two war years, when peasants chose to
see their position in relative terms, they emphasized not their enviable position,
but the undue influence of urban industrial workers on government policy. The
"Turnip Winter" of 1916–17 left urban dwellers in the Ruhr imagining feasts
consumed in the neighboring countryside, but it left peasants angered over the
confiscation of turnips, one of their last remaining sources of livestock feed.[116]
Producers and consumers shared little more than the inability and unwillingness
to consider one another's conditions. Peasant discontent could crystallize politically in opposition to political reforms that would institute de jure the de facto
gains achieved by the representatives of the organized industrial working class;
workers saw those reforms as the absolute minimum necessary to compensate for
their sacrifices during four years of war. There was no clear way to resolve these
conflicts. The failure of the German offensive in the summer of 1918 meant that
an end to the war with the Allies was imminent, as the General Staff finally
conceded—but in the war at home, none of the protagonists seemed ready to
surrender, and the form of a future armistice was far from clear.

FOUR

The Tumultuous Transition from War to Peace

A widely published newspaper story on the "Moral Treatment of Agriculture" undoubtedly expressed the feelings of many peasants at the end of the fourth year of war. The author described the three types of laborers essential to the war effort—the soldier, the worker in the armaments industry, and the peasant. How, he then asked, were these three essential groups treated during the war? The soldier received the honor due him. The worker got higher wages, the respect he deserved, and the attention and concern of government officials. "How do we handle the third?" the author continued rhetorically:

> A year's prison sentence and 10,000-mark fine, expropriation and confiscation, checks, threats of punishments, house searches, mandatory levies, controls of acreage planted, harvest checks, livestock checks, mandatory registration, mandatory deliveries, denial of the right to control one's own food supply. . . . Am I a criminal, the peasant asks himself, and if so, what is my crime? . . . We protect the general welfare from the peasant with maximum prices. But who protects the peasant? . . . The German peasant will begin to get bitter if this continues.[1]

By the late summer of 1918, things did not need to go any further to create bitterness among the west German peasantry, and the final collapse of the war effort in the fall did little to defuse an explosive situation.

Given the antagonism between urban consumers and rural producers before the winter of 1918–19, it is hardly surprising that peasants in the Rhineland and Westphalia did not support the revolutionary movements in nearby cities of the Ruhr initiated by those other two groups of "laborers essential to the war effort," workers and soldiers. The dearth of big estates worked by teams of agricultural laborers also insured that the Rhineland and Westphalia did not experience the strikes of agricultural workers that engulfed some east Elbian districts and parts of Saxony.[2] The one well-documented instance of cooperation between peasants and radical workers, Kurt Eisner's Bavarian Republic, was an exception that proved the rule: peasant support for the revolution in Bavaria was based on long-standing regional antipathy toward a Prussian-dominated national government, the existence of a progressive network of peasant interest groups, and the carefully cultivated ties between Eisner and local peasant leaders. Moreover, even in this instance, peasant support for revolution was quite limited and ultimately short-lived.[3] Far more representative of urban-rural relations in the autumn and winter of 1918 was the situation in the Rhineland and Westphalia, where those peasant councils that did emerge exhibited only antipathy and distrust toward the councils of workers and soldiers in the cities.

Although there was thus little chance that Rhenish and Westphalian peasants would ally themselves with an urban revolution, in the winter of 1918–19 it was not self-evident that rural discontent would be contained by the structures of established interest groups. New organizations aggressively challenged the dominance of the Peasant Associations, and pressure for change came from within existing structures as well. This chapter will assess the forms of interest-group response to these challenges and to the seismic shifts in the political landscape in the year following the end of the war.

"Continuity without a Concept": Agricultural Policy and the Consumer-Producer Conflict

An important element of continuity in the transition from war to peace shaped the reaction of agrarian interest-group leaders and their peasant constituents to the dramatic political changes in late 1918 and 1919. With the signing of the armistice in November 1918, fighting came to an end, but the crisis of the ever-worsening food shortage in Germany did not. There was no immediate suspension of the Allied blockade to foreign imports, and in late 1918 agricultural producers certainly had no more to deliver than they had delivered a year earlier. Matters were made even worse by the fact that many peasants believed that the end of armed conflict meant the end to controls on the economy.[4]

The problems of enforcement were compounded by yet another carryover from the war—the flourishing black market. The situation in early 1919 was effectively summarized at a national meeting of officials charged with overseeing prices: "It's a popular joke that whoever restricts himself to rations ends up in the morgue, whoever doesn't ends up in jail. That's the damned truth. Today, nobody obeys the laws, rather, everyone attempts to get what he needs; the idealism and the patriotic feelings that were present at the beginning are gone, and physiological need is the determining factor."[5] The waves of so-called *Hamsterer*, scroungers from industrial areas who ventured into nearby agricultural regions in search of food, dramatically bore out this observation. Urban residents arrived in rural areas by the trainload in search of agricultural products in amounts however small. Local officials in the countryside blamed the Councils of Workers and

Soldiers and urban police for exacerbating an already chaotic situation by indis-criminately issuing the travel papers still required to reach rural areas from the cities.[6]

With the end of the war, the *Hamster* traffic extended farther and farther from large urban areas into more remote agricultural districts, some as many as 200 kilometers away from the Ruhr.[7] Railroad officials in Essen complained that "all measures to impede the so-called *Hamster* traffic have remained unsuccessful up until now. Thousands of families from the industrial areas leave with the early morning trains for the countryside and come home with the late trains, laden with sacks, crates, and baskets." Conditions on the trains became uncontrollable, and officials feared for the physical well-being of passengers "who cannot find a place in the overfilled compartments that often can no longer be closed [and who] attempt to find a place on the running board, on the roofs of the cars, or near the brakes." Women and children were principal actors in this drama, and in the scramble to return home, they "won't be denied the chance to make the last train and they seize their places with force."[8]

The amounts that disappeared on the black market made it no easier for many rural areas to meet their delivery quotas. A communal official from a district between Münster and Dortmund decried the fact that "grain is carried off by the hundredweight. As soon as they [the *Hamsterer*] hear the sound of a threshing machine, they gather by the hundreds at the farm and demand with threats that the threshed grain be handed over."[9] In another instance, a police official reported grudging forms of collaboration between urban scroungers and peasants as the former assisted the latter with their potato harvest. Aided by ad hoc work teams, the peasant quickly completed his harvest and "sold the potatoes on the spot, thus saving himself trouble and work, and getting a price higher than the official one." Controlling such activity directly on thousands of peasant farms was impossible, and part-time police assistants were in short supply because "no one wants to participate in this unpleasant work."[10] The government president in Cologne described the vicious circle that resulted: "The authorities cannot collect the entire harvest because large parts of it have already been hauled off. The popula-tion cannot survive from what the officials distribute and is left to its own devices to cover its needs. But what . . . [they] seize cannot be collected by the authori-ties, and so it goes." The only feasible solution he could propose to the problem of the black market was to make half the population into police inspectors, charged with controlling the other half.[11]

An expanded black market and the ongoing shortages continued to fuel the tensions between producers and consumers. Escalated rhetorical attacks on agri-cultural producers reflected the dire situations in the cities. Socialist press ac-counts associated the peasantry with the worst enemies of the Republic and charged that widespread peasant participation in the black market indicated collu-sion with usurious middlemen. In one formulation, "Not only the Spartacists on the left but also those on the right threaten to destroy the economy completely with their evil deeds. The latter help to prepare the soil in which the fertile seed of the Spartacists grows."[12] "Traitorous agricultural producers" consumed "sumptuous banquets" and were responsible for the "death of victims of malnutrition." "The profit-hungry peasants, pawning themselves off as Christians, are in reality egotists, usurers, and murderers of coming generations!" The patterns established in wartime survived in the Republic, and "England's ally, the peasant . . . bore the blame for the unfortunate end of the war and will now bring the entire people to disaster, if he's not stopped."[13] Certainly, new imagery had been adapted to a changed situation, but the general tone established long before 1918 had altered little. Neither had the remedies proposed: the only solution acceptable to many angry consumers was the strictest possible control of all agricultural producers "disloyal to their country."[14] In early 1919, such attitudes reflected not only the position of the Majority Socialists but the sentiments of many other urban consumers as well.[15]

Behind this rhetoric was the reality of increasingly sharp conflicts generated by tactics that circumvented not only the controlled economy but also the black market. In the most benign cases, scroungers not eager to aid with the potato harvest and without the resources required to deal on the black market might use forged papers authorizing the confiscation of agricultural products,[16] or might disguise themselves as nurses and plead from farm to farm for food for their hospital, thanking contributors with prayers.[17] Still others resorted to theft from peasant homes, and in the early spring of 1919 a peasant's morning visit to his pastures might reveal the remains of animals butchered on the spot the night before; by the summer, the numbers of such incidents of direct, criminal attacks on peasant property had expanded greatly.[18]

Incidents of this sort followed a pattern established in the last war years. However, peasant accounts that they now involved self-proclaimed "Spartacists," whether a description of reality or a reflection of peasant fears, testified to the political dimension added to such encounters in the wake of the revolution.[19] New forms were also apparent in the collective action of workers to requisition directly the supplies that the authorities could not provide. In one instance, the district administrator in Hamm, a city on the edge of the Ruhr, reported that the entire work force of a mine had walked off the job to look for food. Joined by other workers and numbering over a thousand, they split up into armed groups of two or three hundred and, decked out with red flags and singing revolutionary songs, they set out into the countryside. Teams of four to five went from farm to farm demanding all available reserves; any food taken was divided up immediately. Police attempts to control the situation led to an exchange of gunfire and the death of one peasant member of a local militia.[20]

The willingness of urban workers to take such direct action was an irrefutable indication of the extreme shortages that prevailed in the cities by the spring of

1919, but the response of rural producers was one of defensive fear, not sympathy. Such incidents provided ample material for the rhetorical diatribes of agrarian interest-group leaders, and they also occasionally prompted direct responses by the peasantry. Thus, scroungers who came to the Westphalian village of Emden in May were chased out by a band armed with "flails, clubs, and guns." The success of such direct action encouraged village residents to form a militia and prompted the emulation of their example by peasants in neighboring areas.[21]

In short, relations between city and countryside, already badly strained by the hardships experienced on both sides during the war, only deteriorated further in the immediate postwar period. The problem of shortages continued, and the policy response to shortages did not change.[22] The early governments of the new German republic did not create the controlled economy, but neither did they modify the aspects of it most opposed by peasant producers. Rather, the new order endorsed and maintained a control network that, though clearly inadequate, was at least firmly in place. Thus, as Martin Schumacher has described it, the government's policy was one of "continuity without a concept."[23] The Majority Social Democrats did not assume office with a well-formulated agrarian program, and the insoluble problems of food shortages called for immediate, forceful action, not reflection on the way to fill this void in socialist theory.[24]

The government's reluctance to experiment with relaxing controls in the winter of 1918–19 was not surprising. It confronted a volatile working-class constituency that would hardly have tolerated conciliatory gestures toward rural producers, and it could not anticipate that concessions in this direction would dramatically increase available supplies. The Majority Socialist food minister and former trade-union functionary Robert Schmidt conceded that easing restrictions might increase deliveries, but any signs of compromise met with harsh criticism from the Independent Socialists and from many of his own comrades.[25]

Ironically, it was Otto Braun, the Prussian minister of agriculture after the revolution and a favorite target for the antisocialist diatribes of conservative agrarians, who pushed consistently for a gradual relaxation of controls. In mid-1919, he warned Schmidt that he "would not take responsibility for the outcome of agricultural production in the extremely critical years that directly confront us if some change in the direction outlined is not undertaken. Considerations of a political nature point to the same conclusion."[26]

Braun's proposals, however, represented a minority opinion in Majority Socialist circles, and the consensus view was stated in Schmidt's sharp response to Braun. Schmidt warned that any policy change "in accord with the pressure from producers" would result in the "complete collapse of the provisioning system." The political consequences would be nothing less than the successful "drive of the Independents and Communists to take power, which with effort, we have been able to restrain up until now." An end to the controlled economy would mean price increases that "no industrial worker could bear, given current wage levels."

Schmidt, also Reich minister of economics, predicted that the consequence would be an economically intolerable pressure on wages, bringing about, "among other things, chaos, Bolshevism with all its consequences like we have seen it in Russia and Hungary, and also the collapse of the German Reich and . . . the Prussian state."[27]

Behind Schmidt's hyperbole were fears of the potentially unbearable costs of relaxing the restrictions on agricultural producers. The decision to maintain the controls, however, also had weighty consequences. A policy of "continuity without a concept" provided a common language for agrarian protest against the new government of Weimar. From the perspective of agricultural producers, despite a revolution and changes in the form of government, certain structures remained the same. The spring of 1919 marked the third consecutive annual appearance of control teams—this time expanded to include members of urban Councils of Workers and Soldiers—in the Rhenish and Westphalian countryside. This move was unrealistically intended by Schmidt to allow the peasants to hear firsthand of urban hardships and to promote cooperation and conciliation between city and countryside. Continued declines in the deliveries of all agricultural products also led Schmidt to expand the responsibilities of search committees beyond grains to other products, which only guaranteed that his wistful hopes for urban-rural reconciliation would be disappointed.[28]

Peasants objected vehemently to searches by outsiders, particularly by workers who, in their opinion, had no business evaluating farm production.[29] It was in the interests of workers that the "very last reserves were taken," and it was workers "who initiated senseless strikes at the slightest instigation, who continually reduced working hours, drew unemployment compensation, and bore responsibility in large degree for the intolerable conditions."[30] The officials who fielded such complaints conceded that they were exaggerated, but, confronted with the day-to-day resistance to controls that the protests reflected, they also argued that peasant antipathy had to be taken seriously.[31]

Consumer protest was, of course, equally vehement, and there is much evidence to suggest that local officials attempted to address it as well. Many checked and double-checked the producers who fell behind in their deliveries, and in the case of one village, officials pushed ahead with the prosecution of 130 violators for failure to meet grain delivery quotas by amounts as low as 22 kilograms or less. Again in the spring of 1919, individual expressions of outrage over such treatment took the form of direct appeals protesting these punishments. Wilhelm Busskamp, an agricultural laborer who also farmed a small plot, returned from a Russian prisoner-of-war camp to find himself in a protracted battle with authorities in Recklinghausen who charged that he had planted 1¼ hectares of bread grains, contrary to his reported claim of less than one hectare. Two brothers of Fräulein Maria Mast had been less fortunate than Busskamp and had never returned from prisoner-of-war camps; Mast made no secret of this when she appeared before the county economic council in Recklinghausen in late June to protest the confiscation of the remaining grain reserves from the 1 ¼ hectares that she planted. Others charged that their grain reserves had been depleted by demobilized troops who had taken what they needed as they returned from the front.[32]

Growing rural discontent led some officials to warn that "respect for the law no longer exists and fear of punishment has almost completely disappeared." The speculation that attempts at forceful confiscation would confront "extreme opposition"[33] was based on experiences like those of inspection teams in the governmental district of Minden, where workers and officials were greeted in villages by large- and smallholding peasants brandishing clubs and pitchforks and yelling "Break their bones," and "Kill 'em." Whoever attempted to "spy into their pots," promised angry peasants, "would fly out the window."[34] As the reports of these committees suggest, four years of experience with controls often generated only the heightened anger and bitterness of agricultural producers rather than noticeable increases in deliveries of agricultural products. The basic dimensions of the consumer-producer conflict had changed little, but, with the end of any pretense of a *Burgfrieden*, its angry tone had clearly intensified.[35]

Defining New Forms of Protest and Resistance

As long as the controlled economy remained in place, it defined a central dimension of rural discontent and provided a focus for agrarian protest: all agricultural interest groups shared the demand for its removal. It was against the background of a deepened split between city and countryside and continued market regulation that attempts to organize angry peasants took place in the winter of 1918 and on into the following year. An ambivalent support for the old regime had constrained interest-group protest during the war, but after 1918 this dilemma was resolved. The government responsible for imposing controls was no longer the Kaiser's but that of a socialist provisional government, replaced after January 1919 by a parliamentary coalition that included not only socialists and liberals but also Center representatives. Attacks on controls became attacks on the new order, and the vocabulary of conservative protest could become one of unambiguous resistance.

At the end of the war, however, there existed no clear blueprint for the forms that this resistance would take. A unified opposition to controls did not guarantee a unified basis for collective action or a positive vision of an alternative to the new republican order. In the year following the revolution, established interest groups moved quickly to fill this void lest it be filled more effectively by other organizations.

The tasks of interest-group leaders in the winter of 1918–19 were considerably eased by an important carrot that accompanied the stick of continued controls on agricultural production. The new government's conception of how best to organize agricultural interests revealed even less originality than did its policies for increasing agricultural production. The striking absence of an SPD agrarian program before 1914 was matched by the complete lack of an SPD organizational network among the peasantry, and November 1918 was no time to remedy this situation. Lacking any clear alternative program and fearing a complete collapse of the provisioning system without the cooperation of conservative agrarian leaders, the Council of People's Delegates (Rat der Volksbeauftragten) moved to allow the organizations already in existence virtually free rein in expanding and assuming functions as the representatives of agrarian interests. In retrospect, perhaps no combination of policies could have undermined the government's credibility in the countryside more effectively. The maintenance of controls provided conservative agrarians with a convincing rallying cry to unify discontent, while the government's guarantee that established interest groups could continue to act unimpeded established the basis from which interest-group leaders could launch their attacks on the new order.

Shortly before the revolution, an ad hoc organization of conservative agricultural interest groups, the War Committee of German Agriculture (Kriegsausschuss der deutschen Landwirtschaft), had called for the creation of a network of committees at the local level to oversee the collection of agricultural products in the countryside. After 10 November, these committees were designated as the complement in the countryside to the urban Councils of Workers and Soldiers, but their form was not specified. Not until late November 1918 did the government offer guidelines for founding rural councils, and even then it did not attempt to take a direct part in their establishment.[36] Existing agricultural interest groups quickly attempted to take the lead, and it was no surprise that the councils founded in the Rhenish and Westphalian countryside had little in common with their counterparts in neighboring cities.[37]

Particularly in the Rhineland, the Agricultural Chamber and the Peasant Associations played a direct role in the creation of the councils. Schorlemer-Lieser, head of the Rhenish chamber, had come to this post in 1917 after leaving his position as Prussian minister of agriculture. His departure from Berlin clearly reflected a concession to the storm of protest—from Social Democrats, trade unionists, and other consumer representatives—that had surrounded his intransigent defense of agrarian interests. Schorlemer-Lieser's difficult tenure had made him fully aware of the problems that the agricultural sector would confront in the period of demobilization, and in the wake of the revolution, he was hardly slow to act.

Less than a week after the declaration of the Republic, Schorlemer-Lieser convened a meeting of Rhenish agrarian leaders in the Agricultural Chamber offices in Bonn, stressing that "the agricultural organizations must take the initiative in the creation of Peasant Councils, lest the initiative come from somewhere else." Loë-Bergerhausen, representing the Peasant Association, fully concurred, emphasizing the need for cooperation between local branches of his organization and those of the chamber in order to insure conservative control of the councils. He also stressed the pressing need to reach out to peasants returning from military service, and he emphasized that programmatic demands must be limited to those "appeals that every agricultural producer in a local committee can accept." Although before 1914 interest-group membership had de facto been limited to relatively substantial landholders, now "No agricultural producer can remain outside, today our highest values are at stake."[38]

Within a week after their initial meeting, agrarian leaders advised their members that "since agricultural producers in the Rhineland are already tightly organized," existing organizations should simply take over the functions of the councils. Local Agricultural Chamber officials were offered as recording secretaries and general managers at the local level. At the provincial level, an office was established to coordinate local activity and to serve as the official representative of Rhenish agrarian interests.[39]

When the revolutionary government finally issued its own guidelines for the creation of rural councils,[40] the Agricultural Chamber rejected them, claiming that organizational efforts were already well under way. According to Schorlemer-Lieser, the proposals for parity representation of workers and employers came too late and were, moreover, inappropriate in the Rhineland where few peasants hired large numbers of wage-laborers and even fewer did not participate directly in the work on their own farms.[41] The councils quickly disappointed official hopes that they would provide assistance in food requisitioning,[42] and they explicitly rejected the limitation of their role to economic questions. The chamber prescribed directing efforts "toward the goal of speedy elections to the National Assembly and entry into the bourgeois order. . . . After our recent experience and the pitiful collapse of our governmental structure and parliamentary bodies, we want to take control of our concerns as a Christian occupational estate and to make use of our right to determine our own interests. We will accomplish that if we have a strong, forceful organization behind us." Under a parliamentary system, "Every individual must take a stand, and the best way to do that is with the ballot."[43] In late November, the provincial Peasant Council had still pledged "without exception" its loyalty and service to the new government.[44] Within a month, however, its program of "Demands of Rhenish Agriculture" called for "a strong and steadfast national leadership, schooled in the affairs of state and standing above the parties, and thus not influenced by a dependence on individual economic or social groups."[45]

In Westphalia, neither the Agricultural Chamber nor the Peasant Association took the lead in the creation of the councils in quite so consciously manipulative a fashion. In contrast to the Rhenish experience, Westphalian councils often existed alongside other organizations, as new agents of agrarian protest rather than the blend of old forms achieved in the Rhineland. They also frequently expanded their membership beyond agricultural producers to include teachers, artisans, and agricultural wage-earners.[46] The councils that emerged varied greatly from district to district in their composition and self-perception.

Whatever their differences, however, the Westphalian councils were united in their critical attitude toward the government and their rejection of the controlled economy. The restriction of the councils to economic concerns translated into an aggressive protest against controls and demands for the reduction of mandated quotas. And the calls to coordinate the activities of isolated local organizations at the provincial level in April 1919 emphasized the need to organize the "healthy German people" against the "Bolshevism toward which we are being driven."[47] The would-be director of a provincial council, Carl Rasche, a lawyer, claimed to speak with authority on such matters because, as a soldier, he had been an eyewitness to the ravages of "Russian bolshevism."[48]

Although these political sentiments united the councils with the Westphalian Peasant Association and the Agricultural Chamber, the established organizations nonetheless perceived the council movement as a potential competitor that might present a "certain danger."[49] The plans for a provincial union of local councils were abortive, they claimed, since of thirty-eight rural counties, only fifteen had sent representatives to an organizational meeting in April, and of these, only twelve expressed any enthusiasm for a province-wide federation.[50] To queries from confused local officials unsure of whether to welcome the councils and provide them the financial assistance they requested, the chamber responded unequivocally: "No need of a new representation of agriculture of this sort exists, because the proven, old organizations, which have continued to expand their basis at the bottom and their unity at the top, are in the most effective position now and in the future to represent the interests of agriculture including small farmers and agricultural laborers."[51] Although the Provincial Council attempted to forestall the condemnation of so formidable an opponent by proposing to include chamber representatives in their discussions, neither the Agricultural Chambers nor the Peasant Associations were interested in meaningful collaboration.[52] As long as the Provincial Council survived, they sent official representatives to its meetings, but as Werner Reineke, general secretary of the chamber, reported to Kerckerinck, "The whole movement . . . is to be crushed as effectively as possible."[53] Against such onslaughts, the Provincial Council did not survive past September, and its locals were ultimately absorbed into existing organizations.

In neither the Rhineland nor Westphalia did the councils provide the basis for the conservative unification of agricultural interest groups that was espoused by their initial advocates.[54] Even in the Rhineland, where the council movement progressed under the watchful eyes of the Agricultural Chamber and the Peasant

Association, by the summer of 1919 the chamber's official position was that "the Councils of Peasants and Agricultural Workers must be absorbed into the official organizations."[55] As in Westphalia, the rapid abandonment of the councils in favor of established interest groups reflected the leadership's conviction that they might better ride out the wave of revolution within familiar structures. In the Westphalian case, fear of an institutional competitor was an important additional consideration. From the start, then, it was clear that the councils were at most to supplement, not to supplant, existing organizations.

The leaders of established interest groups deployed more than rhetoric to insure that old frameworks were adapted to new circumstances. In particular they stressed the need to incorporate *all* peasants and even agricultural wage-earners into existing organizations. Both in the last years of the war and after November 1918, these appeals rested not only on a verbal insistence on strength in numbers but also on the objective conditions that confronted all agricultural producers. All remained subject to the same controls, and there is evidence that smallholding peasants, those less likely to be organized before 1914, had suffered the greatest hardships during the war.[56] Common suffering thus provided a firm basis for the repeated insistence on the need for unity in opposition to the controlled economy: what peasants could not achieve through their individual passive resistance, they could accomplish through unified organization. As a student of Max Weber, Wilhelm Mattes, observed in his study of Bavarian peasants completed immediately after the revolution, it was not a feeling of positive solidarity that prompted peasants to organize but rather "parallel egoism."[57]

Repeated emphases on the ever-present threats to private property and the uncertain future of the agricultural sector were, moreover, communicated through an expanded and intentionally decentralized organizational structure that aimed to intensify agrarian representation at every level of the provincial bureaucracy. The Peasant Associations established coordinating offices at the county and district levels and increased membership in the voluntary committees that directed local activities. The number of paid officials, minimal before 1918, increased significantly to include both a permanent provincial staff and heads of district branches. Expansion, however, did not bring a democratization of decision-making. Policy was still formulated at the provincial level by a limited leadership group—but local-level organizations greatly stepped up their activities, holding frequent meetings that often featured speeches by provincial leaders.[58]

The local-level branches of the Agricultural Chambers also participated in this increased organizational work. In Westphalia, by May 1919 the chamber claimed that 130 long-inactive local organizations had been revived and new ones were being created. Existing organizations were also pulled together more tightly in county bodies, which in turn strengthened the representation of local interests in the provincial chamber.[59] Like the Peasant Associations, the chambers attempted to organize those who were left outside their network before 1914. As the Rhenish chamber's general secretary informed his colleagues in the steering committee, there must be a break with the prewar pattern of directing organizational efforts toward well-to-do large landholders. "Leaving the small peasants to themselves," he concluded, "was a mistake that we should have avoided. . . . We are paying for it now, at a time when we should stand unified in defense of our interests."[60]

Dramatic membership gains by both the Agricultural Chambers and the Peasant Associations testified to their success at attracting new members. In June 1919 the Westphalian association boasted 5,187 new members since its last meeting six months earlier, an increase of 17 percent; within a year, the organization registered an additional 11,000 members, bringing the total to 47,000 (excluding family members), a figure that surpassed prewar levels by over 50 percent.[61] The earliest postwar figures for the Rhineland are from 1920, and by that point, membership had expanded to 74,759 heads of family farms and another 13,361 family members. A year later, membership had expanded by another 20,000, an increase of almost 85 percent over the 1907 level.[62]

Although the Rhenish chamber remained tight-lipped about the success of its organizational drive, the figures for Westphalia indicate that there the Agricultural Chamber's plan to organize the previously unorganized was successful. By the end of 1919, membership had increased from 35,000 to 80,000, and the number of local branches had soared from 256 to 612. By the fall of 1920, an additional 121 local-level organizations had been created, and at the county level, 38 regional organizations existed; total membership stood at 113,063, over 70 percent of which was concentrated in the governmental districts of Münster and Arnsberg.[63] Even allowing for the degree of self-advertisement undoubtedly contained in these figures, they are evidence of the success of the chamber and the Peasant Associations at mobilizing a membership excluded from organizational appeals before 1914.

Responding to Pressure from Below

Rapid membership growth did not always reflect firm control from above, however, and the repeated Peasant Association assertions of strength and unity were incomplete descriptions of reality at the local level. Indeed, in the spring and summer of 1919 interest-group leaders continued to confront immense problems, not only with a government that maintained its commitment to the controlled economy but also with their own followers. Decentralized and greatly expanded structures created opportunities for autonomous activity by the network of local branches affiliated with the Peasant Associations. New, independent organizations also questioned association claims to be the sole representative of agrarian interests. In particular, pressure from below took the form of organized opposition to the controlled economy in forms not sanctioned by provincial organizations. Interest-group leaders became increasingly expert at formulating barbed attacks on the controlled economy, but while they scratched away at those "chains on production" with a rhetorical nail file, their constituents were applying a pickax of direct forms of resistance.

In their official pronouncements, provincial leaders continued to encourage compliance with controls in order to insure a peaceful demobilization and to reduce the threat of revolution in the cities, while at the same time they insisted on an end to all controls in the immediate future.[64] Peasants who endorsed the latter appeal did not always heed the former. As Loë-Bergerhausen observed in March 1919, "Soft-spoken and polite petitions are not enough for peasants today. We want to see fast, decisive action."[65] Without coordination or direction from Loë-Bergerhausen or any other provincial leaders, those who were unwilling to wait any longer for a response were taking matters into their own hands.

Characteristic of these tendencies toward direct action were the moves by local-level agricultural organizations in the spring and summer of 1919 toward autonomous price-setting and open refusals to meet delivery quotas. The parallels with the collective action of industrial workers were clear to agricultural producers: if workers could strike to demand higher wages, then peasants could also demand higher prices.[66] Peasants could not achieve their goal by denying an employer their labor power, but they could protest by denying consumers their agricultural products in the form of a "delivery strike." The readiness of local organizations to act independently of their provincial leaders was nowhere clearer than in the conflict over controls on milk prices in the summer of 1919. This is a struggle worth considering in some detail, because it provides a clear index of the radicalization of peasant producers; it also suggests the limits to their independent action and the nature of interest-group response to peasant mobilization.

Both producers and consumers were extremely sensitive to milk prices. Most peasants owned at least a few milk cows that insured a steady source of income throughout the year and provided manure and, in the case of the smallholding peasant, draft power. The acute concern with milk and butter prices made dairy farming a peculiarly "democratic" branch of production.[67] Milk output had declined dramatically during the war: supplies of high-protein feed were scarce, and when they were available the prices were as much as 100 percent above prewar levels; the deterioration of pastures and the increased employment of milk cows as draft animals had further reduced yields. Left uncontrolled, the prices for replacement stock had soared.[68] For urban consumers, milk products had assumed a key role as a source of fat and protein, particularly for children, pregnant women, and lactating mothers.[69] Its highly perishable quality meant that consumers had to go in search of milk almost daily and were thus extremely aware of variations in its price and supply.

A system of maximum prices for milk had been a relative latecomer to the control network, but by 1917 chronic shortages prompted provincial authorities to set farm prices. In both provinces, price-setting committees included agrarian representatives, municipal authorities, and representatives of organized consumer interests. Milk producers faced both fixed prices and provisions that tied them to specific dairies, often connected to the Peasant Association network; dairies in turn were obliged to deliver to certain cities. Price-setting and collection procedures were thus determined at the provincial level, not in Berlin, and were open to direct influence by the representatives of organized agrarian interests.[70]

The problems of regulating milk deliveries were enormous, and from the earliest institution of fixed prices, milk flowed freely around the controls and onto the black market. Overseeing twice-daily collections of milk was virtually impossible, and, unlike a field of grain, milk cows could be driven quickly into a nearby forest at the sight of a coming official. Moreover, milk could easily be converted into butter, a product for which there was a steady demand on the black market. A truly strict regulation of the milk supply, as one government official wryly observed, would have required a full-time inspector in every stall.[71]

With the end of the war, both consumers and producers expected a change, though their conceptions of the form it should take diverged radically. In both the Rhineland and Westphalia, agrarian representatives to provincial price-setting committees from the Peasant Associations and the Agricultural Chamber emphatically demanded price increases, charging that at current levels, prices did not cover production costs. Consumer advocates countered that the "price of milk has considerable political significance," and rejected any talk of price increases.[72] Heated negotiations took place against a background of urban unrest that gave credence to consumer claims. Adequate provisioning of the Ruhr, a major center of strike activity in the spring of 1919, was a high priority in Berlin—but it was not one shared by peasant producers, who indicated their rejection of prices they considered too low by delivering less and less. In the Rhineland, the price-setting committee thus concluded that "political considerations simply had to assume a subordinate role and economic considerations definitely deserved more attention."[73] Costly milk and the potentially negative consumer response were ultimately better than no milk at all.

In Westphalia, however, the provincial high president remained reluctant to raise prices. While conceding that holding the line in his province would potentially channel milk into higher-price Rhenish districts, he feared even more the consumer response to demands for price increases. At the national level, nonetheless, the Rhenish request to increase prices was approved, and officials acknowledged that current prices no longer covered production costs. The Westphalian high president was reminded that, "given the little authority that the power of the state still possesses, the strictest organization for the collection of milk has little chance of success unless we make provision at the same time that the producer does not have to deliver at prices significantly below his costs."[74] Under these pressures, Westphalian officials finally agreed to a price increase to go into effect on 1 July.

By the early summer, it was difficult for the official representatives of agriculture to claim such eleventh-hour concessions as a major victory. Moreover, their inclination toward compromise in talks with consumer representatives contrasted with the far more radical attitudes that were taking on organizational forms at the local level. Thus, while price negotiations proceeded in Cologne, an organization of milk producers in the countryside nearby warned that peasants were "no longer in the mood to accept that the government represents only the interests of industrial workers; peasants count themselves as workers, in fact, as workers in every sense of the word . . . and that is why they can justifiably demand a wage in accord with the fruits of their labors."[75]

Not only this language of protest reflected the influence of industrial trade unions—so too did the tactics of organized refusal to meet delivery quotas at prices deemed too low. The Agricultural Associations in Elberfeld, explained the mayor of that city, had left no doubt that they would stick by their demands for higher prices, "particularly because other groups in the population have shown them how one goes about pushing through one's justified demands these days."[76] In April, the government president in Arnsberg had predicted that "unless they [organized milk producers] win some concessions . . . the peasant strike, which is already dangerously close . . . , will spread."[77] In the Westphalian counties bordering on the Ruhr, local Peasant Councils also played an important part in organizing collective action. A county official concluded that "today intervention by the authorities against this violent movement can no longer promise any success, given that [the movement] already encompasses such wide segments of the agricultural sector."[78]

By May and June, ad hoc organizations of milk producers joined local Peasant Councils and branches of the Agricultural Associations in demanding higher prices and threatening an end to deliveries.[79] The actions followed a common pattern, but there is no evidence that they were coordinated or directed by the Peasant Associations or Agricultural Chambers. Local officials who gave in to this coercion argued that unless prices were raised, "the anger of the agricultural producers will increase to the point where compromise will come too late and will be forced by a peasant strike. . . . The peasant sees that the worker employs this method and reaches his goal. Nothing is more natural for the peasant than to seize upon a similar method since he has to pay for the wage increases of workers in the prices of the goods he buys."[80] Thus, by the time Rhenish and Westphalian officials approved a price increase for 1 July, in many areas their action represented little more than an acknowledgment of a situation that already existed and that had been created by independent pressure from below far more than by the diatribes of agriculture's provincial representatives.

Nonetheless, last-minute intervention by Carl Severing blocked all official price increases that might intensify labor unrest. Severing, the Majority Socialist minister responsible for the western territories still occupied by the Allies, had in mind not only the Ruhr miners' strikes in April but also, in the even less distant past, a strike of railroad workers in which an improvement in the food supply and a ceiling on price increases were major demands.[81] He did not share the opinion of the conservative *Deutsche Tageszeitung* that the threat of a delivery strike in Westphalia was "much more dangerous than the miners' strike,"[82] and he moved quickly to block the price increases so vehemently opposed by workers in the Ruhr. "For reasons of public security," Severing telegraphed from Berlin, price increases for milk and butter were to be suspended.[83]

Severing, as he informed a Council of Peasants and Agricultural Workers in eastern Westphalia, promised forceful action not only against the "Spartacists of the left" but also against the "Spartacists on the right," and vowed that the Berlin government "will find ways to exert its authority in the countryside."[84] Still, though consumer agitation in the cities prompted Severing's intervention, it could not put a halt to producer resistance to controls. The "Spartacists on the right" continued to demand price increases; when their demands were not met, they acted on the threat to stop deliveries.[85] Peasant rejection of Severing's action was widespread, and as the district administrator of one Arnsberg county reported, prosecuting violators "promised as little success as the confiscation of livestock, unless such measures were to be carried out against *all* livestock holders in the county."[86] The district administrator in Solingen, recounting a meeting of some two hundred largely smallholding peasants, concluded that, "given their determination and their indifference to the consequences that would result, the use of force would promise little success, rather it would only pour oil on the fire."[87] By December, when Severing finally agreed that price increases were necessary to extinguish the blaze, his action was too little and came too late. The higher levels that he approved were still far below those that had been demanded and received since September in many of the surrounding areas.[88] As a representative of the Westphalian government admitted in early December, "Milk prices in Westphalia exist only on paper. Everyone has his source in the countryside."[89]

Throughout the winter of 1919–20, this pattern was repeated.[90] The politically volatile struggle over the controlled economy was waged not only by the provincial leaders of agricultural interest groups, but also on other fronts and with other tactics not conceived and not always approved by the Peasant Associations and Agricultural Chambers. The tendency of government leaders to blame peasant discontent on interest-group leaders revealed a failure to recognize the deep-seated nature of rural protest. Provincial leaders were more perceptive, and their understanding of their constituents' anger was reflected in their attempts to channel and contain it.[91]

The continued expansion of established interest groups represented one clear response to grass-roots protest; others included matching the radical rhetoric of local organizations, and stepping up direct attacks on the government. When in the spring of 1919 interest-group leaders declared that "if every German is supposed to have the right to strike, then agricultural producers have the right to strike as well," they showed that they had learned a new vocabulary appropriate to a new age.[92] They were, however, still reluctant to condone such forms of action, and they certainly did not initiate them. In March, the Rhenish chamber's general secretary reminded his colleagues in the steering committee that delivery strikes "might only increase the discontent of the starving masses, thus unleashing a dangerous movement against the countryside."[93]

By the fall of the same year, interest-group leaders realized that appeals for moderation would find no audience. The radicalization of interest-group rhetoric and the abandonment of any pretense of support for controls reflected the attempt by established organizations to stay at least abreast, if not ahead, of those they sought to lead. By September, the Rhenish chamber expressed complete under-standing for the milk producer who overlooked "confused price decrees that fly in the face of economic conditions." Under such circumstances, there was no chance of a profit for the honest producer. No wonder the peasant lost "the last bit of respect for the authorities and for the maximum price policies."[94] Blame for the collapse of controls lay not with agricultural producers but with the "rule of the present government"[95] and the "vanishing authority of the state."[96] Delivery strikes were no more criminal than the work stoppages of Ruhr miners, and the prosecution of peasants for withholding their products represented an unjustifi-able double standard.[97] Indeed, by the fall, a local representative of the chamber might even lead organized peasant resistance against "every mandated delivery of livestock and all other products at fixed prices."[98]

By early 1920, Westphalian chamber officials were even further from counsel-ing compromise. Meeting with government representatives to discuss maximum prices, they came out openly against any piecemeal price increases, "lest we run the risk of losing sight of our goal, the removal of the controlled economy." Disregarding official threats that resistance would be met with "the harshest possible measures," the chamber's general secretary countered that "we cannot get ahead with higher [mandated] prices, but only after suspension of the con-trolled economy."[99] Such open attacks on controls did nothing to increase the peasants' willingness to meet their mandated quotas, but in the first year after the revolution, it was the followers who had heightened their leaders' rhetoric. As it had during the war, the intensified protest of agrarian interest groups reflected a radical pressure from below that leaders had not created and that they could not always control.

The Response to Organizational Competitors

Expanded organizational activity and angry rhetoric were still not enough to insure Peasant Association leadership of a radicalized peasantry. In both the Rhineland and Westphalia, Peasant Association claims to be the most effective and authoritative representative of agricultural interests faced not only the implicit query of unauthorized, independent action at the local level, but also more direct institutional challenges. Particularly in the Rhineland, the spring and summer of 1919 found Loë-Bergerhausen in a series of negotiations to establish his authority. On the one hand, attacks on the Peasant Association came from interests within the Center who opposed Loë-Bergerhausen's hostility toward the party. On the other hand, his organization confronted the competition of the "Free Peasantry," a self-proclaimed "peasant union" that emerged in March 1919 and openly advocated the intensification of active, direct resistance to the controlled economy. Insisting on its complete independence from party politics, the "union" criticized the Peasant Association for being *too* closely tied to Center politics and thus unable to function adequately as an impartial advocate of agrarian interests.[100]

At issue was the relation of conservative agrarian leaders to the Center, a controversial topic suspended only briefly in the immediate wake of the revolution when Center party supporters closed ranks in opposition to the specter of Marxist socialism. Unity in opposition did not survive the spring of 1919. For agrarian leaders, the party's willingness to participate in a coalition government with socialists was prima facie evidence that it was resuming the leftward progression begun in the spring and summer of 1917. The reduction of agrarian representation in the National Assembly in comparison to pre-1914 levels was seen as another dangerous omen.[101] No Rhenish agrarian leader whose political loyalties lay with the Center welcomed these tendencies; opinions diverged widely, however, over how best to stem a leftward tide.

Loë-Bergerhausen's alternative had already emerged during the war in his acrimonious exchanges with the Christian Trade Unions, his open allegiance to the Fatherland party despite official Center disapproval, and his unequivocal rejection of political reform. In the wake of the revolution, his rhetoric intensified as he warned that the "noose is being tied ever more tightly around agriculture's neck. The bleak system of head-count will necessarily choke us." The Center had allowed its left wing to take control; the essential response was the organization of agrarian interests into a "unified occupational estate" tied to no specific party and able to influence both the Center and the German National People's Party (DNVP), the successor to the Conservative party.[102] Loë-Bergerhausen's personal decision not to break completely with the Center and his troubled relation with the party in the early years of Weimar will be of central concern in Chapter 6. His strategy as an interest-group leader was to keep the Center at arm's length.

The fear that such an uncompromising response might only further diminish agrarian influence within the Center led to the creation of the Christian Peasantry in the early months of 1919. Headed by Fritz Bollig, a member of the city council in Cologne and owner of a large farm outside the city, this organization offered itself as a lobby for agrarian interests within the Center party. Bollig was certainly no more enthusiastic than Loë-Bergerhausen about the party's apparent shift to the left, but their strategies for countering that leftward trend differed significantly. The Christian Peasantry should, according to Bollig, become a counterweight to the Christian Trade Unions that indicated the gains to be made through interest-group representation within the party. Bollig candidly admitted, "If we want to follow the path of not organizing ourselves within one of the larger political parties, then, especially in the Rhineland, the problem is not just difficult—rather, in my opinion, it is impossible." Organization should take place, Bollig concluded, "within the Center . . . where 90 percent of all Rhenish peasants are already members. In fact, that is from the start the only possible way—thinking in realistic, political terms—in which we can achieve a unified organization that is powerful and strong and that can really accomplish something. It might be possible to create officers by other means; but in my opinion, this is the only way to get the masses behind us."[103]

Bollig's project received full support and encouragement from the Rhenish Center party leadership. The veteran politician Carl Trimborn, head of the provincial organization in the Rhineland and one of the most forceful liberal voices within the party,[104] heartily endorsed Bollig's conception of the Christian Peasantry as a complement to the Christian Trade Unions and the means to undermine Loë-Bergerhausen. Along with Wilhelm Marx, Trimborn particularly welcomed the split with Loë-Bergerhausen, "who has never been a true Center politician and who has always harbored an animosity toward the Center in his heart."[105] Unfortunately, Trimborn and Marx "had not always found sympathy [for their position] among the peasants loyal to the Center," but now that in the debates over electoral reform Loë-Bergerhausen had revealed himself as the "gravedigger of the Rhenish Center party," Trimborn anticipated that Bollig "will keep the peasantry in the Center."[106] Marx, seconding Trimborn's position, questioned the ability of the Peasant Association to make an effective appeal to smallholding peasants. He saw the Christian Peasantry as the way to organize them and keep them securely within the Center party.[107] With party sanction and with clerical support at the local level, Bollig's efforts enjoyed some success in the Cologne area.[108]

Not surprisingly, Loë-Bergerhausen attacked the new organization head on, vehemently denying charges that the Peasant Association had been unable to represent the political interests of Rhenish agrarians. A completely sympathetic Kerckerinck shared Loë-Bergerhausen's condemnation of the organization. The Westphalian leader judged it to be "nothing more than a peasant offshoot of München-Gladbach [i.e., tied to the People's Association for a Catholic Germany] . . . with the goal of making the peasant movement unthreatening for working-class interests and thus killing it." Warning his friend the Silesian Count Hans Praschma against potential parallel activities in that heavily Catholic province, he underlined his suspicions that the People's Association had a guiding hand in the organization. Condemning the "München-Gladbach half-socialists," he concluded that "trade-union secretaries in peasant movements remind me of the fox preaching to the hens."[109]

Loë-Bergerhausen echoed these sentiments, and argued that the entire structure of the Christian Peasantry was superfluous if political representation was all it had to offer; the Peasant Association already provided this. Marx's charge that the Peasant Associations organized only well-to-do peasants was an ill-fated attempt to create divisions in the countryside. The Peasant Association, Loë-Bergerhausen countered, was intent on representing *all* agricultural producers, and small farmers were actually in a privileged position, given the one-man-one-vote policy in the association and affiliated cooperatives.[110] It was Marx and his party, dominated by trade-union functionaries and lawyers, who should learn to represent the interests of smallholding peasants. Loë-Bergerhausen saw only one motivation behind the founding of the competing organization: "In reality, the tendency represented by the Christian Peasantry would mean undermining the Peasant Association."[111] The Agricultural Chambers were no warmer a friend of the new organization. While vehemently denying charges that their functionaries were instructed to discredit it, chamber spokesmen criticized the Christian Peasantry for threatening the unity among agricultural producers in the Rhineland.[112]

Behind this public posturing negotiations were going on between Bollig and Loë-Bergerhausen that led by late July to a compromise agreement. Bollig was made nominal second-in-command of the Peasant Association, and other loyal Center members joined the steering committee.[113] The association, still headed by the archconservative Loë-Bergerhausen, absorbed all Christian Peasant locals and remained outside the Center; within the association, however, forces true to the party were guaranteed a greater influence than before. In accepting these conditions, Bollig emphasized the need for unity and Loë-Bergerhausen's willingness to meet him halfway, but the agreement also clearly reflected the Peasant Association's position of strength and the Center's unwillingness to force a confrontation. The solution was more a standoff than a heartfelt compromise, again reflecting the uneasy relations between the party and its intransigent conservative agrarian wing.

Although the merger avoided the risk of an open split between conservative agrarians and the Center, it also opened the Peasant Association to charges that it had surrendered all political flexibility by tying itself to a single party. Loë-Bergerhausen and his organization were clearly too conservative and uncompromising for Marx and Trimborn, but they were too moderate and conciliatory for the leaders of the newly created Free Peasantry (Freie Bauernschaft). This "Union for the Protection of the Economic Interests of Agriculture"[114] emerged, like the Christian Peasantry, in the first months of 1919. Concentrating its efforts in the lower Rhine valley, it spread into parts of the governmental district of Aachen as well. Based on the model of the Christian Trade Unions, it nonetheless rejected any identification as a "Center Association" and promised to tie its support for political candidates to the fulfillment of certain conditions. It also understood itself to be an alternative to the Peasant Associations and the Agricultural Chambers, and "gentlemen who were politically burdened or had otherwise played a role in technical, agricultural associations" were excluded from its founding meeting. Outspoken in its attacks on the controlled economy, it advocated activist tactics including delivery strikes. It also established an economic commission to monitor the authorities and to lobby for delivery reductions and price increases. Particularly in the heavily Catholic districts of Moers, Kleve, and Geldern, the organization flourished, and within a month of its founding, twenty local branches shot up. Local organizations joined in a provincial Free Peasantry in March.[115]

From the start, the Rhenish Agricultural Chamber reserved judgment on the new organization, gambling that it might serve as the basis for unified agrarian representation, free of the Peasant Association's party political connections. The new organization might also succeed in organizing smallholders who stood outside existing structures.[116] The chamber saw the Free Peasantry as part of a "new movement" throughout Germany, a response to the "official controlled economy for agricultural products and the fear that this system could be made permanent under the rule of a socialist-oriented majority." Although the chamber encouraged its local heads to join the new organization "in order to prevent it from moving in an extreme direction," for the most part it quite openly endorsed Free Peasantry activities.[117]

Loë-Bergerhausen was far less sympathetic. Still embroiled in negotiations with the Christian Peasantry—which, along with the Center press, rejected the Free Peasantry as a new "Agrarian League"[118]—he correctly understood the Rhenish chamber's support for the Free Peasantry as a challenge to his authority. He hurried to respond directly, proposing a jurisdictional compromise that would relegate the Free Peasantry to the southernmost Rhenish districts, never strongholds of the Peasant Associations. When this proved unsuccessful he agreed to a merger settlement, hammered out in April under Schorlemer-Lieser's guidance, that ostensibly gave the representation of agrarian *political* rights to the Peasant Associations and of *economic* rights to the Free Peasantry.[119]

The difficulties of translating such distinctions into practice became apparent immediately, and by the summer, the working agreement had collapsed into mutually acrimonious exchanges between the leaders of the two organizations. Close to a compromise with Bollig, Loë-Bergerhausen proposed to Free Peasant leaders that the only solution to fights over organizational authority was the alternative nearly realized with the Christian Peasantry—complete merger of all competitors with the Peasant Association. Any justification for the Free Peasantry had vanished with the expanded activities of the Peasant Association.[120] Schorlemer-Lieser's attempts to find a basis for compromise resulted only in Loë-Bergerhausen's explicit proposal to absorb the Free Peasantry completely.[121]

By the late summer, Schorlemer-Lieser's enthusiasm for the Free Peasantry was also beginning to wane. The group's radical activities made it suspect, and the Rhenish chamber president was well aware that the new movement's local branches had played a leading role in the organization of delivery strikes and independent price-setting activity in the months since they had come into existence.[122] Though he remained skeptical of the Peasant Association's claims to represent all agrarian interests in the province, he no longer shared the opinion of the chamber's general secretary that the Free Peasantry was the single best guarantee "that the whole organization [of the agricultural sector] won't be taken in tow by the political parties."[123]

Formal merger of the Peasant Association with the Christian Peasantry by the fall confirmed outside suspicion of the Center ties of Loë-Bergerhausen's organization but also greatly strengthened his position. Denying that the merger implied any concessions to the Center, while claiming a leadership that included several "outspoken Conservatives," Loë-Bergerhausen condemned the Free Peasantry as divisive, and pressured Schorlemer-Lieser to end his support for the new organization.[124] Reflecting on the events of the previous spring, Loë-Bergerhausen now "regretted the explosion of the Free Peasantry. Working with it was very difficult from the very beginning." He attributed its weakness to a failure of strong leadership, and explained to Agricultural Chamber officials that "if we negotiated with it, it was only because it seemed the responsibility of the Peasant Association to prevent the new movement from heading in a completely radical direction."[125] Such hindsight was possible from within a greatly expanded Peasant Association that of course had attempted to steal the Free Peasantry's fire by emulating the competitor's radical posture. Still, from this position of relative strength, Loë-Bergerhausen could have some basis for his rhetorical claims that only "truly stupid people could be taken in by the fairy tale" that stressed the need for a new organization.[126]

Schorlemer-Lieser continued to fear that the Peasant Association's Center connection would scare off potential Protestant members and restrict the organization politically. By late October, however, the Rhenish chamber was willing to back Loë-Bergerhausen's bid to exclude Free Peasantry representatives from a federation of provincial agrarian leaders organized under chamber auspices. Schorlemer-Lieser had opted for unity over his desire to dilute potential Center party influence within the Peasant Association. By the new year, the Free Peasantry locals in the lower Rhine region had merged completely with the Peasant Associations and continued to exist in name only. An independent Free Peasantry withdrew to the southern Rhenish districts outside the Peasant Association sphere of influence, and the organization was ultimately most successful in the Saar, Rheinhessen, the Pfalz, and the Bavarian Palatinate.[127]

Kerckerinck did not face such formidable competitors, but in Westphalia, as in the Rhineland, by late 1919 the Peasant Association was no longer the unquestioned representative of agrarian interests. The association had confronted the threat to its authority by an independent council movement and had absorbed the pressure from below by intensifying its activities and coordinating its efforts with the greatly expanded network of the Agricultural Chamber. Nonetheless, in the summer and fall of 1919 unity against a common foe broke down quickly when Kerckerinck proposed the merger of chamber and Peasant Association under the clear dominance of his organization.

As in the Rhineland, confessional and political concerns blocked the merger. The Agricultural Chamber, headed by Wilhelm von Ledebur, a DNVP sympathizer from the Protestant district of Minden-Ravensberg, rejected the Peasant Association's attempts to transform the informal ties between its organization and the local-level Agricultural Associations into more binding agreements. Ledebur had been relieved of his duties as the Prussian administrator of the eastern Westphalian district of Lübbecke during the war, "because of the increasing gravity of the domestic political situation." Since 1917, he had devoted his full energies to work in the chamber.[128] He perceived Kerckerinck's merger plan as a dangerous move to strengthen the Center's power in rural districts. He rightly understood that the phenomenal growth of the Agricultural Associations in the immediate postwar period meant that the Peasant Associations could only gain from such an agreement.

Within the Westphalian chamber, support for Kerckerinck's proposal came from organizations in the predominantly Catholic regions of Paderborn and Münster. In opposition were the organizations in the Arnsberg region, which included several heavily Protestant districts, and where membership in the Agricultural Association far exceeded that in the Peasant Association. No more enthusiastic was the organization in the Protestant area of Minden-Ravensberg, where Ledebur wielded considerable influence. Ledebur unequivocally opposed what he saw as the effective exclusion of the Agricultural Chamber from policymaking and denied charges that the chamber was in any way compromised by its semiofficial status. Any restriction of the chamber's authority to the benefit of the Westphalian Peasant Association, he claimed, might greatly impede possibilities for coalitions with the Rural League—the successor to the conservative-dominated Agrarian League—and the DNVP.

Ledebur went further, to propose the expansion of a chamber-sponsored organization of provincial agrarian leaders to include Rural League representation. Though the Rural League did not have an extensive organization in Westphalia, he argued that its expansion should not be discouraged. The most effective representation of agricultural interests through all available agencies should be the highest priority. The Agricultural Chamber, of course, had been less tolerant of that other alternative presented by the independent council movement, and behind Ledebur's preferences lurked a clear attack on the Peasant Association's Center ties.[129]

The Peasant Association countered by charging that the chamber was fomenting divisiveness and had become little more than a cover for Rural League interests in the province.[130] If the chamber was not fronting for the Rural League, "that east Elbian growth that despite great care . . . will never take root here in the west," Kerckerinck declared, "then I cannot explain why, on the one hand, the chamber has opposed all attempts to put the Peasant Association at the center of organizational activity in the province, but on the other hand, has aided and apparently favored the creation of new organizations."[131] He opposed the inclusion of Rural League representatives in any provincial umbrella organization and claimed that its insignificance in the province justified disregarding it completely. Indeed, support for the Rural League represented a genuine threat, because "as soon as the agricultural producers of small- and medium-sized caliber—and these constitute the principal mass—realize that they've been drawn into the net of the Agrarian League, they will leave the organization and then run around wild and free, eventually even more susceptible to radical influence."[132] Ledebur might hope to advance the cause of the league in Protestant Minden-Ravensberg, but in Catholic parts of the province, "a too-forceful 'move to the right' would simply have the consequence that the Catholic clergy, united with M. Gladbach, would gather the 'agricultural workers and smallholding peasants' into a new organization."[133]

Private negotiations between Ledebur and Kerckerinck—fostered in particular by that inveterate voice of compromise, Carl Herold—averted an open confrontation. A lukewarm espousal of mutual support, however, fell far short of the Agricultural Chamber's endorsement of Peasant Association dominance initially sought by Kerckerinck.[134] As in the Rhineland, the Westphalian Peasant Association had successfully fended off a threat to its position. It also prevented the chamber from openly encouraging the Rural League. The association's triumph was far from complete, nevertheless, and Kerckerinck had been served notice of the problematic nature of the Westphalian association's Center connection and the chamber's intention of exercising an independent political role.

Limits to Organizational Success

By the end of 1919, both Loë-Bergerhausen and Kerckerinck could pride themselves on maintaining their positions as heads of important agricultural interest groups during the revolutionary transition from Kaiserreich to Republic. Their ability to fight off competitors reflected the skillful use of their position as organizational frontrunners in command of fully articulated institutional networks and their readiness to expand those networks rapidly while adjusting their rhetoric to pressure from their would-be followers. By maintaining controls on the agricultural sector, the early governments of Weimar provided both rural leaders and followers with a common vocabulary of opposition. The controlled economy defined those lines of "parallel egoism" that unified agricultural producers in independent protest actions and that brought them into the organizational framework of the Peasant Associations.

Also important for explaining the substantial membership increases and relative stability of established organizations was the willingness of interest-group leaders to modify pre-1914 conceptions of the "true" peasantry and to organize those who had been excluded from the Peasant Associations before the war. A decentralized structure resulted in few leadership changes at the top of the provincial organization, but it created forms for the expression of radical discontent at the local level that in turn rebounded to shape the program and policy of provincial leaders. In no instance were grass-roots organizations able to survive into 1920. The Peasant Associations effectively met organizational challenges, absorbing a new membership as well as new organizations, restricting the space in which alternatives might have grown, and adapting to the realities of politics in a democratic age.

Compared to other parts of western and southern Germany not dominated by the Agrarian League's successor, the Rural League,[135] the accomplishments of the Peasant Associations in the Rhineland and Westphalia and the relative stability of prewar leadership structures were impressive. In the Bavarian Palatinate and the Saar, for example, the Free Peasantry firmly established itself, outstripping the Catholic Peasant Association and the Rural League in radical rhetoric and exceeding them in membership. In the Palatinate, the Free Peasantry emerged as the most important representative of agrarian interests, and in the Saar, the Trier Peasant Association, unable to fend off the competitor, accepted an agreement that left the Free Peasantry in a position of relative strength. In Hesse as well, the Free Peasantry shaped a merger of competing organizations.[136] In Baden, Bavaria, and Württemberg, pre-1914 organizations matched the success of the Rhenish and Westphalian associations in adjusting to changed circumstances, but even compared to these cases of south German stability, the survival of a noble leadership in the Rhineland and Westphalia was exceptional.

Still, in neither province did the Peasant Associations emerge as the sole representative of agrarian interests. In both, organizational challenges were defeated only with the help of the Agricultural Chambers, which made it clear, in the process, that although they shared many conservative goals with the Peasant Associations, they might disagree on the appropriate tactics for pursuing them. The experience of the Peasant Associations in both the Rhineland and Westphalia indicates that in the postwar period, the chambers intended to take a much more active role as a representative of conservative agrarian interests.

The Agricultural Chambers had maintained a relatively low political profile before the war and had safely claimed an apolitical status as long as the conservative politics of the Kaiserreich were to their liking. They had also remained largely the preserve of wealthy peasants and aristocratic estate owners. The revolution had little impact on the composition of chamber leadership, but it did mark the beginning of significantly expanded organizational activities and direct chamber involvement in the political arena. The rush to insure the conservative organization of the countryside represented in part a reaction to fears of reforms that might increase worker and small peasant participation and influence in the chambers by government decree and, in addition, a concern that the Peasant Associations might not be adequate to the task at hand.[137] The chambers' dramatically increased membership guaranteed them an influence on the forms of agrarian representation and on the direction of conservative agrarian politics in the postwar period.

East of the Elbe, the Agricultural Chambers had been dominated by the Agrarian League before 1914. Whatever the divergence of east Elbian Rural Leagues from prewar patterns, after the revolution their control of the chambers remained secure.[138] In the Rhineland and Westphalia, both before 1918 and after, the personnel in chambers and Peasant Associations often overlapped, but after the war the chambers clearly emerged as independent bodies, capable of presenting a critical commentary on Peasant Association policies. Differences with the Peasant Associations were apparent in both provinces in the chambers' attacks on Peasant Association ties to the Center: chamber leadership in Westphalia was in the hands of a DNVP sympathizer, and in the Rhineland, Schorlemer-Lieser, though nominally outside of the DNVP, made no secret of his rejection of the Center.

Before 1914, however suspect were the reform tendencies of the Center, it had still been a party capable of allying itself on many issues with the Conservatives. After 1917, the Center's move into a coalition that included socialists and that was committed to a democratic parliamentary order made it suspect for those conservative Catholic agrarians who remained within it, but even more dubious for conservative agrarians outside it.[139] These political tensions lay immediately below the surface of organizational fights between the Agricultural Chambers and the Peasant Associations in both the Rhineland and Westphalia. At the end of 1919, they were far from completely resolved.

For the Peasant Associations, successes measured in membership gains and in the ability to ward off organizational challenges were matched with few indications that they could positively influence agrarian policy or dismantle the controlled economy. Controls continued to provide an excellent focus for agrarian protest, but by the end of 1919 that protest had done little to remove them. The disintegration of controls (discussed in detail in Chapter 5) reflected, rather, the practical day-to-day opposition of agricultural producers—not interest-group lobbying attempts at the state, provincial, or local level. Peasant Association leaders could also point to few political triumphs (a subject treated at greater length in Chapter 6). The revolution had failed, but so too had conservative hopes for a return to the status quo antebellum. A year after the revolution, how best to solidify organizational successes and to translate membership gains into political influence remained an open question. Numbers did not mean strength, and the authority of Peasant Association leaders rested on a fragile basis of unity in opposition.

FIVE

Inflation and Peasant Protest in the Early Years of Weimar

In a front-page story, "The Exchange Rate and the Food Supply," in early December 1919, the *Kölnische Volkszeitung* explained to its readers that "as long as an improvement in the mark was not forthcoming, Germany would be forced to pay untold sums to foreigners for food imports." Germany, reliant on food purchased abroad to cover its needs before 1914, could no longer depend on outside sources. Should foreign loans become available, they were needed to rebuild Germany's industrial capacity—not to purchase imported food. The only solution was to curtail food imports and to intensify domestic agricultural production.[1]

The newspaper account stated in simple terms what had long been obvious to government policy makers. There was a straightforward relationship between the price of foreign food and the depreciation of the German currency. Not only was Germany a country impoverished by a lost war and threatened with an unspecified reparations bill; in addition, in contrast to the situation before World War I, domestic food prices were below world market levels, an unusual circumstance that decisively reversed prewar relationships. The mark abroad was depreciating more rapidly than it was within Germany, making imports excessively costly. The discrepancy between the internal and external rates of the mark's depreciation meant that the inflation imposed a levy on food imports, replacing the barrier of the Allied blockade with a barrier of a different sort—in effect, a tariff wall more solid than that imposed before 1914.[2]

The inflation was not a creation of the early Weimar governments. An intentional policy of deficit financing by means of the printing press dated from the early years of the war. The failure of the Kaiser's government to introduce direct forms of taxation before 1914 had left the state without that option once the war began, and war bonds had certainly not bridged the gap between state revenues and expenditures. After 1918, the high costs of demobilization kept the printing presses rolling.

Even after the spring and summer of 1919, there was only lukewarm support for ending the inflation. In the meantime, export-oriented heavy industrialists had learned that the inflation brought them distinct advantages that they were loath to forfeit. The same differential between the internal and external values of the mark that prohibited the import of expensive foreign food made the goods produced in Germany inexpensive on the world market. The result was an export advantage for German industrialists that contributed significantly to their ability to reestablish their position on world markets and to renew and expand their production capacity at home.

The representatives of organized labor also recognized the advantages of inflation: a boom economy meant full employment. The alternative to inflation—a stabilization of the currency—threatened to have ominous consequences, which no policy maker was ready to accept. Stabilization might well lead to economic recession and massive unemployment. The experience of the United States and England in 1920–21 as those countries stabilized their currencies provided ample evidence of this possibility, and in Germany, fears of recession remained coupled with fears of renewed domestic social conflict.

The early Weimar governments could endorse labor's and industry's support for an inflationary policy since they too had an interest in promoting postwar economic reconstruction and maintaining labor peace. In addition, the state benefited directly from the inflation by paying off its sizable domestic war debt with an increasingly worthless currency. Thus, even in the period from the spring of 1920 to the summer of 1921—an unusual interlude of relative currency stabilization amidst phases of very rapid decline—there was no political support for thoroughgoing currency reform and an end to the inflation.[3] On the contrary, an "inflation consensus" of organized labor, heavy industry, and the state continued to support a policy of currency depreciation.

The long-term nature of the inflation is worth emphasizing precisely because the postwar inflation is too often confused with the climax of the process, the hyperinflation that commenced in the summer of 1922 and ended only with currency stabilization in November 1923. To be sure, only the currency's complete collapse prepared the ground for a "stabilization consensus"—a political coalition willing to put an end to the inflation by fiat—but the complete deterioration of the mark and the social conflict that it unleashed were only the final act in an ongoing drama that defined a fundamental continuity in the transition from war to peace.[4]

None of the arguments favoring the continuation of the inflation directly reflected the concerns of agricultural producers, nor were agrarian representatives part of the "inflation consensus." Nonetheless, the ongoing depreciation of the currency directly affected peasant farmers. Most accounts that attempt to determine the winners and losers in the inflation include agricultural producers among those who benefited from the currency depreciation of the immediate postwar period.[5] Like all other property owners, they obviously gained from the virtual elimination of their prewar mortgage debt that could be paid off in depreciated currency. The inflationary barrier to imports guaranteed markets for everything that the peasants could produce and protected German agriculture from foreign competition. Moreover, as this chapter will describe in detail, many of the controls imposed after 1914 were lifted in the postwar years. At the same time, the opening of the "price scissors"—the relationship between agricultural and industrial goods—in agriculture's favor, particularly after 1921, increased agrarian purchasing power.

Any balance sheet of agriculture's experience in the inflation must include these assets, but to overemphasize them is to neglect the liabilities. Most importantly, the inflation justified continued intervention by the state into many aspects of agricultural production. No later than the fall of 1919, officials could observe that the "suspension of the blockade has not had the favorable influence on the provisioning system that we had hoped for." The cause was immediately apparent: "The condition of our currency cuts us off from any substantial imports for the time being." So too was the consequence: "In the interest of the less-well-off members of the population, . . . the controlled economy must definitely be maintained."[6]

The relationship between the inflation and the controlled economy was easily fathomed: one went hand in hand with the other. As long as the inflation lasted, a complete end to controls on agricultural production was not deemed feasible, and controls on grains existed until the summer of 1923. For other products, cumbersome systems of indirect sanctions and price guide-lines replaced direct controls. It was this element of continuity—state intervention in the postwar period—that remained the most important basis of peasant protest and kept alive the conflict between consumers and producers. Nor, for peasant farmers, were controls the only undesirable by-product of the inflation; unpredictable jumps in the value of the currency created a climate of uncertainty and instability that, like controls, united the early years of Weimar with the war years. Chapter 7 will return to the problems of a balance sheet for the agricultural sector in the early years of Weimar. The present chapter will focus on the entries on the ledger's debit side and the forms of peasant protest that accompanied them.

The Collapse of the Controlled Economy

A year after the end of the war food shortages continued, the controlled economy was still in place, and peasant resistance to controls was undiminished. Additions to the repertoire of passive resistance suggest that peasants too were learning to understand the meaning of inflation. For those living on the Dutch and Belgian borders, smuggling augmented the well-established black market. Rhenish and Westphalian producers quickly discovered the discrepancy between prices at home and those across the border and circumvented strict export controls as they had all other parts of the controlled economy. Particularly during the months when livestock was put out to pasture, peasants with property directly on the Dutch border had little difficulty evading customs inspectors and bringing their herds across the border at night to buyers with hard currency. Grains and livestock also found their way through the "hole in the West" into the occupied territories of the left Rhine bank.[7]

As long as Dutch prices were four to five times higher than those in Germany, the temptation to evade export controls was great.[8] When animals that had been smuggled across the border were brought back into Germany to be sold as Dutch livestock at prices far above domestic levels, insult was truly added to injury.[9] Although data on the amounts smuggled allow no precise picture of the illegal trade, such information as does exist suggests that this border traffic followed the fluctuations in the exchange rate, tapering off during the period of the relative stabilization of the mark, from early 1920 until mid-1921, and picking up again after the dramatic fall in the value of the currency in late 1921.[10]

Combined with the already flourishing black market, border smuggling completely undermined restrictions on the meat supply. Controls on products like meat and milk that were always in demand on the black market, had been leaky dams from the start; by early 1920 they were virtually washed away. Since the fall of 1919, some Rhenish cities had been able to cover their needs only by openly violating mandated prices.[11] Monthly reports from the Rhineland throughout 1919 and 1920 reveal that often no livestock was delivered, and in a particularly good month, deliveries might represent 10 percent of the mandated quotas.[12] The difficulty of prosecuting violators grew as the amounts delivered diminished. The passive resistance of nondeliverers was, moreover, consistently accompanied by organized protest against the "controlled economy, put more accurately the prison economy," that made the peasant "the whipping boy of the state."[13]

The official suspension of controls on meat in October 1920 made de jure a situation that already existed de facto.[14] In many districts, peasants had long since ceased "to deliver any animals at the fixed prices."[15] "*The purpose of the controlled economy*," reflected an official in the Reich Ministry of Agriculture, "existed *only on paper*. The suspension of it only represents an acknowledgment of conditions that already exist."[16] The end of controls on milk and butter the following April reflected a similar concession to reality. For more than two years, controls had proved ineffective, and a year earlier the Westphalian high president had estimated that 75 percent of all milk was disappearing on the black market.[17] As Johannes Blum, a Center representative from the Rhineland sympathetic to agrarian interests, reported to his colleagues in the Reichstag, the situation was no longer tenable when a judge in his district could fine the peasant who had sold him black-market butter and advise him afterward "to keep up the deliveries; just make sure you don't get caught."[18]

Whether apocryphal or not, Blum's anecdote testified to the commonly accepted disregard for controls. The ultimate suspension of the regulatory network for meat and milk, like the stepped-up harangues of interest-group leaders, was a clear concession to the widespread discontent and the flouting of controls by thousands of individual producers. As they had during the war, interest-group leaders showed that they correctly understood the reasons for their constituents' protests, and they continued to intensify their attacks on controls. Ultimately, however, it was more peasant resistance than interest-group rhetoric that forced the state to dismantle key parts of the controlled economy.[19]

Attempts at Control after Decontrol

Still, for peasant producers, even these victories in the ongoing battle over controls were far from complete. An end to direct price controls on milk products and meat increased open market supplies, but it also triggered price increases and consumer demands for the reintroduction of restrictions. An improved provisioning system could only slightly mitigate the tensions between consumers and producers.[20] From the beginning of his tenure as the first Reich minister of agriculture in the spring of 1920, Andreas Hermes had conceded that "for the most part, price increases for agricultural products, where daily necessities are concerned, will be examined much more carefully than price increases in the industrial sector."[21] In more direct terms, the *Münsterischer Anzeiger* had warned that "the German agricultural sector had best realize one thing! If its demands for a virtually complete end to the controlled economy are filled . . . , then to a large extent, agriculture will bear the direct responsibility for the provisioning of the population."[22] Reducing the conflict between consumers and producers was one of the most formidable tasks confronting the new minister of agriculture.

Hermes was a native of the Rhineland, a student of agriculture who had worked as a farm manager and had taught in the Agricultural Academy in Bonn-Poppelsdorf before working as a staff member for the German Agricultural Society and serving as Germany's delegate to numerous international economic conferences. He came to the ministerial position strongly recommended by Herold; his appointment was thus seen as a concession to the Center party.[23] Such credentials undoubtedly made him more acceptable in agrarian circles than Robert Schmidt, whose tasks he assumed, and Hermes let it be known that comprehensive controls were a bankrupt system in which he would no longer invest. He resisted pressure to reintroduce those controls that had been lifted, and he attempted to soothe angry organized agrarians by informing the representatives of organized labor that the most appropriate responses to shortages were increased output and agricultural prosperity, not controls. Adopting agrarian interest-group logic, he argued that "given the depressed state of our currency, purchasing foreign food weighs far more heavily on the consumer than granting adequate prices for German agricultural producers to increase the domestic harvest." Hermes conceded that the "deterioration of the reputation of state officials rested largely on the misguided belief that controls would improve the provisioning of the people," and he emphasized that only those controls which were realistic and essential should remain in place.[24]

Nonetheless, like his predecessor, Hermes remained sensitive to consumer interests. As a local official in Dortmund observed in the fall of 1920, "The change in the form of the economy in no way alters the fact that the total supply of food and other items of daily life does not fulfill the present demand. Up until now, this discrepancy between supply and demand has been—and it will continue to be—a source of discontent in large parts of the populace."[25] For Hermes, the policy implications of this situation were clear. He left no doubt in his remarks to a meeting of Peasant Association leaders that "as long as the discrepancy between supply and demand remains so great, a certain form of public control over some essential products will remain indispensable."[26]

The problem confronting Hermes was not only the high cost of imports (see Appendix Table 21); in addition, Germany's agricultural output still lagged far behind prewar levels[27] (see Appendix Tables 18 and 19). Hermes, like his Social Democratic predecessor, saw controls in some form as the only possible response to this dilemma. Thus, despite the suspension of fixed prices and official confiscation schemes for many products by early 1921, no completely free market was introduced for most agricultural products, and direct controls on bread grains were removed only in the midst of the hyperinflation in the spring of 1923.

Only for grains were prices set at the national level. For other products, the mandated price network gave way to a system of price guide-lines that were determined by local price control offices. Established early in the war before the introduction of comprehensive price legislation, these offices had the task of setting "fair prices" based on "social and ethical" considerations. In most instances, this translated into the ability of consumers to pay for the necessities of daily existence.[28] As long as wartime maximum prices were in effect, price control offices had little to do with agricultural farm prices. However, as the branch office in Münster reported in October 1920, "the relaxation and partial suspension of the controlled economy has, contrary to expectations, resulted in greater demands on the price control offices, and has given them a greater significance. The realm of their competence expands continually." The goals of this increased activity were hardly immodest: "Pricing policy should serve as a tool of general economic policy to avoid unhealthy fluctuations in prices and, where possible, to initiate a reasonable reduction of prices."[29] The first objective reflected a large degree of optimism; the second proved to be completely illusory.

Not surprisingly, the price control offices were largely ineffectual. The absence of professional full-time personnel made the collection of relevant data on prices and production costs difficult at best, and the lack of any uniform policy guidelines meant that there could be great discrepancies in the extent of enforcement from one area to the next. The spasmodic fluctuations of the currency further

"The Dutch Peasant Speaks." In this poster, issued during the post–World War I inflation, a Dutch peasant refuses to sell his products for German currency; instead, he offers to exchange them only for German manufactured goods. German workers are reminded that the costs of imported food could be met only by increasing German domestic industrial production. *Courtesy of Bundesarchiv, Koblenz.*

complicated matters. It became almost impossible to sort out inflationary price increases from the potential exploitation by producers of an uncertain economic situation. The meetings of the price control offices, though providing an institutional forum for the exchange of irreconcilable claims by producers and consumers, could do little to regulate farm prices at the point of production. Undoubtedly, most local officials shared the belief that their energies were being "consumed by a Sisyphean task."[30]

The conflict among fruit and vegetable farmers, consumers, and municipal authorities in Cologne in the spring and summer of 1921 demonstrated the difficulty of enforcing price guide-lines. Attempts at unofficial regulation collapsed when producer representatives demanded that price determination be left to market forces,[31] following the confiscation by plainclothes policemen of products being sold at allegedly usurious prices in the Cologne market and the arrest and imprisonment of those selling the goods.[32] Protesting to the Prussian Ministry of Justice, the Rhenish Agricultural Chamber charged that legal bases for prosecution did not exist since official controls had been suspended.[33] Charges of usury were unfounded as long as prices did not exceed those levels determined by "normal market conditions"; surely, in the absence of official controls, such conditions prevailed.[34]

The response from the socialist and communist press in Cologne was predictable. Threats to stop deliveries to the Cologne market amounted to "peasant blackmail politics," aimed at the "starvation of Cologne," and could easily provoke violent reactions.[35] Unified consumer action was essential in the face of this attempt to "realize the immiseration theory," and one socialist paper longed for the "days of Wallenstein" when "greedy peasants" were simply "struck dead if they wouldn't deliver."[36] In only slightly more muted tones, socialist consumer representatives assured the provincial parliament that the fight over agricultural prices was not a "party affair"; on the contrary, in Cologne "the entire consumer public from the extreme left to the extreme right, regardless of their affiliation or religious beliefs, stands together, completely unified." The recommendation that against the usurious peasants of the Rhineland "the best measure is dictatorship" lent rhetorical flair to the intense antagonism that still characterized consumer attitudes toward producers.[37] Agrarian interest-group leaders rightly feared that "agriculture and the consumer public were once again deeply divided,"[38] particularly when the antiagrarian alliance included such a range of "*Mittelstand* organizations."[39] Nonetheless, such fears did not foster a spirit of compromise.

The principal defense against consumer attacks remained the claim that with the end to official controls, the market should be the ultimate source of fair prices. Otherwise, as the Agricultural Association for Rheinpreussen put it, "the present legal basis [for determining price guide-lines] . . . is completely obscure. The agricultural producer does not know how he should behave, whether he is allowed to demand the prices listed in the market, or whether he must comply with prices set by local price committees. This uncertain legal situation is intolerable and is in drastic need of clarification."[40]

Some local authorities continued to rely on the price control offices to bring light into this darkness.[41] Others agreed with the government president of Aachen that "the primary cause [for price increases] of late is the continued fall in the value of the mark"; price increases simply reflected this development, and consequently, "prices in excess of the market price are infrequent."[42] This remained, nonetheless, a minority opinion. The unpredictable fluctuations of the currency made most local officials less sanguine about trusting the price signals generated under such uncertain circumstances.

The provincial officials responsible for fielding the complaints over price increases and shortages were well aware that urban consumers were among those least willing to acknowledge the existence of a "normal market situation," and consumer skepticism was shared by many high-ranking officials in Berlin and at the provincial level.[43] Many believed that leaving price determination to the market was impossible. As the Westphalian high president reported in late 1921, "market prices that are determined by the fully altered economic conditions brought about by the war are not normally based . . . on an effective and just compromise between supply and demand, but rather on a so-called emergency market situation that, as a result of the shortage of goods caused by the war and its consequences, sets the upper limits of the prices of goods solely according to the purchasing power of consumers."[44] As long as one of the war's consequences was an ongoing and unfathomable inflation, few were willing to talk of a normal market situation. Far more common was the opinion that "domestically an emergency market situation exists . . . when it becomes impossible to purchase goods on the world market because of a shortage of currency."[45]

The result, for agricultural producers, was that they remained subject to careful scrutiny by urban consumers and open to charges of exploiting an uncertain situation. The limited effectiveness of price guide-lines was hardly a well-kept secret, and the alternative demanded by many consumers—and, with growing frequency, by some exasperated local officials—was the reinstitution of Reich- or province-wide legally binding price ceilings.[46] The dismal past record of direct controls, however, provided no basis for the hope that such action would greatly reduce prices without also reducing supplies and increasing peasant resistance to controls in any form.

No more successful in providing informal price guide-lines acceptable to both producers and consumers were the committees established to regulate dairy prices after the end of direct controls in the spring of 1921. Created under official auspices in both the Rhineland and Westphalia, these committees consisted of consumers, producers, and dairy representatives. Like the price control committees, they served to focus the acrimony that still infected the relations between consumers and producers, but they were decidedly less effective in regulating supplies and prices of dairy products. By late 1921 conflicting interests could seldom be reconciled within the confines of committee meetings, and refusals of cooperation on both sides led to demands for arbitration.[47]

Agricultural representatives knew all too well that their constituents would reject prices that were substantially below those available on the black market. In this respect, the experience of the summer and fall of 1919 had left indelible impressions. The complete collapse of negotiations with consumer representatives often followed agrarian refusal to accept the results of arbitration.[48] Added to familiar countercharges from consumers was a new element, a comprehension of the inflation: consumer representatives argued vehemently that agricultural producers "would like it best if they could determine prices unilaterally, and in such a way that the milk price . . . would be based on the dollar rate."[49]

Ending the controls on the milk supply seemed to have changed very little. The controls had ceased to be effective before they were suspended, and indirect controls were no successful substitute. The patterns established under the controlled economy—processing milk into butter, selling butter on the black market, and using skim milk as feed—became ever more widely practiced as the attempts to enforce price guide-lines intensified.[50] The flexibility of peasant mixed-farming production patterns continued to deliver a variety of means to circumvent controls, and interest-group representatives did nothing to discourage their constituents from exploiting these fully. On the contrary, responding to tighter restrictions in that province, the press organ of the Westphalian Peasant Association coolly observed that "the agricultural producer will use his product in whatever fashion brings him the economic advantage that he needs to maintain his farm or a particular branch of production. . . . No sealing of milk separators, no sanction against direct milk sales, no obligation to deliver milk in winter, no appeal to producers can force the producer to violate the fundamental economic law that calls for a balance between income and expenditure."[51] The candor of this description indicates clearly how far interest-group spokesmen had come from wartime attempts to encourage compliance with controls. Of course, the economic realities that it outlined had existed as long as the controls themselves.

Continuation of Direct Controls: The Grain Levy System

For peasant producers, the most striking accomplishment of the attempts at enforcing indirect controls was to remind them that the state's desire to defend consumer interests had not vanished with the suspension of the war economy. Prosecution for charging usurious prices was not widespread, but it constituted a punishment by example that let producers know that their relations with consumers were not regulated solely by the market.[52] Controls on grains revealed an even less remote resemblance to wartime measures and, particularly after 1920, they emerged as a central focus for organized peasant protest against the controlled economy. In no other case was the maintenance of controls so directly and explicitly tied to the inflation. No branch of agricultural production was more basic to the food supply, and for no other product were discrepancies between German domestic and world market prices as sensitively felt by policy makers in Berlin.[53]

In January 1920, shortly before turning over the thorny problems of price controls and regulation to Hermes, Robert Schmidt had outlined the government's position to leading agricultural representatives. Like them, he explained, he had hoped that with the end of the war, imports would help to cover Germany's demand for food; nonetheless, he continued, "surely no one reckoned with the depreciation of the currency that has occurred. The food that we lack is available abroad, but we do not have the means to purchase it."[54] An end to controls could only follow an increase in imports, and an increase in imports could only follow an improvement in the health of Germany's currency.

Meanwhile, for the third consecutive winter officials complained that "the agricultural sector simply is not aware of the gravity of the situation and simply fails to recognize the growing danger of a temporary but nonetheless entirely intolerable shortage of bread." Worse yet, there was evidence that the "short-sightedness and bitterness of agricultural producers have brought them to welcome this danger."[55] In particular, the Prussian state commissar for food called for forceful action against the "so-called leaders of agricultural producers who demand nondelivery."[56] Again, Berlin's response was to insist on strict controls of those who were behind in their deliveries.[57]

By the end of 1920, things had not improved. Deliveries of wheat and rye to the Reich Grain Office, the central purchasing agent for foreign and domestic grain, had not reached 60 percent of the levels of the previous year. Only by increasing imports of costly foreign grain was the government able to shore up a crumbling provisioning system.[58] The consequences for Germany's balance-of-payments situation were obvious, given that "the population is in part already living from imported grain. This circumstance leads to an extremely great burden for the Reich and a severe threat to the provisioning of the population, because the financial condition of the Reich restricts the import of grain, and in the face of insufficient domestic deliveries, the need for imports is constantly increasing."[59] For the agricultural sector, the implication was clear. As Hermes expressed it, "The drive for the free economy must find its limit in the needs of the total population."[60] He conceded that "we can get no further with the system for controlling grain that we have employed up until now,"[61] but an end to all controls was out of the question.

Supplies of grain increased slightly in early 1921 when sinking prices on the world market, coupled with the relative stability of the mark, permitted the Reich Grain Office to increase its reserves by expanding its purchases of imports.[62] Nonetheless, the government remained reluctant to increase its reliance on foreign supplies and insisted on maintaining domestic controls.[63] Hermes emphatically defended the suspension of other parts of the controlled economy as prerequisite for improving agricultural output, and as an unavoidable concession to the declining respect for public authority.[64] With equal vehemence, however, he stressed that he did not "for a minute consider suggesting the end to controls on grain production. . . . Today no one would take this step who is serious about his responsibility." He had no sympathy for those producers who were behind in their deliveries and called for continued and systematic prosecution of violators.[65] "The question of the introduction of the free economy," he reiterated, "is in the final analysis the question of the development of our currency and the ability of the German people to pay."[66]

Agriculture's self-interest was also ultimately at stake. In a speech in Cologne in June, Hermes reminded noncooperative peasant farmers that "as soon as our currency has recovered, the pressure of foreign competition will once again make itself known. . . . The agricultural sector should not forget that some day it will not be able to live without the protection of the government." Hermes added the ominous warning that "if agriculture rejects all state intervention into the economy now and desires complete freedom of trade, then the parties on the left will resurrect this argument at a later date, when agriculture again demands state assistance."[67]

The interim measure advocated by Hermes and outlined by the Reich Grain Office was the grain levy system, a transitional step on the way from the controlled economy of mandated prices and confiscation to the complete suspension of controls. The central office in Berlin, after setting a target figure for grain reserves in the entire Reich, distributed this total amount over all state governments. Quotas were based on average harvest yields for the period 1906–20 and reflected regional variations in the relative size of the agricultural and industrial populations and the size structure of agricultural holdings. State governments in turn set provincial quotas; state officials, working in conjunction with provincial Agricultural Chambers, divided up the levy among all administrative districts and—as with all aspects of the regulated economy—the ultimate responsibility rested with the communal official who informed the individual producers of the amounts they were expected to deliver. The price for the mandated deliveries was set at the national level. Individual producers could use the remainder of their grain however they pleased—either for feed on their own farms, or for sale at open market prices.[68]

In short, the levy system created a dual market structure, forcing producers to deliver a part of their grain at fixed prices, while permitting them to sell the remainder on the open market at prices at least two to three times higher. Hermes admitted that such a system would only underline the discrepancy between fixed domestic and free world market prices, "but," he added, "it is undeniable that up until now we have had free grain in the form of black-market grain alongside the system of fixed prices."[69] In effect, the levy system was seen as a way to combat the black market by institutionalizing it. As a precondition for the complete suspension of domestic controls, Hermes proposed either the return of production to prewar levels or the ability to cover deficits with imports. Fulfillment of either condition in the near future was unlikely.

In theory, the levy system was offered as the means to insure grain reserves and to mollify angry agricultural producers by bringing them closer to the end of all controls. Hermes was optimistic that the state's willingness to modify its demands would increase its authority and credibility in the countryside. In practice, however, the levies, once set, evoked a storm of protest from agricultural producers. More than resistance to controls per se was at issue. By 1921, output of the most important cereals still stood substantially below prewar levels (see Appendix

Table 18). Although grains had never constituted a principal source of income in the Rhineland and Westphalia, they had been a significant source of feed; the inflation posed a barrier not only to cereals for human consumption but also to corn, barley, and high-protein feed supplements.[70] Fixed prices for marketed grains created particular resentment because prices for purchased feed grains were left to the open market. Mandated grain prices were not indexed, with the result that prices for other goods continued to rise while grain prices remained fixed, and delays in payment only increased peasant animosity toward controls. Peasants needed no degree in economics to know that late payments were worth less or to fathom the increases in prices for production goods.[71] As a local branch of the Peasant Association in the lower Rhine asked rhetorically, "How should the agricultural producer purchase the goods he needs at prices that follow the depreciating currency if he is only paid 20 percent of the market price for his products?"[72]

Agrarian leaders were intent on insuring that their attacks on the grain levy system did not lag behind the radical actions of their angry constituents. The interest-group press accounts, anticipating the introduction of the system, had occasionally included half-hearted counsels of compliance, stressing the risks involved in further antagonizing consumers,[73] but more frequently they had emphasized the inequity of continued controls in any form.[74] Attacks on controls echoed the catalogue of agrarian demands compiled in the course of the previous seven years.

The record of the grain levy system was, at best, mixed. Ultimately, by the spring of 1922, producers had met delivery quotas, allowing government officials at the national level to breathe more easily[75]—but the price for this compliance had been the continued antagonism of agrarian producers to policies conceived in Berlin. From Moers, an area in the northern part of the Rhineland that had been thoroughly organized by the Free Peasantry during the revolutionary period and a radical stronghold of the Rhenish association thereafter, came the report that "every official intervention is perceived as a new injustice and makes a bad situation worse." Overcoming the peasantry's sense that its "economic existence as a 'free peasantry' is being steadily undermined" presented problems for local officials. Tensions were unavoidable when "the agricultural producer increasingly sees in the representative of the state government and its organs the 'officer of the courts.' " The consequence was a "danger for the state" for which there was no straightforward solution.[76]

Nonetheless, if the suspension of controls had seemed out of the question in the spring of 1921, at a time of relative currency stability and falling foreign prices, it was certainly no more feasible in early 1922. As late as November 1921, Hermes had still held out the possibility that the levy system would be the last step to a completely free economy, "provided that no unexpected circumstances intervene." By early 1922, however, he pointed with anxiety to recent, dramatic price increases, attributable to the fall in the value of the mark. For the agricultural sector, the result was a new form of controlled economy—"a controlled economy [determined by] the currency"—that made it impossible to cover domestic needs with imports and necessitated continued controls.[77] The question of return to the free economy "depends on the conditions of our currency," which, he noted, had depreciated rapidly in late 1921.[78]

Hermes' attitude did not change when he left the Agricultural Ministry in 1922. As the newly appointed finance minister, forced to draw the line on spending foreign currency for costly food imports, he was even less sympathetic to demands for an end to all controls. His successor in the Agricultural Ministry was Anton Fehr, a Reichstag representative with close ties to the Bavarian Peasant League (Bayerischer Bauernbund). Fehr made it clear that he would follow Hermes' lead in dismantling the controlled economy, and he unequivocally rejected appeals for a reintroduction of stricter price regulations; he also, however, acknowledged that some form of controls on grain remained essential.[79]

If Fehr's reluctance to end all controls disappointed agricultural producers in the Rhineland and Westphalia, so too did the position of their parliamentary representatives in the Center party. As negotiations over the renewal of the grain levy progressed in the spring of 1922, the party's Reichstag delegation remained deeply divided. While sensitive to the growing criticism of its agrarian constituents, it could not neglect working-class charges that a relaxation of controls would benefit agriculture at the expense of the poor. As the *Kölnische Volkszeitung* commented, "the danger exists that the parliamentary battle around the issue of the grain levy will lead to a domestic political crisis with completely unpredictable consequences. There are few instances in which the interests of producers and consumers have been so diametrically opposed as in this question—levy [on grain] or not?"[80]

Fears of agrarian resistance to controls, however, were superseded by even greater problems in late June. The assassination of Walther Rathenau created a heightened sense of domestic political crisis and presented the threat of a Reichstag dissolution and new elections. According to Fehr, the rapid depreciation of the currency following the assassination made the summer of 1922 "absolutely the most unsuitable point in time to introduce the free economy."[81] Domestic prices had to be maintained below the world market levels that they would quickly reach if all controls were suspended.

Center leaders argued that their resistance to the maintenance of controls would permit the SPD to campaign against the party with charges of "usury." As Herold reminded his colleagues, new elections might easily return a Reichstag even less sympathetic to agrarian interests. An end to controls was impossible, party spokesmen reasoned, since "there can be no doubt that the bread price that would result would be totally beyond the means of a large part of the consuming public, particularly workers, white-collar employees, and civil servants."[82] This imminent threat, Herold argued, called for unified action and prosecution of the "battle against the radical agrarians."[83] Pressing political considerations, combined with the immediacy of the general crisis, forced the Center to "place the Fatherland above the party."[84] Thus, despite some resistance to party unity by agrarian representatives, including a handful with close ties to the Rhenish and Westphalian Peasant Associations, the Center gave its official support to the continued maintenance of the levy ultimately accepted by the Reichstag.[85]

Long before the Reichstag's decision, it was clear that a continuation of the levy system would find few peasant supporters.[86] The crisis surrounding Rathenau's assassination did nothing to reduce rural protest against any plans for the continuation of controls, and Center attempts to justify its support for Fehr also fell on deaf ears in the Rhenish and Westphalian countryside. Even last-minute attempts to mitigate rural resistance to the legislation by exempting all peasants who farmed under five hectares and those with fewer than ten hectares who planted less than two hectares in grain were to no avail in the Rhineland and Westphalia. On the contrary, interest-group leaders argued that this change would make little difference in east Elbian regions with few small farms, and in western smallholding regions it would only increase the burden on those still subject to controls.[87]

Opposition to the levy system had become such a central part of agrarian protest in the previous year that interest-group leaders could not back down from their ultimatum that controls be ended, and they were in no position to encourage their members to adopt a more compromising attitude.[88] Ledebur, speaking for the Westphalian Agricultural Chamber, warned the Reich Ministry of Agriculture with one familiar, and oft-repeated, formula: "The number of voices is increasing that protest the controlled economy, directed only against agriculture, and the special taxation of agriculture in the amount of many billions; in the coming year, they simply will not put up with it, and if necessary will follow the example of other estates [*Stände*] and oppose it. The longer the grain levy system exists, the greater are the bitterness and the impediments to production increases that it creates."[89]

Moreover, Ledebur's tone was restrained, compared with the Rhenish Peasant Association's promise that "if the agricultural sector is once again brutalized" with the levy system, it would "not only refuse to cooperate in any form, but will employ all available means to oppose this law that is contrary to the natural order."[90] Again, provincial officials were bombarded by protest from local officials who claimed that it would be impossible to meet quotas, given the resistance of agricultural organizations.[91] Local branches of the Peasant Associations and Agricultural Associations made good on their promises not to assist with the collection of materials needed to assess the levies, further complicating matters.[92]

As in the previous year, producers loudly protested the discrepancy between the domestic and world market prices for grain and the prices for grain delivered under the levy. The fixed price for 1,000 kilograms of rye, which had stood at 2,100 marks since August 1921, was finally increased to 6,900 marks a year later; in the meantime, the domestic price on the open market for the same amount had gone from 3,510 marks to 31,500 marks, and the world market price had increased almost ninefold, from 4,660 marks to 38,333 marks.[93] Kerckerinck, addressing the sixtieth anniversary meeting of the Westphalian association, argued that as a consequence, the levy represented an extraordinary "tax that imposed the costs of cheap bread . . . exclusively on one estate, German agriculture." Reckoning the difference between world market and mandated prices, Kerckerinck calculated that the "tax" on Westphalian agriculture alone amounted to "4 billion 193 million marks."[94]

Such open encouragement of disregard for controls prompted a sharp response from Johannes Gronowski, a former Christian Trade Union functionary and Center party loyalist, who had assumed the post of Westphalian high president the previous summer and had been thrown immediately into the conflict over the levy system. At a press conference in late November, he left no doubts that his sympathies were with consumers. Pointing an accusing finger at Peasant Association leaders, he warned that "those who refuse delivery of grain are sabotaging the provisioning system and are revolutionaries."[95] The response was as predictable as the attack, and a chamber spokesman was no less critical of "the completely misguided consumer-oriented policy" pursued by Gronowski and those he represented.[96]

Verbal attacks by provincial agrarian leaders were matched by the direct action of producers. A wave of complaints from hundreds of peasants flooded local officials. Individual petitioners pursued other forms of redress as well, writing directly to high-ranking provincial authorities or to officials in Berlin. Though such appeals to higher authorities did little to relieve local officials, since all protests were first referred back to village and county authorities, these complaints testify to a widespread bitterness that could not be ascribed exclusively to the inflammatory remarks of interest-group leaders.

Karl Wieskotten, who rented a small farm from his former employer (a mining company in Gelsenkirchen), appealed directly to his representative in the Prussian parliament, Franz von Papen, at that point a young right-wing member of the Center party and close personal friend of Kerckerinck. Wieskotten planted only 12½ hectares in grains, but his failure to meet delivery quotas had been answered with a fine of 680,840 marks, the amount necessary to purchase the grain he had yet to deliver, calculated at open market prices. His appeal to a national political figure was only the latest chapter in a long story of frustration and of petitions rejected by local authorities. It was, moreover, not the first time that he had protested the system: a year earlier, he had written to the Prussian minister of agriculture to complain about the confiscation of his grain reserves, the punishment for his failure to meet delivery quotas. At great pains to convince Papen of the legitimacy of his claims, Wieskotten detailed his efforts to improve his land since the war and expressed his fears that "now possibly I will be brought to the poorhouse."[97] Though Papen may have been moved, local officials were not.

No more sympathy was shown to Friedrich Kipper, who farmed 11½ hectares near Dortmund. Kipper's credibility was seriously undermined when a thorough investigation of his claim led to a miner to whom he had boastfully confided, "other agricultural producers are crazy if they properly record the acreage they plant [in grains]." Like Wieskotten, Kipper was assessed a fine for the grain he failed to deliver—astronomically high, because it was reckoned in marks but at open market prices.[98] Anton Lange, who farmed slightly over fifty hectares in the county of Brilon, complained to the Reich agricultural minister of the harsh sanctions of the levy system that threatened "systematically to drive [him] to ruin." Lange's compromise offer—to compensate for a bad grain harvest by selling potatoes at half price to his neighbors—received as short shrift from officials as had Wieskotten's appeal.[99]

Georg Stiess owned a farm roughly as large as Lange's in the neighboring county of Soest. He had failed to meet the deadline for appealing his mandated quota because of illness and a chronic "nervous condition." To the government president in Arnsberg he described his shock as his winter threshing was interrupted by the arrival of a police official and a rural gendarme, who had seized his grain while using the opportunity "to threaten me, to kick me, to address me in such a fashion!" Left with no grain, Stiess was ready to let his livestock starve. "Surely," he added, "it was not the intention of the state simply to destroy a flourishing enterprise." Although local officials conceded that the confiscation was a "harsh blow," they concluded that Stiess "had himself to blame for the consequences" of his negligence. Acting on this opinion, the government president turned down the appeal.[100]

Noble estate owners joined in the chorus of complaint. The estate manager for Fritz Freiherr von Schorlemer-Overhagen protested on his employer's behalf that the harvest had been particularly bad: hail had destroyed fully 40 percent of the crop, making it impossible to meet mandated quotas. Schorlemer-Overhagen was surely better known to local officials than were most other petitioners. He headed the Peasant Association county organization in Lippstadt and also led the county Center party organization. Unlike Wieskotten, Schorlemer-Overhagen's agent did not fear the "poorhouse," but he explained that a fine of 1,903,200 marks, assessed in October 1922, could be paid only if he rented out pasture land formerly made available to the members of the local Association of Goat Owners. Twenty strong, the association members seconded their patron's protest, but this too had no impact on the local authorities.

Confronting official intransigence, Schorlemer-Overhagen's agent petitioned again, this time arguing that his neighbor's quota had been reduced and asking rhetorically, "Doesn't equal justice for all exist under the people's government?

Why are decisions directed against us made behind closed doors? Does one now intend to conduct a real class rule of the sort one always ascribed to the former governments?" Such outbursts may have served to vent Schorlemer-Overhagen's noble spleen, but they won little sympathy from the government president in Arnsberg who treated him as he did other petitioners, firmly reminding him of his formal obligation under the law.[101] Similarly rejected was the appeal of Schorlemer-Overhagen's noble neighbor Count von Plettenberg, whose estate manager threatened that a strict enforcement of the levy system would force him to abandon a 200-year-old tradition of distributing grain to the poor at Christmas and providing for his servant's ten children.[102]

The reliability of these complaints cannot be easily tested, given the undoubtedly exaggerated claims of those who took the time to pursue formal channels and the exasperation of those charged with executing the levy. Still, though unusual for their completeness, these protests are hardly unique in their aggrieved and angry tone. The resentment of agricultural producers was clearly captured not only in individual complaints but also in the refusal of thousands of peasants to meet their quotas, making any thoroughgoing prosecution of violators virtually impossible. The excuses provided by those who were prosecuted were often quite imaginative: Wilhelm Falke, a forester with a smallholding in the Arnsberg region, was not alone in conjuring up herds of grain-eating wild boars and mice that had allegedly destroyed his crop before it could be harvested.[103] But in other cases, exhaustive checks revealed that those appealing for relief had in fact delivered to the best of their ability.[104]

As Wieskotten, Lange, and many others learned, producers were expected to pay for grain not delivered at the free market price. In late 1922 and early 1923 at the height of the inflation, contesting fines on the basis that the initial levies were unjust held an obvious advantage for the producer. Even if he lost his case—the typical outcome—by the time all appeals had been heard and a judgment had been reached, fines could be paid off in inflated marks. Perhaps this comforted Wieskotten when he received word in September 1923 that his fine, reduced by half, now stood at 4,735,674 marks.[105] More likely, neither this nor the news of reductions in the provincial quotas for both Westphalia and the Rhineland, announced the previous spring, did anything to defuse his anger or that of thousands of other Rhenish and Westphalian agricultural producers.[106]

Hyperinflation and the Collapse of Controls

The problems of the hyperinflation that had begun in late 1922 were greatly exacerbated by the French occupation of the Ruhr in early 1923. The printing press financed the policy of passive resistance to the French as it had helped to finance the war and demobilization. By late 1922, even before the French action, domestic prices were increasing as rapidly as the mark's external value was falling. The advantages of the inflation for exporters vanished as the gap between foreign and domestic prices narrowed. By the spring of 1923, domestic prices for grains—and, for that matter, all other products—began to approach world market levels.[107] The end to the discrepancy eliminated a central argument in favor of continued controls on the agricultural sector.

In early December 1922, even before the French occupation, the Reich cabinet had rejected proposals by the Prussian government to maintain controls for another year. The new Reich minister of agriculture, Hans Luther, backed by Hermes (still finance minister), saw the final suspension of the controlled economy as the most appropriate means to increase agricultural production.[108] In justifying its action, the government argued that the gap between supply and demand could be bridged only by stabilizing the currency, not by legally fixing the price of bread.[109] Thus, in the summer of 1923 the last direct official controls on the agricultural sector were lifted, and the formal institution of the controlled economy was finally laid to rest.

It was difficult for agrarian leaders to claim the end to the levy system as a major victory, however diligently they might try. The action came after two years of nonnegotiable demands and vociferous protest that had obviously had little impact on government decision makers.[110] It was the collapse of the currency and the ongoing resistance of peasant producers—not the escalation of protest by agrarian leaders—that had prompted the final suspension of the control network.

Of course, the hyperinflation that made enforcement of the levy system irrelevant also created still other problems, most of which were hardly unfamiliar. The mark's "unstoppable, dizzying plunge into the depths" revived the black market, stimulated a flourishing trade in agricultural products across the border into Holland and Belgium, and once again brought Germany close to a "complete hunger blockade."[111] Following well-established patterns, urban consumers arrived in the countryside in search of any available food, and there were many reports of direct attacks on peasant property, including theft and arson. In the minds of local officials, such violent manifestations of the consumer-producer conflict awakened memories "of the worst years of the war and the immediate postwar period."[112]

The verbal attacks by urban consumers on rural producers were also well rehearsed. A coalition of Christian and Free Trade Unions in Westphalia demanded the reinstitution of maximum prices in the fall of 1922, and charged that "agriculture builds houses and outbuildings, buys machines, hordes goods, buys trousseaus for children still in their mothers' wombs, drives up the prices for food, and the government condones it all." Their question had remained the same since the last years of the war: "Why doesn't the government introduce maximum prices and jail those who charge excessive prices or carry out delivery strikes?"[113]

With the occupation of the Ruhr, the acrimony only intensified.[114] Passive resistance against the French, offered as a national cause and a basis for domestic unity, neither put an end to conflicts within the Center Fortress nor bridged the rift between consumers and producers. According to the central office of the Christian Trade Unions in Westphalia, agriculture's claims to join in support of passive resistance with voluntary food contributions belied the reality that "with one hand, they give us a couple of dried crusts of bread, but with the other, they take it back from the very poorest of the poor with high prices." Such cavalier behavior suggested agriculture's failure to realize that "the outcome of the battle for the Ruhr is also of crucial importance for the future existence of agriculture. But what will happen if agriculture doesn't realize this and leaves us in the lurch?"[115]

Many consumers were not eager to wait long for an answer and loudly demanded that the government take decisive action to counter the uncontrolled price increases that accompanied the hyperinflation.[116] Even before the Ruhr invasion, however, the national government had conceded that any reintroduction of controls would promise little success.[117] Certainly, the provincial and local price control offices were not in a position to accomplish what the Reich government refused to do, and they proved totally incapable of limiting the rapid price increases. As the government president in Arnsberg commented, "the step-by-step upward race of prices has the consequence that calculations are obsolete as soon as they are made."[118] Attempts to enforce maximum prices for milk, for example, only increased the sales of hand-operated milk separators and expanded black-market butter sales. The number of nondeliverers made it difficult to prosecute violators,[119] and when enforcement was attempted, it met with resistance.[120]

By the summer of 1923, the complete impossibility of establishing price guidelines that would satisfy the conflicting interests of producers and consumers resulted in the decision to tie the milk price to the market price for butter.[121] But by the time this measure was put into effect, official action once again trailed events: fresh milk was available increasingly only for real goods or foreign currency.[122] In an action reminiscent of the last war years, the military commander for Westphalia responded in late October 1923 with controls on essential food products—potatoes and milk—and the threat of fines as high as 15,000 gold marks or five years imprisonment for refusals to deliver or to accept "any legal means of payment."[123] In the midst of the chaos of late 1923, such sanctions had little immediate impact on agricultural producers—but before they were countermanded by direct order from Berlin, hundreds of nondeliverers had been issued summonses and faced hearings at the local level, insuring that the unpleasant memories of the controlled economy would live on into the new year.[124]

Also familiar from the last war years were the scenes of urban bands roaming the countryside in search of food and attacking peasant property. Particularly in the areas bordering on Belgium, conditions deteriorated rapidly in the late summer and fall. In the vicinity of Aachen at the height of the hyperinflation, troops of workers took to the fields.[125] For Loë-Bergerhausen, whose estate was in this area, rhetorical descriptions of the consumer-producer conflict took on new meaning as his own property was threatened by the increase of "marauding in the immediate neighborhood, in Düren on one side and in the brown coal mining districts on the other."[126]

Such incidents were only the most striking manifestations of a general crisis. The virtual collapse of the food supply provided a particularly compelling argument in favor of an introduction of currency stabilization sooner rather than later.[127] On 15 November, the government put an end to the inflation by declaring that a gold mark was henceforth equal to one trillion paper marks. The inflationary phase of postwar recovery was over.

For agricultural producers, in key respects the decade of war and inflation ended as it began. The intervention of the state into the agricultural sector that had been initiated with controls on the grain supply in the fall of 1914, lived on in altered states until the winter of 1923. Certainly the tensions between consumers and producers were as pronounced in late 1923 as they had been during the war. Since August 1914, German agricultural producers had not confronted a normally functioning market. State intervention and the inflation combined to create an atmosphere of economic instability. To be sure, the Allied blockade and, after 1919, the artificial tariff barrier of the inflation guaranteed agricultural producers a certain measure of protection and markets for all that they could produce, but the price for this security was high. Barriers to imports also cut off the flow of foreign feeds and fertilizers, and, even more importantly, the unfathomable nature of the currency depreciation undermined any reliable basis for production decisions from one year to the next.

This chapter began with a number of items on the credit side of agriculture's balance sheet in the early years of Weimar, and there is no question that relative to many other groups, agricultural producers fared well.[128] Nonetheless, liabilities were substantial and weighed heavily on agricultural producers who did not choose to see their fate in such rosy or relative terms. For now, this balance sheet remains tentative, and in the concluding chapter we will move beyond these outlines. This subtotal, however, suggests that in the early years of Weimar, even relative winners could see themselves as losers. That perception translated into protest against the state, which was held responsible for imposing controls on peasant producers.[129]

SIX

Rejecting the Republic:
Agrarian Politics, 1920–1923

Agricultural interest groups in the Rhineland and Westphalia could point to no impressive record of shaping the economic policies that affected their members' lives in the immediate postwar period. The most significant opposition to the controlled economy came in the form of passive resistance and, in some cases, the organized collective action of peasant producers, often neither initiated nor directed by established interest groups. To be sure, interest-group leaders encouraged and amplified this protest—but they had not invented its form. Their diatribes echoed peasant discontent as much as they orchestrated it.

In the move from subversion of the controlled economy to the formulation of political protest, interest-group leaders were more influential. As they had during the war and the revolutionary year, 1918–19, the Peasant Associations and the Agricultural Chambers placed peasant economic discontent in a political context. After meeting challenges in the immediate postwar period from both the Center party and new organizations, they confronted few competitors in this role until the second half of the 1920s. The success of conservative agrarians in negotiating the transition from Kaiserreich to Weimar insured their claims as major shapers of political ideology in the countryside. Their response to the events of the Republic's early years represented the one systematic political interpretation of Germany's first democratic experiment to which members of the Peasant Associations were most immediately and consistently exposed, and their message reached a greater rural audience than ever before. For these reasons, it is important to consider in some detail their ideological reception of, and their reaction against, Weimar.

By late 1919, key elements of this response were already in place; in the years that followed, established positions became more firmly entrenched. Economic instability, coupled with the related problem of state intervention into the agricultural sector, provided ample illustration of the dangers of parliamentary government, and a negative critique remained central to interest-group rhetoric. Beyond this, however, conservative agrarians offered few positive solutions short of the Weimar system's complete abolition. By themselves, they could fulfill this aspiration no more successfully than they could bring an end to the controlled economy. Nonetheless, their emphasis on resistance to the parliamentary order did nothing to encourage their peasant constituents to take a sympathetic attitude toward the political parties that were committed to democratic forms.

The Peasant Associations insisted that in the wake of the revolution, "the peasant must become more of a political actor." The new order demanded that peasants "learn how to represent their position and their interests in public life," and essential to this end was "fundamental instruction about politics and citizenship."[1] The associations undertook this educational task in the early years of Weimar. The curriculum they offered stressed the rejection of government by parliamentary institutions. The enemies of agrarian interests included not only the parties of the left, but also those leaders in the Center party who supported the Republic and cooperated with Social Democrats. The Center's own inability to provide an alternative, progressive political schooling in the Rhenish and Westphalian countryside, and its grudging acceptance of the continued authority of the Peasant Associations, created a standoff between a party that was attempting to negotiate its way in a republican order, and agrarian interest-group leaders who rejected the premises on which that order was based.

Agrarian leaders realized that a decision to break ranks with the party could leave them generals without an army—Schorlemer-Alst's experience in the 1890s indicated that peasants might well not follow their lead if it implied abandoning the Center. On the other hand, as long as they remained within the Center they could claim to represent agrarian interests on that party's right wing. Dramatically expanded membership ranks after 1918–19 lent legitimacy to such claims and insured that conservative agrarians could not be neglected or dismissed. Through their defense of a reactionary, antiparliamentary position within the Center, Kerckerinck, Loë-Bergerhausen, and a new generation of Catholic conservatives who joined their attack on Weimar were seldom able to influence party policy decisively. Their presence nonetheless provided a constant reminder of the divisions within the Center Fortress.

In the Rhineland and Westphalia, where the party leadership had continued its leftward progression throughout the war and into the immediate postwar period, splits within the Center were particularly striking. The threat that the departure of agrarian interest-group leaders from the Center might permanently weaken the strength of political Catholicism forced party leaders to tolerate a conservative body within their midst and to avoid direct confrontation on those issues that might have exacerbated the conflict. Conservative agrarians could thus open few doors of discourse, but they could help to close others. There was no easy resolution to this political tension that continued to be fueled by the fundamental economic differences dividing key constituencies within the Center. The forms this conflict assumed and the political posture of conservative agrarian leaders in the early Weimar years will be the topic of this chapter.

Conservative Agrarian Response to Weimar

Formulating the conservative agrarian political response to the Weimar Republic was not the exclusive preserve of an older leadership generation, and younger spokesmen offered new glosses on familiar themes. Hermann Freiherr von Lüninck, an ambitious right-wing Rhenish aristocrat easily young enough to be Loë-Bergerhausen's son, was only in his late twenties at the time of the November revolution. Lüninck began his public career before the war as the district administrator of Neuss, and from the start had a troubled relation with liberal Center leaders in the Rhineland. As Karl Bachem complained to Trimborn, Lüninck was willing "to let himself be backed as a Center candidate and then only directed his speeches *against* the Center."[2] He was to have a checkered career as the head of a regional Peasant Association office, as president of the Rhenish Agricultural Chamber after 1925, and as provincial high president of the Rhine Province after March 1933.[3] His outspoken advocacy of antiparliamentary attitudes was convincing evidence that conservative world views, like aristocratic titles, passed easily from one generation to the next.

In Westphalia, Kerckerinck found an equally zealous youthful ally in the person of Franz von Papen. Papen's career, while no less checkered than Lüninck's, is certainly better known to students of Weimar's collapse. The future chancellor and vice-chancellor under Hitler won his political spurs as a representative of conservative agrarian interests in Westphalia.[4] He was very active on the conservative right wing of the Center, was closely allied both ideologically and personally to Kerckerinck, and was viewed by the Peasant Association leader as an excellent replacement for the aging Carl Herold as a principal spokesman for agrarian interests in the Center.

The political rhetoric of these conservative agrarians was drawn from a limited repertoire. The ties between policies aimed at serving consumer interests and a government of consumer representatives, the scenario sketched out before 1918, remained a familiar theme until controls were suspended in 1923. Not surprisingly, no attempt was made to trace the origins of controls or postwar instability to the Kaiser's government and August 1914; rather, the revolution was quickly enshrined as the root of all evil. The vocabulary employed by agrarian leaders had changed remarkably little since the 1890s and not at all since the spring of 1917. However, in the early years of Weimar the target of antisocialist attacks was not an abstraction but a party of government; the fears imagined in a pre-1914 world had become real.

According to Loë-Bergerhausen and Kerckerinck, the catalogue of crimes of the early Weimar governments also included threats of land reform and, in particular, indirect socialization via taxation. Conservative agrarians worked diligently to keep alive the fears of such predictions. Once any genuine possibility of socialization had passed, attacks on taxation were consciously employed to sustain fears of indirect expropriation.[5] Thus, Kerckerinck claimed that even under a bourgeois government, taxation proposals were formulated according to the motto, "The best minister of finance is the best minister of socialization."[6] Unacceptable to agriculture as well was the eight-hour day—foreign to an economic sector that knew only labor from dawn to dusk, and certainly indefensible at a time when Germany's economic recovery depended on hard work. The swollen ranks of the civil service were another sign of the corruption of the new order. At the same time that the trusted old guard, the Prussian civil servants of the Kaiserreich, had in many cases simply been forced out of office, the senseless and costly expansion of government employment had made it the "grazing grounds for the partisan political herds."[7]

In the ideological constructions of conservative agrarians, guilt by association was presumed, and "Marxist" tendencies were ascribed not only to socialists but to all those willing to cooperate with the SPD in coalition governments. All were responsible for these changes and the economic consequences they entailed for the agricultural sector.[8] Within the Center, the undeniable proof of this connection was provided by Matthias Erzberger, described by Schorlemer-Lieser as a "dyed-in-the-wool red who attempts to hide his scarlet heart under his Christian coat."[9] As finance minister and the architect of comprehensive tax reforms, Erzberger was a priori an enemy of agrarian interests. Kerckerinck proposed that Erzberger literally "be sent to Tokyo, if we can't get rid of him completely," and hoped that such an ambassadorial post would eliminate his influence.[10]

Antisocialism was thus easily fused with an attack on the institutions of a parliamentary democratic order that guaranteed the underrepresentation of the "producing estates" and the rule of city over countryside. The equation between the consumers of political democracy and the consumers of agricultural products, a mainstay in the initial attack on the Prussian electoral reform legislation, was still valid.[11] Last but not least, the parliamentary regime bore responsibility for the collapse of the German currency. Reckless deficit spending seemed another unavoidable consequence of parliamentary rule. Loë-Bergerhausen offered the financial market as a "sensitive barometer for political events," and in November 1921 he pointed to the rapid depreciation of the mark as clear evidence of the bankruptcy of the parliamentary regime.[12]

A year later, in the midst of the hyperinflation, the same claims were easily embellished: "Since the revolution we have lost internal unity and we have lived under the sign of the complete collapse of the state, manifested in the recent past precisely in the catastrophe of the currency." The problem of the clear absence of authority at the helm was compounded by a deeply divided crew. "When a ship is in distress at sea," Loë-Bergerhausen continued, "then the cry is for 'Every man on deck.' Instead of that, we see the pitiful picture of German strife and the absence of leadership." At fault were "the parties . . . stuck in petty quarrels among themselves; they lack the selflessness and discipline, but also the dominating individual who could pull everyone in his wake."[13]

In the formulation of conservative agrarian leaders, the crises confronting postwar Germany were interrelated: all could be traced ultimately to the political tyranny of working-class consumers, an inevitable consequence of parliamentary politics. The inability of Weimar governments to master a chaotic situation was manifested most readily in the maintenance of the controlled economy by "ill-equipped individuals, ignorant of agricultural conditions, indeed in some cases outspoken enemies of agriculture." Those who determined agrarian policy did so without the advice of agrarian representatives and followed "the recipes of the Erfurt catechism,"[14] a reference to the SPD's 1891 party program. A parliamentary system had led to disaster, argued Loë-Bergerhausen, because "following the creed, 'Pursuit of Consumer Interests,' leaders on the left flattered the masses"; the result was the "political disenfranchisement and the economic enserfment of the peasantry."[15]

The policy of passive resistance and calls for national unity following the French invasion in the Ruhr in early 1923 did nothing to tone down conservative agrarian rhetoric; the aftermath of the Ruhr occupation heralded only "stormy times." The Rhenish Peasant Association insisted that "the dangers have become greater, the oppression stronger. The ghost of the controlled economy has still not been banished once and for all," and government measures introduced at the height of the hyperinflation, calling for mandatory food deliveries, showed that agriculture was once again being singled out for particularly harsh treatment.[16] Kerckerinck could barely restrain a sense of vindication in his judgment that by late 1923 the "collapse in all areas of political and economic life" was even worse than in the aftermath of the Thirty Years' War or the "Napoleonic wars of conquest." The resort to an enabling act to maintain order was parliament's final concession of its fundamental inability to govern.[17]

Agrarian leaders did not conjure up the instability of the early years of Weimar; they did, however, interpret that instability for their constituents in a fashion that in no way shored up the credibility of parliamentary institutions. The explanation of Germany's woes formulated by interest-group leaders did not focus on the victorious allies or the reparations question, and it certainly did not trace the problems of the Republic to the decay of the old regime or the Kaiser's responsibility for policies of inflation and market regulation that survived his abdication. The enemy was within, as it had been in the imagery of the right since the invention of the "stab-in-the-back" legend at the end of the war.[18] The Versailles treaty was a document of "Satanic hate," Kerckerinck agreed, but without the aid of the "triumph of Marxism" it could never have created Germany's problems.[19] Responsibility lay first and foremost with those "millions of Germans who still

fundamentally want communism, common ownership of the means of production, expropriation of property owners."[20]

To suggest that there were alternatives to the ideology articulated by interest-
group leaders is not to speculate about ahistorical possibilities, but to stress the
significance of the analysis that *did* emerge. Germany's problems, according to
conservative agrarian leaders, lay neither outside Germany in allegedly unreason-
able reparations demands of the French and British, nor in a past that could be
jettisoned. Rather, the problems were internal—in the political and economic
conflict between consumers and producers, in the clash between workers and the
"producing estates," in the struggle between "Marxism" and the "Christian way of
life." These splits had existed before 1914, and lines of continuity with prewar
conservative political formulae are undeniably clear. Still, reformulated within
the context of Weimar's troubled early history, such established ideological mainstays took on new meaning.

Viewed from this perspective, it would be difficult to overestimate the political
importance of the controlled economy and, after 1919, the inflation that justified
the maintenance of controls and contributed to a climate of economic uncertainty.
Together, they delivered ample material to bear out the conservative interpretation
of Weimar's woes and joined clouds of ideological rhetoric to the solid ground of
economic regulation and the instability of the early years of the Republic. Directing protest at these targets provided little basis for political unity between agricultural producers and other social groups and instead deepened the fault lines in
German society. It is of course unlikely that under the best of circumstances,
conservative agrarians would actively have endorsed a parliamentary system. The
material conditions of the early postwar years, however, provided them with a
well-stocked arsenal for their attacks on the particular form of parliamentary
government introduced in Germany after 1918.

In Search of an Alternative:
Within the Center But against the Republic

The agenda that emerged from the writings of conservative agrarians, young and
old, held as few surprises as their polemics against the controlled economy and
parliamentary politics. The Peasant Associations should maintain a perspective
"above parties" and, if necessary, "against the parties."[21] For Kerckerinck, "a
politician of the highest order in fact . . . feels himself in his innermost self to be
independent from his own party and even despises it, even if he enters into and is
active within the realm of party politics as is necessary today." In Kerckerinck's
view, "politicians of this sort are few and far between in the new Germany,"[22]

though Papen was among the handful who met this requirement. Papen's subsequent career surely justified the high hopes that Kerckerinck placed in him.

Escape from the chaotic horse-trading of electoral politics would be accomplished by removing economic policy making from this sphere and placing it in the hands of an economic parliament. Only a corporatist alternative, an "organic" system, could provide the basis for an acceptable form of "democracy."[23] Specific proposals for the form that this alternative should take focused on the Reich Economic Council (Reichswirtschaftsrat), a creation of the Weimar constitution that included representatives from all major economic interest groups, but was never equipped with any real powers.[24]

Such attempts to tie corporatist fantasies to structures in the Republic reflected the search for new equivalents to old visions. So too did the cry for the "strong man" who need not wear a crown, an ersatz for the Kaiser, who would stand outside the political arena, *above* parties, providing direction and purpose. Crone-Münzebrock, Kerckerinck's chief assistant in Berlin, expressed no sympathy for the "illogical" Bolshevik system, but he conceded his admiration for "the leading men, Lenin and Trotsky, . . . who are in control and who stay at the helm."[25] The agricultural sector in Germany still awaited that "master craftsman," according to Kerckerinck, who would put back together the "stones" of the "wall, torn down by the controlled economy and the levy system."[26]

Models other than a vague corporatist future or a right-wing, German Lenin were not entirely absent, though some options were clearly more acceptable than others. Kerckerinck had little sympathy for extraparliamentary escapades like the Kapp Putsch, and in its aftermath he harshly denounced the "gentlemen from Pomerania, Prussia, Brandenburg, [who] in the interests of the cause that we all serve, would often do well to proceed less autocratically and lend a sympathetic ear to the representatives of other territories of which they have no knowledge."[27]

Of course, in Kerckerinck's own back yard, the uprising of the Red Army in the Ruhr in the aftermath of Kapp's misadventure colored his perception. In late March 1920, from his estate just to the south of Münster, he described "a Red Army, equipped with heavy artillery and in every respect well outfitted, [that] has formed in the industrial region." More than a little distressed, he reported that "our neighboring villages to the south are already in the hands of the Bolsheviks." It was only the certain presence of government troops to the north that reassured him.[28] They undoubtedly carried out their charge to Kerckerinck's satisfaction, but even after the brutal repression of the Ruhr uprising, he had only harsh words for the "east Elbian idiocy of Kapp's followers."[29] In his opinion, *"The movement rightward was marching along well and with no problems*, until these East Elbians, . . . with their blinders up, couldn't wait any longer, and destroyed everything. Now we can begin from the beginning under the most unfavorable circumstances."[30]

For Rhenish and Westphalian interest-group leaders, no more acceptable than

Kapp were proposals to move toward the creation of an independent peasant party. Peasant Association leaders insisted on maintaining ties to no single party and cultivated relations with all major right-of-center bourgeois parties. Any discussion of an independent "Rural party" represented an "unrealizable ideal,"[31] given that Peasant Association members already had established allegiances to the Center and, in certain parts of Westphalia and the Rhineland, to the DNVP.

Undoubtedly Kerckerinck was flattered by overtures from Oswald Spengler, who envisioned Kerckerinck as the head of a peasantry mobilized to counter leftist agitation in the cities. The conservative interest-group leader was nonetheless forced to inform the conservative ideologue that the idea of a "crusade" with the Peasant Associations "collides with practical problems of execution." He reminded Spengler of the decentralized nature of regional Peasant Associations, the spectrum of political opinion each incorporated, and the similar variety of political preferences represented within the loosely federated national umbrella organization. "Welding these masses together," Kerckerinck argued, "will take place via economic postulates and necessities and (but this will take time!) spread more and more into politics." He warned that "to cultivate the purely political terrain today would be to unleash a centrifugal force. To put it briefly, the horses with which I ride are healthy and good, but they want to be driven with care because they are of different race and temperament. The teams of the Prussian Rural League–Junkers are easier to ride, but that isn't to say that they will have the longest endurance."[32]

Of course, in the Rhineland and Westphalia the extremes of "race and temperament" were not as great as those within the federation of all Peasant Associations described by Kerckerinck to Spengler. Kerckerinck and Loë-Bergerhausen were fully aware that their "horses" were most accustomed to grazing in the political pastures of the Center. There were important exceptions, as there had been in the Kaiserreich. Protestant areas that were solidly Conservative before 1914 backed the DNVP just as solidly after 1918, and the conflicts between the Peasant Associations and the Agricultural Chambers in the months following the revolution indicated clearly that the interests of this Protestant minority could not be disregarded. But the bond of Catholic rural voters to the Center had not been ruptured by the pressures of Center support for electoral reform or by the increased domination of working-class and urban middle-class interests within the party during the war. Particularly in the immediate postwar period, concern for the uncertain future of the confessional school and the attitude of socialist governments toward the Catholic church had rallied Center voters to the party. The National Assembly elections in January 1919 provided ample testimony to the continued allegiance of Catholic rural voters to their established political home (see Appendix Table 22).[33]

Equally clear, of course, was the fact that in the new Republic, the balance of power within the Center had shifted in favor of professional politicians, including publishers, representatives of the party press, lawyers, and particularly trade-union functionaries. In the 1912 national elections—the last before the war—of ninety Center party delegates, twenty-one came from the agricultural sector, and of those, twelve were large landholders. In the National Assembly elected in January 1919, in a Center delegation of ninety, there were only five peasants and three large landholders. Kerckerinck's name was among those dropped from the party's national list.[34] In contrast, the number of trade-union functionaries had increased from eleven to thirty-three. The departure of the Bavarian agrarian leaders Georg Heim and Sebastian Schlittenbauer to the Bavarian People's party in 1920 served notice to national party leaders that these developments might provoke defections, but the Bavarian exodus also underlined the increased strength of working-class and urban middle-class interests within the party and eliminated allies for those conservative agrarians who remained.[35]

At the provincial level, the same changes were apparent. Largely restricted to high government officials and heavily weighted toward aristocratic titles by the three-class suffrage before 1914, the provincial parliaments of the new Republic included large numbers of worker representatives, from both the socialist parties and the Center. Even in the subcommittees specializing in agrarian questions, Catholic nobles now sat across from socialist and Catholic workers, and the differences separating them were obvious in the acrimonious exchanges over the controlled economy and the ongoing crisis of food shortages.[36]

Confronted with such unfavorable prospects for influencing policy from within the Center, why did conservative agrarians in the Rhineland and Westphalia not risk following the implications of their own conservative ideology into the DNVP, the party most clearly identified with agrarian interests in the early Weimar years?[37] To be sure, it was an alternative that they carefully considered, and a year after the revolution—in an exchange with the bishop of Paderborn, Karl Joseph Schulte—Kerckerinck explicitly raised this possibility. Perhaps, he suggested, the interests of conservative Catholicism might be better advanced by the infiltration of the "national parties," particularly the DNVP. This idea was already "in the air"; "in the countryside," Kerckerinck informed Schulte, "particularly among largeholding and middle-sized agricultural producers, sentiments have already reached the point where many are open to such an idea. Many younger members of the Catholic aristocracy tend toward the DNVP as well." Kerckerinck hurried to add that he would remain in the party, attempting to anchor the Center on the right, but at the same time he concluded that "those who have up until now held to the Center, but who cannot reconcile themselves to the leftward development of the party, should bring their political allegiance into accord with their political convictions."[38]

Schulte showed little sympathy for such potential heterodoxy, and he emphasized that even the revolution and the existence of a socialist threat could not bridge an historic confessional gap. "It becomes clearer and clearer that the

German National party that you are principally considering harbors serious elements from the *Kulturkampf.*" Schulte reminded Kerckerinck, "[this party] can never do justice to the Catholic population and least of all to the Roman Catholic church." Whatever its shortcomings, the Center Reichstag leadership was firmly committed to the defense of the confessional school. Schulte named as Catholicism's greatest enemy, not the socialists, but the DNVP. The course he recommended was that which Kerckerinck ultimately accepted, "to stay in the party without shying away from emphasizing the basic principles of the old Center program."[39]

Though far less sympathetic to Kerckerinck's conservative dilemma, Karl Brand, the head of the provincial Center office in Westphalia, similarly reminded Kerckerinck in early 1920 that any ties to the DNVP were extremely problematic as long as that party failed to eliminate charges of ultramontanism from its anti-Center rhetoric. In the "German National People's party," Brand explained, "there are *no* representatives who openly commit themselves to the teachings of Leo XIII. The German Nationals *will sooner rely on Martin Luther than Leo XIII.*" Sure of his position, he concluded that "the Catholic nobility has absolutely *no other choice* but to maintain their membership within the Center."[40]

The confessional glue still bound Kerckerinck and Loë-Bergerhausen to the Center, and the strength of this "residual Catholicism" should not be underestimated. As Kerckerinck explained to an aristocratic colleague, "however close we are to them [the DNVP] in economic respects and in some political questions, and whatever I may think of many of them as honorable gentlemen, nonetheless, they can never get out of their Protestant skins, and their hides itch when they hear the word 'Pope' or 'Jesuit.' "[41] In Kerckerinck's case, personal experience lay behind these sentiments: his father had lost his office as Prussian district administrator of the county of Ahaus in 1874, when his mother had signed a petition of sympathy with the local bishop.[42] His allusions to the *Kulturkampf* were not mere rhetoric, and his fears of the DNVP mirrored fundamental confessional convictions.

Short of departure to the DNVP, Kerckerinck and Loë-Bergerhausen also considered a possible alliance in a "Christian" political party outside the Center but not explicitly opposed to it. Such an alternative was offered by Georg Heim and Sebastian Schlittenbauer, who had both played major roles in the exodus of the party's Bavarian branch into the independent Bavarian People's party. Relations between the national party leadership and Heim, the "peasant doctor" and "uncrowned king" who led the Bavarian Peasant Association, had never been good. They rapidly worsened after July 1917. Heim, a Reichstag representative since 1898, and Schlittenbauer, also a Peasant Association leader and the principal spokesman for conservative agrarian interests in the Munich municipal chamber, threatened a complete break with the national party during the last years of the war, lest the party be "Erzbergerized." The revolutionary period only accentuated these tendencies and heightened their discontent with the Center's leftward drift. By January 1920, Schlittenbauer and Heim were ready to issue the founding program for the Bavarian People's party.[43]

Still, as much as Kerckerinck and Loë-Bergerhausen sympathized with this example, they also knew that the circumstances in the Rhineland and Westphalia did not permit its emulation. In Bavaria, before 1914 the Peasant Associations represented the most important source of Center party strength. Kerckerinck and Loë-Bergerhausen's claims to authority within the Westphalian and Rhenish Center had never been so firmly grounded before the war and certainly were not after the revolution. The move from district to proportional representation, the elimination of the Prussian suffrage, and the reapportionment of Reichstag electoral districts only shifted the locus of Center support further away from the Rhenish-Westphalian countryside toward urban centers, undermining agrarian claims to be the backbone of Center support.[44]

Thus, Loë-Bergerhausen and Kerckerinck might side with Heim and Schlittenbauer, tempted by the possibility of a "Catholic Conservative party" which could build bridges to the DNVP,[45] but they realistically conceded that in the Rhineland and Westphalia, any open challenge to the Center was an extremely risky venture. Past experience and the example of their aristocratic predecessors strongly suggested that an aristocratic exodus, even to a Catholic-conservative oasis outside the Center, might provoke not only criticism from party leaders but also the clergy's active opposition.[46] Therefore, along with the overwhelming majority of their followers, Kerckerinck and Loë-Bergerhausen remained in the Center. Alternative political routes remained blocked by confessional loyalties and by fears that even were they to surmount religious and party political hurdles, their peasant constituents might well not follow.

At the same time, as long as conservative agrarians shied away from an open break with the Center, the party avoided directly challenging their claims to represent agrarian interests. The fate of the Christian Peasantry indicated the limited potential for dislodging conservative agrarians from leadership positions, just as memories of Schorlemer-Alst's ill-fated agrarian opposition hampered potential conservative defectors. Party leaders could also exercise little influence on the political rhetoric that conservative agrarians served up to their membership, and continued ties to the Center by no means meant endorsement of any specific political views. Karl Brand, the provincial Center leader who had confidently chastised Kerckerinck for his DNVP leanings, criticized him with equal harshness for his unreconstructed sympathies for the monarchy: "An elected representative of the Center who issues the public confession that he 'will not support Republican endeavors whenever they appear' is unimaginable at the present time; this 'public confession' openly contradicts the . . . position of the Reichstag delegation and the party's commitment to the constitution."[47] In his judgment that confessional bonds held Kerckerinck back from an exodus to the

DNVP, Brand was correct. In his assertion that Center membership implied certain political beliefs, however, his footing was far less sure.

Kerckerinck and Loë-Bergerhausen's positions of strength as agrarian interest-group leaders provided them with a basis on which they could claim authority within the Center without conforming to Brand's political logic. Their explicit objective was to strengthen the Center's right wing, and they repeatedly emphasized the underrepresentation of conservative agrarian interests in the party's policy-making bodies. How best to banish the "revolution psychosis" rife within the party and to block the party's move from a "social-conservative party of the middle" to a "democratic-social party of the left" was, however, far from clear.[48] The deep-seated antagonism of conservative agrarians toward democratic tendencies within the Center was matched by no realistic political strategy.

Within party ranks, agrarian leaders were capable of delivering only the critique clearly articulated by Loë-Bergerhausen at the first postwar party congress of the Center, held in Berlin in January 1920. The congress provided conservative agrarians with the earliest opportunity at the national level to air their distress over the party's development. The list of grievances that they presented held few surprises. Loë-Bergerhausen was outspoken in his attacks on the controlled economy, "the source of contemporary immorality," and he warned that the postwar "peasant movements" that the controls had provoked were directed not only against political parties but also against the clergy and the Peasant Associations. The Center was guilty of "whitewashing a misguided and problem-ridden agricultural program," and should instead exert political pressure to transform the important Reich Economic Council into a powerful corporatist "parliament of estates."[49]

It had already fallen to Herold to make it clear that Loë-Bergerhausen's position would receive little support. Herold continued to represent the conservative spirit of compromise and conciliation within the party, in contrast to Loë-Bergerhausen's unregenerate intransigence. Herold conceded that "in many agrarian circles there is a deep-seated antagonism toward the Center delegation [*Fraktion*] based on the belief that in that group, both in the state and in the Reich, agriculture is not adequately represented." He expressed his concern and regret about this development, but also emphasized that if agriculture was dissatisfied with the treatment it received, then it must become more active at the local level. Moreover, no one could rightfully complain that the Center had not done its all for the agricultural sector, and even the coalition with the Social Democrats favored agrarian interests, since it exerted a moderating influence on the parties of the left. The best strategy for agrarians was "to enter into the party decisively and to exert their influence," and agrarian interests were most effectively represented in a political party that included all social and occupational groups.[50]

Herold was no less a friend of agrarian interests than he had been before 1914, but he realized—particularly in a world in which electoral reforms meant an unavoidable reduction in conservative influence within the Center—that compromise within the party was essential. He stood with others on the party's right in his suspicion of the Center's *Vernunftehe* with the Social Democrats,[51] but he rejected Loë-Bergerhausen's proposals for removing economic policy altogether from the parliamentary arena. At most, he was willing to support plans for the establishment of subcommittees within the party, to be charged with the articulation of the economic interests of varying occupational groups. Even this form of representation, a far cry from Loë-Bergerhausen's corporatist dreams, should never be instituted at the national level, lest it present a challenge to the party's leadership and the Reichstag delegation.[52] Kerckerinck was among the decided minority that joined Loë-Bergerhausen in Berlin, openly expressing his doubts "whether it will be possible in the long term to unify fundamental monarchists with fundamental Republicans in the same party."[53]

Kerckerinck and Loë-Bergerhausen were not ready to act on these threats to leave the party, and they continued to fight for a greater representation of conservative agrarian interests within the Center. In the aftermath of the 1920 Berlin congress, they lobbied to guarantee Crone-Münzebrock a safe seat in the Reichstag elections scheduled for the following June. Crone-Münzebrock would be an acceptable candidate not only for Rhenish-Westphalian interests, but in addition, by virtue of his long service in the Berlin office of the Peasant Association umbrella organization, for that body as well.[54] However, in the negotiations over Crone-Münzebrock's nomination the limits to conservative agrarian influence within the party became clear immediately. The Peasant Associations' proposal met with strong opposition from working-class representatives in the party's national steering committee, but some party leaders, including Trimborn and Herold, promised Crone-Münzebrock support in return for guarantees that conservative agrarians in the Rhineland would tolerate the candidacy of Heinrich Brauns on the Rhenish provincial list. Brauns was a central figure in the People's Association and a key labor advocate within the party, as unpopular with the Peasant Association leadership as Crone-Münzebrock was with labor leaders. Despite this apparent compromise designed to let both stand, Brauns's candidacy was scotched in the Rhineland. Loë-Bergerhausen and the Rhenish Association were blamed, and Crone-Münzebrock was immediately, unanimously, and unceremoniously dropped by the national committee.[55]

The party's inclusion of sixteen safe seats for agrarian representatives on various provincial lists did nothing to tone down Kerckerinck's outraged response. For him, agriculture remained disadvantaged in a political organization increasingly dominated by working-class interests. No Peasant Association leaders were included in the Center Reichstag delegation,[56] and the agrarian representatives who did make it onto the Reichstag list did not meet Kerckerinck's criterion of loyalty to "occupational estate first and party second." Of the twenty-seven Center party candidates from the electoral districts of the Rhineland and Westphalia, only five could be considered representatives of agriculture, and certainly none was a direct lobbyist for the Peasant Associations.[57]

Although the results of the 1920 Reichstag elections revealed clearly how solid the party's rural basis remained, Center leaders perceived any controversy as a threat to party unity (see Appendix Table 23).[58] Particularly in the summer and fall of 1920, they were sensitive to the dangers of deepening divisions. Challenges to party leadership came not only from the conservative right and renegade Bavarians, but also from Catholic labor leaders who proposed the creation of a Christian People's party on an interconfessional basis as an alternative to the Center.[59]

Plagued by such fundamental challenges to party stability, Center leaders were eager to avoid a head-on confrontation with their agrarian right wing. Following the June elections, the party promised to increase agrarian representation in upcoming elections to the Prussian parliament and guaranteed Crone-Münzebrock a seat from the Rhenish district of Düsseldorf-West.[60] Once again, conservative agrarian interests rebuffed were not conservative agrarian interests completely rejected. Such a concession hardly bespoke the surrender of the party to the pressures of agrarian critics, but it did indicate a desire to avoid a divisive confrontation.

Gestures of this magnitude, however, did not lower the decibel level of conservative protests against parliamentary politics in general and the Center in particular. Unable to exert significant political influence from within the Center, agrarian leaders retreated to the ostensibly apolitical ground of the Peasant Associations and, from there, intensified their assaults on the Center Fortress. Their opposition to the party involved a delicate balancing act. Within the Center, they claimed to represent a substantial Catholic peasant constituency that established their legitimacy as the party's agrarian spokesmen. When attacking the Center from without, however, their constituents suddenly knew no specific party political allegiance and were organized exclusively in defense of their apolitical economic interests. Thus, Loë-Bergerhausen had few sympathetic listeners at the 1920 party congress in Berlin, but his audience was captive when it read the text of his remarks to that body a month later in the "apolitical" Rhenish Peasant Association press.[61] If Kerckerinck could not force the Center in the direction of a "conservative-Catholic party," open to the DNVP, he could nonetheless enthusiastically endorse the DNVP presence in the midst of his own organization. Further, he condoned his functionaries' supporting Alfred Hugenberg's Reichstag candidacy from a Westphalian district while he dismissed Herold as "a professional politician . . . not approachable as an agricultural producer."[62]

Responding to demands from the Westphalian provincial party head that he bring his anti-Center charges into the open, Kerckerinck disingenuously contended that as the representative of economic interests, the Peasant Associations "*don't participate in party politics.*" As for allegations of recent attacks on the Center by a Peasant Association functionary, Kerckerinck claimed ignorance of the political affiliations of his staff, though he unhesitatingly admitted that he carefully examined their "economic-political" predilections.[63]

In a similar fashion, it was not as a leader of the Westphalian Center party but as the head of an agrarian interest group that Kerckerinck invited the Bavarian Schlittenbauer, surely an individual with "economic-political" predilections to Kerckerinck's liking, to address the Westphalian general assembly in July 1921. In early 1920 Kerckerinck had still rejected Loë-Bergerhausen's proposal to invite Heim as a keynote speaker to a national meeting of the Peasant Associations, scheduled for March in Cologne. "Of course," he explained, "we can attempt to prove that it would be no war cry [against the Center] but that would do nothing to alter its actual impact." So near the elections, counseled Kerckerinck, it was imprudent to wield the "war ax against one of the bourgeois parties"; for that it was "on the one hand too late, and on the other hand too early."[64] A year later, the time was apparently right.

In front of an enthusiastic audience, Schlittenbauer performed as expected, expressing harsh criticism for the "school master" from Baden, Erzberger. Describing the meeting to Papen, who had been unable to attend, Kerckerinck gleefully reported:

> Schlittenbauer took the cake. . . . In all the years that I have dealt with peasants, I have never experienced a meeting that was continually interrupted with barrages of applause. Schlittenbauer spoke with such candor and bluntness about Erzberger, worker-owned business cooperatives [Erzberger's scheme for *Werksgenossenschaften*], Wirth, the tax burden, Fehrenbach . . . , the Christian Trade Unions, people whose coats are black on the outside and red on the inside, that Herold . . . [was] speechless and couldn't see straight.

Even "dyed-in-the-wool Rural Leaguers" could have no objections to such a tirade. At the luncheon following the meeting, Center loyalists including Herold urged Schlittenbauer to return to the fold "with his Bavarians." But with obvious pleasure, Kerckerinck could recount Schlittenbauer's response that "when lice have nested in a bed, he will leave the bed, find another bed, and only return to the old bed when the owners have reached the decision to rid it of the lice."[65]

Provincial Center leaders did not need to be privy to this conversation to understand the political implications of Schlittenbauer's nominally apolitical appearance. The loyal Center press charged that perhaps the Peasant Association was attempting to infect its members with the attitudes of the DNVP. In response, Kerckerinck again asserted that his organization stood on a plateau above the political arena from which he could endorse Schlittenbauer's views. Indeed, this was entirely appropriate for an "economic-political organization of the agricultural occupational estate." By attacking such activity, it was in fact the provincial Center press that entered into a dangerous alliance with the "extreme left" and, for that matter, with the other harshest critic of the Peasant Association, the Rural League.[66]

That the party faithful could not simply overlook such rearguard actions and unconvincing claims of party political neutrality was clear in an emotionally charged exchange of letters between Kerckerinck and Herold in late 1921. Herold sharply attacked Kerckerinck and other Peasant Association leaders for their unbridled criticism of the Center governments of Konstantin Fehrenbach and Joseph Wirth. Kerckerinck and his associates, warned Herold, were dangerously close to Schorlemer-Alst's unfortunate "secession," based on the "Peasant King's" misguided confusion of "agricultural interests with political goals." Like Schorlemer-Alst, Kerckerinck threatened to exploit "the unrestricted trust of agricultural producers that he enjoyed." Schorlemer-Alst's followers "nonetheless did not fail to recognize the gravity of his action" that had resulted in a "complete fiasco." Agrarian influence within the Center was welcome and essential, but Herold charged that Kerckerinck's right-wing goals brought him dangerously close to "being taken in tow politically by the DNVP." It was essential that Kerckerinck learn the lesson of parliamentary politics: "Agricultural producers can become mobilized in their official organizations in order to obtain a reasonable number of agrarian representatives. But, in the final analysis, the minority must submit itself to the majority."[67]

Herold bluntly exhorted Kerckerinck to abandon "feudal attitudes out of the middle ages." For agricultural interest groups to get their way, power was necessary; "that power," he continued, "no longer exists. Everyone knows that agriculture has no majority by itself. For agriculture—as for other occupational estates— successes can be achieved if other occupational groups are won over to the just demands of agriculture, as we attempt to do in the Center; and by these means we have achieved success in various areas, despite difficult circumstances." Rather than confronting this political reality, Herold charged, Kerckerinck was only "agitating the masses following the example of the Social Democrats." He acknowledged that "of course, all occupational organizations run the risk of demanding more than can be reconciled with the common good," but he reminded Kerckerinck that "it is the task of the politician to find the proper compromise among conflicting interests."[68]

Kerckerinck was not prepared to accept this conception of politics, and he dismissed Herold's criticism as evidence of the "considerable traces remaining . . . after the party's lengthy cooperation with the left."[69] Indeed, he could muster only disdain for party political structures. In an exchange with Alois Löwenstein, the aristocratic head of the national Central Committee of German Catholics (Zentralkomitee der deutschen Katholiken), Kerckerinck clearly articulated his attitude toward the Center. The insights into conservative political Catholicism provided by his remarks justify quoting them at length: "I have a religion, I have a world view, and I have a party to which I belong," he explained to Löwenstein.

> The religion is Catholicism, the world view . . . is Christian-conservative; both are sacred to me and parts of my person. The party is the Center. Parties in my opinion should be confused with neither religions nor world views. Parties are political organs of the lowest order. Parties are means to gather the crowds in order to drive them in a particular direction or pull them behind. Parties, at least modern parties, are not those of conviction but, to put it bluntly for once, means to deceive the people.[70]

The only alternative that Kerckerinck could offer a sympathetic Löwenstein or a critical Herold remained the ostensibly apolitical organization of economic interests into occupationally defined estates. He realized that this option would not soon be realized, and, as did Loë-Bergerhausen, he also recognized that a break with the Center was still out of the question. Like Schlittenbauer, these men despised their lice-filled bed—but in the Rhineland and Westphalia there was nowhere else for them to find even a troubled sleep. As Kerckerinck reminded Crone-Münzebrock in late 1920, it was essential to "establish good, loyal relations with this big party, whether it appeals to us in our hearts or not, for in the last analysis, it is the party to which the overwhelming majority of our members belong."[71]

At the same time, Kerckerinck remained convinced that "the Center does not dare to fight the Peasant Associations in their present forms." Justifying to Rural League leaders his resistance to open alliances with their organization, he explained, "if the Peasant Associations were to go over to the Rural League . . . , they would perhaps take some of the larger holders with them, but at the same time, for the most part, the middle- and smallholding agricultural producers, including the agricultural workers as well, would establish an organization along party political lines with the help of the clergy and the organizational apparatus of München-Gladbach. With that we would lose these masses for the conservative ideal."[72] Peasant Associations could continue to "strike together" with the Rural League, but this would be made much easier "if we march separately and much more difficult if all—in part against their wills—are forced into a uniform straitjacket for the march."[73]

Conservative agrarians thus continued to tread a tightrope drawn between an allegiance to the Center determined by confessional ties, the weight of tradition, and the absence of political options, on one side, and a rejection of that party's commitment to the Weimar constitution on the other. Those who were less ambiguously loyal to the Center could not undermine their position and avoided open conflict with agrarian leaders;[74] whatever their differences with Kerckerinck and Loë-Bergerhausen, they mounted no concerted attempt to wrest control of the Peasant Associations from their archconservative leadership, or to challenge Peasant Association claims as the most important representative of agricultural interests.[75] The result was an implicit truce in which agrarian leaders did not ask their followers to seek political solutions outside the Center and those loyal to the party did not challenge Kerckerinck and Loë-Bergerhausen's claims within their organizations.

At most, the Center could attempt to muster more active and enthusiastic support from its agrarian constituents outside the institutional structure of the Peasant Associations. Examples of such half-hearted efforts were the Center-sponsored "Westphalian Peasant Days" in the summer and fall of 1922, called to allow party leaders to explain their recent support for the continuation of the grain levy system. With Kerckerinck and Crone-Münzebrock conspicuous by their absence, Herold and Konstantin Fehrenbach addressed the party faithful at a meeting in Paderborn. They defended the need for continued cooperation with the SPD and called for compromise in a period of crisis. Center support for the unpopular grain levy system was an eleventh-hour measure essential to avoid dissolution of the Reichstag, they explained, and new elections might easily have returned a majority even less sympathetic to agrarian concerns. Faced with these options, Herold argued, "no one could doubt how the question was answered."[76]

Herold's position reflected not only his commitment to a politics of compromise, but also the knowledge that opposition to the levy system would have resounded negatively within the Center. He could recall the party's losses in the elections of 1903 when Center support for tariffs and responsibility for the "dear loaf" had driven Catholic workers into the socialist camp, and surely it was realistic to anticipate an even more violent consumer reaction to proagrarian policies in the summer of 1922. Brand, who was involved with Herold in the planning of the "Peasant Day" in Paderborn, confided to him his dismay over the defection of some Rhenish Center agrarians in the final votes on the legislation, and fumed "And the consequences? The next time candidates are chosen, who will stop the consumers from declaring: Give no vote to delegates who voted against the grain levy!!!" Such fears were not imagined, Brand explained—in his provincial office "almost daily [he] heard similar sentiments *very* clearly."[77]

For Brand and Herold, of course, it was ruffled agrarian feathers that were to be smoothed in Paderborn in late July. Here the favored line was not to emphasize the potential defection of working-class voters from the Center, but to stress that the levy was essential "to avoid the greater evil, an evil that perhaps would have struck agriculture most harshly."[78] Attempting to broaden the dimensions of the political discussion, Fehrenbach acknowledged the monarchist sympathies that lurked behind agrarian opposition to specific economic policies, but reminded his audience that the Republic also had much to offer. Should his listeners be unconvinced, he added, "Anything other than the Republic is no longer possible."[79]

These attempts to rally peasant support for the levy system and these calls for political realism had at best a hollow ring in the Rhenish and Westphalian countryside in the summer and fall of 1922. The sentiments of Rhenish and Westphalian agricultural producers were better captured at the general assemblies of the Peasant Associations that fall. Both organizations were again celebrating major anniversaries, but this time the self-confident visions of the future and accounts of past accomplishments that had characterized festivities a decade earlier gave way to reviews of "four years of turmoil, and still no rest, no peace, no sunshine."[80] A direct assault on the grain levy was high on the agenda at the Westphalian meeting, which was attended by Peasant Association delegations from throughout Germany. Although Kerckerinck stopped short of openly encouraging his listeners to sabotage the levy, he reaffirmed his pledge to deny Peasant Association assistance in its implementation. Rejecting the Center's "lesser evil" argument, he speculated that "future generations will simply not understand how it was ultimately possible to pass such a law in a civilized country." Kerckerinck countered Fehrenbach's claims of the Republic's virtues with "recent memories of two years past, when Westphalian farms went up in flames and valuable reserves as well as irreplaceable human life were destroyed." Along with the grain levy, such events clearly proved that "the present government is still far from enjoying strong authority."

Any question that these assaults were aimed at the Center was answered by the presence of the Bavarian Georg Heim, as a keynote speaker and a recipient of honorary membership in the Westphalian association. Significantly, this recognition had originally been planned for Herold as well—but Herold's support for the grain levy caused him to be denied the honor. Herold stayed away from the meeting, but not all loyal Center representatives joined his boycott. In attendance was Johannes Gronowski, the former Christian Trade Union functionary and new provincial high president—for conservative agrarians, "a journeyman mechanic from West Prussia" who had no business in Westphalia.[81] If the new high president had any doubts about the future of his relations with agrarian representatives in the province, the tirades delivered by Kerckerinck and Heim quickly laid them to rest. Equally clear two weeks later was the tone of the Rhenish assembly. Combined with the annual meeting of the Peasant Association umbrella organization, this forum provided ample opportunity for a rehearsal of the familiar catalogue of the Republic's woes and reiteration of the ways in which agrarian interests had been abandoned since the revolution.[82]

The Westphalian provincial party press, in its assessment of that province's anti-Center spectacle, regretted Herold's censure and rightly identified its source: Herold was the victim of Peasant Association wrath because he was "a confirmed Center man, not a closet Nationalist who only shares a name with the Center." The meeting left little question that "the Center is no longer trump everywhere in the countryside. Developments are tending toward the right," but, the account predicted, continued attempts at "subversive political activity" might easily back-fire, splitting Peasant Association members from their conservative leaders.[83] Such warnings could silence conservative agrarians within the Peasant Associations no more effectively than could Kerckerinck's diatribes stop Gronowski from proceeding with a conscientious execution of the grain levy and with the reimposition of controls on other agricultural products at the height of the hyperinflation. The Center had become a battleground on which there was little room for negotiation, but from which neither those loyal to the party nor conservative agrarians were willing to depart.

The Retreat from Politics: Maintaining "Balanced Justice" in the Center

During Weimar's early years, the obvious tensions between liberal Center leaders and the party's antiparliamentary conservative agrarian wing were circumvented, not resolved. The priority of unity at all costs was clearly expressed at the party's second postwar congress, convened in early 1922. Rather than directly confronting the conflicts inherent in the party, Center leaders followed the well-established pattern of emphasizing the forces unifying *all* social and occupational groups within their ranks. There were, at times, a few more strident voices, and the confirmed supporter of the Republic, Joseph Wirth, might well have had Kerckerinck, Loë-Bergerhausen, Lüninck, and Papen in mind when he warned that "the gentlemen . . . who stand at the head of big economic organizations should not fail to consider thrice over whether it is possible from a purely economic perspective—and that is usually a partisan perspective—to bring a people, after the biggest catastrophe that its history has ever known, out of these dismal days to better ones."[84] But Wirth stopped short of addressing the conflicts of interests that were present at the party congress, and he added that now was simply not the time to enter into a discussion between right and left. Under the extraordinary circumstances of postwar reconstruction, unity was essential. The Center must remain a party in which "all occupational groups can gather."[85]

The cost of achieving this objective was high. Not only were economic questions skirted, but in addition the party shied away from an unambiguous commitment to the democratic Republic. The discussion of fundamental political questions was generally carried on at a vague, uncontroversial level. The Center program ventured no further than the lowest common denominators acceptable to all members of the party—the need for a "nationalistic consciousness," a support of the common good over individual goals, and the "cornerstone of the entire construction: the Christian way of life and the consciousness of belonging to the German people."[86]

On this basis Kerckerinck and Loë-Bergerhausen could continue to advise against defection from the Center, and they themselves were not forced to leave, even if they were largely powerless to influence party policy. In the early years of Weimar, at best, their position within the party was reduced to that of spoilers. With an eye toward upcoming Reichstag elections in May 1924, Kerckerinck proposed a political strategy of planting a "number of lively and vigorous fleas in the coat of the [Center] Reichstag delegation, who look to the right and . . . serve as bridge builders to the party delegations of the right."[87] His ultimate goal was to create "in the coming Reichstag something above the parties, worthy, agricultural, with a conscious will, . . . which, it is worth noting, will not limit itself to the Center party delegation." This was the only alternative because, "with new splinter parties and the like, . . . we are building on sand. But in this form, with the flea system, our efforts cost relatively little and the success can be extraordinarily great, provided that we have luck in the selection of the fleas."[88] The Center Reichstag delegation was never made to scratch too vigorously, but its discomfort throughout Weimar was nonetheless evident in its reluctance to adopt a clear-cut political program and an open, unequivocal endorsement of the Republic. Such a stand would have forced confrontations among the various constituencies within the Center Fortress, and party leaders were unwilling to risk the consequences.

Measuring peasant reception of these political developments is problematic. In his study of Schleswig-Holstein, Rudolf Heberle discusses the tremendous difficulties in assessing the political inclinations of the peasantry and concludes that "only in voting does the mood of the countryside receive direct and, to some extent, genuine expression."[89] In areas not dominated by the Center, electoral behavior can provide at least one index of peasant political attitudes. Using this measure, it is possible to trace striking continuities in rural voting patterns in the eastern and southern Protestant fringe encompassed by the Westphalian Peasant Association. Unlike some peasants in Weimar who moved rightward after a brief sojourn in the democratic middle,[90] these Protestant rural voters maintained their prewar allegiances, voting for the Conservative party's successor—the DNVP— and the offspring of the National Liberals, the German People's Party (Deutsche Volkspartei) (see Appendix Table 23).[91] In these first elections under the Weimar constitution, neither party was among the unequivocal backers of the parliamentary republic;[92] peasant support of these parties is thus one indication that Protestant rural voters were not outspoken friends of Weimar.

Continuity characterized voting patterns in the Catholic rural districts of the Rhineland and Westphalia as well, but this continuity yields no unambiguous index of rural political attitudes. The Center was by no means free from the political and economic battles that tore apart Weimar's liberal parties and permanently alienated many Protestant peasants from the democratic, republican middle[93]—but the opposition of the Center's rural voters to party policy did not translate into the abandonment of the party at the polls. Had there been an election in the summer of 1922, the fight over the controlled economy might possibly have split open the party, but the Center was spared this test. Between June 1920 and May 1924, there were no national political elections that could indicate the severity of the strains within the party.

The decision of rural voters to remain within the party also reflected the weight of tradition and the power of confessional loyalties. Certainly, the political alternative offered by the DNVP was unacceptable as long as memories of the *Kulturkampf* could be invoked with ease, and other political alternatives were not available in rural areas. An emphasis on confessional ties, combined with a fundamental reluctance to allow political conflicts within the Center to reach clear-cut resolution, allowed the party to remain many different things to its highly diverse electorate. Loyalty to the Center thus less readily yields an unequivocal index of the "mood of the countryside." A Center vote remained a form with ambiguous content. This greatly increases the historian's difficulty in assessing the attitude of party voters, but it permitted those voters to maintain long-standing electoral allegiances without confronting difficult political decisions.

Loë-Bergerhausen and Kerckerinck fully recognized the durability of the bond tying rural voters to the Center, but they also understood that Center loyalty was narrowly defined and without specific political content. A Center vote did not necessarily imply support for the Republic or a commitment to parliamentary institutions; and as the continued resistance of Rhenish and Westphalian peasants to the controlled economy throughout the Republic's early history made clear, it certainly did not imply an endorsement of the economic policies adopted by governments that included Center party representation. The party's decision to eschew a discussion of political issues left the political education of its rural voters to those highly critical of both the party and the Republic. The political instruction provided by the ostensibly apolitical Peasant Associations clearly created no support for a democratic Center party or for Weimar democracy. The Center Fortress continued to stand in the Rhineland and Westphalian countryside, but its political foundation provided no solid support for the Republican order.

The frequently proclaimed strength of the Center—its ability to unify diverse social groups—could also be a profound liability. Unlike the SPD—the other "integrative" party in the political spectrum of the Kaiserreich and the Weimar Republic that accompanied its members "from cradle to grave"[94]—the Center did not demand allegiance to any ideology less abstract than support for a Christian way of life, however that might be defined. Sigmund Neumann, a political scientist who lived through the Weimar period before emigrating to the United States, characterized the Center as a "stranger to the German party system. . . . [I]t approached more the typical patterns and politics of Western constitutional parties. Attracting members from different social strata and divergent ideological leanings, it had to resolve basic conflicts within its own ranks and thus became a school of politics par excellence."[95] In fact, the party's history in the early

Weimar years justifies a quite different judgment. Precisely because of its diverse social composition and the range of ideological positions it encompassed, the party made a political education and the fundamental resolution of conflicts among competing interests impossible. As Wirth realized, an attempt to address openly the differences within the Center might easily have prompted its dissolution. The consequence was to leave unchallenged in the Rhenish and Westphalian countryside a conservative agrarian leadership openly in opposition to the Republic. As Schulte's exchange with Kerckerinck in late 1919 suggested, that other important source of rural ideological orientation, the church, was committed to the Center, but its commitment also implied no loyalty to the Republic.[96]

Rudolf Morsey concludes his study of the Center in the immediate postwar period with the assessment: "By the end of 1923, the majority of those who were loyal to the Center had accommodated themselves to the Weimar constitution in the tradition of a party, true to the constitution."[97] In the Rhineland and Westphalia, however, agrarian interests presented an important exception to this rule. It is possible only to speculate about the political convictions and the content of peasant loyalty to the Center party in the early years of Weimar; but if peasant attitudes diverged widely from those of their elite representatives, those differences left no indelible imprint in the historical record. Peasants and their interest-group leaders did not leave the Center; neither did they willingly enter the Weimar Republic.

SEVEN

Epilogue: Toward 1933

In June 1924 Kerckerinck addressed a festive "Peasant Day" celebration in Hamburg, an event that drew delegations from all member groups of the Federation of German Peasant Associations. Alluding to the stabilization of the German currency the previous November, Kerckerinck described the introduction of the *Rentenmark* as the step absolutely essential to save the currency from "sinking below the Soviet ruble," and to prevent "the wreck of the ship of state." "Is it a question of 'chance,' " he asked rhetorically, "or does the system have a flaw in its construction?"[1]

Despite Kerckerinck's hopes to the contrary, the Weimar ship was to remain afloat until 1933. It would not, however, enjoy smooth sailing, and agricultural producers would remain among its least satisfied passengers. This book can only suggest the nature of that rough passage. A complete account of Weimar's later years exceeds its limits, but the story of agriculture's fate in the war and the postwar inflation cannot end abruptly with the stabilization of the currency. Peasant antagonism toward the Republic, firmly grounded in the resistance to economic controls and democratic politics in Weimar's early years, lived on after the controls had been completely dismantled. The sources of this hostility changed, but its tone did not. The political alternatives offered by conservative agrarians also revealed strikingly little innovation, and a negative political agenda established in the immediate postwar period was modified only little in Weimar's later years. This chapter outlines these developments and sketches the lines of continuity that firmly tied Weimar's troubled early history to its ultimate collapse.

Completing the Balance Sheet: The Economic Fate of Agriculture in the Weimar Republic

Peasant discontent after 1923 remained focused on economic grievances. Was that discontent better founded than the chronic complaints of agricultural producers before 1914, or had agrarians again learned to complain without suffering? At least from the perspective of other groups in German society, the agricultural sector emerged relatively unscathed from the period of postwar inflation.[2] Livestock holdings had almost returned to the levels of the prosperous prewar years (see Appendix Table 10),[3] and a comparison of the first postwar occupational census, in 1925, with the 1907 census (the last conducted before the war) indicates that the "flight from the mark" into real goods during the inflation had often taken the form of the purchase of agricultural machines (see Appendix Table 24). Of even greater significance was agriculture's ability to shed itself of its prewar mortgage debt, paid off by 1923 in worthless currency.

Peasant farms had remained intact, and high land prices had not resulted in a market flooded by peasant owners eager to make paper profits. The evidence suggests that the constant demand for all agricultural products may actually have sustained marginal producers, retarding both their departure from the agricultural sector and any tendency toward the concentration of landholdings.[4] In areas with large numbers of tenant farmers, long-term leases made it profitable for landlords to sell their lands rather than look on as rents were eroded by the inflation. In the Rhineland and Westphalia, however, where tenant farming was never of major importance, such incentives did not exist, and family farmers chose not to break up their holdings in the hopes of quick profits.[5] Government restrictions on sales of farms larger than five hectares—to insure that they not be removed from agricultural production—in part explained this development, but even before 1919 peasants in the Rhineland and Westphalia had resisted the lure of speculative gain (see Appendix Table 25).[6] Both before 1914 and after, the principal market in land was in small parcels, and their sale might be used to finance capital improvements.[7] The scarcity of food during the war and the inflation only increased the demand for such small plots, and the expanded number of households keeping livestock suggests that many sought to supplement their food supply by becoming part-time farmers (see Appendix Table 19). Despite fears that property might become an object of speculation, enclosed farms changed hands very infrequently.[8]

From the perspective of peasant producers, however, even these assets could not outweigh the liabilities on their balance sheets. A gradual *return* of productivity and output to 1913 levels meant the absence of a decade of growth and expansion. In addition, the indices of the recovery were deceptive. The decline in feed imports, coupled with the reduction in bread grains available for use as feeds, resulted in livestock that was often poorly fed;[9] this caused declining slaughter weights and milk yields, which were not reflected in absolute numbers of livestock. Even before stabilization, agricultural economists had warned against holding livestock as a hedge against inflation, especially on farms that could not cover their feed supplies.[10] An excessive commitment to horses for draft power, moreover, might preclude mechanized alternatives at a later date.[11] Furthermore, the "flight from the mark" into purchases of machinery did not always represent a well-considered long-term investment, and after 1923 farms were left with machines that they could not fully exploit.

Even the evaporation of mortgage indebtedness was a mixed blessing. Before the war ended, much mortgage debt had already been paid off, and levels of indebtedness had not been terribly onerous in these west German provinces even before 1914 (see Appendix Tables 14 and 20). The limited market in land sales maintained the prewar patterns, and state-enforced restrictions on these sales represented only one more unwanted control.[12] Finally, whatever the gains of the agricultural sector in the inflation, from the perspective of peasant farmers they were offset by the state intervention into the markets for agricultural products, which was directly related to the inflation.

These elements diminished the apparent benefits of the inflation while it continued, and what followed stabilization provided far more solid grounds for agrarian distress. For the agricultural sector, a harsh stabilization in late 1923 and early 1924 ended the uncertainty of the inflation. Historians may disagree about the impact of the inflation on German agricultural producers, but consensus exists about the severity of the agrarian crisis that followed it. There is also little argument about the most important outlines of this crisis that was triggered by the end to currency depreciation. It began when the income from a relatively bad harvest in 1922–23 proved insufficient to cover the costs of production for the coming year, and when agricultural producers, who like everyone else had been spared the consequences of tax reform as long as the currency continued to depreciate, could no longer escape those consequences. 1923 taxes were due in hard currency, not inflated marks. Moreover, a reassessment aimed at generating additional revenues imposed a higher tax liability on all landowners. After stabilization, agricultural producers dumped their products on the market, driving down prices. Income was not adequate to pay tax bills and production costs, nor could horses and machines purchased during the inflation meet these expenses.[13]

A liquidity crisis forced many peasants to assume new debts at an extremely rapid rate, but credit was no longer available at the 4½ percent interest rates offered by agricultural cooperatives before the war. A potential credit crisis had existed since the summer and fall of 1921, as purchasing and marketing cooperatives faced increasing difficulties in securing loans from credit cooperatives. The flood of savings was clearly beginning to dry up because rural savers realized that there was little chance for an end to the ongoing currency depreciation. At the same time, the demand for credits, long dormant, began to expand rapidly, as cooperative members learned that they were well advised to pay for production goods with money borrowed at low, or virtually negative, interest rates. Coupled with large-scale withdrawals of savings, the result was that by mid-1922 credit cooperatives confronted severe capital shortages and could not meet the demands for new loans. Remaining capital reserves were rendered completely worthless by the hyperinflation.[14] Of course, large reserves of war bonds, the securities "based on the mass of the German people and . . . thus completely safe,"[15] were worthless as well. The advice of the Westphalian Central Bank to its members in early 1923 that they rid themselves of any remaining war bonds was by then long since gratuitous.[16]

Currency stabilization brought no return to prewar circumstances, and rural credit cooperatives were not able to provide their members with low-interest credits as they had before 1914. The credit cooperative network, the most important economic arm of the Peasant Associations in the Kaiserreich, never recovered. After stabilization, the cooperatives, rather than mobilizing reserves among their members, were forced to turn to central banks for whatever funds they could obtain. In competition with other sectors of the economy judged less risky, agriculture fared poorly. Interest rates for short-term capital soared to levels two, three, or even four times higher than before 1914.[17] What loans the cooperatives could provide, moreover, were used not to undertake productive capital improvements that might have offered a profitable return, but rather to cover normal production costs, to pay taxes, and ultimately to meet interest payments on newly acquired debts. By the late 1920s, the total debt burden of agricultural producers still had not achieved prewar levels, but the greatest part of the overwhelmingly short-term obligations at very high interest rates had been accumulated within the first two years after November 1923.[18]

Stabilization also ended the artificial protection for the agricultural sector that had been achieved by the inflation. The barrier to imports had begun to crumble as German domestic prices approached world market levels in late 1922; currency stabilization removed its last remains, leaving German agricultural producers once again in competition with foreign producers. Cheap imports further depressed prices in a market already flooded by domestic producers. At a decided disadvantage were not only grain-producing east Elbian estate owners who confronted a glutted world market, but also west German dairy and livestock farmers who quickly learned that their Dutch and Belgian counterparts had used the intervening decade to standardize their production and marketing techniques.[19]

The agrarian crisis was not unique to German peasants—indeed, Germany's problems were part of a worldwide agricultural crisis. The comparisons with the crisis of the 1870s suggested by some agrarian spokesmen were, however, misleading. In the interwar period price declines reflected, not long-term, gradual downward tendencies, but glutted markets and overproduction. Moreover, prices fluctuated unpredictably. There was also little chance that the crisis would be ended by booming consumer demand as it had been in the second half of the 1890s. On the contrary, the industrial sector in Germany confronted high levels of unemployment as it attempted to rationalize its production in order to remain competitive on world markets.[20]

For peasant producers, the crisis initiated by the sudden and severe form of stabilization meant that there was no respite from the climate of uncertainty and unpredictability that had characterized the decade of war and inflation.[21] The source of agrarian woes was now an international agricultural crisis, depressed prices, high interest rates, and a tax burden well above pre-1914 levels, rather than unforeseeable shifts in government policy and spasmodic drops in the value of the currency.[22] A limited recovery in the mid-1920s was short-lived, and after

1927 a bad situation became worse as prices fluctuated less and instead simply skidded rapidly downward. An already vulnerable agricultural sector was not spared the disastrous impact of the Great Depression of 1929.[23]

From 1924 on, the response to these problems that was demanded with growing vehemence by agricultural interest groups was the complete isolation of Germany from the world market and the "defense of national production."[24] Agrarian spokesmen cited the experience of the war as irrefutable evidence of the need to insure German self-sufficiency in the future. Behind this rhetorical justification was the conviction that only insurmountable tariff walls and central market regulation would allow a return to those stable bases of the pre-1914 world and the prosperity that had accompanied them. With no sense of irony, German agrarians vociferously demanded the state intervention that they had so vigorously rejected during the war and the early years of Weimar.[25]

By themselves, neither peasants nor interest groups could achieve the goal of virtual autarky, nor ultimately—as Hitler too would understand—was it economically feasible for Germany to achieve self-sufficiency in the production of agricultural goods.[26] The tariffs reintroduced in the second half of the 1920s certainly did not provide the stability sought by agricultural producers, nor could they cure the ills of a world agricultural crisis. Moreover, they were won only with the support of, and on the terms of, the industrial community. The form they took was a reflection of complex negotiations as much among camps *within* the industrial community as between industry and agriculture. Agriculture was recruited as an ally in heavy industry's attacks on Social Democratic social programs, but always as a junior partner. The agricultural-industrial alliance in Weimar's later years did not represent a return to the "marriage of rye and iron" of the Kaiserreich.[27]

No Weimar government could provide the economic relief demanded by the agricultural sector, nor is it clear how that relief might have been achieved. The absence of ready solutions, however, greatly intensified agrarian discontent. Particularly after 1930, the Nazis' clear understanding of the sources of this discontent was reflected in their concerted efforts to appeal to rural voters with a program that emphasized autarky, market regulation, and an end to the credit crisis.[28]

The Political Response: Attempts to Reformulate the Conservative Agrarian Interest

Rhenish and Westphalian agricultural producers never returned to the climate of economic prosperity that had characterized the two decades before the First World War, and their attempts to reestablish their prewar political position were no more successful. The decisive role of the Junkers in Weimar's final demise and the rural contribution to the electoral success of the Nazis testify to the continued political significance of a conservative countryside. Still, agriculture's pre-1914 prestige and influence, so clearly diminished in the years of war and inflation, were never restored.[29] Painfully aware of the problem, conservative agrarian leaders could nonetheless offer few positive solutions. Responding at the height of the hyperinflation to Spengler's repeated appeals to lead his followers rightward, Kerckerinck conceded that although it was his "concern night and day to weld together the peasantry," there were problems; "the material from which I shape my figures is not very manageable, either brittle like slate or soft like mush. In reality, the peasant is simply unpolitical; if he were political, he could rule the world."[30]

In the 1920s, not only the world continued to elude the peasantry's political grasp—so too did a decisive role in the Center party. Kerckerinck acknowledged that a massive political mobilization of the peasantry was not immediately forthcoming, and in the shorter term he continued to push for increased representation of conservative agrarian interests within the Center. He hoped to infest the party Reichstag delegation with one of his favorite "fleas," and in the spring of 1924 he lobbied to have Papen nominated for a safe seat in the Reichstag. Kerckerinck favored Papen over the incumbent candidate, Paul Schulz-Gahmen, who was too loyal a party member for Kerckerinck's taste.[31] Papen won nomination from the provincial party subcommittee on agricultural affairs,[32] but when the entire provincial electoral committee met, he went down to defeat by the overwhelming vote of 237 to 8.[33] Not even the agricultural representatives unanimously supported Papen. Kerckerinck's outraged charge that it was unthinkable for Schulz-Gahmen to run "against the unanimous vote of the agricultural subcommittee, propped up by workers and white-collar employees,"[34] could do nothing to reverse the provincial committee's decision. Exasperated, he complained to Loë-Bergerhausen that "we can do what we want, but we just don't make any progress with this party. . . . As long as the peasants are willing to accept anything, they can't be helped."[35]

What peasants accepted in overwhelming numbers in the May 1924 Reichstag elections was once again the Center party. Even slight defections to the DNVP could not seriously challenge the firmly entrenched position of political Catholicism in the Rhenish and Westphalian countryside. In fact, in some heavily Catholic rural districts the Center was able to increase its share of the vote over the high levels of 1920 (see Appendix Table 23). The Rhenish Peasant Association's threat that the Center's continued disregard for agricultural interests would have "entirely unforeseeable" consequences was a bluff that did not translate into the electoral rejection of the party.[36] Marginal Center losses did little to tarnish the reputation of rural areas in the Rhineland and Westphalia as party strongholds.

As in the 1920 Reichstag elections, the solidity of rural support for the Center was even more impressive when compared to the continued defections of disgruntled peasants from the liberal parties of the bourgeois middle. Unlike the Center,

Weimar's liberal parties did not survive the internal conflicts over competing economic interests that divided their constituents; their electoral strength was decimated as their voters departed for one of Weimar's growing array of splinter and special interest parties. The Center Fortress continued to stand, and nowhere more solidly than in the Rhenish and Westphalian countryside.[37]

Attempting to evaluate their generally diminished authority in the Center, Kerckerinck and Papen sought a partial explanation in the outcome of the Hitler putsch attempt in November 1923. Hitler's early endeavor to win credibility for his movement by associating it with the World War I hero Erich Ludendorff did not have the intended impact on Kerckerinck. For him, Ludendorff's *Deutsch-völkisch* connections bordered too closely on "antiultramontanism," and these overtones could be employed by the forces dominant within the Center to discredit the right. Commenting to Spengler on Hitler's trial in the spring of 1924, Kerckerinck expressed his fears that the "ruling wing of the Center will exploit this situation which overnight has become so favorable for it. . . . The beautiful, artistically crafted watchworks were destroyed with the tread of one boot-heel."[38] Kerckerinck clearly overstated the successes of the Center's right wing before 1924. Moreover, if the conservative "watchworks" had functioned only poorly up until then, they ticked even less regularly thereafter, slowed less by Ludendorff than by the strength of the confessional bond tying the peasantry to the Center and the absence of political alternatives that were free from the ghost of the *Kulturkampf.*

The only promising political tactic remained to push rightward in an antiparliamentary direction from within the Center. Papen, like Kerckerinck and Loë-Bergerhausen, still argued that "it will be essential, given the notorious divisiveness within the new Reichstag, to continue the struggle of the estates against western-style democracy with all energy."[39] The fault ultimately lay, as Papen explained to his audience at the general assembly of the Rhenish Peasant Association in early 1924, not with the working class per se, but with the system that allowed the working class to exert its political domination. Awakening still-vivid memories, Papen reminded his listeners that "under the pressure of the masses a ruinous policy of controls was pursued in a variety of areas: policies for producers were subordinated to policies for consumers"—a reflection of the strong influence of socialism. Papen conceded that "parties were not to be expunged from the world," but added that "new wine must be poured in old bottles."[40]

Spengler's hopes that Weimar's bottle might in fact be shattered and that repeated elections "would speed up the dissolution of party machinery" were also shared by Kerckerinck, who predicted that a Reichstag quickly elected would be quickly dissolved. Repeated dissolutions and elections, moreover, would "destroy all treasuries of all parties and trade unions [and] only then could one rule correctly."[41] Perhaps in the first part of 1924, there was some basis for this expectation that Weimar's collapse was imminent, but with the relative economic stabilization that came in 1924 and the political stabilization following the December elections, it became a conservative aspiration not soon to be fulfilled.[42]

Other political options were no more extensive than they had been in Weimar's early years. In his 1924 Hamburg speech, Kerckerinck had invoked the spirit of Bismarck who "sleeps awaiting the second coming." Short of a miracle at Friedrichsruh, Kerckerinck could point to no other possible strategy that promised immediate success or reflected much greater political realism. Returning from an Italian holiday in 1925, he was filled with envy and enthusiasm for the example of fascism in that "wonderful country with its wonderful people under the protective wing of Mussolini's government."[43] As he reported to Count Kanitz, the east Prussian who had become minister of agriculture in October 1923, "Above all, it is immediately apparent and the foreigner is tangibly impressed by how salutary the strong hand of Mussolini has been in this happy land along with the retreat of political parties that [he] has brought about. One is made aware of the gravity of things when one is suddenly submerged into our domestic conditions, where everything is so entirely different."[44] As he confided more candidly to Loë-Bergerhausen, in Germany, by comparison, "a *Schweinehund* leers from every corner."[45] Still, he conceded, although discouraging, the differences that distinguished Italy from Germany precluded serious flirtation with fascist alternatives in his native land.

Kerckerinck and Loë-Bergerhausen continued to ponder the possibility of an alliance with Heim and Schlittenbauer. Reflecting on their defeats in 1924, Papen also speculated that "perhaps we could have been successful with the Center, if we could have threatened to decamp and march to the right with the peasantry." A politically unified peasantry, he proposed, was conceivable in a revised version of the Bavarian People's party, expanded into a "Christian-Federative People's party" that would emphasize its conservatism to bridge the confessional gap.[46] Before the December 1924 elections, an optimistic Schlittenbauer gave Loë-Bergerhausen the same advice, claiming that "the leadership of the Rhenish-Westphalian Peasant Associations are in a position to put a knife to the Center's breast"; should the Center refuse "to pursue an anti-Marxist policy . . . the Peasant Association should put up their own Reichstag candidates, or enter into agreements with the Bavarian People's party."[47]

Loë-Bergerhausen and Kerckerinck were, however, no more in a position to act on the basis of their sympathies for such a plan than they had been when Heim and Schlittenbauer had broken with the Center in 1920. Loë-Bergerhausen reminded Schlittenbauer of the "particular circumstances" in the south, and "the Bavarian monarchist background . . . [that] found its limit at the blue-white border markings." The Bavarian action "is not readily comparable with our possibilities."[48] Kerckerinck could only agree that Heim might "know his Bavarians where everything is simple and clear," but he was clearly "not familiar with our fragmented condition."[49] If this was true before the December elections, there was certainly no denying it after them, once electoral returns made clear that rural Catholics were firmly tied to the Center.

No more successful at turning rural voters against the Center was the support that Loë-Bergerhausen, Kerckerinck, and Papen gave to Hindenburg's presidential candidacy in 1925 against the Center's candidate, Wilhelm Marx. Marx represented the element within the Center that was willing to strike alliances with the SPD and was thus most detested by conservative agrarians.[50] Loyal provincial Center leaders responded to the agrarian challenge by associating Loë-Bergerhausen with defectors to the DNVP and, in Westphalia, threatening that the election of Hindenburg, an east Elbian Junker, would bring the introduction of "enserfment" for the German peasantry.[51] Whatever the impact of such propaganda, the election results once again made clear to conservative agrarians the solidity of Center ties in the countryside (see Appendix Table 23).

Although quick to respond to open challenges against Marx and party unity, Center leaders nonetheless continued to avoid confrontations that might prompt an agrarian defection. They were aware that they could neither assume rural allegiance nor rely exclusively on confessional appeals. The party's support for tariff protection in 1925—over the protests of consumers—was one attempt to placate rural Center voters, to temper right-wing agrarian opposition to party policy, and to block the defection of peasant voters to other parties. The Center also emphasized its decisive role as the only party capable of maintaining a position between the extremes of right and left and leading the "German people . . . toward a true German *Volksgemeinschaft!*"[52] The party kept the SPD at a healthy distance and insisted on its rejection of the "materialistic *Weltanschauung*" of political liberalism as well. On the right, the DNVP and the *völkisch* movement were labeled as sharing an anti-Catholic bias that could be traced back to the *Kulturkampf.*[53]

Center leaders thus sought to undercut the criticism of their own right wing by establishing their claims to a solid middle ground. Defense of a "balanced justice" had changed little since the late nineteenth century. The Center's strength, argued party leaders, was its ability to meet the needs of a diverse constituency and to transcend the narrow, economically defined class interests that characterized other parties.[54] The stalemate between party leaders and conservative agrarians that had been established in Weimar's early years remained unbroken. Conservative agrarians could win some concessions and could limit the party's maneuverability on the left, but they could exercise only little influence on party policy.[55]

Caught between his inability to force the Center more rapidly rightward and his distrust of its commitment to Weimar, an exasperated Kerckerinck complained to Loë-Bergerhausen in April 1925 that, "at present, I am completely without influence within the party and I am unable to influence its policies in any way; publicly, I'm held responsible for those policies, since it's common knowledge that I'm a member of its [national] steering committee. This condition is intolerable for me."[56] At least in part, he accepted the consequences of the situation, by resigning both his national and provincial party positions.[57]

Still, neither Kerckerinck nor Loë-Bergerhausen broke with the Center altogether, and even in leaving his party posts, Kerckerinck carefully differentiated "between an official 'exit' from the party and the 'resignation' of positions of responsibility."[58] His reasons for staying in the Center had not changed since the summer of 1917, and, for that matter, they differed little from those recognized by Schorlemer-Alst in 1893. Along with Loë-Bergerhausen, Kerckerinck continued to fear the consequences of a "crossover" or possibly a "mass exodus" into the German National People's Party.[59] Kerckerinck reported to Loë-Bergerhausen, as he had to Schulte in 1919, that in Westphalia "the larger holders were already with the German Nationals," and slight electoral gains by the DNVP in some Catholic rural districts in the 1924 elections lent credibility to his assessment. Nonetheless, he continued, "the middle, and above all, the smallholders do not do it because of the clergy that hampers them. Already in these parts, they are suddenly systematically preaching against the 'Protestants,' which is the new, spiritual cover name for the German Nationals."[60] If the name was new, the tactic was not. As party leaders threateningly reminded conservative Catholic aristocrats, "Ever since there was a Reformation in Prussia, we Catholics have been mistreated." The defense of the Church implied a readiness *for battle with the right as well as with the left*."[61] Thus, while Kerckerinck predicted definite possibilities for an increase in the number of Catholic agrarians within the DNVP, "given the influence of the clergy, we cannot believe that the great mass of the Center peasantry will swing over to the German Nationals."[62] Despite his deep antipathy for the Rhenish party leadership, Loë-Bergerhausen also agreed, pointing out that "one does not know if the masses will come along [in an exodus to the DNVP], if even the majority of the peasantry will join in step." He added, "We must also consider that the clergy will probably offer unified opposition."[63]

The decision in 1925 to grant Herold the honorary membership in the Westphalian Peasant Association denied him three years earlier was one small gesture of amends to the party faithful, and it was also symptomatic of the dilemma of conservative agrarians unsympathetic to the Center. Explaining the move to an outraged aristocratic Center critic who had left for the DNVP, Kerckerinck conceded that "the problem of Herold cannot be separated from the problem of the Center. One can damn the very bases of this party, but with such tactics, one cannot eliminate it. Whether we like it or not, in coming critical periods, the Center will sit in the government and have influence on the direction of legislative work."[64]

This acknowledgment of their continued reliance on the Center, despite the obvious limits to their influence, did not, however, drive conservative agrarians to seek a rapprochement with party leaders, nor did it mute their diatribes against the Republic.[65] Unable to win the victories they sought within the Center, Loë-Bergerhausen and Kerckerinck could still retreat to their interest groups, that safe ground ostensibly outside the political arena. Here too, however, they could register few tangible gains, and in the second half of the 1920s this power base also showed signs of shrinking. Waning membership totals were one cause for concern: by late 1923, the Rhenish organization had reported a decline in membership to 60,000 heads of family farms, down by 20 percent from 1920 and by more than a third from the postwar high of 1921.[66] The repeated emphasis by the Westphalian association after 1923 on the importance of member loyalty and unity suggests that their silence on membership totals masked the same tendency.[67] Though interest-group leaders might claim the responsibility for the reinstitution of tariff protection, even this only slightly mitigated the agrarian crisis. The collapse of the cooperative network eliminated another basis of member loyalty, and left interest groups ill equipped to meet member demands for credit relief. Lobbying attempts to obtain funds at the national level were of extremely limited success.

Realizing that their claims to authority were increasingly shaky, interest-group leaders attempted to shore up their position through internal reorganization, lest alternatives come from outside the existing structures. In the Rhineland, this took the form of negotiations for closer cooperation between the Peasant Association and the Agricultural Chamber, which built on the basis of a cooperative agreement reached between the two organizations in late 1922.[68] Fears of completely rupturing the Center connection and forfeiting influence within the party had contributed to Loë-Bergerhausen's resistance to this solution in the fall of 1919; the knowledge that by the mid-1920s he had little left to lose undoubtedly led him now to pursue this option. Moreover, the contraction of all agricultural organizations made the arguments for rationalization and elimination of parallel efforts even more compelling.

Loë-Bergerhausen's partner in these negotiations was Hermann von Lüninck, who by 1923 had become his second-in-command in the association and who two years later became chamber president, replacing Dalwigk zu Lichtenfels (who had succeeded Schorlemer-Lieser in 1922 and whose term was ended by his death in 1925). The chamber presidency gave Lüninck the position of prominence and power that he had long sought.[69] The merger of the local branches of the Agricultural Chamber with the Peasant Association, proclaimed as the means to eliminate duplication of efforts and increase the effectiveness of agrarian lobbying attempts, was rightly perceived by the Rhenish Center as a hostile gesture, intended to allow the Peasant Associations to establish even greater distance from the party and to increase their opportunities for collaboration with the Rural League.[70]

Kerckerinck condemned the merger agreement as divisive and a threat to the independence and flexibility of the Peasant Associations, immediately prompting

Loë-Bergerhausen to pull his organization out of the national umbrella federation that Kerckerinck still headed.[71] Plagued by division at the national level, Kerckerinck also confronted increasingly vocal demands for a reorganization of agrarian interest representation in Westphalia. As in the Rhineland, pressure came from those outspokenly critical of the Peasant Association's Center connection. Leading the attack were Ledebur, still chamber president, and Ferdinand von Lüninck, Hermann's cousin and head of the chamber regional organization in the southern part of the province. Both pushed for closer ties with the Rural League and the DNVP.

Organizational fault lines papered over in 1919 quickly reappeared. Cooperation with the Center, Ledebur argued, was possible as long as that party espoused a "truly Christian world view." Since the revolution, the Center's move leftward in support of the Republic suggested that this could no longer be assumed.[72] Openly sympathetic to the Rural League, Ledebur demanded that the Peasant Association disavow its Center ties.[73] Within his own ranks, Kerckerinck confronted a struggle with "the German Nationals from Minden-Ravensberg . . . on the one side, and the unconditionally Center circles on the other," as well as with those who "without approving present Center policies, under no circumstances will tolerate the charge of the Protestant German National calvary." Reflecting on "how strongly and even dangerously the leftward route of the Center can emotionally charge the spirits of the Protestant, right population against us and particularly against all that is Catholic," he once again sought refuge behind avowals of the apolitical status of his organization, and insisted on its continued autonomy.[74]

Ferdinand von Lüninck favored another alternative and pressed Kerckerinck to consider the model established by his cousin and Loë-Bergerhausen in the Rhineland. Along with Ledebur, he believed that the decline of conservative political influence would be checked most effectively by a more resolute demand for a conservative alliance outside, and if necessary against, the Center.[75] As the head of the Agricultural Chamber's regional association for Arnsberg—the branch that had expanded most rapidly after the war—and a Peasant Association functionary, Lüninck claimed a formidable power base. Despite Kerckerinck's warnings against the dangers of divisiveness, by early 1927 Lüninck was ready to defy Kerckerinck and demand the complete merger of the Peasant Association with the Rural League.[76] Lüninck justified his action as a response to pressure from below for the creation of new, unified institutional forms aimed at increasing the effectiveness of agrarian interest representation at the national level. Were existing organizations to provide no alternatives, he predicted, the initiative would surely come from elsewhere.[77]

Behind Lüninck's tactics, endorsed by Ledebur, was an attack not only on the Center but also on Kerckerinck.[78] Again, Kerckerinck countered that closer ties to the Rural League would only antagonize the Center, forcing it to deploy its clerical shock troops and splitting open the Westphalian countryside. Nobles might depart for the DNVP and an alliance with the Rural League, but the peasants, Kerckerinck feared, would remain with their parish priest behind the Center.[79]

Kerckerinck's analysis reflected not only the experience of the postwar period but also the more immediate challenge to his authority from yet another direction: in 1927 he faced attacks from smallholding peasants and tenant farmers who had joined together under the leadership of a Catholic priest, Ferdinand Vorholt, in the Westphalian Peasant League (Westfälischer Bauernbund).[80] The league claimed to represent the interests of the "true" peasantry in contrast to the aristocratic orientation of the association. It openly supported the Republic, and it enjoyed at least the tacit approval of the Center, though not, as Papen feared, of the "Central Soviet in Moscow."[81] Although its numbers remained small, it presented another centrifugal force pulling at the Peasant Associations and threatening Kerckerinck's leadership position.

Kerckerinck thus found himself for the second time since 1918 in a crossfire between those critical of his Center ties, on the one hand, and, on the other, those who claimed that the "route that the Peasant Association is following is irreconcilable with the principles of the Center," as the association became an "organization of nobles, of large landholders . . . that has east Elbian leanings."[82] Herold made no secret of his conviction that "it would be best if Freiherr von Kerckerinck would leave his office,"[83] while Lüninck pressured for the same end but from a different direction. Both called for fundamental changes in the policies of the Peasant Association. In late 1924, Kerckerinck had still prided himself on avoiding the "*agitation against the 'aristocrats'*" that was growing in other parts of Germany;[84] three years later, the embattled Westphalian leader grudgingly admitted the wisdom of "not giving the association an 'aristocratic' head."[85] Accepting the consequences and conceding his growing isolation from his membership, he resigned by the end of 1927.

His disclaimers notwithstanding,[86] Kerckerinck's decision to step down was intended to create a new basis for organizational unity. The form that unity took, however, completely escaped his influence and signaled the Peasant Association's move farther away from the Center. Under Kerckerinck's successor, Heinrich Dieckmann, a long-time association functionary who had served as the head of the regional office for the Ruhr district, the Westphalian association was moving in Ferdinand von Lüninck's direction, not in that favored by Herold.[87] Dieckmann overcame his initial reservations about Lüninck's open criticism of the Center[88] to join with him in creating a common ground for cooperation with both the Rural League and the Rhenish Peasant Association.[89] The appointment of Andreas Hermes, a loyal Center member, to succeed Kerckerinck as head of the national federation of all Peasant Associations was clearly intended to swing the pendulum back in the other direction. However, although he had the backing of Herold, Hermes was to discover that he could not stem the forceful rightward tendencies in the Rhineland and Westphalia.[90]

Even after his departure, Kerckerinck continued to believe that open alliances with the Rural League would have ominous consequences, and he opposed the creation of the "Green Front" (Grüne Front) in the spring of 1929. This national umbrella organization of major agricultural interest groups was created to provide a unified representation of agrarian economic interests and to absorb the pressure from a peasantry increasingly radicalized by the ever-worsening agricultural crisis. The organization was favored by Hermes as the most effective means to forestall a complete merger of the Rural League and regional Peasant Associations. He rightly anticipated that formal unification with the Rural League would provoke an open conflict with the Center because of the league's connections to the DNVP. Kerckerinck saw the "Green Front" differently and warned that even informal cooperation with the Rural League was inadvisable given that "today we have a left government. The possibilities for the Rural League to have any effectiveness in a left direction are at the present time completely blocked." Through the Center, he argued, the Peasant Association could maintain ties to parties on the left. Merger with the Rural League would only prompt charges that the Peasant Associations were controlled by " 'East Elbians,' 'Big Estate Owners,' 'Junkers,' 'Rhenish-Westphalian Barons.' . . ." In response, peasants would be driven to the left.[91]

There is an unavoidable irony in Kerckerinck's pointed emphasis on the importance of close ties between the Peasant Associations and the Center and the necessity of remaining open to the left; he had devoted most of his public career to blocking both of these possibilities. Viewed generously, his reflections perhaps indicate a slow learning experience, but by 1929 it was too late to undo the damage. Kerckerinck was no longer in a position to influence the policy of the Peasant Associations. His prediction of a leftward march by the peasantry was, of course, ultimately as inaccurate as his prediction of the continued dominance of a left government. Indeed, contrary to Hermes' hopes that the "Green Front" would insure Peasant Association autonomy, in the Rhineland and Westphalia it was endorsed as the basis for ever closer cooperation with the Rural League.[92]

This abbreviated account of internal interest-group conflicts in the second half of the 1920s suggests the tenuousness of the compromises struck by Kerckerinck and Loë-Bergerhausen in the immediate postwar period. They had built their structures on a unity of opposition to revolution and the controlled economy, but positive accomplishments were essential for more lasting success and stability. The Rhineland and Westphalia remained immune to the agrarian splinter parties and radical independent agrarian movements that sprang up elsewhere in Germany in the late 1920s, but the established organizations of the region did not survive unchanged in the later years of Weimar.[93] However, the new forms of interest-group coalition, altered from within, were no better able than their predecessors to offer their followers tangible gains.

From the Rejection of Weimar to National Socialism

The sketch of political and economic development after 1923 presented here indicates that the early antipathy toward a democratic Republic among agricultural producers was not overcome in the "golden years" of stability in the mid-1920s. Complete economic collapse after 1929 did nothing to engender peasant loyalty to Weimar. The radical tone of Rhenish and Westphalian interest groups in the years immediately preceding the National Socialist takeover leaves no doubt that they continued to follow the rightward trajectory already distinctly outlined by the end of the decade.

For its part, the Center failed to offer its rural constituents either an effective antidote or arguments in favor of supporting Weimar. Only the party's complete retreat behind its confessional standard insured the solidity of the Center Fortress in the final years of the Republic. The election of Ludwig Kaas in 1928 as the first clerical head of the party was the culmination of this development. Since the establishment of the Republic, the Center had never been one of Weimar's unequivocal supporters; behind Kaas, it moved toward open criticism of parliamentary institutions and a consideration of political alternatives outside a divided Reichstag.[94]

Undoubtedly even these rightward tendencies did not fully satisfy the party's conservative agrarians, and the Center never endorsed conservative agrarian corporatist visions. Under Kaas, however, the party adopted an implicitly anti-democratic rhetoric of *Volksgemeinschaft* and offered a future free from the "unpredictable parliamentary climate." Such appeals, coupled with support for some agrarian economic demands and an emphasis on confessional concerns, maintained the solid block of rural voters that contributed to the Center's ability to play an important role in the governments of Weimar. The party's political maneuverability rested, however, on a fragile basis. It could exercise a decisive influence within a parliamentary system only by avoiding any unequivocal commitment to the principles on which that system was founded. Confessional concerns and a socially diverse constituency still distinguished the Center clearly from right-wing parties, including the National Socialists, but confessional concerns were hardly synonymous with support for democratic institutions. By 1932, the Center had marched only further rightward to join in an antisystem campaign that openly advocated authoritarian solutions.[95]

In the Protestant rural areas and mixed confessional districts of the Rhineland and Westphalia, the progression of peasant voters to the National Socialists via the Christian National Peasant and Rural People's party (Christlich-Nationale

Bauern- und Landvolkpartei) was apparent in the July 1932 Reichstag elections (see Appendix Table 23).[96] The ease with which the Rhenish and Westphalian Peasant Associations actively accepted and supported the Nazis after 1933 suggests that the conversion of their Catholic members had also not taken place overnight. To argue that votes for the Center were votes against National Socialism is to overlook the steady rightward progression of the party's agrarian wing and the extent to which agrarian demands for an end to parliamentary politics were never directly challenged by Center leaders.[97] There were many alternative forms of political Catholicism in the Weimar Republic. That offered by Carl Trimborn, Heinrich Brauns, and Joseph Wirth was poorly represented in the party by the early 1930s and had never taken root in the Rhenish and Westphalian countryside; that offered by Franz von Papen flourished, and Papen's own example indicates how easily the borders between National Socialism and political Catholicism could become blurred and ultimately disregarded.

The collapse of the Republic ended the dilemma of conservative Catholic agrarians within the Center, but Kerckerinck and Loë-Bergerhausen did not witness the denouement: the Westphalian survived the death of his Rhenish counterpart in 1931 by only two years. The final resolution of the troubled relations between the Center and conservative agrarians could hardly have displeased them. How attenuated those relations had become even before Weimar's final demise was indicated by the welcome given by the Westphalian association to a renowned Center renegade at yet another anniversary celebration, in 1932. This time, the honored guest was not a Bavarian "Peasant Doctor," but Franz von Papen, a son of Westphalia, "tied to the soil and the home." Only a month earlier, Papen's break with the Center had become complete when he replaced Heinrich Brüning as chancellor against the wishes of his party. Papen told his audience what they wanted to hear, promising a "new construction of the German state," free from party political connections and based on a conservative, authoritarian, Christian foundation. Such a state could undertake essential economic programs, including the move toward domestic economic self-sufficiency. Although rural Catholics in the Rhineland and Westphalia continued to support the Center with their votes in Weimar's remaining election, they had long since completely abandoned the Republic for the future that Papen promised.[98]

Less than two months after Papen went on to join a cabinet headed by Hitler, the state's attorney ordered that Hermes be arrested—allegedly for expropriating funds earmarked for rationalization of the peasant cooperative network, though his known sympathies for the Center were the more likely cause.[99] Hermann von Lüninck, Hermes' immediate successor, was unencumbered by such a political past, and even before January 1933 his sympathies for the National Socialists were no secret.[100] The Rhenish and Westphalian organizations did not race to Hermes' defense, and the subordination of these regional associations to the Nazi Reich Agricultural Estate (Reichsnährstand), although accompanied by changes in personnel, proceeded without major problems. In fact, this step could justifiably be seen as the realization of the unified interest group that leaders in both provincial associations had long advocated, nor was it only propaganda when the Nazi press claimed that the Peasant Association program was "also the program of our *Führer*."[101] The Nazi triumph marked the beginning of an uncertain future, but for Rhenish and Westphalian peasant farmers, it was far more welcome than the Weimar experiment that it ended.

Conclusion

By 1933, peasants in the Rhineland and Westphalia were neither defenders of the Republic nor opponents of National Socialism. Antagonism toward Weimar united Catholic and Protestant agrarians. Even those who viewed National Socialism with skepticism accepted the abolition of democratic institutions as the essential solution to Weimar's woes. This study has emphasized that the intensity of rural antagonism toward Weimar was neither the exclusive product of the agrarian crisis after 1927–28 nor that of a "proto-fascist" past in the Kaiserreich: both of these alternatives ignore the radical rupture between Kaiserreich and Weimar created by the near-decade of war and inflation, 1914–23. A sustained atmosphere of economic and political uncertainty provided the context within which conservative agrarians experienced the introduction of Germany's first experiment with democratic government, and it shaped the terms of their reaction to parliamentary reform.

No generation creates its past anew, but the survival and success of certain organizational structures, political attitudes, and ideological appeals must be explained in terms of the present in which they are embedded. "A 'tradition' is only as old as the practices and relations which transform its meaning," as Geoff Eley puts it.[1] "The crucial problem," Eley argues, "becomes that of establishing how certain 'traditions' became selected for survival rather than others—how certain beliefs and practices came to reproduce themselves under radically changed circumstances and how they became subtly transformed in the very process of renewal."[2] This book has attempted to specify the "practices and relations" shaped by a decade of war and inflation that gave new meaning to the antidemocratic, antiparliamentary "traditions" of conservative agrarians. Their reaction to democratic political reforms would undoubtedly have been negative under the best of circumstances. The particular conditions of Germany's accelerated advance toward a government of parliamentary institutions, however, created a decidedly unfavorable climate that left little hope for even the most grudging acceptance of these changes in the countryside.

The material background of the war economy, the deep divisions between consumers and producers, and the declining influence of the representatives of agrarian interests on the political decision-making process combined to shape specific opposition to parliamentary government in the years 1917–19. State policies and economic shortages created insurmountable conflicts between city and countryside and defined a fundamental antagonism between urban consumers and rural producers.[3] These dimensions of social conflict were etched in sharp relief in the Rhineland and Westphalia, where rural areas surrounded the industrial heartland of Germany; they were also evident in the Center party, where conservative agrarians had to coexist with liberal and working-class supporters of social and political reform.

The battle over wartime controls was in essence a struggle over the structure of German society.[4] This conflict did not end with the armistice, the end of demobilization, the failure of the revolution, or the establishment of a parliamentary order. The controlled economy, introduced in 1914, lived on in various forms until 1923. It defined a central dimension of peasant experience and unified an almost decade-long period of war and inflation. The decision of the early governments of Weimar to maintain controls created an easily identifiable target for peasant discontent and a ready-made focus for the opposition of conservative interest-group leaders to the parliamentary system.

For conservative agrarians, the transition to Weimar represented "socialism's" triumph. From their perspective, it was the working class, entrenched in the civil service and dominant in parliamentary politics, that had emerged victorious from the struggles over the form of German society in the war and the postwar period. Nowhere could that victory be more readily identified than in controls on agricultural production. Agricultural producers, privileged insiders in the Kaiserreich, saw themselves as abandoned outsiders in the Republic.

To emphasize this self-assessment by conservative agrarian interest-group leaders is not to share or endorse it. In comparison with other social groups in the war and inflation, there is no question that agricultural producers fared relatively well. On the most basic level, during the war the suffering of industrial workers, those on fixed incomes, and civil servants was more severe than that of peasants, who were always insured enough to eat. In the inflation as well, agriculture's losses were relative to its status before 1914, not to many other groups in German society. It was, however, difficult for peasants to see their own position in comparative perspective. Comprehending this myopia is essential for explaining the deep-seated nature of peasant resistance to the economic policies and political reforms of the early Weimar governments, and for grasping the appeal of the reactionary ideology formulated by conservative agrarian leaders.

Agrarian elites accommodated their language to peasant grievances and emphasized the equation between the consumers of agricultural products and the consumers of political democratization. They successfully expanded their interest-group structures to organize the unorganized. As the passive resistance and open opposition to controls in the countryside intensified, so too did the verbal attacks of agrarian leaders on the controlled economy and the institutions of parliamentary rule. These tactics allowed an established agrarian elite to maintain its position in a democratic Weimar and to underline its claims as the most important representative of peasant interests.

The nature of agrarian radicalism created fundamental problems for the Center party. The party feared that it could not live without its agrarian wing, just as conservative agrarians realized that their political survival depended on remaining in the Center. The influence of conservative agrarians within the party steadily declined, but Center leaders sympathetic to the Republic were never sure enough of their position to challenge reactionary conservative agrarians openly. The Center avoided the political dissolution that characterized Weimar's liberal parties by not posing difficult political questions and by retreating to the ostensibly apolitical ground of confessional concerns.[5]

Within the Center, particularly in the cities in and near the Ruhr, there were elements that were Christian *and* democratic, but they made little headway in the Rhenish and Westphalian countryside. The brand of ideological education that agrarian interest groups offered, no small part of the peasantry's political schooling, consistently emphasized unequivocally antidemocratic appeals. Conservative agrarians could register few positive political gains, but together with other antiparliamentary constituencies within the Center, they could act as a coalition blocking the forces loyal to the Republic and willing to work closely together with Social Democrats.

The second half of the 1920s provided no more favorable a climate for the resolution of these fundamental conflicts within either the nation or the Center, that image of the German nation refracted through a confessional glass. Conservative agrarians continued their march to the right and in no way diminished their opposition to Weimar. They could remain within the Center because that party was also on a rightward course. The Center's emphasis on confessional concerns, even more pronounced after 1928, was completely compatible with the advocacy of authoritarian, extraparliamentary political solutions.

What emerges clearly from this study of the agricultural sector in war and inflation is the importance of understanding the period 1914–23 as a unity, defined for the peasantry by state intervention, uncertainty, and unpredictability. Macroeconomic analyses that emphasize the inflation's salutary impact on Germany's postwar recovery seriously understate the inflation's corrosive effect on relations between city and countryside, between consumers and producers, between peasants and workers.[6] Moreover, for the agricultural sector stabilization brought neither recovery nor a return to the bases of prewar prosperity, but rather a decade of uncertainty and crisis defined by different elements but no less profound in its consequences. Seen from the long-term perspective of the German peasantry, by 1933 the nearly two decades of prewar prosperity and confidence had been followed by a period of instability and crisis of equal length.[7]

Generalizing from the political experience of agricultural producers in the Rhineland and Westphalia is more difficult. These regions were distinguished by the predominance of the Center party in a variant that included heavy representation of industrial workers. In addition, unlike the situation in other parts of

Catholic Germany, agrarian interests were organized behind an indigenous Catholic aristocracy that was able to maintain its position within agricultural interest groups despite a democratic revolution and agriculture's declining power within the Center Fortress. These differences are crucial for understanding the nature of conservative agrarian politics in the Rhineland and Westphalia. They did not prevent Catholic peasants from welcoming National Socialism, nor do they allow any equation of Center party loyalty with opposition to the Nazis; they do, however, make it clear that we must carefully specify the paths toward 1933 followed by conservative agrarians in different parts of Germany.

This study has tried to advance an understanding of the immense problems confronting the Weimar Republic, and of the burdens it carried both from the war and from the particular conditions of postwar recovery. An analysis of the crises of Weimar's early history does not inevitably point to the National Socialist triumph, but the knowledge of Weimar's end does raise compelling questions about missed alternatives in Weimar's beginnings. No hidden answer lurks behind this study's conclusions. Indeed, this book suggests that at the very least, to cast an alternative scenario would be to imagine a transition to parliamentary democracy in Germany not prejudiced by a lost war and a postwar inflation. The leap of fancy required for such a counterfactual argument is foreign to the historian intent on explaining what *did* happen.[8] This book does, however, focus attention on the importance of the radical break between Kaiserreich and Weimar, and it warns against the danger of connecting these two periods in German history with a straight line. The particular conditions of economic instability and political upheaval shaped by a decade of war and inflation profoundly influenced agrarian reception of the Weimar experiment. The Republic's early history did not insure its collapse, but in the countryside, it left Weimar with many opponents whose enmity was never overcome.

Appendix

Table 1. Employment in Agriculture and Industry by Districts: 1882, 1907, 1925

| District and Year | Total Employed | % of Females | Agriculture | | | Industry | |
			Total Employed	% Employed	% of Females	% Employed	% of Females
Westphalia							
Münster							
1882	189,413	*	95,928	50.6	*	32.4	*
1907	384,625	28.0	128,194	33.3	44.2	42.8	10.8
1925	626,028	31.3	156,720	25.0	51.9	45.7	11.0
Minden							
1882	184,622	*	93,784	50.8	*	31.2	*
1907	334,425	34.4	123,968	37.1	46.2	37.9	23.5
1925	468,421	40.1	148,980	31.8	54.8	40.5	27.9
Arnsberg							
1882	394,218	*	83,873	21.3	*	60.3	*
1907	887,034	19.0	108,573	12.2	48.2	62.2	5.8
1925	1,299,985	25.4	127,153	9.8	55.8	55.8	8.1
Total for Province							
1882	768,253	*	273,585	35.6	*	46.4	*
1907	1,606,084	24.4	360,735	23.7	46.1	52.5	9.4
1925	2,394,434	29.8	432,853	18.1	54.0	50.1	11.9
Rhineland							
Düsseldorf							
1882	621,280	*	115,439	18.6	*	59.4	*
1907	1,334,556	23.2	136,097	10.2	39.7	59.9	13.8
1925	1,961,660	28.7	138,105	7.0	45.0	55.3	15.9
Cologne							
1882	280,135	*	93,013	33.2	*	38.9	*
1907	534,700	27.6	99,676	18.6	41.1	44.5	14.7
1925	758,678	32.8	101,854	13.4	48.0	40.6	17.1
Aachen							
1882	219,226	*	75,607	34.5	*	46.1	*
1907	314,194	31.4	86,224	27.4	39.6	45.2	21.8
1925	362,635	34.3	79,578	21.9	46.9	44.5	20.8
Total for Province							
1882	1,120,641	*	284,059	25.3	*	51.7	*
1907	2,183,450	25.5	321,997	14.7	40.1	54.0	14.9
1925	3,082,973	30.4	319,537	10.4	46.4	50.4	16.7

Source: *Statistik des Deutschen Reichs*, vol. 2, pp. 430–37; vol. 204, pp. 411, 426, 442, 507, 524–25, 557; vol. 404, pp. 15/72, 15/84, 15/90, 16/86, 16/117, 16/129.

*Data not provided by sex in 1882 census.

Table 2. Heavily Agricultural Counties (*Kreise*): 1882, 1907

District and County	% Employment in Agriculture	
	1882	1907
Westphalia		
Münster		
Tecklenburg	65.6	47.6
Warendorf	66.5	50.0
Beckum	53.3	36.7
Lüdinghausen	56.2	39.5
Münster Land	66.0	43.9
Coesfeld	60.0	36.7
Ahaus	66.5	35.1
Borken	58.8	31.0
Minden		
Minden	45.4	32.9
Lübbecke	73.2	54.9
Halle	69.0	50.5
Bielefeld Land	45.5	40.5
Büren	67.5	50.6
Warburg	57.1	45.5
Höxter	47.1	41.9
Arnsberg		
Meschede	47.6	37.9
Brilon	38.5	35.5
Soest	46.2	35.2
Wittgenstein	59.1	43.9
Rhineland		
Düsseldorf		
Kleve	47.6	29.7
Geldern	48.8	33.4
Cologne		
Wipperfürth	55.3	39.0
Waldbröl	58.5	36.3
Bergheim	60.7	31.0
Rheinbach	61.1	43.6
Aachen		
Erkelenz	47.6	36.2
Heinsberg	52.9	37.2
Geilenkirchen	55.3	35.5
Jülich	50.2	32.4
Monschau	50.8	42.8
Schleiden	50.9	41.9
Malmedy	71.6	39.3

Source: *Statistik des Deutschen Reichs*, vol. 2, pp. 273, 285–86, 293, 302, 310, 317; vol. 212, 2b, pp. 179*–80*.

Note: Counties listed are those with > 30% employment in agriculture according to the 1907 census. For district averages, see Table 1.

Table 3. Regional Origin by Sector of Employment (%): 1907

	Agriculture	Industry
Westphalia		
Born in community of residence	63.6	35.5
Born outside community of residence	36.4	64.5
Born in province	93.9	66.5
Rhineland*		
Born in community of residence	70.3	45.7
Born outside community of residence	29.7	54.3
Born in province	97.2	80.8

Source: *Statistik des Deutschen Reichs*, vol. 210, pp. 418–21, 437–38.

*Figures are for entire Rhineland.

Table 4. Composition of Full-Time Farm Labor Force: 1907, 1925

Size of Holding and Year	Family Members Males (%)	Family Members Females (%)	Contractually Bound Males (%)	Contractually Bound Females (%)	Wage-Laborers Males (%)	Wage-Laborers Females (%)	Number Employed
Westphalia							
2–5 ha.							
1907	49.9	41.7	1.9	5.0	1.1	.4	87,432
1925	46.1	47.7	1.7	3.7	.7	.2	115,522
5–10 ha.							
1907	50.0	34.6	5.0	8.4	1.5	.6	65,706
1925	45.2	41.8	4.9	6.8	1.0	.3	87,995
10–20 ha.							
1907	43.3	26.6	11.5	15.0	2.6	1.0	66,787
1925	39.9	34.0	11.0	12.5	1.8	.7	82,149
20–50 ha.							
1907	33.0	17.4	21.1	21.7	5.4	1.4	53,694
1925	31.0	23.4	20.8	19.3	4.5	1.0	58,252
50–100 ha.							
1907	19.3	8.2	32.4	21.3	14.3	4.4	8,998
1925	17.5	11.4	30.1	18.9	19.7	2.4	9,222
100–200 ha.							
1907	10.0	2.6	38.5	16.3	23.6	9.1	2,113
1925	8.4	4.0	35.9	11.2	35.4	5.1	2,731
> 200 ha.							
1907	4.9	1.0	33.4	8.0	41.4	11.4	1,760
1925	4.9	1.9	27.4	8.7	50.5	6.5	1,308
Rhineland							
2–5 ha.							
1907	53.1	38.7	2.5	3.6	1.6	.4	67,714
1925	49.0	44.2	2.8	2.4	1.4	.2	75,118
5–10 ha.							
1907	52.4	32.4	6.5	6.3	2.0	.4	68,759
1925	48.0	39.7	6.5	4.3	1.3	.2	71,394
10–20 ha.							
1907	44.0	26.0	16.0	10.6	3.0	.4	49,647
1925	41.9	32.1	15.2	8.3	2.2	.4	50,796
20–50 ha.							
1907	29.2	16.0	30.7	14.7	8.6	.8	30,311
1925	29.7	21.2	29.1	13.0	6.3	.8	31,640
50–100 ha.							
1907	15.8	6.9	38.5	13.9	21.1	3.9	9,766
1925	16.8	9.7	35.9	13.1	21.2	3.3	10,496
100–200 ha.							
1907	8.8	2.1	32.8	10.8	36.5	8.9	3,909
1925	9.5	3.9	30.4	11.2	39.9	5.1	3,621
> 200 ha.							
1907	4.6	.5	23.1	5.7	56.0	10.1	593
1925	7.2	2.6	12.2	5.4	65.0	7.6	540

Source: *Statistik des Deutschen Reichs*, vol. 212, 1, pp. 628–30, 638–39; vol. 410, pp. 84–89.

Table 5. Composition of Temporary Farm Labor Force: 1907, 1925

Size of Holding and Year	Family Members		Wage-Laborers		Number Employed
	Males (%)	Females (%)	Males (%)	Females (%)	
Westphalia					
2–5 ha.					
1907	20.6	50.4	16.9	11.7	51,356
1925	37.1	48.3	8.4	6.2	28,537
5–10 ha.					
1907	15.1	40.8	25.2	18.9	25,235
1925	24.8	37.7	20.6	17.0	13,200
10–20 ha.					
1907	8.2	28.9	36.4	26.5	23,019
1925	12.3	23.6	34.7	29.5	13,036
20–50 ha.					
1907	5.5	22.8	42.4	29.3	15,792
1925	7.4	15.1	45.6	31.9	9,956
50–100 ha.					
1907	2.5	11.2	50.9	35.3	2,864
1925	4.4	6.1	50.4	39.1	2,665
100–200 ha.					
1907	1.1	2.5	55.5	40.9	1,246
1925	1.0	1.3	54.8	42.9	1,085
> 200 ha.					
1907	.5	.5	57.3	41.8	1,486
1925	.5	.1	67.1	32.3	803
Rhineland					
2–5 ha.					
1907	16.2	50.9	22.2	10.6	24,900
1925	32.2	45.6	15.2	7.1	12,944
5–10 ha.					
1907	12.1	41.3	28.1	18.5	17,292
1925	21.9	38.9	24.3	14.9	8,475
10–20 ha.					
1907	8.2	28.3	34.4	29.0	11,034
1925	15.1	25.4	33.4	26.0	6,255
20–50 ha.					
1907	4.3	14.7	42.2	38.8	7,309
1925	8.3	13.9	44.4	33.5	4,539
50–100 ha.					
1907	1.0	4.3	47.8	46.9	4,060
1925	3.8	3.5	55.5	37.2	2,734
100–200 ha.					
1907	.6	.7	46.6	52.1	2,472
1925	.7	1.2	58.4	39.7	1,371
> 200 ha.					
1907	.5	.2	40.9	58.4	589
1925	.1	.3	68.7	31.0	316

Source: *Statistik des Deutschen Reichs*, vol. 212, 1, pp. 628–30, 638–39; vol. 410, pp. 84–89.

Table 6. Distribution of Agricultural Landholdings in Westphalia:
1882, 1907, 1925

Size of Holding and Year	Average Size (ha.)	% of Total Agricultural Land[a]	Number of Landholdings[a]	% of Total Agricultural Landholdings[a]
2–5 ha.				
1882	3.2	15.0	44,880	48.9
1907	3.2	15.8	47,492	48.5
1925	3.2	16.4	45,661	47.3
5–10 ha.				
1882	7.0	15.1	19,975	21.7
1907	7.2	17.2	23,038	23.5
1925	7.0	19.1	24,042	24.9
10–20 ha.				
1882	14.0	23.1	15,267	16.6
1907	14.2	24.5	16,626	17.0
1925	14.0	26.6	16,871	17.5
20–50 ha.				
1882	29.2	31.8	10,086	11.0
1907	30.7	30.4	9,506	9.7
1925	27.6	27.8	8,911	9.2
50–100 ha.				
1882	64.4	9.6	1,370	1.5
1907	69.9	7.6	1,044	1.1
1925	63.4	6.3	876	.9
100–200 ha.				
1882	129.3	2.8	197	.2
1907	124.5	2.1	164	.2
1925	134.5	2.3	149	.2
> 200 ha.				
1882	357.4	2.6	79	<.1
1907	304.7	2.3	74	<.1
1925	278.4	1.5	47	<.1

Source: *Statistik des Deutschen Reichs*, vol. 5, pp. 28–31; vol. 212, 1, pp. 64–71; vol. 409, pp. 124–27.

[a]Numbers include only holdings > 2 ha.

Table 7. Distribution of Agricultural Landholdings in the Rhineland:
1882, 1907, 1925

Size of Holding and Year	Average Size (ha.)	% of Total Agricultural Land[a]	Number of Landholdings[a]	% of Total Agricultural Landholdings[a]
2–5 ha.				
1882	3.3	18.3	37,698	48.9
1907	3.3	15.3	32,307	45.3
1925	3.2	15.6	28,549	44.9
5–10 ha.				
1882	7.2	23.7	22,522	29.2
1907	7.4	23.5	21,899	30.7
1925	7.0	22.5	19,132	30.1
10–20 ha.				
1882	14.1	22.0	10,654	13.8
1907	14.4	23.4	11,195	15.7
1925	13.7	23.6	10,223	16.1
20–50 ha.				
1882	30.0	22.3	5,056	6.6
1907	33.1	22.8	4,720	6.6
1925	29.1	22.1	4,507	7.1
50–100 ha.				
1882	67.8	9.5	952	1.2
1907	67.5	9.7	985	1.4
1925	68.7	10.8	936	1.5
100–200 ha.				
1882	126.5	3.3	180	.2
1907	128.1	4.6	246	.3
1925	130.5	4.5	204	.3
> 200 ha.				
1882	257.5	0.8	20	<.1
1907	260.8	0.7	18	<.1
1925	298.1	0.9	17	<.1

Source: *Statistik des Deutschen Reichs*, vol. 5, pp. 36–41; vol. 212, 1, pp. 78–80, 84–87; vol. 409, pp. 136–39.

Note: Declines in 1925 in part reflect the postwar territorial losses of the counties of Eupen and Malmedy.

[a]Numbers include only holdings of > 2 ha.

Table 8. Draft Power Used by Peasants Farming < 20 ha.: 1907

Size of Farm (ha.)	Number of Farms	Farms without Horses (%)	Average Number of Horses per Horse-Owning Farm
		Westphalia	
2–5	47,492	83.8	1.2
5–10	23,038	37.5	1.5
10–20	16,626	6.6	2.3
		Rhineland	
2–5	32,307	73.8	1.1
5–10	21,899	30.1	1.2
10–20	11,195	8.6	2.1

Source: *Statistik des Deutschen Reichs*, vol. 212, 2a, pp. 20–27.

Table 9. Acreage Devoted to Major Crops, 1878–1927

Year	Acreage Planted[a] (ha.)	Wheat (%)[b]	Rye (%)[b]	Oats (%)[b]	Potatoes (%)[b]
		Westphalia			
1878	835,410.7	9.0	27.5	18.2	9.1
1883	833,209.6	9.2	27.7	18.1	9.4
1893	832,809.5	9.6	28.5	18.7	10.2
1900	839,578.3	9.5	28.1	19.6	11.1
1913	841,687.2	9.3	30.2	20.2	12.1
1927	804,625.9	8.7	28.6	20.0	11.9
		Rhineland			
1878	690,279.4	13.0	23.0	18.5	10.8
1883	687,395.8	13.6	20.7	20.1	10.7
1893	676,539.1	13.4	22.1	20.5	11.0
1900	670,413.8	11.8	22.5	22.8	11.4
1913	646,606.4	12.7	23.8	23.1	11.4
1927	588,296.4	14.7	20.6	21.8	10.8

Source: *Preussische Statistik*, vol. 246, pp. xxxiv–xxxv, xxxviii–xl; vol. 291, 1, pp. 40*–44*.

[a]Figures are for major annual planting.

[b]Percentage of *total* agriculturally used land, including arable land, pasture, and meadows.

Table 10. Livestock Holdings: 1882, 1907, 1925

Size of Farm and Year	Horses Total Number	Horses Number per Farm	Cattle Total Number	Cattle Number per Farm	Pigs Total Number	Pigs Number per Farm
Westphalia						
2–5 ha.						
1882	6,718	1.2	108,181	2.5	87,992	2.5
1907	9,182	1.2	144,733	3.2	244,207	5.5
1925	12,070	1.3	132,268	3.1	167,979	4.1
5–10 ha.						
1882	17,391	1.5	84,527	4.3	58,371	3.3
1907	21,126	1.5	131,682	5.8	176,247	8.0
1925	33,470	1.8	138,936	5.8	142,456	6.2
10–20 ha.						
1882	31,931	2.3	107,371	7.1	69,066	4.8
1907	35,484	2.3	166,605	10.1	191,641	12.0
1925	48,273	2.9	176,532	10.5	158,691	9.7
20–50 ha.						
1882	37,536	3.8	117,515	11.7	64,476	6.6
1907	37,655	4.0	169,201	18.0	166,425	18.2
1925	47,025	5.3	164,989	18.6	121,882	13.9
50–100 ha.						
1882	8,124	6.0	26,113	19.2	12,140	9.2
1907	7,070	6.9	32,681	31.9	29,211	29.0
1925	8,414	9.8	28,915	33.5	18,861	22.1
> 100 ha.						
1882	3,351	12.2	8,705	31.5	6,044	23.0
1907	13,261	14.4	13,429	60.5	15,860	73.1
1925	3,874	20.8	12,846	68.3	9,038	48.3
Rhineland						
2–5 ha.						
1882	7,878	1.1	87,084	2.4	50,586	1.9
1907	9,385	1.1	118,315	3.9	87,792	3.4
1925	13,426	1.2	98,721	3.6	56,613	2.5
5–10 ha.						
1882	18,930	1.2	96,840	4.4	51,134	2.7
1907	19,087	1.2	149,175	7.0	102,562	5.3
1925	25,971	1.7	121,104	6.4	66,623	4.0
10–20 ha.						
1882	17,680	1.8	78,440	7.4	41,309	4.3
1907	21,113	2.1	125,826	14.4	108,901	10.7
1925	30,690	3.1	113,570	11.2	73,321	7.6

(continued on next page)

Table 10. continued

Size of Farm and Year	Horses		Cattle		Pigs	
	Total Number	Number per Farm	Total Number	Number per Farm	Total Number	Number per Farm
	Rhineland					
20–50 ha.						
1882	17,638	3.6	69,762	13.9	34,667	7.3
1907	18,726	4.1	107,302	23.4	80,746	18.4
1925	26,223	5.9	94,518	21.3	58,228	13.5
50–100 ha.						
1882	7,314	7.8	24,640	26.0	9,842	10.9
1907	8,837	9.2	39,841	41.8	22,855	25.5
1925	11,360	12.3	33,452	36.4	16,184	18.2
> 100 ha.						
1882	2,450	42.2	7,978	39.9	2,934	15.8
1907	4,345	16.9	16,897	67.1	9,796	42.0
1925	4,732	22.2	11,519	53.6	6,841	33.4

Source: *Statistik des Deutschen Reichs*, vol. 5, pp. 134–38, 146–49; vol. 212, 2a, pp. 24–27, 34–35; vol. 410, pp. 362–65, 396–97.

Table 11. Use of Arable Land: 1907, 1925

Size of Holding and Year	Total Arable Land (ha.)	Wheat (%)	Rye (%)	Oats (%)	Potatoes (%)	Feed Crops (%)
Westphalia						
2–5 ha.						
1907	111,822	5.5	35.7	17.4	16.1	9.2
1925	99,101	6.2	33.4	17.7	15.7	7.4
5–10 ha.						
1907	118,807	6.8	32.4	21.9	11.1	9.1
1925	113,529	7.0	31.0	22.1	11.1	8.0
10–20 ha.						
1907	175,816	8.6	29.9	24.0	8.1	8.8
1925	161,776	9.1	29.1	23.0	8.2	8.2
20–50 ha.						
1907	222,405	11.0	24.1	26.4	6.1	6.4
1925	169,073	11.9	24.4	22.6	6.1	8.7
50–100 ha.						
1907	52,331	12.3	19.6	16.8	13.8	7.8
1925	34,212	13.2	19.8	21.7	5.5	8.9
> 100 ha.						
1907	28,569	12.3	14.5	27.4	4.9	6.9
1925	22,090	13.6	17.6	20.7	5.6	7.9
Rhineland						
2–5 ha.						
1907	77,646	6.0	25.0	23.6	14.3	13.3
1925	62,951	11.0	22.0	20.9	13.9	12.6
5–10 ha.						
1907	129,624	9.2	24.9	25.0	10.6	13.3
1925	100,133	13.6	21.4	22.5	10.1	13.2
10–20 ha.						
1907	130,213	11.9	24.9	23.6	8.8	13.7
1925	108,228	15.8	21.3	21.7	8.5	13.3
20–50 ha.						
1907	124,092	16.4	27.1	29.7	6.4	7.3
1925	94,516	18.6	20.5	20.4	7.3	13.1
50–100 ha.						
1907	52,609	21.5	22.2	25.0	3.6	8.0
1925	48,792	23.5	15.5	20.2	4.5	11.4
> 100 ha.						
1907	30,407	22.2	17.5	22.9	2.9	11.3
1925	25,503	23.1	14.4	20.0	3.9	9.6

Source: *Statistik des Deutschen Reichs*, vol. 212, 1, pp. 428–31; vol. 409, pp. 342–47, 363–68.

Note: Percentages are of total arable, not total agriculturally used, land.

Table 12. Use of Agricultural Machines in Westphalia: 1882, 1907, 1925

| Size of Farm and Year | Number of Farms | % of Farms Using Machines[a] | | | | |
		Sowing	Mowing[b]	Threshing (Motorized)	Threshing (Other)	Milk Separators[c]
2–5 ha.						
1882	44,880	*	*	2.9	2.6	
1907	47,492	*	*	31.4	14.2	23.7
1925	45,661	3.0		20.7	12.2	* 73.2
5–10 ha.						
1882	19,975	*	*	6.7	12.2	
1907	23,038	2.3	8.7	38.7	39.2	39.5
1925	24,042	12.2		35.7	24.5	* 78.5
10–20 ha.						
1882	15,267	*	*	8.7	25.5	
1907	16,626	9.1	45.4	40.8	54.4	47.0
1925	16,871	45.3		50.8	23.3	2.1 81.8
20–50 ha.						
1882	10,086	1.2	9.4	15.2	57.8	
1907	9,506	24.6	81.3	49.0	60.0	54.2
1925	8,911	81.4		63.5	19.5	5.2 80.3
50–100 ha.						
1882	1,370	5.5	26.2	19.3	72.6	
1907	1,044	46.6	93.1	62.3	58.4	51.5
1925	876	94.1		76.5	10.8	16.1 68.0
100–200 ha.						
1882	197	28.4	44.7	32.0	68.0	
1907	164	59.1	81.1	60.4	35.4	44.5
1925	149	93.3		83.2	8.7	24.2 58.4
> 200 ha.						
1882	79	64.6	51.9	50.6	40.5	
1907	74	60.8	85.1	78.4	16.1	37.8
1925	47	91.5		85.1	4.3	29.8 42.6

Source: *Statistik des Deutschen Reichs*, vol. 5, pp. 214–15; vol. 212, 2a, pp. 94–97; vol. 410, pp. 416–17.

Note: Figures include steam-powered machines in 1882 and 1907, and additional forms of motorized machines in 1925. For comparisons of the total number of machines of *all* sorts, see Table 24.

[a]Percentages represent all those *using* machines, not just owners.

[b]The 1925 census includes three varieties of mowing machines not counted separately in 1882 and 1907, making comparison with the other two censuses impossible.

[c]Milk separators are not included in the 1882 census. In the 1925 census they are divided between mechanized (left-hand column) and hand-operated models (right-hand column).

* < 1%.

Table 13. Use of Agricultural Machines in the Rhineland: 1882, 1907, 1925

Size of Farm and Year	Number of Farms	% of Farms Using Machines[a]				
		Sowing	Mowing[b]	Threshing (Motorized)	Threshing (Other)	Milk Separators[c]
2–5 ha.						
1882	37,698	*	*	*	2.7	
1907	32,307	3.0	1.7	2.5	20.6	14.4
1925	28,549	3.7		16.0	23.4	* 56.3
5–10 ha.						
1882	22,522	2.6	*	*	16.2	
1907	21,899	9.5	16.3	6.3	62.0	31.4
1925	19,132	23.2		41.3	38.9	* 62.8
10–20 ha.						
1882	10,654	5.4	3.8	1.2	45.6	
1907	11,195	25.7	54.9	11.8	80.2	40.5
1925	10,223	64.6		62.6	28.3	4.6 59.5
20–50 ha.						
1882	5,056	12.8	26.0	4.7	71.5	
1907	4,720	51.9	84.3	21.5	83.6	36.0
1925	4,507	90.1		79.4	14.7	11.6 48.8
50–100 ha.						
1882	952	46.0	60.9	25.7	72.2	
1907	985	79.1	89.8	53.6	69.7	39.4
1925	936	95.1		81.8	6.2	19.7 49.3
100–200 ha.						
1882	180	74.4	80.0	50.0	58.3	
1907	246	90.2	91.9	78.5	41.1	43.1
1925	204	96.6		83.8	5.4	23.5 45.6
> 200 ha.						
1882	20	95.0	95.0	70.0	40.0	
1907	18	88.9	88.9	83.3	33.3	50.0
1925	17	100.0		100.0		35.3 41.2

Source: Statistik des Deutschen Reichs, vol. 5, pp. 218–19; vol. 212, 2a, pp. 98–101; vol. 410, pp. 420–23.

Note: Figures include steam-powered machines in 1882 and 1907, and additional forms of motorized machines in 1925. For comparisons of the total number of machines of all sorts, see Table 24.

[a]Percentages represent all those using machines, not just owners.

[b]The 1925 census includes three varieties of mowing machines not counted separately in 1882 and 1907, making comparison with the other two censuses impossible.

[c]Milk separators are not included in the 1882 census. In the 1925 census they are divided between mechanized (left-hand column) and hand-operated models (right-hand column).

* < 1%.

Table 14. Indebtedness of Agricultural Producers: 1902

Tax Class (in marks)	Average Farm Size (in ha.)	Number of Farms	Farms with No Debts (%)	Farms with < 50% Indebtedness[a] (%)
		Westphalia		
60–90	7.8	7,543	51.6	40.0
90–150	10.9	9,310	46.7	45.4
150–300	17.7	11,149	39.7	53.1
300–750	30.1	11,841	35.7	58.7
750–1,500	44.0	4,906	34.0	62.0
1,500–3,000	75.3	1,359	27.7	66.5
> 3,000	872.6	354	19.5	70.9
Total		46,462	40.9	52.3
		Rhineland		
60–90	5.1	8,003	79.4	14.5
90–150	6.4	10,890	74.5	17.1
150–300	8.2	12,529	69.5	20.5
300–750	12.4	9,668	59.1	29.3
750–1,500	23.0	3,290	46.0	39.3
1,500–3,000	43.9	1,348	36.0	47.0
> 3,000	192.0	721	34.1	53.0
Total		46,449	67.0	23.1

Source: *Preussische Statistik*, vol. 191, 3, pp. 41–43, 47–48, 50.

[a]Percentage of indebtedness measured in terms of the total value of the farm.

Table 15. Confessional Composition of Heavily Agrarian Counties: 1905

District and County	% Protestant	% Catholic
Westphalia		
Münster		
Tecklenburg	58.6	41.0
Warendorf	1.8	97.9
Beckum	5.3	94.1
Lüdinghausen	3.3	96.3
Münster Land	1.6	98.2
Coesfeld	3.2	96.2
Ahaus	12.6	86.6
Borken	6.7	92.4
District average[a]	18.4	80.9
Minden		
Minden	95.0	4.4
Lübbecke	98.8	.7
Halle	97.3	2.0
Bielefeld Land	95.4	4.0
Büren	1.8	97.3
Warburg	7.7	90.5
Höxter	13.6	84.9
District average[a]	66.5	32.6
Arnsberg		
Meschede	3.5	96.0
Brilon	3.8	94.9
Soest	41.5	57.8
Wittgenstein	95.2	3.2
District average[a]	53.2	45.1
Rhineland		
Düsseldorf		
Kleve	11.4	87.7
Geldern	4.7	94.9
District average[a]	40.8	57.5
Cologne		
Wipperfürth	9.3	90.6
Waldbröl	62.9	36.0
Bergheim	2.5	96.6
Rheinbach	1.1	97.3
District average[a]	17.9	80.2

(continued on next page)

Table 15. continued

District and County	% Protestant	% Catholic
	Rhineland	
Aachen		
Erkelenz	4.8	94.8
Heinsberg	2.1	97.5
Geilenkirchen	2.1	97.1
Jülich	3.9	95.1
Monschau	4.4	95.6
Schleiden	4.0	95.2
Malmedy	1.4	98.6
District average[a]	4.5	94.9

Sources: County figures (for 1905) are from *Statistisches Jahrbuch für den Preussischen Staat*, vol. 5, pp. 275–81. District averages (for 1910) are from Gerhard A. Ritter, ed., *Wahlgeschichtliches Arbeitsbuch: Materialien zur Statistik des Kaiserreichs 1871–1918* (Munich, 1980), pp. 77–78, 80–81.

[a]District averages are for 1910.

Table 16. Voting Patterns in Agrarian Districts in the Kaiserreich

Heavily Catholic Electoral Districts

Year	Population	Voter Turnout (%)	National Liberal (%)	Center (%)	SPD (%)	Other (%)
		Münster-Coesfeld (90.3% Catholic)				
1893	135,240	60.2		84.1		
1898	147,129	49.9		91.7		
1903	158,465	70.4		83.9	7.3	
1907	177,596	81.3		83.6	7.1	
1912	192,327	77.1		83.0	8.2	
		Lüdinghausen-Beckum-Warendorf (95.7% Catholic)				
1893	115,526	60.6		98.0		
1898	118,412	61.5		97.2		
1903	125,198	61.7		95.8		
1907	133,546	80.7		93.7		
1912	153,989	78.0		87.1	11.2	
		Kleve-Geldern (91.1% Catholic)				
1893	106,661	66.4		99.2		
1898	111,340	73.6		87.5		9.8[a]
1903	117,066	75.9		92.3		
1907	124,129	86.4	9.4	87.9		
1912	131,979	82.8		93.3		
		Schleiden-Malmedy-Monschau (96.4% Catholic)				
1893	93,819	62.5		99.7		
1898	94,263	43.3		99.2		
1903	94,029	65.8		96.0		
1907	95,835	79.7		93.9		
1912	100,046	75.4		93.1		

(continued on next page)

Table 16. continued

		Heavily Protestant Electoral District					
		Minden-Lübbecke (96.2% Protestant)					
Year	Population	Voter Turnout (%)	Conservatives (%)	Nat. Liberal (%)	Other Liberal (%)	SPD (%)	Other (%)
1893	132,176	56.5	67.0		14.2	14.3	
1898	140,166	62.1 75.8[b]	37.0 52.9[b]		28.6 47.1[b]	15.7	18.5[a]
1903	149,792	71.2 69.1[b]	39.8 71.4[b]	9.6	18.2	22.9 28.6[b]	9.4[c]
1907	158,647	82.7	52.5		20.8	17.4	9.5[c]
1912	167,166	83.9	31.6		31.4	25.0	12.0[c]

Sources: *Vierteljahrshefte zur Statistik des Deutschen Reichs*, vol. 2, IV, pp. 25–27, 31–33; vol. 7, *Ergänzungsheft zu 1898*, III, pp. 26–28, 30–33; vol. 12, *Ergänzungsheft zu 1903*, IV, pp. 30–32, 35–37, 39; vol. 16, *Ergänzungsheft zu 1907*, III, pp. 36–38, 41, 43, 45, 111–12, 114–16; *Statistik des Deutschen Reichs*, vol. 250, 2, pp. 44–49, 52–58, 62–63.

Note: Percentages are calculated only for the most important political parties in each district.

[a]Bund der Landwirte.

[b]Results of runoff election.

[c]Anti-Semites: Christlich-soziale (1903), Wirtschaftliche Vereinigung (1907, 1912).

Table 17. Confessional Affiliation by Economic Sector: 1907

	Agriculture (%)	Industry (%)	Provincial Average (%)
	Westphalia		
Catholic	61.7	49.1	51.2
Protestant	38.2	50.1	47.8
	Rhineland[a]		
Catholic	75.7	68.3	69.0
Protestant	23.9	30.8	29.8

Source: *Statistik des Deutschen Reichs*, vol. 206, pp. 235–37, 240–42.

[a]Figures are for *total* Rhineland.

Table 18. Yields and Output of Major Grains, 1913–1924 (1913 = 100)

Year	Wheat Acreage (ha.)	Wheat Output (tons)	Wheat Tons/ Ha.	Rye Acreage (ha.)	Rye Output (tons)	Rye Tons/ Ha.	Oats Acreage (ha.)	Oats Output (tons)	Oats Tons/ Ha.
	Westphalia								
Base	(76,696)	(175,237)	(2.28)	(251,490)	(497,034)	(1.98)	(166,778)	(359,099)	(2.15)
1913	100	100	100	100	100	100	100	100	100
1914	94	82	87	100	92	92	108	104	96
1915	96	88	92	100	95	95	108	69	87
1916	70	54	77	81	61	75	77	64	84
1917	67	47	71	74	61	83	77	43	56
1918	68	51	76	76	63	83	72	46	64
1919	65	47	72	71	54	76	72	48	67
1920	75	53	71	76	53	69	81	53	65
1921	69	60	87	70	61	88	75	55	73
1922	64	37	58	69	47	68	82	43	53
1923	78	67	86	77	60	78	86	68	80
1924	81	49	61	79	53	68	96	55	58
	Rhineland								
Base	(79,625)	(206,220)	(2.59)	(151,562)	(343,045)	(2.26)	(146,639)	(383,854)	(2.58)
1913	100	100	100	100	100	100	100	100	100
1914	100	81	81	99	89	90	103	104	101
1915	103	106	103	97	99	101	104	72	69
1916	88	70	79	79	60	77	73	67	93
1917	80	57	71	70	58	82	71	49	69
1918	78	62	79	69	58	84	66	46	69
1919	73	48	66	59	39	65	62	41	66
1920	80	53	66	66	43	65	77	48	62
1921	82	78	64	62	48	77	71	41	58
1922	78	59	75	61	77	47	77	40	52
1923	91	74	82	66	82	54	82	71	87
1924	96	62	65	77	73	56	86	49	57

Source: *Vierteljahrshefte zur Statistik des Deutschen Reichs*, vol. 23, I, pp. 132, 134, 136; vol. 24, II, pp. 220, 222, 224; vol. 25, II, pp. 64, 66, 68; vol. 27, I, pp. 45, 47, 49; vol. 28, I, pp. 30, 32, 34, 48, 50, 52; vol. 29, I, pp. 124, 126, 128; vol. 30, I, pp. 18, 20, 22; vol. 31, I, pp. 86, 88, 90; vol. 32, I, pp. 6, 8; vol. 33, I, pp. 28, 30; vol. 34, I, pp. 36, 38.

Table 19. Pattern of Livestock Holdings, 1913–1924 (1913 = 100)

Year	Households with Livestock	Horses	Cattle	Sheep	Pigs	Goats
Westphalia						
Base	(375,110)	(175,306)	(751,114)	(132,210)	(1,546,087)	(220,533)
1913	100	100	100	100	100	100
1914	97	81	109	102	103	98
1915	92	76	100	91	62	94
1916	110	74	107	86	63	103
1917	119	76	98	93	39	108
1918	117	84	90	110	41	112
1919	119	95	89	131	49	114
1920	128	97	92	157	61	122
1921	132	101	93	129	67	126
1922	127	100	88	114	58	117
1923	114	a	92	138	78	120
1924	130	106	94	108	70	113
Rhineland						
Base	(266,317)	(153,504)	(647,586)	(53,484)	(745,292)	(186,776)
1913	100	100	100	100	100	100
1914	98	79	107	104	100	101
1915	92	71	95	81	63	98
1916	124	66	100	106	71	108
1917	146	68	94	99	42	117
1918	146	84	83	108	38	124
1919	143	88	74	121	47	123
1920	154	89	78	170	64	129
1921	163	91	77	152	72	132
1922	158	90	74	141	64	124
1923	115	a	80	183	82	132
1924	156	99	81	155	74	120

Source: *Vierteljahrshefte zur Statistik des Deutschen Reichs*, vol. 23, IV, pp. 56–59; vol. 24, III, pp. 34, 35; vol. 25, II, pp. 44–45; vol. 26, IV, pp. 4–5, 8–9; vol. 27, IV, pp. 10–11, 14–15, 40–41, 44–45; vol. 29, II, pp. 90–91; vol. 30, II, pp. 20–23; vol. 31, III, pp. 88, 90; vol. 32, III, pp. 64, 66; vol. 33, II, pp. 16, 18; vol. 34, III, pp. 20, 22.

aInformation on horses not available for 1923.

Table 20. Mortgage Indebtedness of Agricultural Producers, 1913–1921
(in Million Marks)

Year	New Debt	Retired Debt
Westphalia		
1913	35.14	19.21
1914	24.70	13.07
1915	10.22	8.35
1916	13.41	12.69
1917	22.94	22.17
1919	31.13	50.70
1920	46.60	58.79
1921	117.60	43.01
Rhineland		
1913	35.44	23.78
1914	22.76	16.67
1915	11.28	13.09
1916	14.88	17.00
1917	18.08	22.75
1919	39.65	55.44
1920	55.52	59.44
1921	124.19	52.29

Source: *Statistisches Jahrbuch für den Preussischen Staat*, vol. 12, p. 96; vol. 13, p. 58; vol. 14, p. 52; vol. 15, p. 58; vol. 16, p. 62; vol. 17, p. 66; vol. 18, p. 74; vol. 19, p. 84.

Note: Information not available for 1918 or after 1921. Figures are preliminary estimates.

Table. 21. World Grain Prices, 1921–1923 (in Dollars per Quintal [= 100 kg])

Grain and Year	Germany	England	France	Belgium	U.S.A.
Wheat					
1921	2.70	6.34	6.61		
1922	4.34	4.87	6.36		
1923	4.76	4.45	5.76		
Rye					
1921	2.34		5.18	5.38	
1922	3.48		4.35	4.36	
1923	4.00		4.05	3.52	
Barley					
1921	2.44	5.56	6.03		
1922	3.78	4.90	5.24		
1923	4.07	4.21	4.11		
Oats					
1921	2.25	4.67	4.25		2.55
1922	3.69	4.55	4.89		2.64
1923	3.64	4.32	3.86		2.97

Source: International Institute of Agriculture, *Agricultural Problems in their International Aspect* (League of Nations, International Economic Conference, Geneva, May 1927, Documentation) (Rome, n.d.), pp. 48–50, 64, 65, 69–71, 78–83, 94–97, 104–7.

Table 22. Voting Patterns in National Assembly Elections: 1919

District	Voter Turnout (%)	Party					
		SPD (%)	Center (%)	DDP (%)	DNVP (%)	DVP (%)	USPD (%)
Westphalia-North	86.8	30.7	41.9	9.8	8.7	6.6	2.1
Westphalia-South	87.3	41.3	28.3	10.0	15.3[a]		5.2
Cologne-Aachen	79.6	25.9	58.9	7.8	3.3	3.4	6.2
Düsseldorf-East	84.6[b]	25.7	27.8	12.2		15.5[c]	18.5
Düsseldorf-West		26.9	50.0	7.0	5.6	9.4	*

Source: *Statistik des Deutschen Reichs*, vol. 291, 1, pp. 96–97. (The Reich *Statistik* provides no county-by-county breakdowns for these elections, as it does for all other elections in Weimar.)

[a]Reflects electoral agreement between DVP and DNVP.

[b]Voter turnout figures for both Düsseldorf districts are combined.

[c]Combined total for DVP and National Association of Essen.

* < 1.0%.

Table 23. Agrarian Voting Patterns in Weimar Elections, 1920–1932 (Percentages in Selected Counties)

		1924					1932	
	1920	May	Dec.	1925	1928	1930	July	Nov.
			Catholic Counties					

Borken
Population (1925): 50,422
Eligible voters (1928): 28,015
Electoral district: Westphalia-North
Confession: 94.6% Catholic
Agricultural population: 49.6%

	1920	May	Dec.	1925	1928	1930	July	Nov.
% Turnout	84.4	89.4	88.6	85.6	81.3	86.2	87.1	80.3
Party								
DNVP	1.1	7.4	6.3		4.9	4.2	2.4	5.0
Center	79.5	83.3	85.8		75.3	75.5	75.2	74.4
SPD	9.5	3.2	3.6		4.4	3.1	2.5	2.4
USPD	3.6							
KPD		1.1	.6		1.0	1.7	2.3	4.4
DVP	4.8	2.2	2.1		2.5	1.4	*	*
DDP	1.5	*	1.0		*	*	*	*
W[a]			*		8.9	6.4	*	*
L[b]					*	*	*	1.9
NSDAP					*	4.3	14.7	10.3
Marx				88.1				
Hindenburg				11.3				

Münster
Population (1925): 51,868
Eligible voters (1928): 30,111
Electoral district: Westphalia-North
Confession: 96.5% Catholic
Agricultural population: 46.4%

	1920	May	Dec.	1925	1928	1930	July	Nov.
% Turnout	89.0	84.4	86.2	83.1	77.6	81.4	83.3	79.5
Party								
DNVP	1.3	5.7	4.3		7.4	2.8	3.3	4.1
Center	85.2	75.2	81.9		72.0	72.1	74.1	70.0
SPD	6.1	3.3	6.7		7.4	5.5	3.9	3.6
USPD	2.1							
KPD		1.9	*		1.1	3.6	3.4	6.0
DVP	4.9	3.3	2.9		3.2	1.8	*	*
DDP	*	1.3	*		1.0	*	*	*
W[a]			*		3.1	1.7	*	*
L[b]					3.1	6.5	1.9	3.2
NSDAP					*	3.9	12.0	11.4
Marx				86.7				
Hindenburg				12.7				

(continued on next page)

Table 23. continued

| | 1920 | 1924 | | 1925 | 1928 | 1930 | 1932 | |
		May	Dec.				July	Nov.
			Catholic Counties					

Büren
Population (1925): 40,670
Eligible voters (1928): 22,636
Electoral district: Westphalia-North
Confession: 97.4% Catholic
Agricultural population: 56.5%

	1920	May	Dec.	1925	1928	1930	July	Nov.
% Turnout	89.9	89.4	86.9	83.2	82.3	83.6	85.1	82.1
Party								
DNVP	1.6	6.1	5.1		3.0	2.2	2.5	3.7
Center	87.7	81.5	84.5		74.0	78.7	77.9	75.2
SPD	5.4	2.9	5.7		7.9	3.4	3.9	3.7
USPD	3.3							
KPD		1.2	*		1.1	3.3	6.4	9.6
DVP	1.1	1.3	1.4		1.4	1.3	*	*
DDP	*	*	*		*	1.4	*	*
Wa			*		2.8	3.2	*	*
Lb					6.0	2.1	*	1.6
NSDAP					*	2.7	7.8	5.3
Marx				90.8				
Hindenburg				8.3				

Rheinbach
Population (1925): 36,755
Eligible voters (1928): 21,950
Electoral district: Cologne-Aachen
Confession: 97.1% Catholic
Agricultural population: 40.0%

	1920	May	Dec.	1925	1928	1930	July	Nov.
% Turnout	78.2	75.3	75.4	74.7	67.8	77.7	78.5	c
Party								
DNVP	4.0	8.3	7.1		10.6	3.3	4.4	
Center	64.9	69.8	73.1		63.0	58.1	59.4	
SPD	13.0	7.4	11.3		14.8	8.3	9.9	
USPD	5.1							
KPD		6.5	2.2		2.5	5.8	6.9	
DVP	1.8	3.3	2.7		3.1	1.9	*	
DDP	2.6	1.4	2.1		1.7	1.4	*	
Wa			*		1.7	1.3	*	
Lb					*	3.8	*	
NSDAP					*	14.3	17.9	
Marx				84.7				
Hindenberg				14.1				

Table 23. continued

	1920	1924		1925	1928	1930	1932	
		May	Dec.				July	Nov.

Catholic Counties

Schleiden
Population (1925): 46,179
Eligible voters (1928): 29,689
Electoral district: Cologne-Aachen
Confession: 95.1% Catholic
Agricultural population: 46.1%

	1920	May	Dec.	1925	1928	1930	July	Nov.
% Turnout	74.9	80.9	77.3	75.4	67.8	78.6	77.3	71.5
Party								
DNVP	3.3	9.2	6.6		7.9	3.0	4.7	4.7
Center	71.1	77.9	78.7		73.4	65.8	67.6	66.8
SPD	4.2	3.2	5.3		4.5	1.8	3.0	3.7
USPD	5.4							
KPD		2.4	1.4		2.3	3.9	5.5	6.5
DVP	2.9	3.3	3.6		3.7	1.8	*	*
DDP	3.6	1.1	2.0		1.2	1.0	*	*
W^a			1.6		3.8	2.7	*	*
L^b					*	5.8	1.8	3.4
NSDAP					*	11.6	15.6	13.0
Marx				86.3				
Hindenburg				12.7				

Wipperfürth
Population (1925): 29,341
Eligible voters (1928): 18,276
Electoral district: Cologne-Aachen
Confession: 90.2% Catholic
Agricultural population: 39.3%

	1920	May	Dec.	1925	1928	1930	July	Nov.
% Turnout	86.3	85.7	84.1	85.0	77.6	86.3	88.5	c
DNVP	4.5	6.2	5.7		6.7	3.9	2.6	
Center	73.0	75.5	76.2		67.3	65.1	65.6	
SPD	10.3	6.6	9.3		10.3	6.4	7.3	
USPD	3.8							
KPD		3.4	1.8		1.6	4.9	7.4	
DVP	1.7	2.6	2.9		2.8	2.1	*	
DDP	2.3	1.7	1.5		1.4	*	*	
W^a			1.1		2.0	2.0	*	
L^b					*	*	1.1	
NSDAP					1.7	7.8	14.0	
Marx				87.5				
Hindenburg				11.6				

(continued on next page)

Table 23. continued

	1920	1924 May	1924 Dec.	1925	1928	1930	1932 July	1932 Nov.
			Mixed Confessional Counties					

Tecklenburg
Population (1925): 68,390
Eligible voters (1928): 40,281
Electoral district: Westphalia-North
Confession: 55.3% Protestant, 44.1% Catholic
Agricultural population: 45.2%

	1920	1924 May	1924 Dec.	1925	1928	1930	1932 July	1932 Nov.
% Turnout	80.9	79.2	79.0	82.0	70.1	75.5	78.8	75.4
Party								
DNVP	9.8	16.8	17.2		7.5	4.3	6.2	7.5
Center	40.3	37.9	38.7		37.4	37.7	37.2	36.0
SPD	20.5	19.7	22.4		24.4	16.9	14.8	13.9
USPD	3.7							
KPD		2.3	2.1		1.0	4.1	6.9	9.4
DVP	19.3	11.5	11.9		7.5	3.5	*	1.3
DDP	6.4	7.0	6.2		3.0	1.2	*	*
W[a]			*		4.8	1.7	*	*
L[b]					10.7	10.1	*	1.6
NSDAP					*	15.1	31.7	28.4
Marx				57.8				
Hindenburg				41.0				

Wiedenbrück
Population (1925): 73,125
Eligible voters (1928): 44,976
Electoral district: Westphalia-North
Confession: 30.0% Protestant, 68.8% Catholic
Agricultural population: 47.3%

	1920	1924 May	1924 Dec.	1925	1928	1930	1932 July	1932 Nov.
% Turnout	91.4	87.6	89.0	88.2	80.7	85.8	83.4	80.2
Party								
DNVP	9.2	11.7	13.9		11.9	5.3	5.5	7.7
Center	59.1	59.1	61.4		55.6	54.7	57.0	55.2
SPD	15.5	8.7	11.1		14.2	11.4	9.0	8.3
USPD	2.1							
KPD		2.8	1.3		1.2	2.7	4.2	7.8
DVP	8.9	8.5	8.4		8.3	5.6	1.3	2.7
DDP	5.1	12.8	2.4		2.1	2.8	*	*
W[a]			*		1.3	2.2	*	*
L[b]					1.6	*	*	*
NSDAP					*	7.7	19.4	14.3
Marx				71.5				
Hindenburg				27.8				

Table 23. continued

	1920	1924 May	1924 Dec.	1925	1928	1930	1932 July	1932 Nov.
			Mixed Confessional Counties					

Rees
Population (1925): 81,253
Eligible voters (1928): 47,949
Electoral district: Düsseldorf-West
Confession: 32.9% Protestant, 65.6% Catholic
Agricultural population: 41.0%

	1920	1924 May	1924 Dec.	1925	1928	1930	1932 July	1932 Nov.
% Turnout	86.7	84.8	84.8	84.8	81.5	87.1	91.2	86.6
Party								
DNVP	7.5	17.3	15.7		12.8	5.9	5.8	7.3
Center	48.6	45.8	49.1		45.7	41.4	43.8	43.0
SPD	12.4	8.3	10.7		13.3	11.5	7.4	6.6
USPD	5.5							
KPD		7.4	4.2		4.8	7.5	9.6	11.7
DVP	17.1	11.3	12.2		12.0	5.0	1.0	1.5
DDP	8.4	4.2	4.7		4.7	2.0	*	*
W[a]			*		4.9	5.0	*	*
L[b]					*	*	-	*
NSDAP					*	18.6	30.6	28.3
Marx				60.8				
Hindenburg				37.0				

			Heavily Protestant Counties					

Halle
Population (1925): 32,962
Eligible voters (1928): 21,621
Electoral district: Westphalia-North
Confession: 96.0% Protestant
Agricultural population: 52.0%

	1920	1924 May	1924 Dec.	1925	1928	1930	1932 July	1932 Nov.
% Turnout	81.8	81.3	81.4	83.5	71.0	76.3	74.7	72.2
Party								
DNVP	30.9	34.1	36.8		24.6	15.2	14.8	15.9
Center	1.3	1.3	2.2		1.5	1.6	1.5	1.5
SPD	26.6	28.8	31.6		33.7	27.6	23.3	22.3
USPD	2.4							
KPD		1.0	1.0		1.1	2.5	4.9	8.1
DVP	21.8	15.8	16.8		10.1	7.6	2.0	3.3
DDP	16.8	11.2	9.4		4.5	2.5	*	*
W[a]			*		7.8	4.1	*	*
L[b]					3.3	1.9	*	*
NSDAP					*	31.2	50.2	45.3
Marx				36.7				
Hindenburg				62.7				

(continued on next page)

Table 23. continued

	1920	1924 May	1924 Dec.	1925	1928	1930	1932 July	1932 Nov.
			Heavily Protestant Counties					

Lübbecke
Population (1925): 55,400
Eligible voters (1928): 33,956
Electoral district: Westphalia-North
Confession: 98.2% Protestant
Agricultural population: 56.7%

	1920	1924 May	1924 Dec.	1925	1928	1930	1932 July	1932 Nov.
% Turnout	73.0	75.0	76.4	85.5	70.9	65.6	78.9	77.4
Party								
DNVP	44.4	51.3	55.5		11.1	7.4	9.6	9.7
Center	*	*	*		*	*	*	*
SPD	25.6	23.4	26.8		24.4	21.7	19.2	17.8
USPD	1.9							
KPD		2.7	1.2		*	2.4	4.0	6.1
DVP	17.6	11.3	9.4		6.0	3.7	1.0	1.2
DDP	9.8	3.7	3.9		2.7	2.8	*	*
W[a]			*		1.2	1.0	*	*
L[b]					46.9	29.0	2.0	3.1
NSDAP					1.5	26.5	60.7	59.1
Marx				24.0				
Hindenburg				75.2				

Wittgenstein
Population (1925): 27,493
Eligible voters (1928): 16,684
Electoral district: Westphalia-South
Confession: 94.4% Protestant
Agricultural population: 40.6%

	1920	1924 May	1924 Dec.	1925	1928	1930	1932 July	1932 Nov.
% Turnout	77.8	77.1	68.6	76.6	55.7	73.1	82.8	81.7
Party								
DNVP	31.4	46.4	47.9		30.5	6.5	6.3	5.9
Center	2.2	2.3	2.3		2.5	2.0	2.2	1.9
SPD	32.5	18.8	21.8		26.3	20.8	16.5	15.9
USPD	6.7							
KPD		5.2	2.9		1.9	1.7	4.3	4.0
DVP	19.4	10.6	10.5		9.2	4.8	1.0	*
DDP	7.6	4.9	5.9		6.8	6.8	1.1	1.5
W[a]			3.6		5.5	1.9	*	*
L[b]					10.9	6.6	*	*
NSDAP					1.9	32.9	63.9	65.7
Marx				21.4				
Hindenburg				77.1				

Table 23. continued

Sources: *Statistisches Jahrbuch für den Preussischen Staat*, vol. 23, pp. 256–65; *Statistik des Deutschen Reichs*, vol. 291, 2, pp. 41–45, 51, 59–63, 67; vol. 315, 2, pp. 35–38, 42, 44–47, 50; vol. 315, 4, pp. 33–36, 39, 42–44, 47; vol. 321, pp. 23, 25, 27, 29; vol. 372, 2, pp. 35–38, 41, 44–46, 50–51; vol. 382, 2, pp. 35–38, 41, 44–46, 49–50; vol. 412, pp. 266–67; vol. 434, pp. 54–58, 121–125.

Note: Because figures have not been presented for all splinter parties and because of rounding, columns may not total 100%.

[a]Wirtschaftspartei.

[b]In 1928, Christlich-Nationale Bauern- und Landvolkpartei; in 1930 and thereafter, Landvolkpartei.

[c]Redistricting in the second 1932 election makes comparisons on the basis of the published statistics impossible.

* < 1.0%.

Table 24. Increase in Number of Agricultural Machines: 1907, 1925

Size of Farm and Year	Machines				
	Sowing	Mowing	Threshing (Motorized)	Threshing (Horse-Drawn)	Milk Separators[a]
Westphalia					
2–5 ha.					
1907	33	169	84	4,710	11,171
1925	935	1,540	3,557	5,310	133 33,408
5–10 ha.					
1907	128	1,599	92	7,624	8,645
1925	2,106	9,831	5,074	5,692	154 18,877
10–20 ha.					
1907	925	7,236	99	8,367	7,782
1925	6,510	16,650	5,962	3,816	360 13,793
20–50 ha.					
1907	2,059	8,334	121	5,470	5,133
1925	6,816	13,943	4,203	1,692	465 7,165
50–100 ha.					
1907	487	1,353	47	577	537
1925	854	2,215	92	503	141 603
100–200 ha.					
1907	110	257	27	54	76
1925	174	592	129	10	36 88
> 200 ha.					
1907	63	158	18	10	30
1925	73	258	45	2	15 21

Table 24. continued

Size of Farm and Year	Machines				
	Sowing	Mowing	Threshing (Motorized)	Threshing (Horse-Drawn)	Milk Separators[a]
			Rhineland		
2–5 ha.					
1907	142	332	31	5,627	4,622
1925	797	3,097	4,118	6,542	61 16,031
5–10 ha.					
1907	517	2,926	48	12,910	6,848
1925	3,798	11,960	7,470	7,384	143 11,996
10–20 ha.					
1907	1,765	5,818	108	8,830	4,511
1925	6,066	12,803	6,169	2,858	471 6,083
20–50 ha.					
1907	2,025	4,302	79	3,960	1,683
1925	3,913	8,317	3,482	641	526 2,204
50–100 ha.					
1907	773	1,302	62	696	389
1925	1,003	2,729	697	57	185 461
100–200 ha.					
1907	262	481	38	104	107
1925	284	887	155	12	48 96
> 200 ha.					
1907	32	57	11	6	9
1925	34	118	20	-	6 7

Source: *Statistik des Deutschen Reichs*, vol. 212, 2a, pp. 94–101; vol. 410, pp. 416–17.

[a]In the 1925 census milk separators are divided between mechanized (left-hand column) and hand-operated models (right-hand column).

Table 25. Land Sales, 1903–1921

Year	Enclosed Farms		Parcels		
	2–5 ha.	> 5 ha.	2 ha.	2–5 ha.	> 5 ha.
	Westphalia				
1903	368	300	2,899	429	177
1907	262	273	4,658	444	278
1912	378	374	4,883	594	277
1915	82	90	2,966	191	107
1916	117	130	2,793	232	114
1917	161	194	2,934	330	163
1918	206	196	3,628	404	208
1919	229	289	5,203	352	173
1920	174	153	4,960	247	104
1921	129	96	4,757	221	82
	Rhineland				
1903	264	257	3,067	328	152
1907	224	240	5,308	385	147
1912	181	190	3,536	628	340
1915	69	62	1,086	197	55
1916	100	98	1,952	323	125
1917	135	156	1,566	233	155
1918	168	200	2,677	273	80
1919	166	159	1,861	251	80
1920	128	104	1,657	206	42
1921	104	90	1,848	175	58

Source: *Statistisches Jahrbuch für den Preussischen Staat*, vol. 3, p. 47; vol. 7, p. 55; vol. 12, p. 101; vol. 15, p. 61; vol. 18, p. 79; vol. 19, p. 87; vol. 20, p. 42.

Note: Information not available after 1921.

Notes

Abbreviations

Abt.	Abteilung
ADGB	Allgemeiner deutscher Gewerkschaftsbund
AK VII	Stellvertretendes Generalkommando, VII. Armee-Korps
BA	Bundesarchiv Koblenz
KA	Kreisausschuss
KEA	Kriegsernährungsamt
KVZ	*Kölnische Volkszeitung*
LAK	Landeshauptarchiv Koblenz
LR	Landrat
LRA	Landratsamt
LVW	Landschaftsverband Westfalen-Lippe
LWKR	Landwirtschaftskammer für die Rheinprovinz
LWKW	Landwirtschaftskammer für die Provinz Westfalen
LWZR	*Landwirtschaftliche Zeitschrift für die Rheinprovinz*
LWZW	*Landwirtschaftliche Zeitschrift für Westfalen-Lippe*
MA	*Münsterischer Anzeiger*
NL	Nachlass
NWHStA	Nordrhein-Westfälisches Hauptstaatsarchiv (Düsseldorf)
OB	Oberbürgermeister
OP	Oberpräsidium
Op	Oberpräsident
PPS	Preisprüfungsstelle
PSV	Preussischer Staatskommissar für Volksernährung
R	Rhineland
RB	Regierungsbezirk
Reg.	Regierung
RhB	*Rheinischer Bauer*
RhGB	*Rheinisches Genossenschaftsblatt*
RMELW	Reichsministerium für Ernährung und Landwirtschaft
RMI	Reichsministerium des Innern
RP	Regierungspräsident
RWM	Reichswirtschaftsministerium
StAD	Staatsarchiv Detmold

StAK	Stadtarchiv Cologne
StAM	Staatsarchiv Münster
VDDB	Vereinigung der deutschen Bauernvereine
VdRT	*Verhandlungen des Reichstags*
W	Westphalia
WB	*Westfälischer Bauer*
WBV	Westfälischer Bauernverein
WGZ	*Westfälische Genossenschafts-Zeitung*
ZStA I	Zentrales Staatsarchiv. Dienststelle Potsdam
ZStA II	Zentrales Staatsarchiv. Dienststelle Merseburg

Introduction

1. An important exception is Rudolf Heberle's work on Schleswig-Holstein, completed in the 1930s, but published only in full thirty years later as *Landbevölkerung und Nationalsozialismus*. Two other recent works that provide an essential background for this study and illuminate Weimar's early years are Flemming, *Landwirtschaftliche Interessen*, which concentrates particularly on the politics of the Agrarian League (Bund der Landwirte) and its successor, the Rural League (Reichslandbund); and Schumacher, *Land und Politik*, a broad review of interest-group politics in all of Germany.

2. On the later years of Weimar, see Gessner, *Agrarverbände*; Gessner, "Dilemma"; Klemm, *Ursachen und Verlauf*; Klemm, "Entwicklung der landwirtschaftlichen Produktion"; Farquharson, *Plough and the Swastika*; Grill, "Nazi Party's Rural Propaganda"; Zofka, *Ausbreitung des Nationalsozialismus*, pp. 111–32; Gies, "NSDAP und landwirtschaftliche Organisationen"; Fröhlich and Broszat, "Politische und soziale Macht." This is also the emphasis in such regional studies as Noakes, *Nazi Party*; Grill, *Nazi Movement*, pp. 135–50; and Pridham, *Hitler's Rise*. In general, see the recent, very useful overview by Holmes, "Forsaken Past."

3. See in particular, Gerschenkron, *Bread and Democracy*, a study that appeared in 1943 and has continued to exert an immense influence on the English-language literature. See also the extensive references in Chapter 1 below, note 22. More sophisticated variants of this continuity thesis can be found in Hans Rosenberg, "Pseudodemokratisierung"; Puhle, *Politische Agrarbewegungen*, pp. 77–94; Puhle, *Von der Agrarkrise*; Stegmann, *Erben Bismarcks*, pp. 519–22; and with application to other parts of the *Mittelstand*, Winkler, *Mittelstand, Demokratie und Nationalsozialismus*; Winkler, "From Social Protectionism"; and Volkov, *Rise of Popular Antimodernism*. Critical reviews of this approach are presented by Eley, *Reshaping*, pp. 1–16; Richard J. Evans, "Introduction," pp. 11–36; Blackbourn, *Class, Religion*, pp. 1–18; and Blackbourn and Eley, *Mythen*. These works concentrate on the Kaiserreich, but both Blackbourn and Eley have emphasized the significance of the war and postwar upheaval for explaining the instability of the Weimar Republic. See Eley, "What Produces Fascism"; and Blackbourn, "The *Mittelstand*," p. 433. For a critical assessment of their position, see Moeller, "Besonderheiten der Deutschen?"; and Moeller, "Kaiserreich Recast?"

4. On the gaps still remaining in the history of the agricultural sector in this period, see

Feldman, "Gegenwärtiger Forschungsstand," pp. 14–15; and Flemming, Krohn, and Witt, "Sozialverhalten und politische Reaktionen," pp. 349–53.

5. Thus, this study excludes the two southernmost districts of the Rhine Province, Regierungsbezirk (RB) Coblenz and RB Trier. These areas were characterized by small farms, attributable to the practice of partible inheritance, and limited market orientation, due to the absence of large urban centers. For reasons that will be made clear in Chapter 1, this distinguishes them from the northern Rhineland and the Province of Westphalia. Throughout this study, unless otherwise specified, references to the Rhineland will be to its three northern districts, RB Düsseldorf, Cologne, and Aachen.

6. The most important single study is Puhle, *Agrarische Interessenpolitik*, which concentrates on the Kaiserreich. On Weimar's early years, see Flemming, *Landwirtschaftliche Interessen*.

7. See, e.g., Blackbourn, "Peasants and Politics," p. 50; Richard J. Evans, "Introduction," pp. 24–25.

8. Transferred into a North American context and judged by the structure of their landholdings and patterns of production, these agricultural producers might be called farmers. They will be called peasants in this book because this is how they referred to themselves. The use of the term "peasant" is not, however, an historicist retreat. Rather, it is intended to convey an important element of the ideological self-perception of German agricultural producers in the late nineteenth and early twentieth centuries. It indicated their ties to a preindustrial past that survived—transformed, modified, reinterpreted—in an industrial society. My choice of nomenclature is heavily influenced by the discussions in Berger, *Peasants against Politics*, p. 4; Berger, "Traditional Sector," pp. 88–93; Berger, "Regime and Interest Representation," pp. 84–86; Eley, "What Produces Fascism," pp. 61–63; Shanin, *Awkward Class*, p. 207; and in general, Mendras, *Vanishing Peasant*.

9. The only comprehensive treatment of Catholic peasant associations concentrates exclusively on the Kaiserreich. See Hendon, "Center Party" and "German Catholics." Highly instructive as well are the regional studies of Bavaria in the Wilhelmine period by Farr: "Populism," "Peasant Protest," and "From Anti-Catholicism"; on Württemberg, the excellent work of Blackbourn, *Class, Religion*; and on the Rhineland, Klaus Müller: "Zentrumspartei" and "Politische Strömungen." On Weimar, see Osmond, "Second Agrarian Mobilization?"; Müller, "Agrarische Interessenverbände"; and Schumacher, *Land und Politik*, pp. 387–431. See also additional references below in Chapters 2, 4, and 6.

10. For other recent studies that clearly reveal the value of a regional focus, see White, *Splintered Party*; Hunt, *People's Party*; Blackbourn, *Class, Religion*; Farr's work on Bavaria, cited above in note 9; and Sperber, *Popular Catholicism*.

11. Kirch, "Person und Individualität," pp. 23–24.

12. Koshar, "Two 'Nazisms,'" p. 35. See also Lepsius, *Extremer Nationalismus*, pp. 22–25; and the useful comparative perspective offered by Eugen Weber, *Peasants into Frenchmen*, p. 242. Great strides in such local level research have been made primarily by working-class historians. See, e.g., the following excellent examples: Nolan, *Social Democracy*; Crew, *Town in the Ruhr*; and the interesting collections, Evans and Lee, *German Family*; and Richard J. Evans, *German Working Class*.

13. My thought on these topics has been particularly influenced by the work of anthropologists and economists who study peasants in the third world. See, e.g., Wolf, *Peasants*; Wolf, *Peasant Wars*; Migdal, *Peasants, Politics*; Ennew, Hirst, and Tribe, "'Peasantry'";

and Galeski, *Basic Concepts*. Also extremely useful are the works of historians of peasants outside Germany who have borrowed heavily from social science theory. See, e.g., Hobsbawm, "Peasants and Politics"; Tilly, *Vendée*; Jackson, "Peasant Political Movements"; Berger, *Peasants against Politics*; and Judt, *Socialism in Provence*. In addition, see the older works of German authors: Wrede, *Eifler Volkskunde*, pp. 222–23; Diener, *Hunsrücker Volkskunde*, pp. 40–62, 154; Mattes, *Die bayerischen Bauernräte*, pp. 6–33; the contributions in Wiese, *Dorf als soziales Gebilde*, and Wurzbacher, *Dorf im Spannungsfeld*; and more recently, Fried, "Sozialentwicklung im Bauerntum."

14. See the lucid, insightful discussion by Berger, "Traditional Sector"; Mayer, "Lower Middle Class"; and the suggestive historical applications of theory by Eley, "What Produces Fascism"; Gellately, *Politics of Economic Despair*; Blackbourn, "The *Mittelstand*"; and Roberts, "Petty Bourgeois Fascism."

15. Berger, *Peasants against Politics*, p. 34. Also Ferguson, "Rural/Urban Relations," pp. 111–14; and Heberle, *Landbevölkerung und Nationalsozialismus*, pp. 46–47.

16. See the recent, insightful discussion and numerous references in Anderson and Barkin, "Myth of the Puttkamer Purge"; and Ross, "Enforcing the Kulturkampf." On the background of political Catholicism in these two provinces, see Winfried Becker, "Der politische Katholizismus"; Sperber, "Shaping of Political Catholicism"; and Sperber, *Political Catholicism*, esp. pp. 156–297.

17. Berger, *Peasants against Politics*, pp. 4–5.

18. The concept of "political immunization" is borrowed from Burnham, "Political Immunization," who credits it to McPhee, *Public Opinion*, pp. 155–79. As this book will argue, in the case of the Center's rural voters, a confessional immunization to competing electoral appeals did not have an unambiguous political content in the Weimar Republic.

Chapter One

1. See Hohorst, Kocka, and Ritter, *Sozialgeschichtliches Arbeitsbuch*, vol. 2, p. 45. For general descriptions of the region and discussions of its economic development, see Pounds, *Ruhr*, pp. 84, 89, 96ff., 129; Croon, "Versorgung der Grosstädte," pp. 356–57; Dickinson, *Germany*, p. 380; Croon, "Einwirkungen der Industriealisierung," pp. 305–6; and Köllmann, "Rheinland und Westfalen," pp. 218–19.

2. See, e.g., Lucas, *Zwei Formen*, pp. 21–136; and Tampke, *Ruhr and Revolution*, pp. 4–18. In addition, the studies of Crew, *Town in the Ruhr*; Nolan, *Social Democracy*; Tenfelde, *Sozialgeschichte*; Reulecke, *Arbeiterbewegung*; Moore, *Injustice*, pp. 227–74; and on other parts of these provinces, Karl Ditt, *Industrialisierung, Arbeiterschaft*; Köllmann, *Sozialgeschichte*; and Mooser, "Weg vom proto-industriellen."

3. This definition is taken from Pounds, *Ruhr*, pp. 25–26.

4. Köllmann, "Bevölkerung Rheinland-Westfalens," pp. 230–33; Tipton, *Regional Variations*, pp. 47, 65, 89–91. See the interesting comparisons with Judt, *Socialism in Provence*, pp. 45, 52, 273–74; also the discussion in Wurzbacher, "Die berufliche Gliederung," pp. 44–47.

5. Reekers, *Westfalens Bevölkerung*, p. 142; Wehler, "Polen im Ruhrgebiet," pp. 220–26.

6. Köllmann, "Rheinland-Westfalen in der deutschen Binnenwanderungsbewegung,"

pp. 251, 253, 255; and in general, Bade, "Transnationale Migration," pp. 183–88. For comparisons with the very high regional mobility characteristic of the urban, industrial working class in these same areas, see Crew, *Town in the Ruhr*, pp. 59–74; and Nolan, *Social Democracy*, pp. 113–18.

7. See Bergmann, *Agrarromantik*; and Barkin, *Controversy*.

8. On the nature of women's agricultural work, see Otto Kaufmann, "Frauenarbeit im 19. Jahrhundert," pp. 76–102; Karl Müller, *Die Frauenarbeit*, pp. 17–24; Golde, *Catholics and Protestants*, pp. 113–16; and the interesting comparison offered by Regina Schulte, "Bauernmägde in Bayern," pp. 110–27.

9. Useful comparisons are offered by Dillwitz, "Struktur der Bauernschaft," pp. 47–127; and Ballwanz, "Sozialökonomische Kennziffern," pp. 467–72.

10. Of those holding between one-half and two hectares in Westphalia, only 16.8 percent were employed full time in agriculture, and 40 percent were employed primarily in industry. The figures for the Rhineland are 29.2 percent and 35.1 percent, respectively. See *Statistik des Deutschen Reichs*, vol. 212, 1, pp. 189–91.

11. Henkelmann, *Zur Frage*, pp. 28–31; Rogge, "Gestaltung," and "Gegenwartsfragen der Realteilung," pp. 293–384.

12. See Aussel, *Die landwirtschaftlichen Betriebe*, p. 6; Havenstein, "Personalkredit," p. 76; Winkelmann and Jaspers, "Personalkredit," pp. 135–36.

13. Albrecht, "Bauerntum im Zeitalter," pp. 45–50, 64. In fact, the type of draft power employed was the basis for terminology used in defining social stratification in the countryside, and contemporaries distinguished between *Pferdebauer* (those using draft teams of horses, the "true" peasants) and *Kuhbauer* (those using oxen or cattle). On the nineteenth-century background to the social differentiation in the countryside associated with the form of the end of the feudal order in these west Elbian districts, see Mooser, *Ländliche Klassengesellschaft*, and Mooser, "Gleichheit und Ungleichheit," pp. 231–33. The restrictive nature of this definition of the "true" peasantry is suggested by Appendix Table 8, which makes clear that most peasants farming less than five hectares did not meet the criterion set for a *Pferdebauer*. See Borchert, *Die landwirtschaftlichen Betriebsverhältnisse*, pp. 42–43; Wilms, "Grossbauern und Kleingrundbesitz," pp. 117–18; Bussmeyer, "Die betriebswirtschaftliche Bedeutung," p. 12; and Neuhaus, "Entwicklungstendenzen," p. 14.

14. See the discussions in Albrecht, "Bauerntum im Zeitalter," passim; Dillwitz, "Struktur der Bauernschaft," pp. 91–92; Sølta, *Bauern der Lausitz*, pp. 76, 97–98; Golde, *Catholics and Protestants*, p. 92; Ballwanz, "Bauernschaft," pp. 10–11; and in general, the discussion in Conze, "Bauer, Bauernstand," pp. 407–39.

15. As the description that follows makes clear, peasants in these areas had little in common with those described by most development economists or by such theorists as the Russian agricultural economist A. V. Chayanov. See Chayanov, *Theory of Peasant Economy*, and the discussion, heavily influenced by Chayanov, in Shanin, *Awkward Class*. The inappropriateness of Chayanov's theory for understanding the German peasantry was stressed by critics in the 1920s. See Skalweit, "Familienwirtschaft als Grundlage," pp. 231–46; Studensky, "Die ökonomische Natur," pp. 318–19; Heinz Becker, "Zu Tshajanows Lehre," pp. 563–75; and Münzinger, *Arbeitsertrag*, p. 785.

16. See the lucid, succinct discussion in Schissler, "Junkers."

17. Gieselmann, "Aufbau und Verflechtung," pp. 20, 24.

18. See Hans Rosenberg, *Grosse Depression*, pp. 178–87; Puhle, *Agrarische Interessenpolitik*, pp. 14–17; and Henning, "Produktionskosten," pp. 214–36.

19. Flemming, *Landwirtschaftliche Interessen*, pp. 20–22; Helling, "Berechnung eines Index," pp. 125–51; Helling, "Zur Entwicklung," pp. 129–41; Baudis and Nussbaum, *Wirtschaft und Staat*, p. 206; Webb, "Agricultural Protection," pp. 309–26; Webb, "Tariff Protection," pp. 336–57; and Perkins, "Agricultural Revolution," pp. 71–129.

20. The works cited above in note 19 suggest that the inflexibility of east Elbian agriculture has been overstated, but a revision of that conventional wisdom lies outside the scope of this study.

21. See the much more nuanced interpretation by Karl Hardach, *Bedeutung wirtschaftlicher Faktoren*, pp. 111–19.

22. This line of argument, stated most forcefully by Gerschenkron, *Bread and Democracy*, pp. 16, 26–27, 57–58, 74–76, 85, 87, continues to wield a pervasive influence. See, e.g., Gourevitch, "International Trade," pp. 285–92; Barkin, *Controversy*, pp. 120–21; Wehler, *Das deutsche Kaiserreich*, pp. 45–48; Moore, *Social Origins*, pp. 448–50; Kindleberger, "Group Behavior," pp. 22–23, 24; and Urwin, *From Ploughshare to Ballotbox*, pp. 96–97. For a similarly negative assessment of the rationality of peasant producers in the 1920s see Gessner, *Agrarverbände*, pp. 87–88. In addition to the criticism of this view offered by Webb and Perkins, cited above in note 19, see the excellent discussion in Hunt, "Peasants, Grain Tariffs," pp. 311–31.

23. See the critical perspective offered by Baudis and Nussbaum, *Wirtschaft und Staat*, p. 227.

24. Hunt, "Peasants, Grain Tariffs," passim; Esslen, *Fleischversorgung*; Teichmann, *Politik der Agrarpreisstützung*, pp. 571–72.

25. Hunt, "Peasants, Grain Tariffs," stresses this point, and it holds true for these regions as well.

26. For complete references to the regional studies on which this description is based, see Moeller, "Peasants and Tariffs," pp. 376–81.

27. Münzberg, *Deutschlands Verbrauch*, p. 68; Henkelmann, "Fütterung und Tierzucht," pp. 674–76.

28. Beckmann, *Futtermittelzölle*, pp. 66–68.

29. Moeller, "Peasants and Tariffs," pp. 378–79.

30. In Westphalia, large-scale pig-fattening concerns were not completely absent but were restricted to the northern part of RB Münster and the northern part of RB Minden—the counties of Halle, Wiedenbrück, Lübbecke, and Minden. See Gieselmann, "Aufbau und Verflechtung," p. 21; and in general, Baade, "Roggenpolitik," pp. 211–16.

31. Heinrichs, "Entwicklung der landwirtschaftlichen Betriebsverhältnisse," p. 116.

32. Moeller, "Peasants and Tariffs," p. 381.

33. Vogel and Boehm, "Einfluss der Preise," pp. 48–49; Spee, "Die landwirtschaftlichen Betriebsverhältnisse," pp. 22–23; Vasters, *Landwirtschaft in den Kreisen*, pp. 144–45; Howard, *Produktionskosten*, p. 6; Gläsel, "Preise landwirtschaftlicher Produkte," p. 33.

34. Aussel, *Die landwirtschaftlichen Betriebe*, p. 45; Avereck, "Landwirtschaft unter dem Einflusse," p. 86; Linneweber, *Landwirtschaft in den Kreisen*, p. 111; Altkemper, "Landwirtschaft in den Kreisen," p. 105; Wilms, "Grossbauern und Kleingrundbesitz," p. 24; Neuhaus, "Entwicklungstendenzen," p. 36; Buer, "Die gegenwärtige landwirtschaftliche Betriebesweise," pp. 32–33.

35. See, e.g., the descriptions in Buer, "Die gegenwärtige landwirtschaftliche Betriebsweise," pp. 75–85.

36. Brinkmann, "Oekonomik des landwirtschaftlichen Betriebes," pp. 30–31, 99. Nor did peasant producers abandon this system in the 1920s: see, e.g., the descriptions in Pritzel, "Wie reagierte die Landwirtschaft"; Rolfes, *Bodennutzung*, esp. pp. 16–19, 24, 29–32, 46–50, 61–66; and Henkelmann, "Zusammenhang," pp. 852–76, 918–19. Even into the 1970s German agricultural producers continued to devote considerable acreage to cereal grains, and the ratio of arable to permanent pasture has remained fairly constant. See Henning, *Landwirtschaft*, pp. 232–45, 258–69; and Priebe, "Modern Family Farm," pp. 209–33.

37. E.g., those proposed by German Social Democrats. See Kautsky, *Agrarfrage*, and the comprehensive treatment in Lehmann, *Agrarfrage*.

38. Karl-Heinz Fischer, "Untersuchungen über die Viehhaltung," pp. 879–80; and in general, on the viability of the family farm, the discussions in Franklin, *European Peasantry*, p. 45; Renborg, "Tendencies Towards Concentration," p. 214; Priebe, "Modern Family Farm," p. 260; Vergopoulos, "Capitalism and Peasant Productivity," pp. 457–58.

39. Karl Hardach, *Bedeutung wirtschaftlicher Faktoren*, pp. 85, 114–15; Heyermann, "Landarbeiterfrage in Westfalen," pp. 18–19, 49; Schlotter, *Die ländliche Arbeiterfrage*, pp. 112, 128ff. For contemporary observations on labor shortages, see the reports of the district administrators in RB Aachen from 1894 and 1900 in NWHStA, Reg. Aachen 909; similar reports from a 1900 survey in Westphalia, StAM, OP 2970, and for the 1890s, StAM, Reg. Münster 2635; and reports from 1908 for RB Düsseldorf, NWHStA, Reg. Düsseldorf 36703; also *RhB*, 15 February 1884.

40. Schlotter, *Die ländliche Arbeiterfrage*, pp. 44–50, 178–85; Münchmeyer and Spaetgens, "Lohnentwicklung," pp. 435–537; Altkemper, "Landwirtschaft in den Kreisen," pp. 48ff.

41. Borchert, *Die landwirtschaftlichen Betriebsverhältnisse*, p. 31; on the Rhineland, see Münchmeyer and Spaetgens, "Lohnentwicklung," p. 451; and in general, Karl Ditt, *Industrialisierung, Arbeiterschaft*, pp. 9–26, 78–122, 179–220; and Mooser, "Weg vom proto-industriellen."

42. See the descriptions in Kaerger, "Die ländlichen Arbeiterverhältnisse," pp. 109, 118; Görnandt, *Landarbeiter*; Albrecht and Meyer-Johann, "Heuerlingswesen," pp. 177–231; Seraphim, *Heuerlingswesen*; Wilms, "Grossbauern und Kleingrundbesitz," pp. 52–70; Dartmann, "Landarbeiterverhältnisse Westfalens," p. 65; Schlotter, *Die ländliche Arbeiterfrage*, pp. 81–82; and on the Rhineland, Münchmeyer and Spaetgens, "Lohnentwicklung," pp. 454–55.

43. See the descriptions in Lindner, "Die bäuerliche Wohnkultur," pp. 727–28; and Henkelmann, *Zur Frage*, p. 27.

44. See the examples in Schlotter, *Die ländliche Arbeiterfrage*, pp. 75, 87–90; Dartmann, "Landarbeiterverhältnisse Westfalens," p. 62; Seraphim, *Heuerlingswesen*, pp. 14–15; and Wilms, "Grossbauern und Kleingrundbesitz," pp. 53–56.

45. Görnandt, *Landarbeiter*, pp. 45–46. Indeed, there is much evidence that the institution had lost its paternalistic patina long before the late nineteenth century. See Mooser: "Property and Wood Theft," and *Ländliche Klassengesellschaft*, pp. 246–80.

46. Quoted in Görnandt, *Landarbeiter*, p. 62.

47. *Verhandlungen der am 20. und 21. März 1893*, p. 66, in response to the comments of G. F. Knapp, pp. 6–23.

48. Wilms, "Grossbauern und Kleingrundbesitz," pp. 67–68; Schlotter, *Die ländliche Arbeiterfrage*, p. 104.

49. In general on this development see Nichtweiss, *Die ausländischen Saisonarbeiter*.

50. Münchmeyer and Spaetgens, "Lohnentwicklung," p. 461; Vasters, *Landwirtschaft in den Kreisen*, pp. 123–24.

51. Dix, *Untersuchungen*, p. 34; Kroeger, "Entwicklung der landwirtschaftlichen Bodennutzung," pp. 85–86.

52. This and the next two paragraphs draw on Münchmeyer and Spaetgens, "Lohnentwicklung," pp. 447–50, 458–62, 516–18, 527–29, 532; Kaerger, "Die ländlichen Arbeiterverhältnisse," pp. 3, 133, 140, 151–52, 166; and Sauermann, *Knechte und Mägde*, pp. 17–19 and passim.

53. That unionization was not a particular problem in these areas was stressed repeatedly in the reports of the district administrators in Düsseldorf responding to a 1908 survey of labor conditions. See NWHStA, Reg. Düsseldorf 36703. See also the useful theoretical discussion in Galeski, *Basic Concepts*, p. 126, and the comparison with the Bavarian experience in Blessing, "Umwelt und Mentalität," pp. 37, 41–42. On the problems of unionization and the repressive legal framework (the Gesindeordnung), which impeded organization, see Flemming, *Landwirtschaftliche Interessen*, pp. 55–62; Flemming, "Landarbeiter," pp. 351–418, and Saul, "Kampf um das Landproletariat," pp. 162–208.

54. Beckmann, "Bauer im Zeitalter," pp. 726, 739.

55. Heinrichs, "Entwicklung der landwirtschaftlichen Betriebsverhältnisse," p. 104; Gläsel, "Preise landwirtschaftlicher Produkte," passim; Farnsworth, "Wheat," p. 326; Walther G. Hoffmann, *Wachstum der deutschen Wirtschaft*, pp. 561–62.

56. Hehnsen, "Strukturwandel der Landwirtschaft," pp. 174–76.

57. Baade, "System der agrarpolitischen Mittel," p. 236.

58. Dix, *Untersuchungen*, p. 29; Beckmann, *Einfuhrscheinsysteme*, pp. 140–41; Frenzen, *Untersuchungen*, p. 64; Kroeger, "Entwicklung der landwirtschaftlichen Bodennutzung," pp. 69–71; Leonhards, "Die landwirtschaftlichen Betriebsformen," p. 156; and in general, Ballwanz, "Sozialstruktur," pp. 148, 155.

59. Laer, "Die wirtschaftlichen Verhältnisse," p. 200; Rothkegel, "Bewegung der Kaufpreise," pp. 1689–1747; Aereboe, *Beurteilung von Landgütern*, Figs. 20–23, 26, 46–49, 52.

60. Kroeger, "Entwicklung der landwirtschaftlichen Bodennutzung," p. 88; Wilken, *Volkswirtschaftliche Theorie*, pp. 109–10; Winkel, "Zur Anwendung," pp. 19–31.

61. See the discussion in *Preussische Statistik*, vol. 191, 2, pp. xliii–xliv, xlvi–xlvii.

62. Beckmann, "Bauer im Zeitalter," p. 747.

63. Henning, *Landwirtschaft*, pp. 148–50; Haushofer, *Die deutsche Landwirtschaft*, pp. 219–20, 251–55; Klein, *Geschichte der deutschen Landwirtschaft*, pp. 127–32.

64. Puhle, *Agrarische Interessenpolitik*, p. 242.

Chapter Two

1. Stegmann, *Erben Bismarcks*; also Puhle, "Parlament, Parteien," pp. 340–77; Nipperdey, "Interessenverbände und Parteien," pp. 369–88.

2. See the comprehensive treatment by Puhle, *Agrarische Interessenpolitik*; also Tirrell,

German Agrarian Politics; Flemming, *Landwirtschaftliche Interessen*, pp. 1–75; and the critical reappraisal of Puhle, emphasizing the league's successes *west* of the Elbe, by Eley, "Anti-Semitism, Agrarian Mobilization." See also Hunt, " 'Egalitarianism,' " pp. 513–30.

3. This is the tone in Gerschenkron, *Bread and Democracy*. See also Stegmann, *Erben Bismarcks*, pp. 38–39; and in general, the critical discussion in Blackbourn, "Peasants and Politics," pp. 47–75.

4. Count Hoensbroech, reported in *RhB*, 15 May 1898; in general, see Puhle, *Agrarische Interessenpolitik*, p. 147.

5. Ross, *Beleaguered Tower*, p. 45; Schauff, *Wahlverhalten der deutschen Katholiken*, pp. 43, 83, 88, 134; Schumacher, *Land und Politik*, p. 238. In general, on the origins of political Catholicism in the Rhineland and Westphalia, see Sperber, "Shaping of Political Catholicism"; and Sperber, *Popular Catholicism*.

6. Gabler, "Entwicklung der deutschen Parteien," pp. 54–55.

7. See the excellent study by Blackbourn, *Class, Religion*. Württemberg was distinguished not only by the parallels between occupational and confessional splits but also by the late appearance of the Center as a political force. Its origins lay in the 1890s, not in the *Kulturkampf*. Both qualities make it difficult to transfer Blackbourn's findings into the Rhenish-Westphalian context. See the general discussion and review of Blackbourn's argument in Moeller, "Kaiserreich Recast?" p. 668. On the very different background of political Catholicism in the Rhineland and Westphalia, see Sperber's recent work. On Bavaria, see the excellent recent studies by Farr: "Populism," "Peasant Protest," and "From Anti-Catholicism"; also Haushofer, "Der Bayerische Bauernbund," pp. 562–69; and in general, Hendon, "German Catholics," and Hendon, "Center Party."

8. See also Neher, *Die wirtschaftliche und soziale Lage*, pp. 25, 28, 62–63, 71–73, 75, 115–16.

9. Count Strachwitz at a meeting of the Catholic Nobles of Silesia in 1895, quoted in Mittmann, *Fraktion und Partei*, p. 168.

10. Cited in Naumann, *Die politischen Parteien*, p. 29.

11. In general, see Heckart, *From Bassermann to Bebel*, and Gustav Schmidt, "Parlamentarisierung."

12. See the discussions in Johanns, "Organisation des landwirtschaftlichen Vereinswesens"; Bäcker, "Wesen und Entwicklungstendenzen," pp. 66ff., 103–6; Lessmann, "Die deutschen christlichen Bauernvereine," pp. 25–43; Wygodzinski, "Die rheinische Landwirtschaft," pp. 256f.; Wygodzinski, "Landwirtschaftskammer," pp. 1361–1420; Crone-Münzebrock, "Landwirtschaftliches Vereinswesen," pp. 561–63; Reif, "Adel und landwirtschaftliches Vereinswesen," pp. 39–60; Braun, "Die historische Entwicklung"; and Schleh, "Entwicklung des landwirtschaftlichen Vereinswesens," pp. 112–39.

13. See the useful discussion in Molt, *Reichstag*, pp. 82–96.

14. Anderson and Barkin, "Myth of the Puttkamer Purge," pp. 660–61. See also Muncy, "Prussian *Landräte*," pp. 299–338.

15. This discussion draws heavily on the important work of Reif, *Westfälischer Adel*, esp. pp. 398–456, and Reif, " 'Erhaltung adligen Stamms und Namens,' " pp. 275–308. On the general trend toward increasing religiosity and Catholic self-identification in which nobles actively participated, see Sperber, "Transformation of Catholic Associations," pp. 253–64; Sperber, "Roman Catholic Religious Identity," pp. 305–18; and Sperber, *Political Catholicism*, pp. 73–98.

16. Schorlemer-Alst's "Promemoria und Motive zu dem Statut für einen zu bildenden Bauernverein," quoted in Wesemann, "Der Westfälische Bauernverein," p. 22.

17. Schorlemer-Alst to Wilhelm Emmanuel von Ketteler, 14 February 1862, cited in ibid., p. 16. See also *WB*, November 1912, a special *Fest-Nummer: 50 Jahre Westfälischer Bauernverein 1862–1912* (cited hereafter as *Fest-Nummer*), which provides much useful information on the organization's background. In general, on the foundation of the organization, see in addition, Ferdinand Jacobs, *Von Schorlemer*; Jürgens, "Politischer Konservatismus," pp. 127–47; and Hendon, "Center Party," pp. 37–42. On corporatist ideology, see Emil Ritter, *Die katholisch-soziale Bewegung*, pp. 88ff., and Bowen, *German Theories*, p. 80. For an excellent comparative perspective, see Berger, *Peasants against Politics*.

18. The phrase comes from Judt, *Socialism in Provence*, pp. 278–79. In general, see Jacobs, *Von Schorlemer*, p. 10. On the very different situation in the southern Rhenish district of Trier, where the Trier Peasant Association was founded by a Catholic priest, Georg Dasbach, see *Entwickelung und Tätigkeit*; Hendon, "Center Party," pp. 55–59; and Bäcker, "Wesen und Entwicklungstendenzen," pp. 97–100. For another example, see Muth, "Zur Geschichte," pp. 178–219.

19. See Winfried Becker, "Der politische Katholizismus," pp. 281–84; and the general discussion and references in Ellen Lovell Evans, *German Center Party*, pp. 31–32.

20. See, e.g., the recent discussion and references in Anderson, *Windthorst*, pp. 130–200; Ross, "Enforcing the Kulturkampf"; Ellen Lovell Evans, *German Center Party*, pp. 36–94; and Klaus Müller, "Rheinland als Gegenstand," pp. 401–2. Sperber provides an excellent treatment of these regions in *Political Catholicism*, pp. 206–76.

21. Figures are from *Fest-Nummer*, p. 395.

22. Jacobs, *Deutsche Bauernführer*, p. 60; Kissling, *Geschichte der deutschen Katholikentage*, p. 51; and Emil Ritter, *Die katholisch-soziale Bewegung*, p. 138.

23. The original organization included members from the administrative districts of Kempen, Crefeld, Cologne, Gladbach, Moers, Geldern, and Kleve, all predominantly Catholic districts. See the special issue of *RhB*, 1907, *Der Rheinische Bauern-Verein: Jubiläumsbericht zur Feier seines 25jährigen Bestehens* (cited hereafter as *Jubiläumsbericht*), issued as part of the twenty-fifth anniversary of the organization. In general, see also the recent summary provided by Küppers, "Zur Entstehung," pp. 1–31; Bäcker, "Wesen und Entwicklungstendenzen," passim; and Hendon, "Center Party," pp. 53–55.

24. Such information was not even made available to Wesemann for his completely sympathetic treatment, undertaken with the full cooperation of the association in the 1920s.

25. From the original statute, reprinted in *Fest-Nummer*, p. 365. The reformed 1871 statute continued to insist on a "selbständigen Grundbesitz"; see *Fest-Nummer*, p. 380. Lessmann, "Die deutschen christlichen Bauernvereine," p. 134, concluded: "Während die grösseren Landwirte fast restlos im Vereinswesen organisiert sind, entziehen sich die kleineren Landwirte, man möchte fast sagen, im Verhältnis zur abnehmenden Betriebsfläche, ihrem Zusammenschluss." The limitations that this placed on potential membership are suggested in Appendix Tables 6, 7, and 8.

26. Kellermann, "Der Westfälische Bauernverein," pp. 376–447.

27. Küppers, "Zur Entstehung," pp. 27–28, n. 72; Muth, "Führungsschichten," p. 310; Kerckerinck, *Beiträge zur Geschichte*, p. 857; and Winkelmann and Jaspers, "Personalkredit," p. 135.

28. Küppers, "Zur Entstehung," pp. 14–15; Jürgens, "Politischer Konservatismus," p. 132; Muth, "Führungsschichten," pp. 299, 304–5; Latten, "Dorf als Lebensgemeinschaft," p. 42; Reif, " 'Erhaltung adligen Stamms und Namens,' " p. 281; and Grabein, *Wirtschaftliche und soziale Bedeutung*, p. 157.

29. See the discussion in Muth, "Führungsschichten," passim; and on Trier, the works cited above in note 18.

30. These are constant themes in the Peasant Association press. See, e.g., the series of articles, "Was will der Rheinische Bauernverein?" in *RhB*, 1888–89; a typical description of the corporatist ideal in the series in *RhB*, June–September 1893; a series attacking Social Democracy in *WB* throughout 1891; characteristic anti-Semitism in "Das Volk der Juden," a series in *RhB*, 1892; and for a good summary of Loë-Terporten's position, his speech at the general assembly meeting of the association in December 1886, reported in *RhB*, 15 February 1887.

31. See the useful discussion in Puhle, *Agrarische Interessenpolitik*, p. 130.

32. Moore, *Social Origins*, p. 495. Also very informative on the relationship between conservative ideology and interest-group organization is the work of Lewis on Austria, "Peasantry, Rural Change," pp. 119–43. The material bases of peasant life are described above in Chapter 1. See also Sauermann, "Hofidee," pp. 58–78; and the general discussion in Fried, "Sozialentwicklung im Bauerntum," pp. 755–59, 764–72. For an analysis that differs from the argument presented here in its emphasis on the manipulative quality of agrarian ideology, see Ziche, "Kritik der deutschen Bauerntumsideologie," pp. 105–42.

33. The phrase comes from Koshar, "Two 'Nazisms,' " p. 35. On other forms of Catholic associational life and the profound influence of the church, see the works by Sperber, cited above in note 15.

34. On the limited success of SPD attempts to organize even in Protestant parts of eastern Westphalia, see Karl Ditt, *Industrialisierung, Arbeiterschaft*, pp. 266–68; and on Social Democratic agrarian policy in general, in addition to Lehmann's exhaustive study, *Agrarfrage*, see Maehl, "German Social Democratic Agrarian Policy," pp. 121–57.

35. No good study of the democratic German Peasant League exists. See the brief treatment and references in Schwab, "Deutscher Bauernbund," pp. 415–21; and Schumacher, *Land und Politik*, p. 435.

36. See, e.g., the protocol of the steering committee of the Westphalian association, 28 March 1893, reported in *WB*, April 1893; and a similar story in *WB*, December 1893. See also the account of "Die agrarische Bewegung" in *RhB*, 15 March 1893; and the reassertions of these positions, *RhB*, 15 June 1901, and *WB*, March 1900, and October 1902. For a detailed treatment of Agrarian League ideology, see Puhle, *Agrarische Interessenpolitik*, pp. 72–110.

37. See, e.g., attacks on Agrarian League proposals, particularly for the canal and graduated freight rates: *WB*, April 1894, February 1895, and November 1895; and in general, Horn, *Kampf um den Bau*, pp. 28, 40, 48–49; Hendon, "German Catholics," passim; and Gerschenkron, *Bread and Democracy*, p. 69.

38. Hendon, "Center Party," pp. 72–73.

39. Puhle records that in 1906, 17 percent of Agrarian League members were artisans, over half of whom were not even employed part-time in the agricultural sector: Puhle, *Agrarische Interessenpolitik*, p. 39.

40. Puhle rightly emphasizes the ability of the Agrarian League to employ the tactics appropriate to politics in a mass society, but although this part of Agrarian League activity

contained a blueprint for other forms of interest organization, its direct political involvement had no precedents and few successors in Germany. See the general discussion in Puhle, *Agrarische Interessenpolitik*, pp. 293–94; the comparative perspectives suggested by Gollwitzer, "Europäische Bauerndemokratie," pp. 1–82; and Puhle, "Warum gibt es in Westeuropa," pp. 603–67.

41. *Fest-Nummer*, p. 395. One of the two acting organizational heads always came from Minden-Ravensberg.

42. See in particular, Vierhaus, "Wahlen und Wählerverhalten," pp. 61–62; Helmut Busch, *Stoeckerbewegung*, pp. 87–102; Wolfgang Hofmann, *Bielefelder Stadtverordneten*, pp. 65–66; and Hoener, "Geschichte der christlich-konservativen Partei," esp. pp. 79–96. Stoecker remained quite successful in the district of Siegen in the southern tip of Westphalia, which, with a break from 1893 to 1898, sent him to the Reichstag from 1881 until 1907. This was a heavily industrial area; see Busch, *Stoeckerbewegung*, pp. 3–4.

43. Wesemann, "Der Westfälische Bauernverein," p. 44.

44. Winkelmann and Jaspers, "Personalkredit," p. 149. In general, see Lessmann, "Die deutschen christlichen Bauernvereine," pp. 101–16.

45. Quabeck, "Das landwirtschaftliche Genossenschaftswesen," pp. 506–8. Along with Winkelmann and Jaspers, Quabeck provides a good summary of the development of the cooperative network (he was its head in Westphalia).

46. Quabeck, "Das landwirtschaftliche Genossenschaftswesen," pp. 466, 498.

47. See Grabein, *Wirtschaftliche und soziale Bedeutung*, pp. 44–45, 121–26.

48. Wygodzinski and Müller, *Genossenschaftswesen*, p. 140.

49. For an interesting comparative perspective, see the work of Lewis, "Peasantry, Rural Change."

50. Quabeck, "Das landwirtschaftliche Genossenschaftswesen," pp. 464, 467–68.

51. Figures are provided in *Jubiläumsbericht*, pp. 110–12. In general, see also Hendon, "Center Party," pp. 78–79; and Havenstein, "Personalkredit," pp. 75–134.

52. Linneweber, *Landwirtschaft in den Kreisen*, pp. 112–15. See also Wygodzinski and Müller, *Genossenschaftswesen*, pp. 225ff; and Grabein, *Wirtschaftliche und soziale Bedeutung*, pp. 29–30, 46–47, 51.

53. *Jubiläumsbericht*, pp. 109–23; *Fest-Nummer*, pp. 418–24; Dix, *Untersuchungen*, p. 63; Quabeck, "Das landwirtschaftliche Genossenschaftswesen," pp. 494, 510–11; Borchert, *Die landwirtschaftlichen Betriebsverhältnisse*, pp. 93, 95; and *WGZ*, 7 September 1915. In general, see Lessmann, "Die deutschen christlichen Bauernvereine," pp. 116–26.

54. Hendon, "Center Party," pp. 94ff; Bäcker, "Wesen und Entwicklungstendenzen," p. 89; Wesemann, "Der Westfälische Bauernverein," pp. 46, 50; Kellermann, "Der Westfälische Bauernverein," pp. 420, 422, 434, 437–38; and Lessmann, "Die deutschen christlichen Bauernvereine," pp. 51–86.

55. *RhB*, 15 October 1901.

56. Front-page banner headline, *WB*, June 1897.

57. *Beilage zu RhB*, 15 January 1885.

58. Front-page headline and story in *Beilage zu RhB*, 15 August 1886.

59. The political sociologist M. Rainer Lepsius writes, "The organization of the peasant social milieu, the peasant associations, civic associations, cooperatives, livestock breeding associations, mediate the political integration of the peasantry into the total society; they are the real agents of political orientation" (Lepsius, *Extremer Nationalismus*, p. 22).

See also Eley, *Reshaping*, pp. 137–38, who describes the "economic defence leagues of the peasantry" as "an organic part of their members' lives, deeply embedded in the social fabric of their daily existence."

60. On this, see the subtle discussion in Nolan's study of Düsseldorf, *Social Democracy*, pp. 126–45; and Lidtke, *Alternative Culture*.

61. Figures are in *Fest-Nummer*, p. 396. This figure excludes those living outside the provincial borders in Oldenburg, Waldeck, Pyrmont, and Lippe.

62. *Jubiläumsbericht*, pp. 78–79.

63. The phrase comes from Blackbourn, *Class, Religion*. Blackbourn's tendency to dismiss its importance, however, is far more appropriate to the context that he studies, Württemberg, than it is to the Rhineland and Westphalia.

64. For general discussions of the Center in the Wilhelmine period, see Blackbourn, *Class, Religion*, pp. 23–60; Ross, *Beleaguered Tower*; Zeender, *German Center Party*; Mittmann's interesting comparative approach, *Fraktion und Partei*; Ellen Lovell Evans, *German Center Party*, pp. 117–202; Morsey, "Die deutschen Katholiken," pp. 270–98; Morsey, "Zentrumspartei in Rheinland," pp. 11–50; and Morsey, *Deutsche Zentrumspartei*, pp. 33–52. Unfortunately, no complement to Blackbourn's fine study exists for the Rhineland and Westphalia. Sperber's work, cited above in note 15, concentrates on the period 1848–80.

65. See Farr's works on Bavaria.

66. Zeender, *German Center Party*, pp. 28–35.

67. Tirrell, *German Agrarian Politics*, pp. 119–23, 245. See the general discussion in Barkin, *Controversy*, pp. 44ff.; and Puhle, *Agrarische Interessenpolitik*, pp. 28–33.

68. This and the following paragraph draw heavily on Jacobs, *Von Schorlemer*, p. 29 and passim. See also Mittmann, *Fraktion und Partei*, p. 168; Bachem, *Vorgeschichte, Geschichte*, vol. 5, pp. 23–24, 26–27, 291–93, 352; and Hendon, "Center Party," pp. 348–50, 439–40.

69. Bachem, *Vorgeschichte, Geschichte*, vol. 3, p. 149.

70. Bachem, *Vorgeschichte, Geschichte*, vol. 5, pp. 352–54. In general on these events, see Klaus Müller: "Zentrumspartei," and "Politische Strömungen."

71. On Loë-Terporten's corporatist alternative, borrowed from a Cologne priest, Peter Oberdörffer, see Bachem, *Vorgeschichte, Geschichte*, vol. 9, p. 346; Hendon, "Center Party," pp. 372ff.; Bowen, *German Theories*, pp. 113–16; and Emil Ritter, *Die katholisch-soziale Bewegung*, pp. 203–5.

72. See the works cited in note 71; also Bachem's notes on the matter following the Katholikentag the following year in Munich, StAK, NL Bachem, Abt. 1006 Nr. 15.

73. See, e.g., Loë-Terporten's proposals for state market regulation, the Neuss Program, named for the site of the meeting where it was adopted: *RhB*, 15 February and 15 June 1896, 15 February 1897; and the official party critique in *KVZ*, 16 and 17 January 1896.

74. Klaus Müller, "Zentrumspartei," pp. 854–56; Hendon, "Center Party," pp. 497–503.

75. Count Hoensbroech, reported in *RhB*, 15 May 1898.

76. See Ross, *Beleaguered Tower*, p. 62; Nipperdey, *Organisation der deutschen Parteien*, pp. 265, 270; Gabler, "Entwicklung der deutschen Parteien," pp. 54, 58; and on the importance of Catholic self-identification, the works by Sperber. The power of the clergy is

also stressed by Klaus Müller in "Politische Strömungen" and "Rheinland als Gegenstand."

77. On the concept of a "sociocultural milieu," see Lepsius, "Parteiensystem und Sozialstruktur," pp. 56–80, esp. pp. 64–65 and 69–70.

78. Müller, "Politische Strömungen," p. 372.

79. E.g., Nipperdey, "Interessenverbände und Parteien," p. 384.

80. Morsey, *Deutsche Zentrumspartei*, p. 42; Schauff, *Wahlverhalten der deutschen Katholiken*, pp. 26–27, 36–37; and in general, Milatz, "Reichstagswahlen," pp. 207–23.

81. See Hendon, "Center Party," pp. 122–23, 131–38, 147–49, 160–63; Müller, "Politische Strömungen," pp. 190–91, 396–98; and Bachem, *Vorgeschichte, Geschichte*, vol. 5, pp. 354–56.

82. See Jacobs, *Deutsche Bauernführer*, pp. 86–87. Herold's double leadership role in the Prussian parliament and the Reichstag won him the name "Hin- und Herold"; Morsey, *Deutsche Zentrumspartei*, p. 164.

83. See Bachem's notes on the meeting of Reichstag leaders, 23 November 1902, StAK, NL Bachem, Abt. 1006 Nr. 178. Also Bachem's notes on his discussion with Bülow about the Center's position on upcoming tariff debates, 30 November 1901, StAK, NL Bachem, Abt. 1006 Nr. 173 and the meeting of the Reichstag delegation, 27 November 1901, StAK, NL Bachem, Abt. 1006 Nr. 172.

84. *Niederrheinische Volkszeitung*, 16 June 1903, in StAK, NL Bachem, Abt. 1006 Nr. 346. See also Herold's address to leaders of the Westphalian Association, 10 February 1903, in *WB*, March 1903; and the general discussions of the tariff, *WB*, August 1901 and January 1903, and *RhB*, 15 January 1903; also Zeender, *German Center Party*, pp. 87–93, and Hendon, "Center Party," pp. 472–99. For an account of the negotiations see Barkin, *Controversy*, pp. 211–52.

85. Anderson, *Windthorst*, pp. 371–72.

86. See Blackbourn, *Class, Religion*, pp. 16, 25. His point of reference and the phrase come from Arthur Rosenberg, *Imperial Germany*, p. 18.

87. E.g., in the years after 1900, the major battles within the Center—the *Zentrumsstreit*, the conflict over plans for an interconfessional political party, and the *Gewerkschaftsstreit*, the fight over proposals for interconfessional unions—represented attempts to transform the party into an explicitly political body, less dependent on confessional ties and with a greater appeal to working-class voters. In both conflicts, Rhenish liberals and Catholic working-class leaders played leading roles. Neither the Rhenish nor the Westphalian Peasant Association became directly involved in these controversies, but it is safe to assume that they would have had little sympathy for movements away from the self-definition of the Center as a confessional interest group toward an identity as a mass political party that supported democratic reforms. In general, see Ross, *Beleaguered Tower*, and Ellen Lovell Evans, *German Center Party*, pp. 178–202.

88. See the recent study of Heitzer, *Volksverein*, pp. 49, 54–57, 312–15. See also Ross, *Beleaguered Tower*, pp. 79–118; Focke, *Sozialismus aus christlicher Verantwortung*, pp. 35–59; Anderson, *Windthorst*, pp. 391–92; and most recently, Schneider, *Die Christlichen Gewerkschaften*, pp. 11–362, and Schneider, "Religion and Labour," pp. 345–69.

89. Nipperdey, *Organisation der deutschen Parteien*, pp. 271, 284, 287, 290–92; Morsey, *Deutsche Zentrumspartei*, p. 52; Blackbourn, *Class, Religion*, p. 114; Mittmann, *Fraktion und Partei*, pp. 273–86; Winfried Becker, "Der politische Katholizismus," p. 286; and Puhle, "Conservatism," pp. 694, 697–98.

90. Nolan, *Social Democracy*, pp. 157–66; Blackbourn, *Class, Religion*, pp. 52–53; Nipperdey, *Organisation der deutschen Parteien*, p. 280; Klaus Müller, "Politische Strömungen," p. 396; Mittmann, *Fraktion und Partei*, pp. 166–67.

91. See the discussion in Ross, *Beleaguered Tower*, pp. 33–48; also Blackbourn, *Class, Religion*, pp. 196–241.

92. Cited in Ross, *Beleaguered Tower*, p. 116.

93. On increased demands for democratic reforms, see Ross, *Beleaguered Tower*, p. 82; Hendon, "Center Party," p. 584; Schauff, *Wahlverhalten der deutschen Katholiken*, pp. 80–83, 90; Focke, *Sozialismus aus christlicher Verantwortung*, pp. 60–61; Heitzer, *Volksverein*, pp. 124–25, 160–64, 279–91; and Epstein, *Matthias Erzberger*, pp. 38–44, 65, 89–95. On continued resistance to reforms, see Dietzel, "Die preussischen Wahlrechtsreformbestrebungen," pp. 37–39, 64, 68–72, 74–79. On the 1912 electoral losses, see Bertram, *Wahlen zum Deutschen Reichstag*, pp. 22–28, 212–13, 217–18; and on the steady losses in urban areas before 1914, the figures in Gerhard A. Ritter, *Wahlgeschichtliches Arbeitsbuch*, pp. 109–10. In general, see also Gottwald, "Umfall des Zentrums," pp. 182–84. In Westphalia, where worker interests were not as heavily represented as in the Rhineland, a tally of the party's provincial committee before the war still revealed seventeen nobles and another twenty-eight agricultural producers, but they confronted nineteen workers, twenty-two artisans, fifty-eight from commerce and industry, forty-seven clerics, sixty-three professionals—including lawyers, academics, and civil servants—and six white-collar workers. In the nine-member provincial steering committee, Herold was joined by only one other agrarian representative, Engelbert Freiherr Kerckerinck zu Borg, who also sat in the Reichstag delegation but seldom had much to say in Berlin. Kerckerinck became head of the Westphalian association in 1916 and will play a central role in later chapters. See *Mitteilungen der Zentralstelle der Westfälischen Zentrumspartei*, 1 February 1914, BA, NL Herold, Nr. 7. Stegmann overestimates the continued authority of conservative aristocrats in the Party: see Stegmann, *Erben Bismarcks*, pp. 30–31.

94. Speech in Cologne, 20 April 1906, cited in Heitzer, *Volksverein*, p. 128; and in general, ibid., pp. 120–29. See also the brief biographical sketch of Trimborn in Morsey, *Deutsche Zentrumspartei*, pp. 570–76.

95. Dietzel, "Die preussischen Wahlrechtsreformbestrebungen," pp. 74–79; Hendon, "Center Party," pp. 607, 615, 623–26; Hendon, "German Catholics"; Heckart, *From Bassermann to Bebel*, pp. 238–39; Stegmann, *Erben Bismarcks*, p. 327.

96. On the so-called "National Catholics," see Hendon, "Center Party," pp. 562–63; and Molt, *Reichstag*, pp. 106–7.

97. Ross, *Beleaguered Tower*, pp. xiv, 137.

98. From the electoral platform for the 1903 elections, published in full in Bachem, *Vorgeschichte, Geschichte*, vol. 7, p. 459. See also Zeender, "German Center Party during World War I," pp. 446–47; and Müller, "Rheinland als Gegenstand," pp. 401–2.

99. Schorlemer-Lieser to the Westphalian association, 13 November 1912, reported in *WB*, 1 December 1912.

100. Loë-Bergerhausen, reported in *RhB*, 16 November 1912.

Chapter Three

1. In general, see Farrar, *Short-War Illusion*.

2. See Winkler, *Organisierter Kapitalismus*, esp. the critical perspective offered by Feldman, "Der deutsche Organisierte Kapitalismus," pp. 150–71.

3. Tyszka, *Konsument*, p. 5; Aereboe, *Einfluss des Krieges*, p. 37. On the greatly expanded authority of local officials, see Lindemann, *Die deutsche Stadtgemeinde*; Hassel, *Einrichtungen der preussischen Landkreise*; and Gündell, *Organisation der deutschen Ernährungswirtschaft*. In general, on the politicization of economic relations during the war, see the insightful comments of Cronin, "Labor Insurgency," p. 29; and Gramsci, *Selections*, pp. 83–85.

4. In general, see Feldman, *Army, Industry*; and Kocka, *Klassengesellschaft im Krieg*.

5. See in particular Lindemann, *Die deutsche Stadtgemeinde*; and Hassel, *Einrichtungen der preussischen Landkreise*.

6. See Aereboe, *Einfluss des Krieges*, and the companion study in the Carnegie Foundation series on the First World War, Skalweit, *Die deutsche Kriegsernährungswirtschaft*. See also the recent discussions in Flemming, *Landwirtschaftliche Interessen*, pp. 80–105; and Schumacher, *Land und Politik*, pp. 33–84.

7. The so-called *Schweinemord* unleashed an extended debate over food policy. See, e.g., Beckmann, "Organisation der agraren Produktion," pp. 700, 703, who called it the "Bartholomäusnacht der Borstentiere." For a more detailed discussion and additional references, see Moeller, "Dimensions of Social Conflict," pp. 147–48.

8. Beckmann, "Organisation der agraren Produktion," pp. 495ff.

9. This is a common theme in the monthly reports on economic conditions provided to Reich authorities by district government presidents. These reports, along with the information from local authorities on which they were based, provide the single most important source for a consideration of the peasantry's reaction to the war economy at the local level. See, e.g., materials for 1917 and 1918 in StAM, OP 3944, and LAK, 403/12326 and 12328.

10. This is emphasized by LWKW report of 22 October 1917, StAM, OP 3940.

11. Skalweit, *Die deutsche Kriegsernährungswirtschaft*, p. 107; Skalweit, *Schwein*, pp. 19–20; Beckmann, "Organisation der agraren Produktion," pp. 777–79; and LWKW report of 22 May 1917, StAM, OP 3940.

12. For a summary of these declines see Flemming, *Landwirtschaftliche Interessen*, pp. 80–83; Berthold, "Zur Entwicklung," pp. 83–111; and the lengthy reports, prepared for the Reichsernährungsministerium, which include not only a detailed overview but also some materials for the Rhineland and Westphalia: "Grundlagen für Preisbemessung der landwirtschaftlichen Erzeugnisse im Jahre 1919," and "Untersuchungen über die Steigerung des landwirtschaftlichen Betriebsaufwandes in den Jahren 1913/14 bis 1917/18 auf Grund buchmässig ermittelter Betriebsergebnisse," dated 21 May 1919, in BA, R 43 I/ 1254, pp. 15–77, 124–53.

13. See LWKW report of 14 July 1915, StAM, OP 1843; also report of RP Minden, 1 January 1915, StAM, OP 1842, I. Ernst Klein claims that of 3.4 million male workers in the agricultural sector before the war, two million were drafted, but he provides no source for this estimate: Klein, *Geschichte der deutschen Landwirtschaft*, p. 155. Martin Sogemeir provides yet another figure, again without a source, claiming that of 612,691 men

conscripted into the army from the Rhenish and Westphalian industrial districts, 81,713 were heads of farms and an additional 29,945 were workers. He also states that in the district he studies, 40 percent of all male agricultural workers were drafted; see *Entwicklung und Regelung*, pp. 11–13, 116–17. Tallies of those drafted from a county-by-county survey of eastern Westphalia for the first half of 1917 range from a low of 26 percent to a high of 39 percent for heads of family farms, and from 43 percent to 50 percent for agricultural workers: see StAD, M1 IIIE Nr. 492, and results from a similar survey for StAM, Kreis Steinfurt, LRA Nr. 367; RP Cologne report of 30 January 1917, LAK, 403/9046, p. 393; and RP Düsseldorf, 23 May 1917, LAK, 403/12326, p. 435.

14. Report of LR München-Gladbach, 4 December 1914, NWHStA, Reg. Düsseldorf 15080.

15. E.g., AK VII rejected all 699 petitions from the district of Herford in the spring of 1916: see StAD, M1 IIIE, Nr. 489.

16. The first postwar census, conducted in 1925, revealed that this trend had not been reversed: see Appendix Tables 4 and 5. And on postwar developments, see Bridenthal, "Beyond *Kinder*," pp. 148–66.

17. See report of RP Düsseldorf to the Prussian minister of the interior and similar reports from RP Arnsberg, Aachen, and Münster from September 1916, in ZStA II, Rep. 197A Teil II K Nr. 17, pp. 46–47, 121.

18. See the discussion in *Preussische Statistik*, vol. 257, pp. 1*–12*.

19. See Appendix Table 18.

20. The increase in the number of nonpeasant households keeping animals for their personal food needs means that the absolute figures understate the decline in holdings on peasant farms; see Appendix Table 19.

21. RP Arnsberg, 23 September 1917, and similar accounts in StAM, Reg. Münster 4833; also RP Aachen, 24 June 1918, LAK, 403/12327, p. 697.

22. See, e.g., an early report of this from the Rheinischer Viehhandelsverband, the official purchasing agent for meat, to the Reich Meat Office, 1 August 1916, LAK, 403/12580, pp. 365–67; and the report from the Prussian Meat Office to OpR of 12 August 1918, estimating the deficits from outside sources in the period since 15 December 1917 at 2,682,923 kilograms: LAK, 403/12585, p. 353.

23. Reports from LR Höxter, 2 June 1916, StAM, OP 4080; from Westfälischer Viehhandelsverband, 8 October 1917, StAM, Reg. Münster 4833; from RP Münster, 24 October 1917, StAM, OP 3940; and for the Rhineland, from RP Aachen, 2 February 1917, StAM, Reg. Münster 1314. See also materials in LAK, 403/12327, 12579–12580.

24. Reports of RP Arnsberg, 25 March 1918, and LWKW, 22 May 1918, StAM, OP 3943; LWKW, 20 September 1918, StAM, OP 3944; and RP Cologne, 29 April 1917, LAK, 403/12326, p. 370.

25. Tyszka, *Konsument*, p. 47. Such a judgment implicitly raises the question of alternatives. Although that question does not lie within the scope of this study, it might ultimately be best answered in a comparative analysis: for example, by committing labor, fertilizer, and machines to the agricultural sector, and by delaying the introduction of fixed prices—which were coupled from the first with confiscation and a system of *minimum*, not maximum, prices—the British were actually able to increase output during the war; see Hibbard, *Effects of the Great War*, and Litman, *Prices and Price Controls*. France's consumer-oriented maximum prices and tough controls on producers more closely ap-

proximated the German experience; see Augé-Laribé, "Agriculture in France," esp. pp. 69–99, and Barral, "Les conséquences," pp. 551–65. Very useful for a general comparative overview is Hardach, *First World War*, pp. 108–38.

26. See *MA*, 14 February 1917, story by Thiel.

27. *Stenographische Berichte über die Verhandlungen des Preussischen Hauses der Abgeordneten*, 22. Legislaturperiode, session of 16 February 1916, vol. 1, p. 367.

28. See, e.g., Prussian Minister of Agriculture Schorlemer-Lieser to all RP, 30 October 1915, StAM, OP 1821, 1. See also Baumgarten, "Der sittliche Zustand," p. 47; and in general, Aereboe, *Einfluss des Krieges*, pp. 99–100. This is also a constant theme of the monthly reports of RP throughout 1917 and 1918.

29. Kocka, *Klassengesellschaft im Krieg*, pp. 71, 73, 83, 92–93. See also Kocka, "First World War," pp. 101–24, and Kocka, "Weltkrieg und Mittelstand," pp. 431–57. Excellent in general on the civil servants is Kunz, "Verteilungskampf," pp. 347–84. The impact of food shortages on the middle classes became a constant theme in the monthly reports of the RP throughout 1917 and 1918.

30. Letter of 7 June 1917 from Adolf von Batocki to von Eisenhardt, who forwarded a copy to Kerckerinck, LVW, NL Kerckerinck, III Blb: Ako 38. See also the circular from Michaelis to all presidents of LWK, 9 May 1917, ZStA II, Rep. 197A, Generalia AI, Nr. 20, pp. 55–56; and the remarks by von Gayl reported in *WB*, 1 June 1916.

31. LR Halle, quoted in report of RP Minden, 22 July 1917, StAM, OP 3938; also similar complaints in StAM, OP 3936, and StAM, Kreis Siegen, LRA Nr. 1072.

32. Speech of LR Mayen to Rhenish Landfrauentag in Bonn, reported in *LWZR*, 23 March 1917. See also the discussion in Wiedtfeldt, *Bewirtschaftung von Korn*, p. 63; Baumgarten, "Der sittliche Zustand," p. 47; and Cronin, "Labor Insurgency," p. 29.

33. RP Cologne, 30 April 1917, LAK, 403/9046.

34. Quoted in *Kirchliches Amtsblatt* for the dioceses of Münster in a special issue directed at agrarian parishioners in 1916. This was part of the clergy's general efforts at encouraging compliance with the controlled economy, the so-called "Aufklärungsarbeit." See relevant materials in StAM, OP 3932, 3934, and 4098; StAM, Reg. Münster 1304; and StAM, Reg. Arnsberg I 15 Nr. 38. On the Rhineland, see the report of LR Schleiden, 3 March 1917, LAK, 403/12321; and of the Königliches Konsistorium der Rheinprovinz, 15 December 1916, LAK, 403/12319, p. 177. Regrettably, these materials yield only a sketchy picture of how the system actually functioned.

35. Aereboe, *Einfluss des Krieges*, p. 102; see also Baumgarten, "Der sittliche Zustand," pp. 27, 29.

36. Report of RP Düsseldorf, 3 March 1917, LAK, 403/12319, pp. 283ff. See also the general descriptions in Budde, "Landwirtschaft im Kreise," p. 29; Dartmann, "Landarbeiterverhältnisse Westfalens," p. 10; Lindner, "Die bäuerliche Wohnkultur," pp. 727–28; Busch, *Landbauzonen*, p. 65; and Henkelmann, *Zur Frage*, p. 27.

37. LR Lüdinghausen, report of 6 April 1917, StAM, Reg. Münster 4836; LR Waldbröl, report of 21 September 1917, LAK, 403/12320, p. 229; and regional reports to the Prussian Ministry of Justice for 1916 in Geheimes Staatsarchiv Berlin-Dahlem, Rep. 84a 1831.

38. LR Recklinghausen, 16 April 1917, StAM, Reg. Münster 4836.

39. See the vivid description in Eduard Schulte, *Kriegschronik*, pp. 299–300.

40. Reported in Tampke, *Ruhr and Revolution*, p. 41.

41. The archival record abounds with evidence of such violations. See, for example, the

report of the Westphalian PPS in Dortmund to the KEA, 26 November 1917, StAM, OP 3941; OpW, 4 December 1917, and Amtmann Delbrück to LR Paderborn, 7 April 1917, ZStA II, Rep. 197A Ii 8f vol. 1, pp. 133, 137; and materials for the Rhineland in LAK, 403/12321, pp. 525, 539, 565.

42. Report of RP Arnsberg, 30 September 1918, and RP Münster, 30 September 1918, both in StAM, OP 3944; similar report from RP Düsseldorf, 23 August 1918, LAK, 403/12328, p. 111.

43. Report of Westphalian PPS, June 1917, ZStA I, RMELW 458, p. 55.

44. See, e.g., RP Arnsberg, 10 August 1917, and RP Minden, 31 August 1917, StAM, OP 3938; and OpW at a meeting of provincial LR, 9 January 1918, StAM, OP 3941.

45. Report of 23 July 1917, StAM, OP 3938. See also Lindemann, *Die deutsche Stadtgemeinde*, pp. 83–84; Baumgarten, "Der sittliche Zustand," p. 26; the discussion in Liepmann, *Krieg und Kriminalität*, pp. 10, 164ff.; and Kohler, "Inflation," pp. 49–50.

46. RP Aachen, report of 26 November 1917, LAK, 403/12327, p. 279; RP Münster in speech to Landwirtschaftlicher Hauptverein für den Regierungsbezirk Münster, *MA*, 3 January 1918; OpW to Provincial Meat Office, 11 December 1917, StAM, OP 3941.

47. See appeals of Carl Legien, head of the socialist Free Trade Union movement, to KEA, February 1917, StAM, OP 3934; also protest of "Teuerungsausschuss" of Center party in Düsseldorf, 11 February 1916, LAK, 403/12314, p. 339.

48. See, e.g., Aereboe and Warmbold, *Preisverhältnisse*, pp. 26–27. See also reports of RP Minden, 20 January 1917, StAM, Reg. Münster 1313; and RP Arnsberg, 24 February 1917, StAM, OP 3934.

49. Emphasis on the food supply as the best barometer of urban unrest was a constant theme in official reports in the last two years of the war. On the conditions of Rhenish and Westphalian workers, see Tampke, *Ruhr and Revolution*, pp. 47–66; Lucas, *Zwei Formen*, pp. 237–52; and Nolan, *Social Democracy*, pp. 250–60.

50. Report from von Gayl, 3 April 1917, StAM, OP 3935. See also reports in *Rheinische Zeitung*, 13 December 1916 and 23 February 1917.

51. For the demands for the so-called "Anbauzwang," see *Volkswacht*, an SPD paper in Bielefeld, 5 December 1916; and RP Cologne, 24 February 1917, LAK, 403/12326, pp. 125ff. Konrad Adenauer, of course best known as the architect of a conservative German recovery in the post–World War II era, earned a reputation during the First World War as a special enemy of agriculture for advocating such direct controls on production decisions while he was a member of Cologne's city council and later mayor of the city. See the sharp response in *RhB*, 10 and 24 June 1916.

52. Michaelis's order of 23 March 1917, StAM, OP 3935; also *MA*, 26 and 28 March 1917.

53. See the descriptions in Lindner, "Die bäuerliche Wohnkultur"; and Weber-Kellermann, *Die deutsche Familie*, pp. 91–96.

54. LR Münster, report of 4 April 1917, StAM, Reg. Münster 4836. On the minimal results of searches, see RP Cologne, report of 23 March 1917, LAK, 403/12326; RP Düsseldorf, report of 30 April 1917, LAK, 403/9049, p. 964; LR Siegen, report of 15 December 1917, StAM, Kreis Siegen, LRA Nr. 1672; and *KVZ*, 25 June 1917. *MA* of 27 June 1917 reported an increase of only 4 percent for Westphalia.

55. See reports of the prosecution of violators in *MA*, 12 April, 12 and 13 May, and 17 June 1917.

56. OpW to all RP, 25 April 1918, StAM, OP 3943.

57. In the words of a local official in Krefeld, report of 7 October 1917, StAM, OP 3940.

58. Letter of 15 February 1918, together with related materials in LAK, 403/12582, pp. 165–69.

59. Letter of 25 April 1916, to LR Höxter, StAM, OP 4080. See also the list of similar complaints provided by Vereinigung der landwirtschaftlichen Kasinos von Barmen, 28 June 1916, LAK, 403/12580, pp. 553–60.

60. Letter dated 16 May 1916, StAM, OP 4080.

61. Report of 15 June 1918, StAM, Kreis Wittgenstein, LRA Nr. 133.

62. Report of 2 November 1918, ibid.

63. Her letter of 12 April 1918, and the official response of 15 April 1918, in ibid.

64. See Klein's letter to OpR, 9 January 1917, and response of LR Waldbröl, 3 February 1917, LAK, 403/12581, pp. 471–72.

65. See note 15 above.

66. See one case in which this measure was imposed on an entire area in the government district of Düsseldorf, behind in its collective deliveries: ZStA II, Rep. 197A III Nr. 16, pp. 152–55; the materials in StAD, M 2 Minden B 88; and StAM, Kreis Meschede, LRA Nr. 65.

67. Report from Städtisches Lebensmittelamt, Aachen, 4 March 1917, StAM, Reg. Münster 1314; RP Minden, 24 January 1917, and LR Lüdinghausen, 16 January 1917, StAM, Reg. Münster 4837; RP Minden, 22 September 1917, StAM, OP 3940.

68. LR Herford, report of 17 January 1915, StAM, OP 3926.

69. Letter dated 11 August 1918, StAM, Kreis Wittgenstein, LRA Nr. 133.

70. And a systematic review of relevant provincial archives, including the county-level record, indicates that such materials were not among those that officials felt particularly concerned to preserve for posterity. For other scattered examples from 1917, see StAD, M2 B 88 Kreis Minden. For 1916, see LAK, 403/12580, pp. 11, 571–76; and materials in StAM, Kreis Recklinghausen, Nr. 257.

71. The phrase "passive resistance" is used by Skalweit, *Die deutsche Kriegsernährungswirtschaft*, p. 3; see also *Rheinische Zeitung*, 13 December 1916, clipping in LAK, 403/12701.

72. Reported in *LWZR*, 9 May and 17 October 1919. See also comments of Chamber General Secretary Reinhardt, ibid., 2 May 1919.

73. For a contrasting view that puts a tremendous emphasis on the manipulative impact of interest-group leaders, see Münch, "Die agitatorische Tätigkeit," p. 343.

74. Wolf, *Peasant Wars*, p. 295.

75. Kocka points to these democratizing tendencies as one important piece of evidence against a model of increasing class tensions in the war: *Klassengesellschaft im Krieg*, pp. 112–15, 118. See also Flemming, *Landwirtschaftliche Interessen*, pp. 105–7; Schramm, "Militarisierung und Demokratisierung," pp. 376–97. On the unity of industry and labor behind strict controls, see Feldman: "German Business," p. 322, and "Economic and Social Problems," p. 13.

76. For the details of the proposal, see Flemming, *Landwirtschaftliche Interessen*, pp. 126–32. On the unanimous official rejection of the suggestion in the spring of 1918, see reports in StAM, OP 3943.

77. Report of RP Düsseldorf, 18 May 1918, and similar sentiments expressed by RP Aachen, LAK, 403/12309, pp. 181, 195.

78. From 1913 to 1918, the member savings in cooperatives associated with the Rhenish Peasant Association increased from 89 million marks to 158 million marks; see *RhGB*, 31 July 1919. In Westphalia, the increase was even greater, from 238 million marks in 1913 to over 516 million marks at the end of the war; see *MA*, 12 June 1918 and 8 August 1920; *WGZ*, 1 August 1918.

79. See also report of RP Cologne, 31 October 1917, and similar report of 30 January 1917, StAM, Reg. Münster 4834.

80. For an excellent summary of this convincing argument, see Beckmann, "Kreditpolitik und Kreditlage," pp. 79–140, 211–72. This was also a constant theme in the press of the cooperative associations. We will return to this topic in Chapter 7.

81. *WB*, 1 October 1917. This propaganda message was repeated ad nauseam throughout the war, appearing in the pages of the *RhB* as well.

82. *RhGB*, 31 July 1919; *WGZ*, 21 August 1919.

83. Along with the RP, they submitted monthly reports to the provincial high president, and their press organs were used for official publication of government regulations and prices. Meetings of local branches did provide an opportunity for airing complaints over specific wartime measures, particularly pricing policies; see, e.g., reports in *MA*, 6 and 16 March, 12 September, and 6 November 1917.

84. See Deist, *Militär- und Innenpolitik*, esp. pp. 264–67, 279–82, 668–89.

85. For characteristic expressions of the need to comply with restrictions out of informed self-interest see Crone-Münzebrock and Kerckerinck at the Westphalian general assembly meeting of December 1916, reported in *WB*, 1 January 1917; Crone-Münzebrock a year later, *WB*, 15 February 1918; the open letter from von Gayl, *RhB*, 31 October 1914; and *RhB*, 19 January 1918. Such public avowals are also explained in part by the fact that leading provincial officials were regularly in attendance at association meetings and undoubtedly carefully monitored the interest-group press.

86. *RhB*, 28 October 1916.

87. See, e.g., *RhB*, 4 August 1917.

88. *MA*, 8 July 1917; *RhB*, 5 February 1916, 31 August and 9 November 1918. See also responses to charges of the Christian Trade Unions in *RhB*, 8 May 1915, and 28 September 1918; Zeender, "German Center Party during World War I," passim; Schneider, *Die Christlichen Gewerkschaften*, pp. 425–27; and in general, Dülmen, "Der deutsche Katholizismus," pp. 347–76.

89. See the complaint of RP Münster, 31 March 1918, and Kreisausschuss Münster, 11 March 1918, over the public statements of Carl Herold, StAM, OP 3943; also report of the Christian Trade Union leader, Adam Stegerwald, after touring the Ruhr area in the summer of 1917, LAK, 403/12326, p. 627.

90. See Tampke, *Ruhr and Revolution*, pp. 33–70.

91. Quoted in Feldman, *Army, Industry*, p. 369.

92. See the stories in *WB*, 1 June and 1 July 1916.

93. See the biographical sketch of Kerckerinck in Jacobs, *Deutsche Bauernführer*, pp. 129–35.

94. Speech to Westphalian general assembly in Münster, 5 June 1917, reported in *RhB*, 9 June 1917. See also Loë-Bergerhausen's relentless elaboration of these themes in *RhB*, 8 and 22 December 1917, and 5 and 19 January 1918; also, Loë-Bergerhausen, *Organisation*, pp. 49ff.

95. On the nature of nineteenth-century conservatism, see the useful conceptual discus-

sion by Bowman, "Antebellum Planters," pp. 779–808.

96. *RhB*, 21 July 1917.

97. Notes from Freiherr von Twickel, Kerckerinck's predecessor, probably from 1916, in LVW, NL Kerckerinck, III Blb: Ako 37. See also Kerckerinck's "Gedanken zur innenpolitischen Lage," prepared for Ludendorff in July 1917, LVW, NL Kerckerinck, III A2: Polko 30.

98. *WB*, 15 June 1917.

99. At meeting of 19 December 1917, reported in *WB*, 1 January 1918; see also Schneider, *Die Christlichen Gewerkschaften*, pp. 403–4. München-Gladbach, referred to also as M.-Gladbach, is the present-day city of Mönchengladbach. The nineteenth- and early twentieth-century usage has been employed here throughout.

100. See Karl Bachem's letter to Felix Porsch, 18 April 1917, StAK, NL Bachem, Abt. 1006 Nr. 584; and Marx's reflections on the controversy over electoral reform, written in 1935, StAK, NL Marx, Abt. 1070 Nr. 222. On the clerical opposition to electoral reform, see Dülmen, "Der deutsche Katholizismus," p. 368; and Patemann, *Kampf um die preussische Wahlrechtsreform*, pp. 196–97.

101. In Weimar, Brauns would serve in many cabinets as Reich minister of labor. On the controversy between Loë-Bergerhausen and Brauns, see Bachem's notes on this meeting, 2 April 1918, and his account of a private meeting with Loë-Bergerhausen two days later, StAK, NL Bachem, Abt. 1006 Nr. 854. See also Schneider, *Die Christlichen Gewerkschaften*, pp. 434–36, 439–40.

102. For a discussion of these proposals, see Kerckerinck to Georg von Hertling, 19 May 1918, to Herold, 28 January 1918, and to Loë-Bergerhausen, 29 January 1918, LVW, NL Kerckerinck, III A1: Polko 14; and in general, Patemann, *Kampf um die preussische Wahlrechtsreform*, pp. 171, 196–97, 207.

103. *Bericht über die erste Tagung der Arbeiter-Zentrumswähler*, remarks of Albersmann, a trade-union functionary from Hagen, p. 23.

104. Ibid., Klost, a trade-union functionary from Essen, p. 7.

105. Ibid., Vogelsang, a representative to the Prussian parliament, p. 31.

106. Ibid., Vogelsang, p. 32.

107. Ibid., Klost, pp. 7–11. See also Kerckerinck's specific responses at the Westphalian association's general assembly in late October, reported in *WB*, 1 December 1918; Stegerwald's comments at a meeting of trade-union leaders in Düsseldorf, *MA*, 6 March 1917; Nipperdey, *Organisation der deutschen Parteien*, p. 282; Morsey, *Deutsche Zentrumspartei*, pp. 25–28; Focke, *Sozialismus aus christlicher Verantwortung*, pp. 61–63; Patemann, *Kampf um die preussische Wahlrechtsreform*, pp. 72, 168–69, 194; and in general, Mendershausen, "German Political Catholicism."

108. See letter of Stegerwald to Trimborn, 11 September 1915, StAK, NL Marx, Abt. 1070 Nr. 222, p. 25.

109. *MA*, 8 November 1917.

110. See Loë-Bergerhausen's correspondence with party leaders Gröber and Lensing in the spring of 1918, and Lensing to Kerckerinck, 8 March 1918, LVW, NL Kerckerinck, III A1: Polko 14. In general, see Heinen, "Zentrumspresse," esp. pp. 148ff; and Zeender, "German Center Party during World War I," pp. 450–67.

111. Morsey, *Deutsche Zentrumspartei*, pp. 58ff; Patemann, *Kampf um die preussische Wahlrechtsreform*, pp. 82–83; Mittmann, *Fraktion und Partei*, pp. 80, 321–22, 325–26,

332–33; Epstein, *Matthias Erzberger*, pp. 182ff; Zeender, "German Center Party during World War I," p. 464.

112. *Arbeiterwähler und Zentrumspartei. Vortrag (27 Juli 1918)* (Krefeld, 1918), p. 7, quoted in Morsey, *Deutsche Zentrumspartei*, p. 68.

113. *RhB*, 23 June 1917.

114. 28 June 1918, LVW, NL Kerckerinck, III A1: Polko 14.

115. See Kerckerinck's "Denkschrift über die Bauernbewegung im allgemeinen und den westfälischen Bauernverein im besonderen während der letzten zwei Jahre," dated July 1918, BA, NL Herold, Nr. 24; and Loë-Bergerhausen's thoughts, in *Organisation*.

116. LR Tecklenburg, report of 19 January 1917, StAM, Reg. Münster 4837; also RP Münster, report of 30 January 1917, StAM, Reg. Münster 4834.

Chapter Four

1. *KVZ*, 1 August 1918; *LWZR*, 26 July 1918; *WB*, 15 August 1918. Kerckerinck also cited the story at the general assembly meeting of 30 October 1918, reported in *WB*, 1 December 1918.

2. See Mantzke, "Zur Landarbeiterbewegung," pp. 87–96; Kohler, "Revolutionary Pomerania," pp. 250–93; and on the limited success of these incidents and the attempts of east Elbian estate owners to block worker organization, Flemming, *Landwirtschaftliche Interessen*, pp. 275–315.

3. See in particular Mattes, *Die bayerischen Bauernräte*; and Mitchell, *Revolution in Bavaria*, esp. pp. 24–25, 119–20. On other parts of Germany where councils showed no sympathy for the revolution and agrarian organization moved rapidly in a reactionary direction, see Osmond, "Second Agrarian Mobilization?"; Muth, "Entstehung der Bauern- und Landarbeiterräte," pp. 1–38; and Flemming, "Landwirtschaftskammer."

4. See, e.g., reports from LR Kempen, 1 January 1919, NWHStA, Reg. Düsseldorf 15087; RP Münster, 25 February 1919, StAM, Reg. Münster 2659; and RP Minden, 27 February 1919, StAM, OP 3945.

5. Protocol of meeting of all state PPS in Munich, 16 January 1919, ZStA I, RWM 378. This sentiment was clearly echoed at the meeting of the steering committee of the Reichsernährungsministerium, 11 July 1919, BA, R 43 I/1255, pp. 56ff.

6. Reports from LR Paderborn, 11 March 1919, StAM, OP 3945; Demobilmachungskommissar for Minden, 4 February 1919, StAM, Reg. Münster 3776; and KA Coesfeld, 29 March 1919, StAM, Reg. Münster 3777.

7. See, e.g., report from RP Münster to PSV, 16 October 1918, StAM, Reg. Münster 3780.

8. Eisenbahndirektion Essen to Reichsernährungsminister, RWM, RMI, Prussian MI, 12 March 1919; also reports from Minister der öffentlichen Arbeiten to RMI, 29 March 1919, 20 April 1919, and 26 May 1919, ZStA I, RMI 13090/ 7, pp. 2, 4, 6, 16.

9. Reports from Lüdinghausen, 1 March 1919, StAM, Reg. Münster 3776; LR Tecklenburg, 30 January 1919, and similar reports in StAM, Reg. Münster 3780; also LR Ahaus, 4 March 1919, and KA Höxter, 2 March 1919, StAM, OP 3945.

10. Oberwachmeister of Borken to LR Borken, 4 August 1919, StAM, Reg. Münster 3780.

11. Reported in *KVZ*, 3 October 1918.

12. *Westfälische Allgemeine Volks-Zeitung*, 26 February 1919. See also ibid., 13 March 1919; and report of Council of Workers and Soldiers in Cologne, *KVZ*, 11 November 1918.

13. *Westfälische Allgemeine Volks-Zeitung*, 5 August 1919.

14. Ibid., 29 February 1919.

15. See, e.g., reports of Council of Workers and Soldiers in Münster, 7 and 13 March 1919, StAM, Reg. Münster 3777. See also *MA*, 5 April 1919.

16. Reported in *MA*, 10 July 1919.

17. Ibid., 10 August 1919.

18. *MA*, 11 July 1919; reports of such criminal cases are numerous in *MA* throughout the winter, spring, and summer of 1919.

19. See, e.g., incidents reported in *MA*, 30 March, 12 and 13 July 1919.

20. See the accounts from local officials in StAM, OP 3945; and the report of similar events in Olpe in the Rhineland the following fall, *KVZ*, 21 October 1919.

21. *MA*, 1 May 1919. See also the discussion of peasants arming themselves for protection against theft at a conference of LR from RB Minden, 3 February 1919, StAM, OP 3945, and the approval of such efforts in *WB*, 15 February, 15 June, and 1 August 1919; also the discussion focusing on east Elbian districts and the paramilitary overtones of these militia organizations in Flemming, "Bewaffnung des 'Landvolks,'" pp. 7–36.

22. See, e.g., report of RP Arnsberg, 16 January 1920, StAM, OP 3970. The same conclusion was reached at a conference attended by all Westphalian LR in Dortmund, March 1920: protocol dated 30 March 1920, StAM, OP 3947. This topic will be discussed at length in Chapter 5.

23. Schumacher, *Land und Politik*, p. 141; Mathews, "German Social Democrats," pp. 562–67.

24. On the background to SPD agrarian policy in the Wilhelmine period, see Lehmann, *Agrarfrage*. On agrarian policy during the revolution and the early years of Weimar see, in particular, Schumacher, *Land und Politik*, pp. 317–53; Mathews, "German Social Democrats," esp. pp. 533–78.

25. Schumacher, *Land und Politik*, pp. 137ff. See also Schmidt's insistence on maintaining the controlled economy, *Sitzungsberichte der verfassungsgebenden Preussischen Landesversammlung*, session of 29 March 1919, vol. 1, pp. 1049ff.

26. BA, R 43 I/ 2534, pp. 18ff.

27. BA, R 43 I/ 1255, pp. 117ff., and Reichsministerium meeting of 16 June 1919, ibid., p. 153. In general, see also Breitman, *German Socialism*, pp. 64–65.

28. See the measures ordering controls and the record of peasant protest throughout the spring and summer in StAM, Kreis Meschede, LRA Nr. 65; StAM, Kreis Recklinghausen, Nr. 238 and Nr. 240; and StAM, Kreis Coesfeld, LRA Nr. 447.

29. Peasant and Agricultural Workers Council in Düsseldorf to OpR, LAK, 403/12605, p. 325. The council movement will be discussed in detail below. See accounts of similar protests in *MA*, 9 April and 22 July 1919; and from the summer and fall of 1919, in StAM, OP 3970.

30. Report of RP Minden on conditions in the county of Herford, 16 August 1919, StAM, OP 3970; see also report of Amtmann Wulfen, 16 May 1919, StAM, Kreis Recklinghausen, Nr. 240.

31. RP Minden, 17 October 1919, StAM, OP 3970.

32. Materials in StAM, Kreis Recklinghausen, Nr. 240, and records of similar complaints from the spring of 1919 in Nr. 238; also StAM, Kreis Meschede, LRA Nr. 65.

33. From a local official in Schleiden to OpR, 29 August 1919, LAK, 403/12584, pp. 209–10.

34. Reported in *Volkswacht*, an SPD paper in Bielefeld, 28 July 1919. See also the report of another incident in the same region, ibid., 2 August and 11 August 1919; and reports of these events from Versmold, 11 August 1919, and RP Minden, 16 August and 28 August 1919, StAM, OP 3970.

35. See, e.g., report of RP Minden, 17 October 1919, StAM, OP 3970.

36. Schumacher, *Land und Politik*, pp. 90ff. See also Flemming, *Landwirtschaftliche Interessen*, pp. 162–69; Flemming, "Landwirtschaftskammer," pp. 315–18; and Kovan, "Reichs-Landbund," pp. 70–82.

37. On these see Rürup, *Arbeiter- und Soldatenräte*, and Moore, *Injustice*, pp. 316–53. In general, see Rürup, "Demokratische Revolution," pp. 278–301; and Mommsen, "German Revolution," pp. 21–54.

38. Protocol in NWHStA, RW 152/ 167, pp. 193–94. See also *LWZR*, 15 November 1918; *RhB*, 23 November 1918; and the discussions in Schumacher, *Land und Politik*, pp. 395–98; Osmond, "Second Agrarian Mobilization?"; and Muth, "Entstehung der Bauern- und Landarbeiterräte."

39. See the protocols of the initial meetings of provincial leaders, 16 and 27 November 1918, and Schorlemer-Lieser's account to the steering committee of the chamber, NWHStA, RW 152/ 167, pp. 194, 217, 212. For examples of the forms that these organizations took, in some instances, under direction of the chamber's official in charge of the local agricultural school, see the collection of reports in NWHStA, RW 152/ 167.

40. General letter from Wurm, state secretary in the KEA, 16 January 1919, StAM, Reg. Arnsberg I 15 Nr. 14; copy of the appeal, 12 November 1918, NWHStA, RW 152/ 167.

41. LWKR to OpR, 16 December 1918; also Schorlemer-Lieser to Preussisches Landes-Oekonomie Collegium, 12 December 1918, both in NWHStA, RW 152/ 167, pp. 286–87, 315.

42. See, e.g., "I. Bericht über die Versammlung des Vertrauensmänner-Ausschusses der Landwirte der Kreise M. Gladbach, Gladbach und Rheydt am Sonntag, den 15ten September 1918," as well as the exchange over the organization's activities between LWKR and LR Gladbach in December and January, NWHStA, RW 152/ 167, pp. 225–36, 340–41.

43. *LWZR*, 22 November 1918.

44. Ibid., 29 November 1918.

45. Published in ibid., 20 December 1918. See the even more outspoken draft version, NWHStA, RW 152/ 167, p. 290.

46. Evidence on the councils is scanty: reports on them typically include nothing more than the sketchiest information on their membership and activities. In addition to the materials cited below, the account here is based largely on the scattered reports of local officials in StAM, Reg. Arnsberg I 15 Nr. 14; StAM, Kreis Tecklenburg, Kreis Ausschuss, Nr. 24 and Nr. 25; StAM, Kreis Wittgenstein, LRA Nr. 679; the collection of reports in Landesarchiv Berlin, Deutscher Landkreistag 19; from eastern Westphalia, StAD, M2

Höxter Nr. 279; an unsigned report giving provincial totals by county for November 1919, in StAM, OP 3945; isolated reports in StAM, OP 4046, and StAM, Reg. Münster 2659; and the report in *LWZW*, 22 August 1919.

47. Report of meeting of Provincial and County Councils of Peasants and Agricultural Workers in Hamm, 11 April 1919, StAM, Kreis Steinfurt, LRA Nr. 1557.

48. Letter of Carl Rasche to LR Steinfurt, 28 April 1919, ibid.

49. LWKW to RP Arnsberg, 17 March 1919, StAM, Kreis Steinfurt, LRA Nr. 1557.

50. Ledebur, head of LWKW, to RP Arnsberg, 16 April 1919, StAM, Reg. Arnsberg I 15 Nr. 14; also report in *MA*, 22 March 1919.

51. Circular of 13 May 1919, LWKW to all RP, StAM, Kreis Gelsenkirchen, LRA Nr. 68.

52. See the report of the meeting of the Provincial Council, 20 May 1919, StAM, Reg. Arnsberg I 15 Nr. 14.

53. Letter of 4 May 1919, LVW, NL Kerckerinck, III Bla: Ako 25.

54. See the comments of Reinhardt, general secretary of the Rhenish chamber, at the chamber steering committee meeting, 20 March 1919, NWHStA, RW 152/ 408; and Reinhardt's letters to Oekonomierat Bürgsens, 6 March 1919, and to Trier Peasant Association, 4 December 1918, NWHStA, RW 152/ 167, pp. 42, 248.

55. See the protocol of steering committee meeting of Rhenish chamber, 17 July 1919, NWHStA, RW 152/ 408; also Schorlemer-Lieser in response to questions from Deutscher Landwirtschaftsrat about the progress of the council movement in the Rhineland, 16 July 1919, NWHStA, RW 152/ 167, pp. 276–77.

56. This is a central argument in Moeller, "Dimensions of Social Conflict," pp. 159–63.

57. Mattes, *Die bayerischen Bauernräte*, pp. 49–50.

58. Kerckerinck to the Silesian Count Hans Praschma, 1 July 1919, LVW, NL Kerckerinck, III A1: Polko 15. On Westphalia, see *WB*, 1 February, 15 February, and 1 August 1919; *MA*, 15 May 1920. On the Rhineland, see *RhB*, 20 July 1918; materials in "Rheinische Bauernbewegung 1920–1922," in particular the report of RP Düsseldorf, September 1921, on the expansion of the Rhenish association up to that point, NWHStA, Reg. Düsseldorf 15776; and RB Aachen to OpR, 28 May 1920, LAK, 403/13312, p. 32. On the structure of decision-making in the organization, see Kerckerinck's reflections at the provincial steering committee meeting in November 1927, reported in *WB*, 30 November 1927.

59. *LWZW*, 9 June 1920.

60. Reinhardt's remarks, reported in *LWZR*, 9 May 1919; see also his lengthy draft "Zur Bildung der landwirtschaftlichen Berufsvertretung," dated 30 March 1919, NWHStA, RW 152/ 87, vol. 1, pp. 25–30.

61. *WB*, 1 August 1919, and 1 June 1920.

62. Reported in *Rheinische Volksstimme*, 13 December 1921, copy in ZStA I, RLB 1685; *RhB*, 3 September and 9 December 1921. At this time, almost 80 percent of Peasant Association membership was concentrated in the governmental districts of Cologne, Aachen, and Düsseldorf.

63. See LR Steinfurt, report of 26 May 1919, StAM, LRA Steinfurt, Nr. 1557; also reports in *LWZW*, 5 September, 26 September, and 10 October 1919, and 4 June and 8 October 1920.

64. See, e.g., *RhB*, 1 February 1919, and Herold to Landwirtschaftlicher Hauptverein für den Regierungsbezirk Münster, *MA*, 24 January 1919.

65. *RhB*, 29 March 1919.

66. On the strikes of industrial workers in the Ruhr, see, e.g., Lucas, *Zwei Formen*, pp. 155–236; Tampke, *Ruhr and Revolution*, pp. 69–143; Moore, *Injustice*, pp. 328–53; Feldman, "Arbeitskonflikte im Ruhrbergbau," pp. 168–223; Oertzen, "Die grossen Streiks," pp. 238–45; and Eliasberg, *Ruhrkrieg*, pp. 47–64.

67. Beckmann, "Bauer im Zeitalter," p. 747.

68. Figures are provided in "Grundlage für die Preismessung," BA, R 43 I/ 1254, pp. 15ff. On declines of feed imports in general, see League of Nations, *Agricultural Production*, p. 43.

69. See in general, Ostertag, "Versorgung," pp. 43–76.

70. On the background to controls, see the materials in StAM, OP 4046, and LAK, 403/12596; also *LWZR*, 3 May 1918.

71. Ostertag, "Versorgung," p. 72.

72. Meeting of Provinzialfettstelle, 17 May 1919, LAK, 403/12604.

73. Ibid.

74. Reich Fettstelle to PSV, 26 April 1919, and OpW to PSV, 28 May 1919, ZStA II, Rep. 197A, Va, Nr. 12, vol. 1.

75. From the steering committee of the Ortsgruppen des bergischen Milchverwertungsverbandes, 3 June 1919, LAK, 403/12604; also story in *MA*, 6 June 1919.

76. OB Elberfeld to RP Düsseldorf, 4 May 1919, LAK, 403/12604, pp. 117–18.

77. Report of 12 April 1919, StAM, OP 4046; and a similar report from LR Opladen to OpR, 28 May 1919, LAK, 403/12604, p. 171. In his words, "Auf dem Gebiet der Milchpreise herrscht volle Anarchie."

78. LR Altena to OpW, 20 June 1919, StAM, OP 4046; see also resolution of Landwirtschaftliche Lokalabteilung Elberfeld-Barmen, Lennep-Remscheid, calling for an end to all controls, ZStA II, Rep. 87B, Nr. 15909, p. 57.

79. See the numerous reports of outright refusals to deliver, as well as many reports of independent price-setting action, in LAK, 403/12603–12605, and StAM, OP 4046.

80. LR Arnsberg, 17 June 1919, StAM, OP 4046.

81. Mathews, "German Social Democrats," p. 548.

82. *Deutsche Tageszeitung*, 23 February 1919.

83. Telegram dated 1 July 1919, StAM, OP 4046. See also complaint from OpW to PSV, 21 July 1919, contesting Severing's authority, and Severing's response to a similar complaint from OpR, LAK, 403/12605, pp. 261, 287.

84. *Volksblatt*, Bochum, citing Severing's letter to the Peasant and Agricultural Workers Council in Bielefeld, 4 September 1919.

85. See, e.g., protest of Landwirtschaftlicher Lokalverein in Balve, 4 August 1919, StAM, OP 4047; telegram from OB Cologne over lack of milk at fixed prices, 28 August 1919, LAK, 403/12604.

86. Report of LR Brilon, 1 August 1919, StAM, OP 4047.

87. Report of 8 August 1919, LAK, 403/12604.

88. See, e.g., telegram of OB Cologne, 3 January 1920, LAK, 403/12605, p. 532.

89. Protocol in ibid., p. 508.

90. Renewed threats to halt all deliveries from the Interessengemeinschaft der Kreis-

bauernschaften Köln-Stadt and Köln-Mühlheim, reported by RP Cologne, 12 May 1920, LAK, 403/13312. See also Freie Bauernschaft, Kreisgruppe Geldern to OpR, 27 September 1919, LAK, 403/12605, p. 5; and similar accounts in StAM, OP 4076.

91. LWKW to RP Arnsberg, 17 March 1919, StAM, Reg. Arnsberg I 15 Nr. 14.

92. *VdRT*, session of 12 April 1919, vol. 327, pp. 1001ff.

93. Reinhardt at meeting of 20 March 1919, NWHStA, RW 152/ 408.

94. *LWZR*, 9 September 1919.

95. Protocol of meeting of LWKR steering committee, 21 and 22 November 1919, NWHStA, RW 152/ 408. See similar stories in *LWZW*, 3 October 1919, and *LWZR*, 17 October 1919.

96. Resolution of LWKR opposing the controlled economy, *LWZR*, 2 February 1920.

97. *RhB*, 20 January 1920.

98. Report of RP Aachen to OpR on activities of a "neutrale Bauernschaft," headed by the director of the local agricultural school, 3 September 1919, LAK, 403/12584, pp. 283–84.

99. Meeting of a subcommittee of Landwirtschaftlicher Hauptverein für den Regierungsbezirk Münster, 3 January 1920, reported in *LWZW*, 30 January 1920.

100. In general, see Osmond, "Second Agrarian Mobilization?"

101. See in general, Morsey, *Deutsche Zentrumspartei*, pp. 79–99, 159–67, 163–64; and Gerhard A. Ritter, "Kontinuität und Umformung," p. 371. These topics will be discussed in greater detail in Chapter 6.

102. *RhB*, 5 April 1919. See also the attack on Heinrich Brauns, *RhB*, 19 April 1919, as well as 2 February, 10 May, and 6 June 1919.

103. Christliche Bauernschaft der Rheinlande, *Bericht über die erste vorbereitende Versammlung*, pp. 3–12.

104. He became head of the national party organization in 1920. See Morsey, *Deutsche Zentrumspartei*, pp. 570–76.

105. Trimborn to the Silesian Count Hans Praschma, 11 June 1919. Praschma apparently forwarded the letter immediately to Kerckerinck: copy in LVW, NL Kerckerinck, III Bla: Ako 25.

106. Ibid.

107. See Marx's notes on the meeting of Rhenish Center party leaders, StAK, NL Marx, Abt. 1070, Nr. 209, pp. 5–6. Another clear indication of the Center connection of the Christian Peasantry was the open support given it by the *KVZ*; see, e.g., 30 March and 23 April 1919.

108. Christliche Bauernschaft der Rheinlande, *Jahresbericht für das Geschäftsjahr 1919*, p. 11. By July, seven "Bauernsekretäre" had been created in Schleiden, Bonn-Land, Euskirchen, Geilenkirchen, München-Gladbach, Rheinbach, and Köln-Land.

109. Kerckerinck to Praschma, 1 July 1919, LVW, NL Kerckerinck, III A1: Polko 15.

110. *RhB*, 12 December 1918.

111. *RhB*, 14 June 1919. See also ibid., 26 April; 10, 17, and 24 May; and 7 June 1919.

112. See Reinhardt's comments at steering committee meeting of LWKR, 20 March 1919, protocol in NWHStA, RW 152/ 408; also critical queries from Bollig, 24 May 1919, and Wilhelm Busch, a loyal Center party member and under secretary in the Prussian Ministry of Agriculture, 31 May 1919, about the chamber's interference with the work of the Christian Peasantry, as well as Schorlemer-Lieser's response, 17 June 1919, emphasiz-

ing the need for severing ties to all political parties: all in NWHStA, RW 152/ 87, vol. 1, pp. 162–68.

113. *RhB*, 31 May, 7 June, and 9 August 1919. See also *KVZ*, 3 August 1919; and Schumacher, *Land und Politik*, pp. 402ff.

114. *LWZR*, 4 April 1919; and *RhB*, 15 May 1919.

115. See the accounts in *LWZR*, 4 April and 9 May 1919; and Osmond, "Second Agrarian Mobilization?" pp. 177–79.

116. See notes of Reinhardt, general secretary of LWKR, on meeting of 2 April 1919, NWHStA, RW 152/ 87, vol. 1, pp. 65–66.

117. LWKR to RP Aachen, 28 April 1919, LAK, 403/12597, and *LWZR*, 2 May 1919.

118. See *KVZ*, 2, 5, 16, and 17 May 1919.

119. Protocol of meeting of 2 April 1919, NWHStA, RW 152/ 87, vol. 1, pp. 65–66.

120. *RhB*, 12 and 19 July 1919; also Heinrich Pflug of the Free Peasantry to Schorlemer-Lieser, 20 June 1919, NWHStA, RW 152/ 87, vol. 1, p. 215.

121. Loë-Bergerhausen's account of meeting with Free Peasantry leaders in letter to Schorlemer-Lieser, 16 August 1919, NWHStA, RW 152/ 87, vol. 2, pp. 51–61.

122. See, in particular, the discussion above, pp. 81–83. Also see, e.g., letter of OpR to PSV, 6 October 1919, LAK, 403/12584; and scattered accounts of the Free Peasantry's activities in LAK, 403/12603; LAK, 403/12597; LAK, 403/12604; and LAK, 403/13312.

123. Notes to Schorlemer-Lieser on August meeting of Peasant Association and Free Peasantry representatives, NWHStA, RW 152/ 87, vol. 2, pp. 62–64.

124. Loë-Bergerhausen to Schorlemer-Lieser, 13 September 1919, NWHStA, RW 152/ 87, vol. 2, p. 84.

125. Ibid.

126. *KVZ*, 2 November 1919.

127. See, in general, the exchanges between Schorlemer-Lieser and Reinhardt in October 1919, NWHStA, RW 152/ 87, vol. 2, pp. 145–46; Osmond, "Second Agrarian Mobilization?" pp. 179–81; and Rhenish Peasant Association to OpR, 26 March 1920, LAK, 441/25519, p. 575.

128. Wegmann, *Die leitenden staatlichen Verwaltungsbeamten*, p. 302.

129. See *LWZW*, 22 August, 5 September, and 10 October 1919.

130. *WB*, 1 October 1919.

131. *WB*, 1 September 1919.

132. Kerckerinck to Praschma, 31 July 1919, LVW, NL Kerckerinck, III B1a: Ako 25.

133. Letter of Kerckerinck to Ledebur, 16 January 1920, LVW, NL Kerckerinck, III B1a: Ako 25.

134. *LWZW*, 31 October 1919.

135. On its activities, see Flemming, *Landwirtschaftliche Interessen*, pp. 161ff.

136. See the summary of these developments in Osmond, "Second Agrarian Mobilization?"

137. On the discussion of laws governing chamber membership, see Flemming, *Landwirtschaftliche Interessen*, pp. 171–74; and Flemming, "Landwirtschaftskammer," pp. 318–21.

138. See Flemming, "Grossagrarische Interessen," p. 757.

139. A complete discussion of conservative agrarian politics and the Center occupies Chapter 6.

Chapter Five

1. *KVZ*, 2 December 1919.

2. See the comments of the PSV in a letter to all RP, 2 April 1919, StAM, OP 3945.

3. See, in particular, Feldman, "Political Economy," pp. 180–206.

4. This brief summary draws heavily on the excellent account of Holtfrerich, *Die deutsche Inflation*, esp. pp. 97–115, 118–20, 167, 198–99, 219–20, 227, 328–29. Holtfrerich's treatment critically assesses and surpasses the works of Laursen and Pedersen, *German Inflation*, and Graham, *Exchange, Prices*. Still extremely useful is Bresciani-Turroni, *Economics of Inflation*. On heavy industry in the inflation, see Feldman, *Iron and Steel*; and Feldman and Homburg, *Industrie und Inflation*. For a comparison of the process of decontrol for agriculture and for industry, see Schieck, "Kampf um die deutsche Wirtschaftspolitik," pp. 233–35.

5. See the references and excellent critical discussion in Osmond, "German Peasant Farmers," pp. 289–307.

6. OpW, 11 October 1919, LAK, 403/12238, p. 25. See also the general description in Dade, "Preiskonjunktur," pp. 243–48.

7. See reports on this phenomenon from LR in border regions, NWHStA, Reg. Düsseldorf 9079. Also complaint from Prussian Provincial Meat Office, 23 February 1920, StAM, Reg. Münster 3781; report from a customs inspector in Vreden, 15 December 1919, StAM, Reg. Münster 3779; and in general, Kohler, "Inflation."

8. This according to the minister of the interior, 19 January 1920, LAK, 403/12237, p. 135.

9. Report of Reichs- und Staatskommissar für den Befehlsbereich des VII. AK Münster, 9 September 1919, StAM, Reg. Münster 3779; and protocol of meeting of RWM representatives with government authorities in Aachen, 30 April 1920, ZStA I, RWM 12208, p. 69.

10. Report of LR Meppen, a district in Lower Saxony bordering on Westphalia, 9 September 1919, StAM, Reg. Münster 3779; also RP Aachen, 4 November 1920, LAK, 403/12237, p. 329, and stories in *MA*, 22 January and 30 June 1921, that falling prices in Germany led to an increase in smuggling. See also RP Aachen to PSV, 6 June 1920, ZStA I, RWM 12208, p. 94; RP Aachen to OpR, 16 December 1921, LAK, 403/13331; RP Münster, 5 December 1922, StAM, OP 3972; and reports in *MA*, 24 August and 21 October 1922.

11. RP Cologne to OpR, 9 September 1919, LAK, 403/12584, pp. 277–78.

12. For these records of 1919 and 1920, see LAK, 403/12584–12585. See also reports of explicit refusals to deliver animals at fixed prices from the Vorstand des landwirtschaftlichen Kreisvereins, Warendorf, reported in *MA*, 2 August 1920.

13. See the protests from the local agricultural association in Dielingen, 5 May 1920, StAM, OP 3948; and from the same organization, 26 May 1920, StAM, OP 3947.

14. *Reichsgesetzblatt*, 1920/II, Nr. 194, 22 September 1920.

15. LR Krefeld to RB Düsseldorf, 16 February 1920, LAK, 403/12385; for similar assessments from Westphalia, see materials in StAM, OP 4077 and OP 3947.

16. 1 October 1920, BA, R 43 I/ 1257, p. 259.

17. To LR and RP, 23 May 1920, StAM, OP 3971.

18. *VdRT*, session of 7 December 1920, vol. 346, p. 1504.

19. This assessment contrasts with the judgments of Gessner, *Agrarverbände*, p. 19; of Kovan, "Reichs-Landbund," pp. 289ff.; and with the claims of VDDB, reported in *RhB*, 11 September 1920. On the limited influence of agrarian spokesmen, see Schumacher, *Land und Politik*, p. 166.

20. See, e.g., the annual report of the office for control of usurious prices for the Rhenish-Westphalian area, attached to the office of the Police President in Essen, for 1922, StAM, Reg. Arnsberg I 15 Nr. 42, p. 407; reports from local authorities in 1920–21 in StAM, OP 3972; LAK, 403/13305, pp. 39–41; and the general discussion in Holtfrerich, *Die deutsche Inflation*, pp. 86–87, 90–91. For early demands for reinstitution of controls, see official reports from late 1920 in LAK, 403/13328, pp. 65–69; reports of similar demands from consumer groups in Westphalia, in *MA*, late 1920 into 1921; and a report from OpW on conditions in Westphalia in the late summer of that year, 14 August 1921, BA, R 43 I/ 1259, pp. 175–78.

21. *VdRT*, session of 26 April 1920, vol. 333, p. 5455.

22. *MA*, 12 August 1920.

23. See Barmeyer, *Andreas Hermes*, pp. 29–30; and Topf, *Die Grüne Front*, pp. 109–11.

24. To executive committee of ADGB, 18 August 1920, *Kabinett Fehrenbach*, p. 127; see also his comments to the meeting of the Center's parliamentary steering committee, 26 June 1920, in *Protokolle der Reichstagsfraktion*, pp. 23–26.

25. "Bericht über die erste Sitzung der Arbeitskammer westfälischer Preisprüfungsstellen am 5. Oktober 1920 in Dortmund," NWHStA, Reg. Düsseldorf 9075, pp. 173ff.

26. Meeting of 5 June 1920, reported in *RhB*, 15 May 1920.

27. There are regrettably few regional treatments of agriculture in the inflation (or, for that matter, in the 1920s) to compare with the detailed studies of the prewar period that form the basis of the discussion in Chapter 1. For exceptions, see Plattmann, "Entwicklung und Stand," esp. pp. 457–64; Willy Schmidt, "Die landwirtschaftlichen Verhältnisse"; and Oberhansberg, "Die landwirtschaftlichen Betriebsverhältnisse."

28. Briefs, "Aufbau und Tätigkeit," p. 60.

29. Reports from Westphalian PPS in Dortmund, 28 September 1920, NWHStA, Reg. Düsseldorf 9075; and from PPS Münster, 7 October 1920, StAM, OP 3971.

30. Report of district PPS, 10 February 1922, NWHStA, Reg. Düsseldorf 41712, pp. 147ff.; see also report from OB Düren to RP Aachen, 24 December 1921, ZStA I, RWM 11976, p. 73.

31. Report of meeting of producer and consumer representatives under the aegis of municipal authorities, 15 June 1921, LAK, 403/13331.

32. See the reports of those arrested in LAK, 403/13331, pp. 38–39, 497, 543, 573, 581, 583.

33. Letter dated 2 June 1921, and the response, upholding the action, dated 21 July 1921, ibid., pp. 497, 543.

34. Official resolution of LWKR, quoted in *LWZR*, 24 June 1921, and related story, "Marktpreis oder Preiswucher?" in ibid., 6 June 1921; see also *RhB*, 28 May 1921.

35. Reported in *Rheinische Zeitung*, 14 July 1921, copy in LAK, 403/13360.

36. *Sozialistische Republik*, Nr. 130, and *Kölner Tageblatt*, Nr. 265, cited in *RhB*, 16 July 1921.

37. *Stenographische Berichte über die Verhandlungen des 61. Rheinischen Provinzial-*

landtags, meeting of 15 July 1921, pp. 235, 238.

38. Bollig at meeting of Rhenish Center party provincial congress, reported in *KVZ*, 3 November 1921.

39. *RhB*, 15 October 1921. See reports of similar tensions in Westphalia in the fall of 1921, *MA*, 5 October 1920, and the materials in StAM, OP 4010.

40. To Prussian minister of agriculture, 23 May 1921, StAM, OP 4010.

41. See, e.g., RP Cologne, report of 12 October 1921, LAK, 403/13331, p. 665.

42. Report of RP Aachen, 5 January 1922, LAK, 403/13331, p. 757; see also Hermes' comments at the cabinet meeting of 26 November 1921, *Kabinett Wirth*, vol. 1, p. 438.

43. See the circular from Prussian minister of the interior to all Op, 14 September 1921, LAK, 403/13331, pp. 717–19.

44. Report of 8 December 1921, StAM, OP 4010.

45. Niklas, an expert on livestock markets, in discussions of meat imports in the RMELW, 22 December 1921, Geheimes Staatsarchiv, Berlin-Dahlem, Rep. 84a 1797.

46. See, e.g., report from LR Hattingen, 7 November 1921, StAM, OP 3980.

47. For the background on these committees see, for Westphalia, StAM, OP 4043, and for the Rhineland, LAK, 403/13339–13341 and 13343.

48. This was the case in Westphalia by September 1922: see materials in StAM, OP 4043. The Rhenish Peasant Association suspended all support for the Rhenish committee the following summer; see letter of 5 June 1923, LAK, 403/13340.

49. Letter from Verbraucherkammer für die Provinz Westfalen, 23 May 1922, StAM, OP 4043.

50. See, e.g., reports of RP Düsseldorf to OpR, 23 June and 17 October 1922, LAK, 403/13340.

51. *WB*, 1 November 1922.

52. See records of hearings for nondeliverers, LAK, 403/13343, pp. 75ff., and LAK, 403/13340. Those producing more than fifty liters a day were not subject to obligations to deliver to specific dairies, and they were less easily supervised; prosecution, thus, usually had a greater impact on peasants with smaller holdings of land and livestock.

53. On the discrepancy between German domestic and world market prices, see Appendix Table 21; also *Wirtschaft und Statistik* 1 (1921), p. 376.

54. "Bericht über die Sitzung im Reichswirtschaftsministerium über die Kundgebung der landwirtschaftlichen Körperschaften zu der Frage der Bewirtschaftung landwirtschaft-licher Erzeugnisse am 13.1.20," issued by the Reichsassuschuss der deutschen Landwirts-chaft, LVW, NL Kerckerinck, III B1b: Ako 14.

55. Letter from Wilhelm Peters, successor to Schmidt as PSV, to all Op, 12 January 1920, StAM, OP 3981.

56. See the order from PSV to OpR, 2 February 1920, LAK, 403/13348, pp. 1–7; also circular of 30 March 1920, LAK, 403/13312, pp. 277–78.

57. Hermes to PSV, Hagedorn, 14 August 1920, ZStA II, Rep. 197A, IIo, Nr. 1, vol. 1, p. 326.

58. Meeting of the supervisory council of the Reich Grain Office (Reichsgetreidestelle), 13 December 1920, ZStA II, Rep. 197A, IIo, Nr. 1, vol. 2, pp. 53ff.

59. RMELW report of 27 November 1920, BA, R 43 I/ 1258, p. 39.

60. At a meeting in the Reichstag with agrarian representatives, including Schorlemer-Lieser, Crone-Münzebrock, and Herold, ZStA II, Rep. 197A, IIo, Nr. 1, vol. 2, pp. 67ff.

61. Meeting of supervisory board of Reich Grain Office, 23 November 1920, ibid., pp. 37ff.

62. Meeting of same organization, 14 February 1921, ibid., pp. 144ff. See also Bresciani-Turroni, *Economics of Inflation*, pp. 30–32.

63. See the call for continued controls on all grain reserves from RP Aachen, 21 January 1921, LAK, 403/13305, p. 114.

64. Speech to Reichstag, *VdRT*, session of 6 December 1920, vol. 346, pp. 1469ff.

65. Speech to Reichstag, *VdRT*, session of 29 January 1921, vol. 347, p. 2283.

66. Speech to Reichstag, *VdRT*, session of 14 June 1921, vol. 349, p. 3850; also Herold's report of Hermes' position to meeting of Center parliamentary steering committee, 12 May 1921, in *Protokolle der Reichstagsfraktion*, p. 206.

67. Reported in *RhB*, 4 June 1921.

68. See the description of the system in the circular from the Reich Grain Office, 24 March 1921, StAM, OP 3982; also cabinet meeting of 13 April 1921, *Kabinett Fehrenbach*, pp. 638–39, and the report in *LWZW*, 1 July 1921.

69. Speech to Reichstag, *VdRT*, session of 16 June 1921, vol. 349, p. 3906.

70. On declines in imports, see *Wirtschaft und Statistik* 1 (1921), pp. 408–9. See also Kurt Ritter, *Einwirkungen*, pp. 109–10.

71. See the report from LR Moers, 16 December 1921, NWHStA, Reg. Düsseldorf 14920, p. 503; and *LWZW*, 24 February 1922.

72. Letter of 9 March 1922, LAK, 403/13348. See also *KVZ*, 18 March 1922, and LWKR to OpR, 6 May 1922, LAK, 403/13307, p. 29.

73. See, e.g., Crone-Münzebrock's comments in *RhB*, 29 January 1921, and his comments at VDDB meeting, 28 October 1920, protocol in LVW, NL Kerckerinck, IIIB 1b: Ako 53.

74. See *WB*, 15 January and 1 April 1921; *LWZW*, 10 June 1921; and *RhB*, 21 and 28 May 1921. The critique of controls dominated the interest-group press throughout the late summer and fall of 1921. See also the numerous reports from local organizations throughout the fall and winter of 1921 in LAK, 403/13306–13307, and StAM, OP 3983.

75. OpR to minister of interior, 20 May 1920, LAK, 403/13308, pp. 685–86; and reports from RP Aachen, 27 March 1922, and RP Düsseldorf, 11 April 1922, LAK, 403/13307, pp. 779–83, 823.

76. LR Moers, 16 December 1921, NWHStA, Reg. Düsseldorf 14920, p. 503.

77. Speech to Reichstag, *VdRT*, session of 11 November 1921, vol. 351, pp. 4997–99, 5002. See also Fehr's comments, *KVZ*, 3 December 1921.

78. Speech to Reichstag, *VdRT*, session of 21 February 1922, vol. 353, p. 5998.

79. Speech to Reichstag, *VdRT*, session of 22 May 1922, vol. 355, p. 7514. See also Schumacher, *Land und Politik*, pp. 168–72.

80. *KVZ*, 19 June 1922. See also report by Reinhardt, general secretary of LWKR, to Schorlemer-Lieser, on an acrimonious meeting with Christian Trade Union leaders in Cologne, 6 June 1922, NWHStA, RW 52/ 105, pp. 81–83.

81. Speech to Reichstag, session of 30 June 1922, *VdRT*, vol. 356, pp. 8189–90.

82. See Adam Stegerwald, "Zur Getreideumlage: Ein Wort an die Landwirte," *KVZ*, 3 July 1922, and Theodor v. Guérard, "Die Getreideumlage 1922/23 und die politische Lage," ibid., 9 July 1922, as well as Loë-Bergerhausen's negative response, ibid., 15 July 1922. See also the account, sympathetic to the Center, in *MA*, 20 June 1922; and Steger-

wald's comments, *VdRT*, vol. 356, 30 June 1922, pp. 8179–80.

83. Meeting of Center parliamentary steering committee, 28 June 1922, *Protokolle der Reichstagsfraktion*, p. 374.

84. Ibid., pp. 370–71.

85. The levy system was a major preoccupation of the Center's parliamentary steering committee throughout May and June, and the summary here is based on the meetings of 17 and 23 May and 19, 27, and 28 June, *Protokolle der Reichstagsfraktion*, pp. 338–41, 361–62, 369–74.

86. Again, the topic had dominated the interest-group press throughout the winter, spring, and early summer of 1922, and resolutions rejecting a maintenance of the system in any form had become commonplace. See, e.g., *WB*, 15 April 1922; *RhB*, 2 February and 1 and 22 April 1922.

87. See the discussion of this in Jones, "Democracy and Liberalism." See also *WB*, 1 August and 1 September 1922; *LWZW*, 11 August 1922; and report of OpR to PSV, 16 July 1922, LAK, 403/13347.

88. No theme had been more dominant in interest-group pronouncements and resolutions throughout the winter, spring, and early summer of 1922. See, in addition to numerous stories in *RhB* and *WB*, the comments by Papen, reported in *WB*, 15 April 1922; *LWZW*, 24 February 1922; and the report on agrarian resistance from OpR to the Prussian minister of the interior, 3 March 1922, LAK, 403/13348.

89. Letter of 16 February 1922, StAM, OP 3984.

90. *KVZ*, 18 March 1922; and similarly ominous rumblings from Westphalia, *MA*, 15 April 1922.

91. For numerous examples from the summer of 1922, see LAK, 403/13349.

92. See, e.g., the complaint of KA Rees zu Wesel to OpR, 8 September 1922, ibid.; report in *Niederrheinische Bauernzeitung*, Nr. 202; and report from Kreisbauernschaft Krefeld, 29 July 1922, in LAK, 403/13308.

93. Materials prepared for a meeting of the Reich cabinet, 1 September 1922, BA, R 43 I/ 1260, pp. 264–65.

94. Reported in *WB*, 1 October 1922.

95. *MA*, 1 October 1922.

96. *WB*, 1 November 1922.

97. Wieskotten's letter to Papen is dated 21 June 1923; his initial petition is dated 12 April 1922, StAM, Reg. Arnsberg I 15 Nr. 23; see also his earlier protest, dated 1 January 1922, StAM, Reg. Arnsberg I 15 Nr. 21.

98. Correspondence from August 1923, final rejection by RP Arnsberg, 29 August 1923, StAM, Reg. Arnsberg I 15 Nr. 23.

99. Letter of 12 September 1922, and rejection by RP Arnsberg, 30 October 1922, StAM, Reg. Arnsberg I 15 Nr. 22.

100. Letter of 16 January 1923, and the official response, 27 January 1923, ibid.

101. See exchange from late 1922 and early 1923, ibid.

102. Rejection by local officials in Oeslinghausen to LR Soest, 3 March 1923, ibid.

103. See the record of Falke's protest, 22 January 1922, StAM, Reg. Arnsberg I 15 Nr. 21.

104. See the long list from the district office in Warburg in May 1923, StAM, OP 3985. Similar materials can be found in StAD, M2 Lübbecke Nr. 2570.

105. See letter from OB Gelsenkirchen, 6 September 1923, StAM, Reg. Arnsberg, I 15 Nr. 23, and examples of other cases and the prolonged appeals process, in StAM, Reg. Arnsberg I 15 Nr. 22–23; also StAD, M2 Lübbecke Nr. 2570.

106. From Prussian minister of agriculture, 27 October 1922, LAK, 403/13350; and StAM, OP 3985.

107. Bresciani-Turroni, *Economics of Inflation*, pp. 136–37.

108. As a former mayor of Essen during the war, Luther had ample experience with the problems of the provisioning system; see his thoughts on ending controls in *Kabinett Cuno*, pp. 243–50. See also discussion at cabinet meeting, 19 March 1923, ibid., pp. 314–15. On the hyperinflation, see Holtfrerich, *Die deutsche Inflation*, pp. 298–315. The parliamentary steering committee of the Center was also unified in its support of this position: see meeting of 22 March 1923, *Protokolle der Reichstagsfraktion*, pp. 445–46.

109. See the detailed discussion of the events leading up to this in Schumacher, *Land und Politik*, pp. 176–86.

110. See Crone-Münzebrock's letter to Kerckerinck, 12 January 1923, and the letter of the same date from the steering committee of the VDDB to Luther, complaining over his failure to consult with them, LVW, NL Kerckerinck, III B1b: Ako 44.

111. *KVZ*, 10 November 1922.

112. LWKW to minister of agriculture, 4 December 1922, StAM, OP 3972; similar reports from Westphalian officials, StAM, OP 3985, and *MA*, 3 December 1922; and for the Rhineland, LAK, 403/13340 and 403/13311.

113. Letter of 10 October 1922, StAM, OP 3949.

114. See the general description in Pabst, "Ruhrkampf," pp. 8–10.

115. Christian Trade Unions in Dortmund, letter of 22 March 1923, StAM, OP 4044.

116. Calebow, representative of the regional PPS for Düsseldorf, "Niederschrift über die Tagung der Preisprüfungsstellen der alt- und neu besetzten Gebiete am 20. und 21. März 1923 im Oberpräsidium Münster (Westf.)," StAM, OP 3996.

117. See the discussion of this at the cabinet meeting of 17 January 1923, *Kabinett Cuno*, pp. 156–57.

118. RP Arnsberg, 15 September 1922, StAM, OP 3972.

119. See, e.g., report from an organization of dairy owners for the counties of Warendorf, Wiedenbrück, and Halle, 14 October 1922, ZStA II, Rep. 197A Va Nr. 12, vol. 4, pp. 11–12. In another case, a dairy in Espeln reported in June 1923 that of 500 producers legally tied to it, only eight regularly met their obligations; see letter of 10 June 1923, StAM, OP 4054. KA Ahaus reported that as of 28 November 1922, of 320 producers obliged to deliver to a dairy in its district, 249 had stopped deliveries completely; for this and similar reports, see StAM, OP 4055 and 4056.

120. See reports of the interrogations of smallholders, many with only one to three cows, KA Burgsteinfurt, 3 March 1923, StAM, OP 4054.

121. *KVZ*, 27 July 1923; and report of PPS Westfalen, 20 July 1923, StAM, OP 4044.

122. See reports of RP Düsseldorf, 28 October 1923, LAK, 403/13347; of OpW, 18 December 1923, StAM, Reg. Arnsberg I 15 Nr. 43, p. 231; of Rhenish officials, NWHStA, Reg. Düsseldorf 36192; and of Polizeiverwaltung Minden, 29 November 1923, StAD, M2 Minden (LRA) Nr. 76.

123. See a copy of the order, dated 27 October 1923, and OpW order calling for strict enforcement at the local level, 29 November 1923, StAD, M2 Minden (LRA) Nr. 79.

124. For many reports of prosecution dragging on into 1924, see StAM, OP 4055 and 4056.

125. See Plum, *Gesellschaftsstruktur*, p. 49, and *KVZ*, 11 August 1923. See also *KVZ*, 15 and 31 August 1923; and telegram from OB Aachen, 15 August 1923, BA, R 43 I/ 1263, p. 17. By September, the supply situation was truly critical; see report of RMELW, 29 October 1923, "Bericht über den Stand des Wirtschaftslebens und der Volksernährung im September 1923," BA, R 43 I/ 1263, pp. 238–39.

126. Letter to Kerckerinck, 15 August 1923, LVW, NL Kerckerinck, III B1b: Ako 44. See also the description of similar events in Upper Bavaria, in Tenfelde, *Proletarische Provinz*, pp. 135–41, 144–45.

127. See Luther's comments at the cabinet meeting of 15 August 1923, *Kabinett Stresemann*, vol. 1, pp. 4–7; also his letter to the Reich Chancellor, 8 August 1923, ibid., pp. 60–63, and his comments at the cabinet meetings of 30 August and 9 September 1923, ibid., pp. 162–63, 226–27. Holtfrerich quotes Paul Beusch: "Die Frage spitzte sich auf die kürzeste aber fruchtbarste Formel zu: Währung—Ernährung. Wurde die Währungsfrage nicht bald eine Lösung zugeführt, so musste die Hungersnot in Deutschland einsetzen" (*Währungsverfall und Währungsstabilisierung* [Berlin, 1928], p. 50, quoted in Holtfrerich, *Die deutsche Inflation*, p. 311).

128. Whether this included workers has recently been open to question. See the discussion in Abelshauser, "Verelendung der Handarbeiter?" pp. 445–76; Holtfrerich, *Die deutsche Inflation*, pp. 264–77; and Kunz, "Verteilungskampf," pp. 347–84.

129. See also Moeller, "Winners as Losers," pp. 255–88; and Kohler, "Inflation."

Chapter Six

1. *WB*, 1 September 1920.

2. Letter of 10 February 1920, StAK, NL Bachem, 465, quoted in Morsey, *Deutsche Zentrumspartei*, p. 314.

3. See Jacobs, *Von Schorlemer*, p. 10; and Flemming, "Landwirtschaftskammer," pp. 323–38.

4. See the recent, largely sympathetic biography by Bach, *Franz von Papen*; and Papen, *Der Wahrheit*, pp. 123, 149–51.

5. See the letter from Obermeyer, a functionary of the Westphalian Agricultural Association, to Kerckerinck, 5 July 1923, LVW, NL Kerckerinck, III B1a: Ako 29; also Kerckerinck to Erzberger, 14 July 1919, LVW, NL Kerckerinck, III A1: Polko 15.

6. At the general assembly, 19 November 1920, reported in *WB*, 1 December 1920.

7. Kerckerinck at the Kreisversammlung in Burgsteinfurt, 8 November 1923, reported in *WB*, 15 November 1923.

8. Ibid.

9. Letter to Kerckerinck of 13 May 1921, LVW, NL Kerckerinck, III A1: Polko 17.

10. To Silesian Center party and Peasant Association leader Count Hans Praschma, 20 February 1920, LVW, NL Kerckerinck, III A1: Polko 17.

11. See, e.g., Loë-Bergerhausen at the extraordinary general assembly in Aachen, 14 November 1921, reported in *RhB*, 23 November 1921.

12. Ibid.

13. Fortieth anniversary general assembly of the Rhenish association, held 8 November 1922, reported in *RhB*, 18 November 1922. For variations on these themes, see Lüninck, "Das Zentrum," pp. 53–68, 107–22; his speech to Verein katholischer Edelleute, 1 March 1920, reported in *KVZ*, 1 March 1920; and Morsey, *Deutsche Zentrumspartei*, pp. 314–15.

14. *Zeitungs-Korrespondenz des Rheinischen Bauernvereins*, 28 April 1923; Loë-Bergerhausen at first postwar meeting of Rhenish general assembly, reported in *RhB*, 4 March 1920. See also *LWZW*, 3 March 1920.

15. *RhB*, 4 March 1920.

16. *RhB*, 6 October 1923.

17. *WB*, 15 November 1923.

18. See, e.g., Lüninck's comments at an extraordinary general assembly of the Rhenish association, 13 January 1922, reported in *RhB*, 28 January 1922.

19. *WB*, 15 November 1923.

20. Kerckerinck at general assembly of Westphalian association, 8 November 1922, reported in *WB*, 18 November 1922. See also Lüninck's speech to the Free Peasantry county organization in Moers, 21 December 1922, reported in *Niederrheinische Bauernzeitung*; and Lüninck at 19 June 1923 meeting of Westphalian association's general assembly, *WB*, 7 July 1923.

21. *RhB*, 25 June 1921; also Loë-Bergerhausen's letter to Kerckerinck, 29 January 1920, LVW, NL Kerckerinck, III B1a: Ako 26.

22. Letter to Papen of 25 April 1921, LVW, NL Kerckerinck, III B1b: Ako 42.

23. Lüninck, "Das Zentrum."

24. See comments by Loë-Bergerhausen and Lüninck at Rhenish general assembly, 4 March 1920, reported in *RhB*, 13 March 1920. In general, see Schulz, "Räte, Wirtschaftsstände," pp. 355–66; Nocken, "Corporatism and Pluralism," pp. 37–56; and Maier, *Recasting Bourgeois Europe*, pp. 207–8.

25. *RhB*, 23 November 1921.

26. Ibid., 18 November 1922.

27. Kerckerinck to Carl Mehnert, 20 March 1920, LVW, NL Kerckerinck, III B1b: Ako 41; for the parallels with the attitude of the business community, see Feldman, "Big Business," pp. 99–130.

28. Kerckerinck to Mehnert, 20 March 1920, LVW, NL Kerckerinck, III B1b: Ako 41; also the report of attacks on peasant property in the wake of the Kapp Putsch, Wehrkommando VI to Op, RP, 30 March 1920, StAM, Reg. Münster 3781.

29. To general assembly, 15 May 1920, reported in *WB*, 6 June 1920. On the events in the Ruhr, see Eliasberg, *Ruhrkrieg*; Lucas, *Zwei Formen*, pp. 236–41; and Lucas, *Märzrevolution*.

30. Kerckerinck to Mehnert, 20 March 1920, LVW, NL Kerckerinck, III B1b: Ako 41; also Kerckerinck's remarks at meeting of VDDB, 8 April 1920, protocol in LVW, NL Kerckerinck, III B1b: Ako 53; and Schorlemer-Lieser to Kerckerinck, 9 April 1920, LVW, NL Kerckerinck, III A1: Polko 16.

31. Protocol of meeting with Rural League representatives, 1 April 1921, LVW, NL Kerckerinck, III B1b: Ako 42.

32. Letter of 24 September 1923, LVW, NL Kerckerinck, III A1: Polko 19.

33. Morsey, *Deutsche Zentrumspartei*, pp. 133–49; Hömig, *Das Preussische Zentrum*,

pp. 33–34; Stump, *Geschichte und Organisation*, pp. 29–31; and Kühr, *Parteien und Wahlen*, pp. 57–62.

34. See the tables compiled by Alfred Milatz, in Gerhard A. Ritter, "Kontinuität und Umformung," pp. 342–84; and in general, Schumacher, *Land und Politik*, pp. 411, 414. County-by-county results, comparable to those for the Kaiserreich or subsequent elections in Weimar, are not provided in the Reich statistics. Appendix Table 22 summarizes results for the major electoral districts.

35. Schumacher, *Land und Politik*, p. 431; in general, see Klaus Müller, "Agrarische Interessenverbände," pp. 391–95.

36. E.g., in Westphalia the agricultural subcommittee consisted of fifteen members, three of whom were estate owners, and another five of whom were agricultural producers. The balance consisted of three SPD representatives, one from the USPD, a smattering from the liberal parties, and a Center trade union secretary. See "Verzeichnis des Provinziallandtags-Abgeordneten für die Provinz Westfalen für die Wahlperiode 1919 bis 1924," in *Verhandlungen des im Jahr 1919 abgehaltenen 61. Westfälischen Provinziallandtags*, p. 8. Within provincial Center party institutions, agrarian influence was also greatly reduced. Information for party county committee chairmen in the Rhineland reveals that by 1920, of forty-nine in the RB Düsseldorf, Cologne, and Aachen, only two were clearly involved in the agricultural sector: one was an estate owner, and the other, a well-to-do largeholder. See *Mitteilungen der Zentralstelle*, vol. 6, Nr. 1, April 1920.

37. Schorlemer-Lieser to Kerckerinck, 9 April 1920, LVW, NL Kerckerinck, III A1: Polko 16; also Martin Spahn, another conservative who openly split with the party, to Kerckerinck, 14 March 1921, LVW, NL Kerckerinck, III A1: Polko 17.

38. Kerckerinck to Schulte, 24 April 1919, LVW, NL Kerckerinck, III A1: Polko 15.

39. Schulte to Kerckerinck, 2 November 1919, ibid.

40. Brand to Kerckerinck, 12 March 1920, LVW, NL Kerckerinck, III A1: Polko 16.

41. Kerckerinck to Adolf von Oer, 12 November 1919, and to Clemens Graf Droste zu Vischering, 15 December 1919, LVW, NL Kerckerinck, III A1: Polko 15.

42. Anderson and Barkin, "Myth of the Puttkamer Purge," p. 660.

43. Schumacher, *Land und Politik*, pp. 428–31. See also Schönhoven, *Bayerische Volkspartei*, pp. 21–22, 54; Zofka, *Ausbreitung des Nationalsozialismus*, pp. 22–25; Morsey, *Deutsche Zentrumspartei*, pp. 280–85; and on Heim, Jacobs, *Deutsche Bauernführer*, pp. 112–28.

44. On these formal changes, see Gerhard A. Ritter, "Kontinuität und Umformung."

45. See also Lüninck to Verein katholischer Edelleute, reported in *KVZ*, 1 March 1920.

46. Kerckerinck's speech to Ordentliche Generalversammlung des Kreises katholischer Edelleute, in Münster, 4 February 1919, LVW, NL Kerckerinck, III A2: Polko 30.

47. Brand to Kerckerinck, 12 March 1920, LVW, NL Kerckerinck, III A1: Polko 16.

48. Kerckerinck's speech at the general assembly of Kreis katholischer Edelleute in Münster, 4 February 1919, LVW, NL Kerckerinck, III A2: Polko 30; and Lüninck, "Das Zentrum." See also Lüninck, "Die politische Vertretung," pp. 555–72.

49. *Offizieller Bericht des ersten Reichsparteitages*, p. 56.

50. Ibid., pp. 43–45.

51. E.g., Rudolf ten Hompel; see his remarks, ibid., pp. 58–59.

52. Morsey, *Die Deutsche Zentrumspartei*, pp. 595–98; Schumacher, *Land und Politik*, p. 428; and Stump, *Geschichte und Organisation*, pp. 126–34.

53. *Offizieller Bericht des ersten Reichsparteitages*, p. 19.

54. This discussion is based on a collection of correspondence on this issue, including exchanges between Loë-Bergerhausen and Trimborn, published with a lengthy explanation of the entire affair, and sent by Kerckerinck to all member organizations of the VDDB as well as to all leaders of the Center party. His cover letter is dated 28 July 1920. A copy is in Teil II W, "Reichsausschuss der Katholiken in der DNVP," Landwirtschaftskammer Westfalen-Lippe, Schorlemer-Archiv. See also lengthy parts of the exchange published in *RhB*, 29 May and 17 July 1920; and the discussion in Schumacher, *Land und Politik*, pp. 413ff.

55. Letter from Loë-Bergerhausen to Kerckerinck, 16 May 1920, LVW, NL Kerckerinck, III A1: Polko 16.

56. Kerckerinck to Loë-Bergerhausen, 18 May 1920, LVW, NL Kerckerinck, III A1: Polko 16.

57. Figures compiled from information in *Statistik des deutschen Reichs*, vol. 291, II, pp. 41–43; see also Kerckerinck to Loë-Bergerhausen, 18 May 1920, LVW, NL Kerckerinck, III A1: Polko 16.

58. See Jones, "Dissolution," pp. 273–74, for comparisons with the liberal parties.

59. See, in particular, Jones, "Adam Stegerwald," pp. 1–29; Zeender, "German Catholics and the Concept," pp. 424–39; and Morsey, *Deutsche Zentrumspartei*, pp. 360–78.

60. Schumacher, *Land und Politik*, pp. 419–20; record of this meeting, 20 December 1920, in LVW, NL Kerckerinck, III B1b: Ako 47; and Hömig, *Das Preussische Zentrum*, pp. 93–94.

61. *RhB*, 7 February 1920.

62. Brand complaining over this to Kerckerinck, 5 May 1920, LVW, NL Kerckerinck, III A1: Polko 16.

63. Kerckerinck to Brand, 18 December 1919, LVW, NL Kerckerinck, III A1: Polko 15, in response to Brand's letter of 15 December 1919; see also the continued exchange, Brand's letter of 26 February 1920 and Kerckerinck's of 28 February 1920, all in LVW, NL Kerckerinck, III A1: Polko 16.

64. Kerckerinck to Loë-Bergerhausen, 2 January 1920, LVW, NL Kerckerinck, III B1a: Ako 26.

65. Kerckerinck to Papen, 22 July 1921, LVW, NL Kerckerinck, III A1: Polko 17. See also the account of Schlittenbauer's speech, *WB*, 1 August 1921; and in general, on Erzberger's policies that prompted this rabid criticism, Epstein, *Matthias Erzberger*, pp. 346–47, 373–79.

66. Kerckerinck to Theodor Warnecke, quoting *Westfälischer Merkur*, 2 August 1921, in letter of 7 August 1921, LVW, NL Kerckerinck, III B1a: Ako 27.

67. Herold's letter of 9 February 1922, responding to Kerckerinck's original letter of 8 November 1921, LVW, NL Kerckerinck, III A1: Polko 18. See also Schumacher, *Land und Politik*, pp. 425–26.

68. Herold to Kerckerinck, 9 February 1922, LVW, NL Kerckerinck, III A1: Polko 18.

69. Kerckerinck to Herold, 27 February 1922, LVW, NL Kerckerinck, III B1a: Ako 28.

70. Kerckerinck to Löwenstein, 24 June 1921, LVW, NL Kerckerinck, III A1: Polko 17.

71. Kerckerinck to Crone-Münzebrock, 15 November 1920, LVW, NL Kerckerinck, III B1b: Ako 41.

72. Protocol of meeting of 1 April 1921, in LVW, NL Kerckerinck, III B1b: Ako 42.

73. Ibid.; see also criticisms of Rural League proposals for closer cooperation, *WB*, 15 September 1921 and 15 March 1922.

74. See the discussion in Schumacher, *Land und Politik*, pp. 421–26.

75. See remarks of Paul Schulz-Gahmen, meeting of Center Reichstag delegation, protocol of 27 September 1921, in StAK, NL Marx, Abt. 1070 Nr. 227, pp. 8–11.

76. *MA*, 22 July 1922. See also the discussion and references in Chapter 5.

77. Brand to Herold, 10 July 1922, BA, NL Herold, Nr. 12.

78. Pennemann, reported in *Westfälisches Volksblatt*, 22 July 1922, copy in ibid., and *MA*, 22 and 23 July 1922.

79. *Westfälisches Volksblatt*, 22 July 1922, in BA, NL Herold, Nr. 12; also Brand's comments in *Meschede Zeitung*, 27 September 1922, copy in ibid.

80. A full account is provided in *WB*, 15 October 1922. This serves as the basis for the discussion in the next paragraph as well.

81. The phrase is from Schorlemer-Lieser in a letter to Kerckerinck, 26 April 1922, LVW, NL Kerckerinck, III B1b: Ako 43. On the debates over Gronowski's appointment, vehemently resisted by Peasant Association leaders but supported by Herold, see the remarks by Lambert Lensing, a publisher, and Herold in *Verhandlungen der 1. Vollsitzung des 65. Westfälischen Provinziallandtags*, vol. 65, pp. 3–4; extended correspondence between Brand and Herold as well as between Brand and Westphalian labor leaders in April and May 1922, BA, NL Herold, Nr. 12; and the brief biographical sketch of Gronowski in Gruna, "Johannes Gronowski," pp. 162–68.

82. See Loë-Bergerhausen's speech in *RhB*, 18 November 1922.

83. *MA*, 17 October 1922.

84. *Offizieller Bericht des zweiten Reichsparteitages*, p. 96 and passim.

85. Ibid.; also Morsey, *Deutsche Zentrumspartei*, pp. 430–32.

86. Emil Ritter in *Offizieller Bericht des zweiten Reichsparteitages*, p. 62 and, in general, pp. 61–70. See also Junker, *Die deutsche Zentrumspartei*, pp. 141–42, 145–48; and Stump, *Geschichte und Organisation*, pp. 54–55.

87. Kerckerinck to Alexander Elverfeld, second-in-command of the district branch of the Westphalian association in Brilon, 21 March 1924, LVW, NL Kerckerinck, III B1a: Ako 30.

88. Ibid.

89. Heberle, *Landbevölkerung und Nationalsozialismus*, pp. 11–12 (translation from Tilton, *Nazism, Neo-Nazism*, p. 7).

90. See Heberle, *Landbevölkerung und Nationalsozialismus*.

91. See particularly the results for Halle, Lübbecke, and Wittgenstein.

92. On the early history of political liberalism in Weimar, see Albertin, *Liberalismus und Demokratie*; Jones, "Democracy and Liberalism"; Hartenstein, *Anfänge der Deutschen Volkspartei*; and Romeyk, "Deutsche Volkspartei," pp. 189–236. On the DNVP, see Hertzmann, *DNVP*, and Liebe, *Die Deutschnationale Volkspartei*; and in general, Gerhard A. Ritter, "Kontinuität und Umformung."

93. Jones, "Democracy and Liberalism."

94. The comparison is suggested by Neumann, *Die deutschen Parteien*, p. 109. In general, see also Mittmann, *Fraktion und Partei*.

95. Neumann, *Modern Political Parties*, p. 358; for a sharply contrasting view, see Decker, "Zentrumskrise," p. 412. See also Grebing, "Die Konservativen und Christlichen," p. 485; and Schumacher, *Land und Politik*, pp. 426–28.

96. In general, see also Hans Müller, "Der deutsche Katholizismus," pp. 521–36; and Dülmen, "Der deutsche Katholizismus," pp. 361–76.

97. Morsey, *Deutsche Zentrumspartei*, p. 613.

Chapter Seven

1. *WB*, 11 June 1924.

2. See Osmond, "German Peasant Farmers"; also Sering, *Die deutsche Landwirtschaft*, p. 40; Aereboe, *Einfluss des Krieges*, pp. 14ff; and Meyer, *Die deutsche Landwirtschaft*, esp. pp. 6–17.

3. Kupperberg, "Viehhaltung," pp. 423–25, 428–29, 432–33.

4. Sølta, *Bauern der Lausitz*, pp. 134–35, 238, 240.

5. Osmond, "German Peasant Farmers," pp. 299–300; Bresciani-Turroni, *Economics of Inflation*, p. 299. For comparisons with areas of tenant farming in Italy, where land sales accelerated in the war and the postwar period, see Maier, *Recasting Bourgeois Europe*, p. 311; Corner, *Fascism in Ferrara*, pp. 154–55; the description of Italian landlord-tenant relations in Tuscany in Snowden, "From Sharecropper to Proletarian," pp. 136–71; and Cardoza, *Agrarian Elites*, esp. pp. 245–386. The appeals of Italian fascists, " 'the land to him who works it and makes it bear fruit' " (quoted in Corner, *Fascism in Ferrara*, p. 147), could have little resonance in the Rhenish and Westphalian countryside, where family farmers already owned the land they worked.

6. See, e.g., materials on land sale and the restrictions imposed near the end of the war in NWHStA, LRA Mettmann, Nr. 145; NWHStA, LRA Düsseldorf, Nr. 516; NWHStA, LRA Bonn, Nr. 1683; and NWHStA, LRA Bonn, Nr. 1504.

7. See references in Chapter 1, note 34.

8. Report of LWKR, 27 April 1919, NWHStA, LRA Grevenbroich, Nr. 525. See also *WGZ*, 12 February 1918; *LWZR*, 7 and 21 December 1917; and *RhB*, 7 July 1917.

9. Kuczynski, *Deutschlands Versorgung*, pp. 75–76, 113–15, 277–80, 287, 296.

10. Beckmann, *Die weltwirtschaftlichen Beziehungen*, pp. 55–57, 61, 113, 118; Beckmann, "Kapitalbildung," p. 129; Feierabend, *Die volkswirtschaftlichen Bedingungen*, pp. 34–35.

11. Bussmeyer, "Die betriebswirtschaftliche Bedeutung," p. 12; Bismarck, "Mechanisierung der Landwirtschaft," p. 811.

12. In general, on the economic impact of the inflation on agricultural production and investment decisions, see Osmond, "German Peasant Farmers"; Dietze, "Bedeutung der Preisverhältnisse," pp. 302–3; Bramstedt, "Kaufkraftschwankungen," pp. 110, 136–39, 144–45; Schumacher, "Thesen zur Lage," pp. 215–17; and Boelcke, "Wandlungen," pp. 498–532.

13. In particular, see Beckmann, "Agrarkrise," pp. 397–451, 525–70; Beckmann, "Kreditpolitik und Kreditlage"; Sering, *Die deutsche Landwirtschaft*, pp. 70ff.; Sering, *Agrarkrisen*; *Ausschuss zur Untersuchung*, vol. 12, pp. 12–14; Gerloff, "Besteuerung der Landwirtschaft," pp. 156–95; and the lucid summary in Childers, *Nazi Voter*, pp. 73–74.

14. This account is based on stories in the press of the cooperative network. See comments by Loë-Bergerhausen at the general assembly of the Rhenish organization, reported in *RhGB*, 31 July 1921, and in *KVZ*, 25 June 1922. See also *RhGB*, 31 March 1923; *RhB*, 20 and 27 January 1923; *KVZ*, 27 February and 28 July 1923; Quabeck at

Westphalian general assembly, *WGZ*, 26 August 1922; *WGZ*, 19 June and 3 August 1922; *Der Münsterländer* (supplement to *MA*), 28 July 1923; *LWZW*, 14 June 1923; and Bollig's comments, *Verhandlungen des 63. Rheinischen Provinziallandtags*, 14 July 1922, pp. 211–16.

15. *RhGB*, 30 November 1918.

16. *WGZ*, 24 January 1923.

17. On the disastrous conditions of the Westphalian network, see the findings of the Prussian Central Bank audit, summarized in a lengthy report of 31 August 1927, LVW, NL Kerckerinck, III B1a: Ako 33. See also the protocol of a meeting prior to this of the Direktorium of the Prussian Central Bank with Kerckerinck and Reineke, 9 March 1926, LVW, NL Kerckerinck, III B1a: Ako 32; and Kerckerinck's account to Crone-Münzebrock, 12 March 1926, LVW, NL Kerckerinck, III B1b: Ako 48.

18. *Ausschuss zur Untersuchung*, vol. 12, p. 79; Beckmann, "Agrarkrise," p. 437; Beckmann, "Kreditpolitik und Kreditlage," pp. 80–81, 131–33; Fabian, "Verschuldung der deutschen Landwirtschaft"; Mahnke, "Entstehen der Kreditnot"; Rossberg, *Anteil der Genossenschaften*, pp. 22–37, 124–57; preliminary report of the *Ausschuss zur Untersuchung* on indebtedness, *VdRT*, vol. 422, Drucksache Nr. 4058; and Hellwig, "Das landwirtschaftliche Kreditwesen."

19. Brinkmann, "Veränderungen in den Methoden," p. 643; Beckmann, "Notlage der Bauernwirtschaften," pp. 310–11; Schindler, "Standardisierung," pp. 749–50; Beckmann, "West-Deutschland," p. 232; Boelcke, "Wandlungen," pp. 528–29.

20. See the discussion in Sering, *Internationale Preisbewegung*, pp. 3–46, 97–132.

21. In general, on the severity of stabilization for other parts of German society, see Jones, "Inflation, Revaluation"; Southern, "Impact of the Inflation"; Childers, "Inflation, Stabilization"; Hughes, "Economic Interest"; and Childers, *Nazi Voter*, pp. 50–101.

22. On the international dimensions of the agrarian crisis, see Kindleberger, *World in Depression*, pp. 83–107; Timoshenko, *World Agriculture*; and Wolfram Fischer, "Weimarer Republik," pp. 34–36. On the climate of uncertainty, see Beckmann, "Kapitalbildung," p. 120; Aereboe, *Einfluss des Krieges*, pp. 115–17; Fabian, "Verschuldung der deutschen Landwirtschaft," p. 43; Beckmann, "Kreditpolitik und Kreditlage," pp. 83, 234; and Baade, "Stabilisierung der Getreidepreise," pp. 250–52.

23. See *Ausschuss zur Untersuchung*, vol. 2, pp. 39, 203–44, and 297–314. In each instance, conditions on a variety of farms, mostly largeholdings, are reported. See also, e.g., Heinrich David, "Entwicklung des Kreditgenossenschaftswesens"; Fuchs, "Untersuchungen über die Kreditlage"; Husen, *Belastung des Kreises Rees*, pp. 25–84, 105–16; and Montag, "Die steuerliche Belastung." In general, see Gessner, *Agrarverbände*, pp. 83–96; Henning, *Landwirtschaft*, pp. 189–98; Sering, *Die deutsche Landwirtschaft*, pp. 78ff; Heberle, *Landbevölkerung und Nationalsozialismus*, pp. 118–29; Klemm, *Ursachen und Verlauf*; and Klemm, "Entwicklung der landwirtschaftlichen Produktion."

24. See, e.g., Hermann von Lüninck's speech to general assembly of Rhenish association, 3 March 1925, reported in *RhB*, 4 April 1925. This was a constant theme in the press of both the Rhenish and Westphalian associations throughout the second half of the 1920s. Appeals for strict market regulation and ever-higher tariffs only intensified in the last years of Weimar.

25. See in general, Kretschmar, *Deutsche Agrarprogramme*.

26. See, e.g., the discussion in Farquharson, "Agrarian Policy."

27. See the details of tariff agreements and the debates surrounding them in Panzer, *Ringen um die deutsche Agrarpolitik*; Gessner, *Agrarverbände*, pp. 150–51, 200–215; Nocken, "Corporatism and Pluralism," p. 49; Stegmann, "Deutsche Zoll- und Handelspolitik," pp. 499–513; and Abraham, *Collapse*, pp. 180–228. The theme of agriculture's eclipsed position by the mid-1920s is also stressed by Maier, *Recasting Bourgeois Europe*.

28. See, in particular, Gies, "NSDAP und landwirtschaftliche Organisationen."

29. See the interesting comments by Geyer, "Professionals and Junkers," p. 80. For one variant of the standard interpretation, emphasizing the Junkers' contribution to Weimar's demise, see Buchta, *Junker*; and in general, Gerschenkron, *Bread and Democracy*.

30. 15 July 1923, LVW, NL Kerckerinck, III A1: Polko 19.

31. Kerckerinck to Loë-Bergerhausen, 19 March 1924, LVW, NL Kerckerinck, III A1: Polko 20. See also Schulz-Gahmen to Kerckerinck, protesting Kerckerinck's opposition, 25 March 1924, LVW, NL Kerckerinck, III B1a: Ako 30.

32. Kerckerinck to Hennecke, an official of the Peasant Association, 30 March 1924, and also to Crone-Münzebrock, 30 March 1924, LVW, NL Kerckerinck, III A1: Polko 20.

33. Brand to Schorlemer-Overhagen, 13 May 1924, ibid.

34. Kerckerinck to Hennecke, 30 March 1924, ibid.

35. Kerckerinck to Loë-Bergerhausen, 14 April 1924, ibid.

36. Letter to Reich Party Executive Committee, signed by Bollig and Loë-Bergerhausen, 9 April 1924, and Lüninck to Kerckerinck, 10 April 1924, both in ibid.

37. Childers, *Nazi Voter*, pp. 76–77; Childers, "Inflation, Stabilization," pp. 409–31; and, in general, Jones, "Inflation, Revaluation," pp. 143–68, and Jones, "Dissolution," pp. 268–88.

38. Kerckerinck to Spengler, 17 March 1924, and Spengler's letters on the putsch and the Hitler trial, 23 March and 11 April 1924, LVW, NL Kerckerinck, III A1: Polko 19.

39. Papen to Kerckerinck, Charsamstag [Saturday before Easter], 1924, LVW, NL Kerckerinck, III A1: Polko 20.

40. *RhB*, 16 February 1924.

41. Spengler to Kerckerinck, 23 March 1924, and Kerckerinck to Spengler, 14 November 1923, LVW, NL Kerckerinck, III A1: Polko 19.

42. In general, see Stürmer, *Koalition und Opposition*.

43. Kerckerinck to Loë-Bergerhausen, 5 June 1925, LVW, NL Kerckerinck, III B1b: Ako 49.

44. Kerckerinck to Count Kanitz, 6 June 1925, LVW, NL Kerckerinck, III A1: Polko 21.

45. Kerckerinck to Loë-Bergerhausen, 5 June 1925, LVW, NL Kerckerinck, III B1b: Ako 49.

46. Papen to Kerckerinck, Charsamstag 1924, LVW, NL Kerckerinck, III A1: Polko 20.

47. Schlittenbauer to Loë-Bergerhausen, 22 October 1924, LVW, NL Kerckerinck, III B1b: Ako 46.

48. Loë-Bergerhausen to Schlittenbauer, 28 October 1924, ibid.

49. Kerckerinck to Loë-Bergerhausen, 17 March 1925, LVW, NL Kerckerinck, III B1b: Ako 48.

50. See Loë-Bergerhausen's public attacks on the Marx candidacy, *KVZ*, 20 April and 5 May 1925; and Kerckerinck to Loë-Bergerhausen, 6 June 1925, on the stir created by the

publication by Papen of a flier that defended support for Hindenburg, LVW, NL Kercke-rinck, III A1: Polko 21. See also Zeender, "German Catholics and the Presidential Election," pp. 367–68, 375.

51. "Politische Parteien und berufsständische Bewegung," in *Mitteilungen der Zentral-stelle*, second series, Nr. 7/8, May/June 1925, pp. 81–83.

52. *Wähler und Wählerinnen*, Center leaflet, 1924, Landesarchiv Berlin, Rep. 240, Acc. 1962, Nr. 21, cited in Childers, *Nazi Voter*, p. 114.

53. Childers, *Nazi Voter*, pp. 113–14.

54. See, e.g., "Politik der Mitte, Partei der Mitte," in *Mitteilungen der Zentralstelle*, Nr. 9/10, September/October 1925.

55. Klaus Müller, "Agrarische Interessenverbände," p. 395. In general, see also Stürmer, *Koalition und Opposition*, pp. 99–100, 104–6; and Pies, "Sozialpolitik und Zentrum," pp. 260–61.

56. Kerckerinck to Loë-Bergerhausen, 17 April 1925, LVW, NL Kerckerinck, III A1: Polko 21.

57. Kerckerinck to Marx as head of the national party organization, 19 April 1925, ibid.

58. Kerckerinck to Brand, informing him that he would also remain in the party's subcommittee on agricultural affairs at the provincial level, 20 May 1925, ibid.

59. Loë-Bergerhausen to Kerckerinck, 13 May 1925, LVW, NL Kerckerinck, III B1b: Ako 49.

60. Kerckerinck to Loë-Bergerhausen, 5 June 1925, ibid.

61. Joseph Hess to Adolf von Oer, 14 March 1925, LVW, NL Kerckerinck, III A1: Polko 21.

62. Kerckerinck to Loë-Bergerhausen, 5 June 1925, and Loë-Bergerhausen to Kercke-rinck, 13 May 1925, LVW, NL Kerckerinck, III B1b: Ako 49.

63. Loë-Bergerhausen to Kerckerinck, 13 May 1925, ibid.

64. Kerckerinck to Euer Durchlaut (?), 11 November 1925, LVW, NL Kerckerinck, III B1b: Ako 31. I have been unable to identify the aristocratic recipient of this letter.

65. See, e.g., the sharp exchange between Loë-Bergerhausen and Mönnig, the Rhenish party head, *Mitteilungen der Zentralstelle*, second series, Nr. 1, October 1924, pp. 6–8.

66. Report by Loë-Bergerhausen to Dalwigk, 27 July 1923, NWHStA, RW 152/ 153.

67. See, e.g., the speeches at "Deutscher Bauerntag" in Recklinghausen, 1 January 1927, reported in *WB*, 2 February 1927; also *WB*, "Mehr Aktivität," 6 July 1927, and *WB*, "Bauer und sein Bauernverein," 2 November 1927.

68. Flemming, "Landwirtschaftskammer," pp. 323–25.

69. Ibid.

70. See the accounts of this step in *RhB*, 4 September and 2 October 1926.

71. *WB*, 8 and 15 September and 6 October 1926; Kerckerinck's speech to executive committee of VDDB, undated but probably 1926, LVW, NL Kerckerinck, III B1b: Ako 49; and his "Aktenmässiger Beweis betr. die Organisationsabsichten des Frhr. v. Loë," dated October 1927, LVW, NL Kerckerinck, III B1b: Ako 50.

72. See *Dülmener Zeitung*, 4 February 1925, copy in LVW, NL Kerckerinck, III B3: Nr. 65; also *MA*, 11 March 1925.

73. Ledebur to Kerckerinck, 27 January, in response to Kerckerinck, 24 January 1925, LVW, NL Kerckerinck, III B1a: Ako 31.

74. Kerckerinck to Loë-Bergerhausen, 7 March 1925, LVW, NL Kerckerinck, III B1b:

Ako 48. See also protocol of executive meeting of the Westphalian association, 6 March 1925, LVW, NL Kerckerinck, III B1a: Ako 31; and Ledebur's public statement of reconciliation, *MA*, 11 March 1925.

75. See letter of Count Westphalen to Kerckerinck, 11 February 1924, and Schorlemer-Overhagen to Kerckerinck, 2 June 1924, LVW, NL Kerckerinck, III A1: Polko 20; Golte, head of the Peasant Association office for the Arnsberg region, to Kerckerinck, 7 October 1926, LVW, NL Kerckerinck, III B1b: Ako 49; and Crone-Münzebrock to Kerckerinck, 8 February 1927, and Kerckerinck's response, 10 February 1927, LVW, NL Kerckerinck, III B1b: Ako 50. Lüninck also headed the Westphalian branch of the right-wing Stahlhelm. From 1933 to 1938, he was a firm supporter of the Third Reich. Ultimately, he joined the aristocratic resistance to National Socialism and was executed for his participation in the attempt on Hitler's life on 20 July 1944. See Berghahn, *Stahlhelm*, pp. 65, 281.

76. Account in *WB*, 16 March 1927. See also protocol of executive committee meeting, 25 February 1927, LVW, NL Kerckerinck, III B1a: Ako 33; and Gessner, *Agrarverbände*, pp. 120–22.

77. Lüninck to Kerckerinck, 3 March 1927, LVW, NL Kerckerinck, III B1a: Ako 33.

78. Alex Vogelsang, leader of the Peasant Association county level organization in Steinfurt, to Kerckerinck, 22 February 1927; and Lüninck to Kerckerinck, 6 March 1927, ibid.

79. See the criticism of Ledebur and Lüninck, *KVZ*, 12 February 1927; also Kerckerinck's correspondence with Crone-Münzebrock in February and March 1927, LVW, NL Kerckerinck, III B1b: Ako 50; the exchange between Lüninck and Kerckerinck in early March 1927, and Herold's comments at the meeting of the Westphalian Center party subcommittee on agricultural problems, according to Alex Vogelsang's account, 5 November 1927, LVW, NL Kerckerinck, III B1a: Ako 33.

80. Account of its meeting in *MA*, 15 October 1928. See also *Westdeutsche Landwacht*, April 1927; this publication was superseded in Westphalia by a provincial publication, *Westdeutscher Bauer*. For biographical information on Vorholt, see Jacobs, *Deutsche Bauernführer*, pp. 79–85. Johannes Brockmann, a Peasant League leader, was among those active in the reconstitution of the Center and the founding of the CDU after 1945; see Wieck, *Entstehung der CDU*, pp. 108–9.

81. Alex Vogelsang's account of meeting of agricultural subcommittee of provincial Center party, 5 November 1927, LVW, NL Kerckerinck, III B1a: Ako 33.

82. Josef Schmelzer, a WBV leader from Olpe and a representative to the Prussian parliament, at meeting of Westphalian Center subcommittee on agricultural affairs, according to notes of Alex Vogelsang, 5 November 1927, LVW, NL Kerckerinck, III B1a: Ako 33; and Franz Bornefeld-Ettmann, a Westphalian representative to the Reichstag, at executive committee meeting of Westphalian association, 19 November 1927, reported in *WB*, 7 December 1927.

83. According to Vogelsang's notes, 5 November 1927, LVW, NL Kerckerinck, III B1a: Ako 33; also Müller, "Agrarische Interessenverbände," p. 397.

84. Kerckerinck to Hermann von Lüninck, 8 October 1924, LVW, NL Kerckerinck, III B1b: Ako 46.

85. In a speech to the Westphalian association steering committee, 19 November 1927, reported in *WB*, 30 November 1927.

86. Kerckerinck to Gennes, lawyer for the Reichsverband der deutschen landwirtschaft-

lichen Genossenschaften, the national organization with which the Westphalian cooperatives were affiliated, 24 October 1928, LVW, NL Kerckerinck, III B1a: Ako 34; also *WB*,
8 February and 26 September 1928.

87. See Vorholt to Kerckerinck, 17 September 1928, and the account of the meeting
between Vorholt and Kerckerinck's sister, undated, LVW, NL Kerckerinck, III B1a: Ako
34.

88. Dieckmann to Kerckerinck, 26 February 1927, and Kerckerinck's response, 1
March 1927, LVW, NL Kerckerinck, III B1a: Ako 33.

89. Gessner, *Agrarverbände*, pp. 125–26. See also the protocols of the executive
committee of the Westphalian association, 13 February, 1 March, and 29 April 1929,
LVW, NL Kerckerinck, III B1a: Ako 35; and background in *WB*, 17 October 1928 and 12
June 1929, and *RhB*, 3 and 24 March 1928.

90. Topf, *Die grüne Front*, p. 112; Barmeyer, *Andreas Hermes*, pp. 29–30, 59–128.

91. Kerckerinck to steering committee of WBV, cited in Barmeyer, *Andreas Hermes*, p.
70. See also Hermes to Kerckerinck, letter of 28 March 1929, LVW, NL Kerckerinck, III
B1a: Ako 35; Hermes to Kerckerinck, 13 March 1929, and Kerckerinck to Hermes, 20
April and 24 June 1929, LVW, NL Kerckerinck, III B1b: Ako 51; and the debate at the
steering committee of the WBV, 29 April 1929, LVW, NL Kerckerinck, III B1a: Ako 35.

92. Klaus Müller, "Agrarische Interessenverbände," pp. 398–99, 403–4; Barmeyer,
Andreas Hermes, pp. 80–110. Bollig, former head of the Christian Peasantry and still a
Center loyalist, resigned all his positions in the Rhenish organization in protest over
cooperation between the league and the Peasant Association; see *MA*, 19 March 1929.

93. For comparative perspectives, see the work of Heberle, *Landbevölkerung und
Nationalsozialismus*, and Stoltenberg, *Politische Strömungen*, on Schleswig-Holstein. See
also Farquharson, *Plough and the Swastika*, pp. 1–42; Gies, "NSDAP und landwirtschaftliche Organisation"; and the fictionalized account by Fallada, *Bauern, Bonzen*.

94. See, in general, Morsey, "Deutsche Zentrumspartei," pp. 281–453; Junker, *Die
deutsche Zentrumspartei*; Kühr, *Parteien und Wahlen*, pp. 67–74; Childers, *Nazi Voter*,
pp. 189–90; and the interesting local study by Plum, *Gesellschaftsstruktur*.

95. Childers, *Nazi Voter*, pp. 189–90, 259–60.

96. The Nazi vote ran as high as 60.7 percent in Lübbecke and 63.9 percent in
Wittgenstein, both heavily Protestant districts. On developments in RB Aachen, see Plum,
Gesellschaftsstruktur, pp. 23–24. On the agrarian splinter parties, see Methfessel,
"Christlich-Nationale Bauern- und Landvolkpartei," pp. 241–44; Gessner, *Agrarver-
bände*, pp. 111–20; and the insightful analysis of Jones, "Crisis and Realignment."

97. The opposite has been argued at length most recently by Hamilton, *Who Voted for
Hitler?* pp. 43, 50, 371–73, 420, 427. See the alternative offered by Childers, "Social
Bases," p. 29; and Childers, *Nazi Voter*.

98. Papen's speech of 8 August 1932, reported in *WB*, 31 August and 7 September
1932. On Papen's break with the Center, see Morsey, "Deutsche Zentrumspartei," pp.
306–14; Morsey, *Untergang*, pp. 45–55; Bracher, *Auflösung*, pp. 455–71; and Papen, *Der
Wahrheit*, pp. 225–27.

99. Barmeyer, *Andreas Hermes*, p. 123.

100. Vogelsang, *Reichswehr, Staat*, pp. 206–7, 466.

101. *WB*, 10 and 17 May and 5 July 1933. See also the stories by Papen, *WB*, 30 August
1933, and by Dieckmann, "Die Stunde der Erfüllung," *WB*, 25. Gilbhart/October 1933;

RhB, 8 April and 6 May 1933; Klaus Müller, "Agrarische Interessenverbände," p. 404; and Bürger, "Die landwirtschaftliche Interessenvertretung," pp. 34, 36–37. This contrasts with the less willing acceptance of the Reichsnährstand (Reich Agricultural Estate) in Schleswig-Holstein. See Stoltenberg, *Politische Strömungen*, pp. 168, 190; and for comparisons with one Bavarian case study, see Zofka, *Ausbreitung des Nationalsozialismus*, pp. 321–27. On the organization of the Reichsnährstand, see Farquharson, "Agrarian Policy"; Lovin, "Agricultural Reorganization"; and Gies, "Reichsnährstand."

Conclusion

1. Eley, *Reshaping*, p. 353.

2. Eley, "What Produces Fascism," p. 63.

3. Berger, writing of the "traditional sector" in France and Italy, observes that the "coherence and unity" of the groups that compose it are political creations that owe "their existence only in part to real, objective similarities in the economic interests of the members of the class but mainly to the members' common perception of having the same situation in society and to society's seeing them as the same and establishing rules that identify them as a political and social entity." See Berger, "Traditional Sector," p. 93; Berger, "Regime and Interest Representation," pp. 83–102; and, in general, Mayer, "Lower Middle Class," pp. 425–26, 436. The same argument has been applied convincingly to German white-collar workers in the writings of Kocka; see, e.g., most recently, Kocka, "Class Formation," pp. 63–82.

4. Feldman, *Army, Industry*, p. 4.

5. On the dissolution of the middle, see the work of Jones, in particular " 'Dying Middle' " and "Dissolution." In general, see Childers, "Inflation, Stabilization"; and Childers, *Nazi Voter*.

6. See, e.g., Abelshauser, "Inflation und Stabilisierung"; this point is also emphasized by Laursen and Pedersen, *German Inflation*.

7. An insightful discussion of the importance of these *repeated* crises is offered by Vierhaus, "Auswirkungen der Krise," p. 158.

8. Barrington Moore, Jr., writes, "The historian's reluctance to engage in debate about why something did not happen is quite understandable. Historians justifiably feel that they have enough work to do explaining what did happen. But any explanation of what actually took place connotes an explanation of why something else failed to occur" (*Injustice*, p. 377).

Bibliography

Archival Sources

Berlin
  Geheimes Staatsarchiv, Preussischer Kulturbesitz
    Preussisches Ministerium der Justiz
  Landesarchiv
    Deutscher Landkreistag
Cologne
  Stadtarchiv
    Nachlass Karl Bachem
    Nachlass Wilhelm Marx
Detmold
  Staatsarchiv
    Regierung Minden
    Kreisverwaltungen (Bielefeld, Büren, Höxter, Lübbecke, Minden, Warburg)
Düsseldorf
  Nordrhein-Westfälisches Hauptstaatsarchiv
    Regierung Aachen
    Regierung Düsseldorf
    Landwirtschaftskammer Rheinland
    Landratsämter (Bonn, Cologne, Dinslaken, Düren, Düsseldorf, Erkelenz, Geldern,
      Grevenbroich, Mettmann, Moers, Waldbröl, Wipperfürth)
Koblenz
  Bundesarchiv
    Reichskanzlei
    Nachlass Carl Herold
    Nachlass Rudolf ten Hompel
  Landeshauptarchiv
    Oberpräsidium für die Provinz Rheinland
    Regierung Koblenz
Merseburg
  Zentrales Staatsarchiv
    Ministerium des Innern
    Ministerium für Landwirtschaft, Domänen und Forsten
    Preussischer Staatskommissar für Volksernährung
Münster
  Landschaftsverband Westfalen-Lippe
    Nachlass Engelbert Freiherr Kerckerinck zu Borg

Staatsarchiv
    Oberpräsidium für die Provinz Westfalen
    Regierung Münster
    Regierung Arnsberg
    Kreisverwaltungen (Beckum, Borken, Coesfeld, Dortmund, Hagen, Hamm, Hattin-
        gen, Lüdinghausen, Meschede, Recklinghausen, Schwelm, Siegen, Soest, Stein-
        furt, Tecklenburg, Wittgenstein)
    Westfälisch-Lippischer Landwirtschaftsverband
    Schorlemer-Archiv
Potsdam
    Zentrales Staatsarchiv
    Archiv des Reichslandbundes
    Reichskanzlei
    Reichsministerium für Ernährung und Landwirtschaft
    Reichswirtschaftsministerium
    Reichswirtschaftsrat

Published Primary Sources

Akten der Reichskanzlei: Weimarer Republik. Edited by Karl Dietrich Erdmann.
    —*Das Kabinett Scheidemann: 13. Februar bis 20. Juni 1919.* Edited by Hagen
        Schulze. Boppard am Rhein, 1971.
    —*Das Kabinett Müller I: 27. März bis 21. Juni 1920.* Edited by Martin Vogt. Bop-
        pard am Rhein, 1971.
    —*Das Kabinett Fehrenbach: 25. Juni 1920 bis 4. Mai 1921.* Edited by Peter Wulf.
        Boppard am Rhein, 1972.
    —*Die Kabinette Wirth I und II: 10. Mai 1921 bis 26. Oktober 1921, 26. Oktober 1921
        bis 22. November 1922.* 2 vols. Edited by Ingrid Schulze-Bidlingmaier. Boppard
        am Rhein, 1973.
    —*Das Kabinett Cuno: 22. November 1922 bis 12. August 1923.* Edited by Karl-Heinz
        Harbeck. Boppard am Rhein, 1968.
    —*Die Kabinette Stresemann I und II: 13. August bis 6. Oktober 1923.* 2 vols. Edited
        by Karl Dietrich Erdmann and Martin Vogt. Boppard am Rhein, 1978.
*Ausschuss zur Untersuchung der Erzeugungs- und Absatzbedingungen der deutschen
    Wirtschaft (Enquête Ausschuss): Verhandlungen und Berichte des Unterausschusses
    für Landwirtschaft (II. Unterauschuss). Vols. 2–4, Landwirtschaftliche Buch-
    führungsergebnisse: Untersuchungen zur Lage der Landwirtschaft. Vol. 7, Unter-
    suchungen über Landarbeiterverhältnisse. Vol. 12, Die Verschuldungs- und Kredit-
    lage der deutschen Landwirtschaft in ihrer Entwicklung von der Währungsbefestigung
    bis Ende 1928. Vol. 15, Die Lage der deutschen Milchwirtschaft. Berlin, 1929–31.*
*Bericht über die erste Tagung der Arbeiter-Zentrumswähler Westdeutschlands in Bochum
    am 23. Juni 1918. Krefeld, n.d.*
Christliche Bauernschaft der Rheinlande. *Bericht über die erste vorbereitende Versamm-
    lung am 29. Januar 1919 zu Köln.* Cologne, n.d.
_____. *Christliche Bauernschaft der Rheinlande.* N.p., n.d.

————. *Jahresbericht für das Geschäftsjahr 1919 erstattet in der Generalversammlung vom 18. Februar 1920.* N.p., n.d.

Entwickelung und Tätigkeit des Trierischen Bauern-Vereins und seiner Institute. Trier, 1907.

Mitteilungen der Zentralstelle der Rheinischen Zentrumspartei. Cologne, 1920, 1924–25.

Offizieller Bericht des ersten Reichsparteitages der Deutschen Zentrumspartei: Tagung zu Berlin vom 19. bis 20. Januar. Berlin, n.d. [1920].

Offizieller Bericht des zweiten Reichsparteitages der Deutschen Zentrumspartei: Tagung zu Berlin vom 15. bis 17. Januar. Berlin, n.d. [1922].

Preussische Statistik. Berlin, 1896–1924.

Die Protokolle der Reichstagsfraktion der Deutschen Zentrumspartei 1920–1925. Edited by Rudolf Morsey and Karsten Ruppert. Mainz, 1981.

Sitzungsberichte des Preussischen Landtags. I. Wahlperiode. Berlin, 1922–24.

Sitzungsberichte der verfassungsgebenden Preussichen Landesversammlung: Tagung 1919/21. Vol. 5, 67. bis 83. Sitzung (17. Oktober bis 15. November 1919). Berlin, 1921.

Statistisches Jahrbuch für den preussichen Staat. Berlin, 1897–1925.

Statistik des Deutschen Reichs. Berlin, 1885–1935.

Stenographische Berichte über die Verhandlungen des Preussischen Hauses der Abgeordneten. 22. Legislaturperiode. Berlin, 1917.

Stenographische Berichte über die Verhandlungen des Rheinischen Provinziallandtags. Düsseldorf, 1918–24.

Verhandlungen des Reichstags. XIII. Legislaturperiode, II. Session; I. Wahlperiode, 1920. Berlin, 1914–18, 1921–24.

Verhandlungen der verfassungsgebenden Deutschen Nationalversammlung. Berlin, 1920.

Verhandlungen des Westfälischen Provinziallandtags. Münster, 1914–24.

Vierteljahrshefte zur Statistik des Deutschen Reichs. Berlin, 1893–1925.

Newspapers

Kölnische Volks-Zeitung (1914–24)

Kölnische Zeitung (1918–23)

Landwirtschaftliche Zeitung für die Rheinprovinz (1914–24)

Landwirtschaftliche Zeitung für Westfalen-Lippe (1914–24)

Münsterischer Anzeiger (1914–24)

Rheinischer Bauer (1882–1933)

Rheinisches Genossenschaftsblatt (1914–24)

Westdeutsche Landwacht (1927)

Westdeutscher Bauer (1927–32)

Westfälische Allgemeine Volks-Zeitung (1918–23)

Westfälische Genossenschafts-Zeitung (1918–23)

Westfälischer Bauer (1888–1933)

Books and Articles

Abelshauser, Werner. "Inflation und Stabilisierung: Zum Problem ihrer makroökonomischen Auswirkungen auf die Rekonstruktion der deutschen Wirtschaft nach dem Ersten Weltkrieg." In *Historische Prozesse der deutschen Inflation 1914 bis 1924: Ein Tagungsbericht*, edited by Otto Büsch and Gerald D. Feldman, pp. 161–74. Berlin, 1978.

_____. "Verelendung der Handarbeiter? Zur sozialen Lage der deutschen Arbeiter in der grossen Inflation der frühen zwanziger Jahre." In *Vom Elend der Handarbeit: Probleme historischer Unterschichtenforschung*, edited by Hans Mommsen and Winfried Schulze, pp. 445–76. Stuttgart, 1981.

Abraham, David. *The Collapse of the Weimar Republic: Political Economy and Crisis*. Princeton, 1981.

Aereboe, Friedrich. *Agrarpolitik: Ein Lehrbuch*. Berlin, 1928.

_____. *Die Beurteilung von Landgütern und Grundstücken: Ein Lehrbuch für Landwirte, Volkswirte, Kataster- und Steuerbeamte, Gebäudetaxatoren, Angestellten ländlicher Kreditanstalten usw*. Berlin, 1924.

_____. *Der Einfluss des Krieges auf die landwirtschaftliche Produktion in Deutschland*. Stuttgart, 1927.

_____. *Über den Einfluss der neuzeitlichen Preisgestaltung auf Organisation und Führung der Landgutswirtschaft*. Berlin, 1922.

Aereboe, Friedrich; Hansen, J.; and Roemer, Th., eds. *Handbuch der Landwirtschaft*. 5 vols. Berlin, 1928–30.

Aereboe, Friedrich, and Warmbold, H. *Preisverhältnisse landwirtschaftlicher Erzeugnisse im Kriege*. Berlin, 1917.

Albertin, Lothar. *Liberalismus und Demokratie am Anfang der Weimarer Republik: Eine vergleichende Analyse der Deutschen Demokratischen Partei und der Deutschen Volkspartei*. Düsseldorf, 1972.

Albrecht, Gerhard. "Das Bauerntum im Zeitalter des Kapitalismus." In *Grundriss der Sozialökonomik*, IX Abteilung, pp. 35–69. Tübingen, 1926.

_____. *Zur Krisis der deutschen Landwirtschaft*. Jena, 1924.

Albrecht, Gerhard, and Meyer-Johann, Martin. "Das Heuerlingswesen in Westfalen." *Berichte über Landwirtschaft* New Series 2 (1924): 177–231.

Altkemper, Johannes. "Die Landwirtschaft in den Kreisen Recklinghausen und Gelsenkirchen." Dissertation, Bonn, 1905.

Anderson, Margaret Lavinia. *Windthorst: A Political Biography*. Oxford, 1981.

Anderson, Margaret Lavinia, and Barkin, Kenneth. "The Myth of the Puttkamer Purge and the Reality of the *Kulturkampf*: Some Reflections on the Historiography of Imperial Germany." *Journal of Modern History* 54 (1982): 647–86.

Angress, Werner T. "The Political Role of the Peasantry in the Weimar Republic." *Review of Politics* 21 (1959): 530–49.

_____. "Weimar Coalition and Ruhr Insurrection." *Journal of Modern History* 29 (1957): 1–20.

Aubin, Hermann; Buhler, Ottmar; Kuske, Bruno; and Schulte, Aloys, eds. *Der Raum Westfalen*. Vols. 1 and 3. Berlin, 1931–32.

Augé-Laribé, Michel. "Agriculture in France during the War." In *Agriculture and Food*

Supply in France during the War, pp. 1–154. New Haven, 1927.

Aussel, H. *Die landwirtschaftlichen Betriebe im Bezirk Münster.* Berlin, 1906.

Avereck, Heinrich Wilhelm. "Die Landwirtschaft unter dem Einflusse von Bergbau und Industrie im rheinischen Ruhrkohlengebiet." Dissertation, Leipzig, 1912.

Ay, Karl-Ludwig. *Die Entstehung einer Revolution: Die Volksstimmung in Bayern während des ersten Weltkrieges.* Berlin, 1968.

Baade, Fritz. "Die deutsche Landwirtschaft nach dem Kriege." *Sozialistische Monatshefte* 29 (1923): 657–66.

―――. "Die gegenwärtige Lage der deutschen Landwirtschaft." *Sozialistische Monatshefte* 30 (1924): 81–90.

―――. "Hat die deutsche Landwirtschaft versagt?" *Sozialistische Monatshefte* 30 (1924): 355–63.

―――. "Landwirtschaft und Volksernährung." *Die Gesellschaft* 1928/II: 132–49.

―――. "Roggenpolitik und bäuerliche Veredlungswirtschaft: Deutsche Roggenpolitik II." *Der deutsche Volkswirt* 5 (1930): 211–16.

―――. "Stabilisierung der Getreidepreise." *Die Gesellschaft* 1927/I: 250–80.

―――. "Das System der agrarpolitischen Mittel." In *Deutsche Agrarpolitik im Rahmen der inneren und äusseren Wirtschaftspolitik*, edited by Fritz Beckmann, Bernhard Harms, Theodor Brinkmann, Hermann Bente, Edgar Salin, and Werner Henkelmann, vol. 2, pp. 218–96. Berlin, 1932.

Bach, Jürgen A. *Franz von Papen in der Weimarer Republik: Aktivitäten in Politik und Presse, 1918–1932.* Düsseldorf, 1977.

Bachem, Karl. *Vorgeschichte, Geschichte und Politik der Deutschen Zentrumspartei: Zugleich ein Beitrag zur Geschichte der katholischen Bewegung sowie zur allgemeinen Geschichte des neueren und neuesten Deutschlands 1815–1914.* 9 vols. Cologne, 1927–32.

Bade, Klaus J. "Transnationale Migration und Arbeitsmarkt im Kaiserreich: Vom Agrarstaat mit starker Industrie zum Industriestaat mit starker agrarischer Basis." In *Historische Arbeitsmarktforschung: Entstehung, Entwicklung und Probleme der Vermarktung von Arbeitskraft*, edited by Toni Pierenkemper and Richard Tilly, pp. 182–211. Göttingen, 1982.

Bäcker, Walter. "Wesen und Entwicklungstendenzen der landwirtschaftlichen Berufsvertretung in der Rheinprovinz." Dissertation, Bonn, 1928.

Ballwanz, Ilona. "Bauernschaft und soziale Schichten des Dorfes im Kapitalismus." *Jahrbuch für Wirtschaftsgeschichte* 1980/III: 9–24.

―――. "Sozialökonomische Kennziffern der Betriebsgrössengruppen in der kapitalistischen Landwirtschaft des Deutschen Reiches 1871–1914." *Wissenschaftliche Zeitschrift der Universität Rostock, Gesellschafts- und sprachwissenschaftliche Reihe* 28 (1979): 465–72.

―――. "Sozialstruktur und Produktionsentwicklung der deutschen Landwirtschaft von 1871 bis 1914." Dissertation, Wilhelm-Pieck-Universität Rostock, 1977.

Barkin, Kenneth D. *The Controversy over German Industrialization 1890–1902.* Chicago, 1970.

Barmeyer, Heide. *Andreas Hermes und die Organisation der deutschen Landwirtschaft: Christliche Bauernvereine, Grüne Front, Reichsnährstand 1928–1933.* Stuttgart, 1971.

Barral, Pierre. "Les conséquences de la première guerre mondiale dans l'agriculture française." *Francia* 2 (1974): 551–65.

Baudis, Dieter, and Nussbaum, Helga. *Wirtschaft und Staat in Deutschland vom Ende des 19. Jahrhunderts bis 1918/19.* Vaduz/Liechtenstein, 1978.

Baumgarten, Otto. "Der sittliche Zustand des deutschen Volkes unter dem Einfluss des Krieges." In *Geistige und sittliche Wirkungen des Krieges in Deutschland*, pp. 1–88. Stuttgart, 1927.

Becker, Heinz. "Zu Tschajanows Lehre von der bäuerlichen Wirtschaft." *Landwirtschaftliche Jahrbücher* 63 (1926): 563–75.

Becker, Winfried. "Der politische Katholizismus in Rheinland-Westfalen vor 1890—Programmatische Entwicklung und regionale Verankerung." In *Rheinland-Westfalen im Industriezeitalter: Beiträge zur Landesgeschichte des 19. und 20. Jahrhunderts*, edited by Kurt Düwell and Wolfgang Köllmann, vol. 2, pp. 271–92. Wuppertal, 1984.

Beckmann, Fritz. "Agrarkrise und Agrarzölle." *Berichte über Landwirtschaft* New Series 2 (1925): 397–451, 525–70.

———. "Der Bauer im Zeitalter des Kapitalismus." *Schmollers Jahrbuch* 50 (1926): 719–48.

———. *Einfuhrscheinsysteme: Kritische Betrachtung mit besonderer Berücksichtigung der Getreideeinfuhrscheine.* Karlsruhe, 1911.

———. *Die Futtermittelzölle: Eine wirtschaftspolitische Untersuchung.* Munich, 1913.

———. "Die Kapitalbildung der deutschen Landwirtschaft während der Inflation." *Schmollers Jahrbuch* 48 (1924): 111–33.

———. "Kreditpolitik und Kreditlage der deutschen Landwirtschaft seit der Währungsstabilisierung." *Berichte über Landwirtschaft* New Series 3 (1926): 79–140, 211–72.

———. "Die Notlage der Bauernwirtschaften in den westdeutschen Höhengebieten (Eifel, Hunsrück, Taunus, Westerwald, Sauerland)." In *Die deutsche Landwirtschaft unter volks- und weltwirtschaftlichen Gesichtspunkten*, edited by Max Sering, pp. 308–30. Berlin, 1932.

———. "Die Organisation der agraren Produktion im Kriege." *Zeitschrift für Sozialwissenschaft* New Series 7 (1916): 477–516, 611–26, 698–716, 771–98.

———. *Die weltwirtschaftlichen Beziehungen der deutschen Landwirtschaft und ihre wirtschaftliche Lage, 1919–1926.* Berlin, 1926.

———. *Die weltwirtschaftlichen Beziehungen der Landwirtschaft des westfälischen Industriegebietes.* Leipzig, 1929.

———. "West-Deutschland: Grundlagen und Formen der westdeutschen Landwirtschaft." In *Grundlagen und Formen der deutschen Landwirtschaft*, pp. 229–72. Berlin, 1933.

———. "Zum Führerproblem in der deutschen Landwirtschaft." *Die Gesellschaft* 1927/I: 433–52.

Beckmann, Fritz; Harms, Bernhard; Brinkmann, Theodor; Bente, Hermann; Salin, Edgar; and Henkelmann, Werner, eds. *Deutsche Agrarpolitik im Rahmen der inneren und äusseren Wirtschaftspolitik.* 3 vols. Berlin, 1932.

Beidler, F. W. "Der Kampf um den Zolltarif im Reichstag 1902." Dissertation, Berlin, 1929.

Berdahl, Robert M. "Conservative Politics and Aristocratic Landholders in Bismarckian Germany." *Journal of Modern History* 44 (1972): 1–20.

Berger, Suzanne. *Peasants against Politics: Rural Organization in Brittany 1911–1967.* Cambridge, Mass., 1972.

———. "Regime and Interest Representation: The French Traditional Middle Classes." In *Organizing Interests in Western Europe: Pluralism, Corporatism and the Transformation of Politics*, edited by Suzanne Berger, pp. 83–102. Cambridge, 1981.

———. "The Traditional Sector in France and Italy." In *Dualism and Discontinuity in Industrial Societies*, edited by Suzanne Berger and Michael Piore, pp. 83–131. Cambridge, 1980.

———, ed. *Organizing Interests in Western Europe: Pluralism, Corporatism and the Transformation of Politics.* Cambridge, 1981.

Berger, Suzanne, and Piore, Michael, eds. *Dualism and Discontinuity in Industrial Societies.* Cambridge, 1980.

Berghahn, Volker R. *Der Stahlhelm: Bund der Frontsoldaten, 1918–1935.* Düsseldorf, 1970.

Bergmann, Klaus. *Agrarromantik und Grossstadtfeindschaft.* Meisenheim am Glan, 1970.

Berthold, Rudolf. "Zur Entwicklung der deutschen Agrarproduktion und der Ernährungswirtschaft zwischen 1907 und 1925." *Jahrbuch für Wirtschaftsgeschichte* 1974/IV: 83–111.

———. "Zur sozialökonomischen Struktur des kapitalistischen Systems der deutschen Landwirtschaft zwischen 1907 und 1925." *Jahrbuch für Wirtschaftsgeschichte* 1974/III: 105–25.

Berthold, Rudolf, and Hombach, Wilfried. "Landwirtschaft und Agrarpolitik im imperialistischen Deutschland während des ersten Weltkrieges und der revolutionären Nachkriegskrise: Teil I." *Wissenschaftliche Zeitschrift der Universität Rostock, Gesellschafts- und sprachwissenschaftliche Reihe* 23 (1974): 571–78.

Bertram, Jürgen. *Die Wahlen zum Deutschen Reichstag vom Jahre 1912.* Düsseldorf, 1964.

Bessel, Richard, and Feuchtwanger, E. J., eds. *Social Change and Political Development in Weimar Germany.* London, 1981.

Béteille, André. *Six Essays in Comparative Sociology.* Oxford, 1974.

Beyer, Hans. "Die Agrarkrise und das Ende der Weimarer Republik." *Zeitschrift für Agrargeschichte und Agrarsoziologie* 13 (1965): 62–92.

———. *Die Agrarkrise und die Landvolkbewegung in den Jahren 1928–1932: Ein Beitrag zur Geschichte "revolutionärer" Bauernbewegungen zwischen den beiden Weltkriegen.* Wedel bei Hamburg, 1962.

———. "Landbevölkerung und Nationalsozialismus in Schleswig-Holstein." *Zeitschrift für Agrargeschichte und Agrarsoziologie* 12 (1964): 69–74.

Biberfeld, Erich. "Die Frage der Intensivierung der deutschen Landwirtschaft nach dem Kriege." Dissertation, Leipzig, 1933.

Bismarck, Ludolf von. "Die Mechanisierung der Landwirtschaft." In *Die deutsche Landwirtschaft unter volks- und weltwirtschaftlichen Gesichtspunkten*, edited by Max Sering, pp. 806–17. Berlin, 1932.

Bissing, W. M. Freiherr von. *Der Realkredit der deutschen Landwirtschaft.* Berlin, 1930.

Blackbourn, David. "Class and Politics in Wilhelmine Germany: The Center Party and the Social Democrats in Württemberg." *Central European History* 9 (1976): 220–49.

––––––. *Class, Religion and Local Politics in Wilhelmine Germany: The Centre Party in Württemberg.* New Haven, 1980.

––––––. "The *Mittelstand* in German Society and Politics, 1871–1914." *Social History* 2 (1977): 409–33.

––––––. "Peasants and Politics in Germany, 1871–1914." *European Studies Quarterly* 14 (1984): 47–75.

––––––. "The Political Alignment of the Centre Party in Wilhelmine Germany: A Study of the Party's Emergence in Nineteenth-Century Württemberg." *Historical Journal* 18 (1975): 821–50.

––––––. "The Problem of Democratisation: German Catholics and the Role of the Center Party." In *Society and Politics in Wilhelmine Germany*, edited by Richard J. Evans, pp. 160–85. London, 1978.

Blackbourn, David, and Eley, Geoff. *Mythen deutscher Geschichtsschreibung: Die gescheiterte bürgerliche Revolution von 1848.* Frankfurt am Main, 1980.

Blessing, Werner K. "Umwelt und Mentalität im ländlichen Bayern: Eine Skizze zum Alltagswandel im 19. Jahrhundert." *Archiv für Sozialgeschichte* 19 (1979): 1–42.

Böckenförde, Ernst Wolfgang. "Der deutsche Katholizismus im Jahre 1933." In *Von Weimar zu Hitler*, edited by Gotthard Jaspar, pp. 344–76. Cologne, 1968.

Boelcke, Willi A. "Wandlungen der deutschen Agrarwirtschaft in der Folge des Ersten Weltkrieges." *Francia* 3 (1975): 498–532.

Borchert, Gerhard. *Die landwirtschaftlichen Betriebsverhältnisse im Kreise Steinfurt.* Berlin, 1912.

Bowen, Ralph H. *German Theories of the Corporative State with Special Reference to the Period 1870–1919.* New York, 1947.

Bowman, Shearer Davis. "Antebellum Planters and *Vormärz* Junkers in Comparative Perspective." *American Historical Review* 85 (1980): 779–808.

Bracher, Karl-Dietrich. *Die Auflösung der Weimarer Republik: Eine Studie zum Problem des Machtverfalls in der Demokratie.* Düsseldorf, 1978 (reprint of fifth edition, 1971).

Bramstedt, Paul. "Die Kaufkraftschwankungen von Gold, Roggen und Kohle." *Berichte über Landwirtschaft* New Series 1 (1923): 85–145.

Braun, Theo. "Die historische Entwicklung der deutschen Landwirtschaftskammer bis zur Gegenwart unter besonderer Berücksichtigung der Landwirtschaftskammer Rheinland." Dissertation, Cologne, 1952.

Breitman, Richard. *German Socialism and Weimar Democracy.* Chapel Hill, 1981.

Brentano, Lujo. *Die deutschen Getreidezölle: Eine Denkschrift.* Stuttgart, 1910.

Brepohl, Wilhelm. *Bäuerliche Heilkunde in einem Dorfe des Mindener Landes um die Jahrhundertwende: Ein Beitrag zur Volkskunde von Minden-Ravensberg.* Minden, 1964.

––––––. *Industrievolk im Wandel von der agraren zur industriellen Daseinsform dargestellt am Ruhrgebiet.* Tübingen, 1957.

Bresciani-Turroni, Costatino. *The Economics of Inflation: A Study of Currency Depreciation in Post-War Germany.* London, 1937.

Bridenthal, Renate. "Beyond *Kinder, Küche, Kirche*: Weimar Women at Work." *Central European History* 16 (1973): 148–66.

Briefs, Goetz. "Aufbau und Tätigkeit der Preisprüfungsstellen in der Praxis." In *Die*

Preisprüfungsstellen, pp. 35–94. Berlin, 1917.

Brinkmann, Theodor. *Betriebsführung und Geldwirtschaft des Landwirtes im Zeichen der Geldentwertung.* Berlin, 1923.

————. "Geldüberschuss und Reinertrag des landwirtschaftlichen Betriebes unter dem Einfluss der Geldentwertung." In Theodor Brinkmann, Hugo Hagmann, and Emil Lang, *Landwirtschaft und Geldentwertung*, pp. 7–25. Stuttgart, 1921.

————. "Die Oekonomik des landwirtschaftlichen Betriebes." In *Grundriss der Sozial-ökonomik*, VII Abteilung, pp. 27–124. Tübingen, 1922.

————. "Veränderungen in den Methoden und der Organisation des Absatzes landwirt-schaftlicher Erzeugnisse." In *Die deutsche Landwirtschaft unter volks- und weltwirt-schaftlichen Gesichtspunkten*, edited by Max Sering, pp. 643–59. Berlin, 1932.

Brodbeck, Walter. *Deutsche Getreidestatistik seit 1878.* Berlin, 1939.

Broszat, Martin; Fröhlich, Elke; and Wiesemann, Falk. *Bayern in der NS-Zeit: Soziale Lage und politisches Verhalten der Bevölkerung im Spiegel vertraulicher Berichte.* Munich, 1977.

Buchheim, Karl. *Geschichte der christlichen Parteien in Deutschland.* Munich, 1953.

————. *Ultramontanismus und Demokratie: Der Weg der deutschen Katholiken im 19. Jahrhundert.* Munich, 1963.

Buchta, Bruno. *Die Junker und die Weimarer Republik: Charakter und Bedeutung der Osthilfe in den Jahren 1928–1933.* Berlin, 1959.

Budde, Paul. "Die Landwirtschaft im Kreise Lüdinghausen." Dissertation, Giessen, 1925.

Buer, Heinrich. "Die gegenwärtige landwirtschaftliche Betriebsweise im Landkreise Bonn unter Vergleichung mit der vor 50 Jahren üblich gewesenen, von Hartstein in seiner statistisch-landwirtschaftlichen Topographie des Kreises Bonn beschriebenen Betriebsweise." Dissertation, Bonn, 1901.

————. *Die Heimstättenversicherung: Eine soziale Einrichtung zur Bekämpfung der Landflucht.* Bonn, 1908.

Bürger, Hans. "Die landwirtschaftliche Interessenvertretung in der Zeit von 1933 bis zur Gegenwart unter besonderer Berücksichtigung der westdeutschen Verhältnisse." Dis-sertation, Erlangen-Nürnberg, 1967.

Büsch, Otto, and Feldman, Gerald D. *Historische Prozesse der deutschen Inflation 1914 bis 1924: Ein Tagungsbericht.* Berlin, 1978.

Büsch, Otto; Wölk, Monika; and Wölk, Wolfgang, eds. *Wählerbewegungen in der deutschen Geschichte: Analysen und Berichte zu den Reichstagswahlen 1871–1933.* Berlin, 1978.

Bumm, Franz, ed. *Deutschlands Gesundheitsverhältnisse unter dem Einfluss des Welt-krieges.* Stuttgart, 1928.

Burnham, Walter Dean. "Political Immunization and Political Confessionalism: The United States and Weimar Germany." *Journal of Interdisciplinary History* 3 (1972): 1–30.

Busch, Helmut. *Die Stoeckerbewegung im Siegerland: Ein Beitrag zur Siegerländer Geschichte in der zweiten Hälfte des 19. Jahrhunderts.* Hüttental-Wiedenau, 1968.

Busch, Wilhelm. *Das Gefüge der westfälischen Landwirtschaft.* Münster, 1939.

————. *Die Landbauzonen im deutschen Lebensraum.* Stuttgart, 1936.

Bussmeyer, Heinrich. "Die betriebswirtschaftliche Bedeutung der Nutzviehhaltung und ihre Gestaltung unter den neuzeitlichen wirtschaftlichen Verhältnissen (dargestellt an den bäuerlichen Betriebsverhältnissen des Kreises Halle i. Westf.)." Dissertation, Münster, 1934.

Butz, Otto. *Die Landwirtschaft des Kreises Rees am Niederrhein.* Halle an der Saale, 1905.

Caplan, Jane. " 'The Imaginary Universality of Particular Interests': The 'Tradition' of the Civil Service in German History." *Social History* 4 (1979): 299–317.

Cardoza, Anthony L. *Agrarian Elites and Italian Fascism: The Province of Bologna, 1901–1926.* Princeton, 1982.

Chayanov, A. V. *The Theory of Peasant Economy.* Edited by Daniel Thorner, Basile Kerblay, and R. E. F. Smith. Homewood, Ill., 1966.

Childers, Thomas. "Inflation, Stabilization, and Political Realignment in Germany 1919–1928." In *Die deutsche Inflation: Eine Zwischenbilanz,* edited by Gerald D. Feldman, Carl-Ludwig Holtfrerich, Gerhard A. Ritter, and Peter-Christian Witt, pp. 409–31. Berlin, 1982.

_____. *The Nazi Voter: The Social Foundations of Fascism in Germany, 1919–1933.* Chapel Hill, 1983.

_____. "The Social Bases of the National Socialist Vote." *Journal of Contemporary History* 11 (1976): 17–42.

Conze, Werner. "Bauer, Bauernstand, Bauerntum." In *Geschichtliche Grundbegriffe: Historisches Lexikon zur politisch-sozialen Sprache in Deutschland,* edited by Otto Brunner, Werner Conze, and Reinhart Koselleck, vol. 1, pp. 407–39. Stuttgart, 1972.

Corner, Paul. *Fascism in Ferrara 1915–1925.* London, 1975.

Crew, David F. *Town in the Ruhr: A Social History of Bochum, 1860–1914.* New York, 1979.

Crone-Münzebrock, August. "Landwirtschaftliches Vereinswesen und Landwirtschaftskammer." In *Beiträge zur Geschichte des westfälischen Bauernstandes,* edited by Engelbert Freiherr Kerckerinck zu Borg, pp. 531–63. Berlin, 1912.

_____. *Die Organisation des deutschen Bauernstandes.* Berlin, n.d. [1920?].

Cronin, James E. "Labor Insurgency and Class Formation: Comparative Perspectives on the Crisis of 1917–1920 in Europe." In *Work, Community, and Power: The Experience of Labor in Europe and America, 1900–1925,* edited by James E. Cronin and Carmen Sirianni, pp. 20–48. Philadelphia, 1983.

Croon, Helmuth. "Die Einwirkungen der Industriealisierung auf die gesellschaftliche Schichtung der Bevölkerung im rheinisch-westfälischen Industriegebiet." *Rheinische Vierteljahrsblätter* 20 (1955): 301–16.

_____. "Die Versorgung der Grossstädte des Ruhrgebietes im 19. und 20. Jahrhundert." *Jahrbücher für Nationalökonomie und Statistik* 179 (1966): 356–68.

_____. "Vom Werden des Ruhrgebiets." In *Rheinisch-Westfälische Rückblende,* edited by Walter Först, pp. 175–226. Cologne, 1967.

Czada, Peter. "Grosse Inflation und Wirtschaftswachstum." In *Industrielles System und politische Entwicklung in der Weimarer Republik,* edited by Hans Mommsen, Dietmar Petzina, and Bernd Weisbrod, pp. 386–95. Düsseldorf, 1974.

Dade, Heinrich. "Die Preiskonjunktur für landwirtschaftliche Erzeugnisse in Deutschland nach der Entwicklung des Weltmarktes und der Valuta." *Archiv des Deutschen Landwirtschaftsrats* 41 (1921): 243–48.

Dahrendorf, Ralf. *Society and Democracy in Germany*. Garden City, 1967.

Dartmann, Heinrich. "Die Landarbeiterverhältnisse Westfalens vor und nach dem Kriege in betriebswirtschaftlicher Hinsicht." Dissertation, Giessen, 1932.

David, Eduard. *Sozialismus und Landwirtschaft*. Berlin, 1903.

David, Heinrich. "Die Entwicklung des Kreditgenossenschaftswesens in Westfalen unter besonderer Berücksichtigung der Nachkriegsinflation." Dissertation, Bonn, 1931.

Decker, Georg. "Die Zentrumskrise." *Die Gesellschaft* 1925/II: 410–28.

Deist, Wilhelm, ed. *Militär- und Innenpolitik im Weltkrieg, 1914–1918*. Düsseldorf, 1970.

Dickinson, Robert E. *Germany: A General and Regional Geography*. New York, 1953.

———. *The Regions of Germany*. London, 1945.

Diener, G. Walter. *Hunsrücker Volkskunde*. 2nd ed. Bonn, 1962.

Dietze, Constantin von. "Die Bedeutung der Preisverhältnisse für die Lage der deutschen Landwirtschaft." *Berichte über Landwirtschaft* New Series 4 (1926): 273–321.

Dietzel, Hans. "Die preussischen Wahlrechtsreformbestrebungen von der Oktroyierung des Dreiklassenwahlrechts bis zum Beginn des Weltkrieges." Dissertation, Cologne, 1934.

Dillwitz, Sigrid. "Quellen zur sozialökonomischen Struktur der Bauernschaft im deutschen Reich nach 1871." *Jahrbuch für Wirtschaftsgeschichte* 1977/II: 237–69.

———. "Quellen zur Verschuldung der Bauernschaft im Deutschen Reich von 1871 bis 1914." *Wissenschaftliche Zeitschrift der Universität Rostock, Gesellschafts- und sprachwissenschaftliche Reihe* 25 (1976): 773–88.

———. "Die Struktur der Bauernschaft von 1871 bis 1914: Dargestellt auf der Grundlage der deutschen Reichsstatistik." *Jahrbuch für Geschichte* 9 (1973): 47–127.

Dirks, Walter. "Katholizismus und Nationalsozialismus." *Die Arbeit* 8 (1931): 201–9.

Ditt, Hildegard. *Struktur und Wandel westfälischer Agrarlandschaften*. Münster, 1965.

Ditt, Karl. *Industrialisierung, Arbeiterschaft und Arbeiterbewegung in Bielefeld 1850–1914*. Dortmund, 1982.

Dix, Walther. *Untersuchungen über die Betriebsorganisation der Landwirtschaft am Niederrhein*. Berlin, 1911.

Dülmen, Richard von. "Der deutsche Katholizismus und der Erste Weltkrieg." *Francia* 2 (1974): 347–76.

———. "Die Wirkung des ersten Weltkrieges auf den deutschen Katholizismus." *Zeitschrift für bayerische Landesgeschichte* 38 (1975): 982–1001.

Eley, Geoff. "Anti-Semitism, Agrarian Mobilization, and the Crisis of the Conservative Party: Radicalism and Containment in the Foundation of the *Bund der Landwirte* 1892–1893." In *Politics, Parties and the Authoritarian State: Imperial Germany 1871–1918*, edited by John C. Fout. Forthcoming.

———. *Reshaping the German Right: Radical Nationalism and Political Change after Bismarck*. New Haven, 1980.

———. "What Produces Fascism: Preindustrial Traditions or a Crisis of the Capitalist State." *Politics and Society* 12 (1983): 53–82.

———. "The Wilhelmine Right: How it Changed." In *Society and Politics in Wilhelmine Germany*, edited by Richard J. Evans, pp. 112–35. London, 1978.

———. "Zum Problem der Verbände im Kaiserreich." *Sozialwissenschaftliche Informationen für Unterricht und Studium* 11 (1982): 22–28.

Eliasberg, Georg. *Der Ruhrkrieg von 1920*. With an introduction by Richard Löwenthal. Bonn–Bad Godesberg, 1974.

Ennew, Judith; Hirst, Paul; and Tribe, Keith, " 'Peasantry' as an Economic Category." *Journal of Peasant Studies* 4 (1977): 295–322.

Epstein, Klaus. *Matthias Erzberger and the Dilemma of German Democracy*. Princeton, 1959.

Erdmann, August. *Die christlichen Gewerkschaften insbesondere ihr Verhältnis zu Zentrum und Kirche*. Stuttgart, 1914.

Esslen, Joseph B. *Die Fleischversorgung des Deutschen Reiches: Eine Untersuchung der Ursachen und Wirkungen der Fleischteuerung und der Mittel zur Abhilfe*. Stuttgart, 1912.

Eulenberg, Franz. "Die sozialen Wirkungen der Währungsverhältnisse." *Jahrbücher für Nationalökonomie und Statistik* 122 (1924): 748–94.

Evans, Ellen Lovell. *The German Center Party 1870–1933: A Study in Political Catholicism*. Carbondale, 1981.

Evans, Richard J. "Introduction: Wilhelm II's Germany and the Historians." In *Society and Politics in Wilhelmine Germany*, edited by Richard J. Evans, pp. 11–39. London, 1978.

———. "Religion and Modern Society in Germany." *European Studies Review* 12 (1982): 249–88.

———, ed. *The German Working Class 1888–1933: The Politics of Everyday Life*. London, 1982.

———, ed. *Society and Politics in Wilhelmine Germany*. London, 1978.

Evans, Richard J., and Lee, W. R., eds. *The German Family: Essays on the Social History of the Family in Nineteenth- and Twentieth-Century Germany*. London, 1981.

Fabian, Friedrich. "Die Verschuldung der deutschen Landwirtschaft vor und nach dem Kriege." Dissertation, Leipzig, 1930.

Fallada, Hans. *Bauern, Bonzen und Bomben*. Berlin, 1931.

Farnsworth, H. C. "Decline and Recovery of Wheat Prices in the 'Nineties." *Wheat Studies* 10 (1933/34): 289–352.

———. "Wheat in the Post-Surplus Period 1900–1909 with Recent Analogies and Contrasts." *Wheat Studies* 17 (1940/41): 315–86.

Farquharson, J. E. "The Agrarian Policy of National Socialist Germany." In *Peasants and Lords in Modern Germany: Recent Studies in Agricultural History*, edited by Robert G. Moeller, pp. 233–59. Boston, 1986.

———. *The Plough and the Swastika: The NSDAP and Agriculture in Germany 1928–1945*. Beverly Hills, 1976.

Farr, Ian. "From Anti-Catholicism to Anticlericalism: Catholic Politics and the Peasantry in Bavaria, 1890–1900." *European Studies Review* 13 (1983): 249–69.

———. "Peasant Protest in the Empire—The Bavarian Example." In *Peasants and Lords in Modern Germany: Recent Studies in Agricultural History*, edited by Robert G. Moeller, pp. 110–39. Boston, 1986.

———. "Populism in the Countryside: The Peasant Leagues in Bavaria in the 1890s." In *Society and Politics in Wilhelmine Germany*, edited by Richard J. Evans, pp. 136–59. London, 1978.

Farrar, Lancelot F. *The Short-War Illusion: German Policy, Strategy and Domestic Affairs, August–December 1914*. Santa Barbara, 1973.

Fassbender, Martin, and Fassbender, Christian. "Der westfälische Bauernstand in seinem Verhältnis zum allgemeinen Kulturleben." In *Beiträge zur Geschichte des westfälischen Bauernstandes*, edited by Engelbert Freiherr Kerckerinck zu Borg, pp. 564– 614. Berlin, 1912.

Feierabend, Hans. *Die volkswirtschaftlichen Bedingungen und die Entwicklung des Fleischverbrauchs in Deutschland seit Beginn des Weltkrieges*. Berlin, 1928.

Feldman, Gerald D. "Arbeitskonflikte im Ruhrbergbau 1919–1922: Zur Politik von Zechenverband und Gewerkschaften in der Überschichtenfrage." *Vierteljahrshefte für Zeitgeschichte* 28 (1980): 168–223.

―――. *Army, Industry and Labor in Germany 1914–1918*. Princeton, 1966.

―――. "Big Business and the Kapp Putsch." *Central European History* 4 (1971): 99– 130.

―――. "Die Demobilmachung in der Zwischenkriegszeit in Europa." *Geschichte und Gesellschaft* 9 (1983): 156–77.

―――. "Der deutsche Organisierte Kapitalismus während der Kriegs- und Inflationsjahre 1914–1923." In *Organisierter Kapitalismus: Voraussetzungen und Anfänge*, edited by Heinrich August Winkler, pp. 150–71. Göttingen, 1974.

―――. "Economic and Social Problems of the German Demobilization 1918–1919" (with comments). *Journal of Modern History* 47 (1975): 1–45.

―――. "Gegenwärtiger Forschungsstand und künftige Forschungsprobleme zur deutschen Inflation." In *Historische Prozesse der deutschen Inflation 1914 bis 1924: Ein Tagungsbericht*, edited by Otto Büsch and Gerald D. Feldman, pp. 3–21. Berlin, 1978.

―――. "German Business between War and Revolution: The Origins of the Stinnes-Legien Agreement." In *Entstehung und Wandel der modernen Gesellschaft: Festschrift für Hans Rosenberg zum 65. Geburtstag*, edited by Gerhard A. Ritter, pp. 312–41. Berlin, 1970.

―――. *Iron and Steel in the German Inflation 1916–1923*. Princeton, 1977.

―――. "The Political Economy of Germany's Relative Stabilization during the 1920/21 Depression." In *Die deutsche Inflation: Eine Zwischenbilanz*, edited by Gerald D. Feldman, Carl-Ludwig Holtfrerich, Gerhard A. Ritter, and Peter-Christian Witt, pp. 180–206. Berlin, 1982.

―――. "The Social and Economic Policies of German Big Business, 1918–1929." *American Historical Review* 75 (1969): 47–55.

―――. "Social-economic Structures in the Industrial Sector and Revolutionary Potentialities, 1917–1922." In *Revolutionary Situations in Europe, 1917–1921: Germany, Italy, Austria-Hungary*, edited by Charles L. Bertrand, pp. 159–68. Quebec, 1977.

―――. "Wirtschafts- und sozialpolitische Probleme der deutschen Demobilmachung 1918/19." In *Industrielles System und politische Entwicklung in der Weimarer Republik*, edited by Hans Mommsen, Dietmar Petzina, and Bernd Weisbrod, pp. 618–36. Düsseldorf, 1974.

Feldman, Gerald D.; Holtfrerich, Carl-Ludwig; Ritter, Gerhard A.; and Witt, Peter-Christian, eds. *Die Erfahrung der Inflation im internationalen Zusammenhang und Vergleich*. Berlin, 1984.

Feldman, Gerald D., and Homburg, Heidrun. *Industrie und Inflation: Studien und Dokumente zur Politik der deutschen Unternehmer 1916–1923*. Hamburg, 1977.

Feldman, Gerald D.; Kolb, Eberhard; and Rürup, Reinhard. "Die Massenbewegungen der Arbeiterschaft in Deutschland am Ende des Ersten Weltkrieges (1917–1920)." *Politische Vierteljahresschrift* 13 (1972): 84–105.

Fensch, H. L. "Bauernbetrieb und Grossbetrieb als Versorger des deutschen Marktes." *Archiv des Deutschen Landwirtschaftsrats* 48 (1930): 160–85.

————. *Die Entwicklung der landwirtschaftlichen Betriebsergebnisse seit der Neugestaltung der Währung*. Berlin, 1932.

————. *Die Preisbildung in der Landwirtschaft in den Wirtschaftsjahren 20/21 – 22/23*. Berlin, 1923.

————. *Die Verwendung der deutschen Getreideernte*. Berlin, 1930.

Ferguson, D. Frances. "Rural/Urban Relations and Peasant Radicalism: A Preliminary Statement." *Comparative Studies in Society and History* 18 (1976): 106–18.

Finckenstein, H. W. Graf Finck von. *Die Entwicklung der Landwirtschaft in Preussen und Deutschland 1800–1930*. Würzburg, 1960.

Fischer, Karl-Heinz. "Untersuchungen über die Viehhaltung in 130 bäuerlichen Betrieben." *Landwirtschaftliche Jahrbücher* 76 (1932/33): 897–951.

Fischer, Wolfram. *Deutsche Wirtschaftspolitik 1918–1945*. Opladen, 1968.

————. "Die Weimarer Republik unter den weltwirtschaftlichen Bedingungen der Zwischenkriegszeit." In *Industrielles System und politische Entwicklung in der Weimarer Republik*, edited by Hans Mommsen, Dietmar Petzina, and Bernd Weisbrod, pp. 26–50. Düsseldorf, 1974.

Flemming, Jens. "Die Bewaffnung des 'Landvolkes': Ländliche Schutzwehren und agrarischer Konservatismus in der Anfangsphase der Weimarer Republik." *Militärgeschichtliche Mitteilungen* 1979/2: 7–36.

————. "Grossagrarische Interessen und Landarbeiterbewegung: Überlegungen zur Arbeiterpolitik des Bundes der Landwirte und des Reichslandbundes in der Anfangsphase der Weimarer Republik." In *Industrielles System und politische Entwicklung in der Weimarer Republik*, edited by Hans Mommsen, Dietmar Petzina, and Bernd Weisbrod, pp. 745–62. Düsseldorf, 1974.

————. "Landarbeiter zwischen Gewerkschaften und 'Werksgemeinschaft': Zum Verhältnis von Agrarunternehmern und Landarbeiterbewegung im Übergang vom Kaiserreich zur Weimarer Republik." *Archiv für Sozialgeschichte* 14 (1974): 351–418.

————. *Landwirtschaftliche Interessen und Demokratie: Ländliche Gesellschaft, Agrarverbände und Staat 1890–1925*. Bonn, 1978.

————. "Landwirtschaftskammer und ländliche Organisationspolitik in der Rheinprovinz, 1918–1927: Ein Beitrag zur Vorgeschichte der 'Grünen Front.'" In *Rheinland-Westfalen im Industriezeitalter: Beiträge zur Landesgeschichte des 19. und 20. Jahrhunderts*, edited by Kurt Düwell and Wolfgang Köllmann, vol. 2, pp. 314–32. Düsseldorf, 1983.

————. "Zwischen Industrie und christlich-nationaler Arbeiterschaft: Alternativen landwirtschaftlicher Bündnispolitik in der Weimarer Republik." In *Industrielle Gesellschaft und politisches System: Festschrift für F. Fischer zum siebzigsten Geburtstag*, edited by Dirk Stegmann, Peter-Christian Witt, and Bernd-Jürgen Wendt, pp. 259–76. Bonn, 1978.

Flemming, Jens; Krohn, Claus-Dieter; and Witt, Peter-Christian. "Sozialverhalten und politische Reaktionen von Gruppen und Institutionen im Inflationsprozess: Anmerkungen zum Forschungsstand." In *Historische Prozesse der deutschen Inflation, 1914 bis*

1924: Ein Tagungsbericht, edited by Otto Büsch and Gerald D. Feldman, pp. 239–63. Berlin, 1978.

Focke, Franz. *Sozialismus aus christlicher Verantwortung: Die Idee eines christlichen Sozialismus in der katholisch-sozialen Bewegung und in der CDU*. Wuppertal, 1978.

Först, Walter, ed. *Politik und Landschaft*. Cologne, 1969.

————, ed. *Provinz und Staat*. Cologne, 1971.

————, ed. *Zwischen Ruhrkampf und Wiederaufbau*. Cologne, 1972.

Franklin, S. H. *The European Peasantry: The Final Phase*. London, 1969.

Franz, Günther, ed. *Bauernschaft und Bauernstand 1500–1970*. Limburg/Lahn, 1975.

Frenzen, Peter. *Untersuchungen über die Entwicklung der Landwirtschaft im Kreise Gladbach*. München-Gladbach, 1907.

Freyberg, Freiherr von. *Die Futtermittelwirtschaft im Kriege*. Berlin, 1919.

Fricke, Dieter, ed. *Die bürgerlichen Parteien in Deutschland: Handbuch der Geschichte der bürgerlichen Parteien und anderer bürgerlicher Interessenorganisationen vom Vormärz bis zum Jahre 1945*. 2 vols. Leipzig, 1968 and 1970.

Fried, Pankraz. "Die Sozialentwicklung im Bauerntum und Landvolk." In *Handbuch der bayerischen Geschichte*, edited by Max Spindler, vol. 4, pp. 749–80. Munich, 1975.

Friedrich, Carl J. "The Agricultural Basis of Emotional Nationalism." *Public Opinion Quarterly* 2 (1937): 50–61.

————. "The Peasant as Evil Genius of Dictatorship." *Yale Review* New Series 26 (1937): 729–40.

Fröhlich, Elke, and Broszat, Martin. "Politische und soziale Macht auf dem Lande: Die Durchsetzung der NSDAP im Kreis Memmingen." *Vierteljahrshefte für Zeitgeschichte* 25 (1977): 546–72.

Fuchs, Walter. "Untersuchungen über die Kreditlage der Landwirtschaft im rheinischen Flachland mit Einschluss des bergischen Landes." Dissertation, Bonn, 1933.

Gabler, Hans. "Die Entwicklung der deutschen Parteien auf landschaftlicher Grundlage von 1871–1912." Dissertation, Berlin, 1934.

Galeski, Boguslaw. *Basic Concepts of Rural Sociology*. Edited by Teodor Shanin and Peter Worsley. Manchester, 1972.

Geary, Dick. *European Labour Protest 1848–1939*. London, 1981.

Geiger, Theodor. *Die soziale Schichtung des deutschen Volkes: Soziographischer Versuch auf statistischer Grundlage*. Stuttgart, 1932.

Gellately, Robert. *The Politics of Economic Despair: Shopkeepers and German Politics 1890–1914*. Beverly Hills, 1974.

Gerloff, Wilhelm. "Die Besteuerung der Landwirtschaft vor und nach dem Krieg." In *Die deutsche Landwirtschaft unter volks- und weltwirtschaftlichen Gesichtspunkten*, edited by Max Sering, pp. 156–95. Berlin, 1932.

————. *Die Finanz und Zollpolitik des Deutschen Reiches nebst ihren Beziehungen zur Landes- und Gemeindefinanzen von der Gründung des Norddeutschen Bundes bis zur Gegenwart*. Jena, 1913.

Gerschenkron, Alexander. *Bread and Democracy in Germany*. Berkeley, 1943.

Gessner, Dieter. *Agrardepression, Agrarideologie und konservative Politik in der Weimarer Republik: Zur Legitimationsproblematik konservativer Politik in der Zwischenkriegszeit*. Wiesbaden, 1976.

————. *Agrardepression und Präsidialregierungen in Deutschland 1930 bis 1933:*

Probleme des Agrarprotektionismus am Ende der Weimarer Republik. Düsseldorf,
1977.

————. "Agrarprotektionismus und Welthandelskrise 1929/32: Zum Verhältnis von
Agrarpolitik und Handelspolitik in der Endphase der Weimarer Republik." *Zeitschrift
für Agrargeschichte und Agrarsoziologie* 26 (1978): 161–87.

————. *Agrarverbände in der Weimarer Republik: Wirtschaftliche und soziale Voraussetzungen agrarkonservativer Politik vor 1933.* Düsseldorf, 1976.

————. "The Dilemma of German Agriculture during the Weimar Republic." In *Social
Change and Political Development in Weimar Germany*, edited by Richard Bessel and
E. J. Feuchtwanger, pp. 134–54. London, 1981.

————. "Industrie und Landwirtschaft 1928–1930." In *Industrielles System und politische Entwicklung in der Weimarer Republik*, edited by Hans Mommsen, Dietmar Petzina, and Bernd Weisbrod, pp. 762–78. Düsseldorf, 1974.

Geyer, Michael. "Professionals and Junkers: German Rearmament and Politics in the
Weimar Republic." In *Social Change and Political Development in Weimar Germany*,
edited by Richard Bessel and E. J. Feuchtwanger, pp. 77–133. London, 1981.

Gies, Horst. "Die nationalsozialistische Machtergreifung auf dem agrarpolitischen Sek-
tor." *Zeitschrift für Agrargeschichte und Agrarsoziologie* 16 (1968): 210–32.

————. "NSDAP und landwirtschaftliche Organisationen in der Endphase der Weimarer
Republik." *Vierteljahrshefte für Zeitgeschichte* 15 (1967): 341–76.

————. "Der Reichsnährstand—Organ berufsständischer Selbstverwaltung oder Instru-
ment staatlicher Wirtschaftslenkung?" *Zeitschrift für Agrargeschichte und Agrarsoziologie* 21 (1973): 216–33.

————. "Revolution oder Kontinuität—Die personelle Struktur des Reichsnährstandes."
In *Bauernschaft und Bauernstand 1500–1970*, edited by Günther Franz, pp. 323–30.
Limburg/Lahn, 1975.

Gieselmann, F. J. "Aufbau und Verflechtung der Wirtschaft." In *Der Raum Westfalen*,
edited by Hermann Aubin, Ottmar Buhler, Bruno Kuske, and Aloys Schulte, vol. 3,
pp. 5–146. Berlin, 1932.

Gläsel, Ernst. "Die Preise landwirtschaftlicher Produkte und Produktionsmittel während
der letzten 50 Jahre und deren Einfluss auf Bodennutzung und Viehhaltung im deutschen Reich." Dissertation, Breslau, 1917.

Görnandt, Rudolf. *Der Landarbeiter mit eigener Wirtschaft in Nordwest- und Ost-
deutschland.* Berlin, 1910.

Golde, Guenther. *Catholics and Protestants: Agricultural Modernization in Two German
Villages.* New York, 1975.

Gollwitzer, Heinz. "Europäische Bauerndemokratie im 20. Jahrhundert." In *Europäische
Bauernparteien im 20. Jahrhundert*, edited by Heinz Gollwitzer, pp. 1–82. Stuttgart,
1977.

————, ed. *Europäische Bauernparteien im 20. Jahrhundert.* Stuttgart, 1977.

Golte, Wilhelm. "Die Gestaltung der landwirtschaftlichen Betriebsorganisation unter
verschiedener Höhenlage untersucht an 37 Betrieben des Regierungsbezirkes Arnsberg." Dissertation, Giessen, 1909.

Gottwald, Herbert. "Der Umfall des Zentrums: Die Stellung der Zentrumspartei zur Flot-
tenvorlage von 1897." In *Studien zum deutschen Imperialismus*, edited by Fritz Klein,
pp. 181–223. Berlin, 1976.

Gourevitch, Peter Alexis. "International Trade, Domestic Coalitions, and Liberty: Comparative Responses to the Crisis of 1873–1896." *Journal of Interdisciplinary History* 7 (1977): 281–313.

Grabein, Max. *Wirtschaftliche und soziale Bedeutung der ländlichen Genossenschaften in Deutschland.* Tübingen, 1908.

Graham, Frank D. *Exchange, Prices, and Production in Hyper-Inflation: Germany 1920–1923.* Princeton, 1930.

Gramsci, Antonio. *Selections from Political Writings (1910–1920).* Edited by Quintin Hoare. Trans. by John Mathews. New York, 1977.

Grebing, Helga. "Die Konservativen und Christlichen seit 1918." *Politische Studien* 9 (1958): 482–91.

Grill, Johnpeter Horst. *The Nazi Movement in Baden, 1920–1945.* Chapel Hill, 1983.

————. "The Nazi Party's Rural Propaganda before 1928." *Central European History* 15 (1982): 149–85.

Grosse-Lümern, Gottfried. *Die Landwirtschaft im Kreise Wiedenbrück: Ein Beitrag zur Kenntnis der modernen Sandbodenwirtschaft.* Münster, 1913.

Gruna, Klaus. "Johannes Gronowski." In *Politik und Landschaft*, edited by Walter Först, pp. 162–68. Cologne, 1969.

Gündell, Gisela. *Die Organisation der deutschen Ernährungswirtschaft im Weltkriege.* Leipzig, 1939.

Günther, Adolf. "Die Folgen des Krieges für Einkommen und Lebenshaltung der mittleren Volksschichten Deutschlands." In *Die Einwirkung des Krieges auf Bevölkerungsbewegung, Einkommen und Lebenshaltung in Deutschland*, edited by R. Meerwarth, A. Günther, and W. Zimmermann, pp. 103–279. Stuttgart, 1932.

Hagmann, Franz. "Zur Frage des Risikos in der rheinischen Landwirtschaft: Untersuchung an Hand 10jähriger Buchführungsergebnisse rheinischer Betriebe." Dissertation, Bonn, 1939.

Hagmann, H. *30 Wirtschaftsrechnungen von Kleinbauern und Landarbeitern.* Bonn, 1911.

————. *Landwirtschaftliche Statistik für die Kreise der Rheinprovinz.* Bonn, 1912.

————. "Löhne der einheimischen und der Wander-Arbeiter in Schlesien und der Rheinprovinz." *Landwirtschaftliche Jahrbücher* 40 (1911): 611–730.

————. *Wirtschaftsrechnungen rheinischer Kleinbauern.* Bonn, 1917.

Hagmann, Hugo. "Einfluss der Preisgestaltung auf den Reinertrag des Landgutes." In *Landwirtschaft und Geldentwertung*, edited by T. Brinkmann, H. Hagmann, and E. Lang, pp. 1–6. Stuttgart, 1921.

Hamann, Karl Otto. "Der Arbeitsmarkt in der westfälischen Landwirtschaft." Dissertation, Bonn, 1932.

Hamilton, Richard F. *Who Voted for Hitler?* Princeton, 1982.

Hansen, Joseph. *Preussen und Rheinland von 1815 bis 1915.* Bonn, 1918.

————, ed. *Die Rheinprovinz 1815–1915: Hundert Jahre preussischer Herrschaft am Rhein.* Vol. 1. Bonn, 1917.

Hardach, Gerd. *The First World War 1914–1918.* Berkeley, 1977.

Hardach, Karl W. *Die Bedeutung wirtschaftlicher Faktoren bei der Wiedereinführung der Eisen- und Getreidezölle in Deutschland 1879.* Berlin, 1967.

Harrison, Mark. "Chayanov and the Marxists." *Journal of Peasant Studies* 7 (1979): 86–100.

————. "The Peasant Mode of Production in the Work of A. V. Chayanov." *Journal of*

Peasant Studies 4 (1977): 323–36.

————. "Resource Allocation and Agrarian Class Formation: The Problem of Social Mobility among Russian Peasant Households, 1880–1930." *Journal of Peasant Studies* 4 (1977): 127–61.

Hartenstein, Wolfgang. *Die Anfänge der Deutschen Volkspartei 1918–1920*. Düsseldorf, 1962.

Haselhoff, Emil, and Breme, H., eds. *Die Entwicklung der Landeskultur in der Provinz Westfalen im 19. Jahrhundert*. Münster, 1900.

Hassel, von. *Die Einrichtungen der preussischen Landkreise auf dem Gebiete der Kriegswirtschaft*. Berlin, 1918.

Haushofer, Heinz. "Der Bayerische Bauernbund 1893–1933." In *Europäische Bauern-parteien im 20. Jahrhundert*, edited by Heinz Gollwitzer, pp. 562–86. Stuttgart, 1977.

————. *Die deutsche Landwirtschaft im technischen Zeitalter*. Stuttgart, 1963.

Havenstein, Gustav. "Der Personalkredit des ländlichen Kleingrundbesitzes in der Rhein-provinz." In *Der Personalkredit des ländlichen Kleingrundbesitzes in Deutschland*, Schriften des Vereins für Sozialpolitik, vol. 74, pp. 75–134. Leipzig, 1896.

Heberle, Rudolf. *Landbevölkerung und Nationalsozialismus: Eine soziologische Unter-suchung der politischen Willensbildung in Schleswig-Holstein 1918–1932*. Stuttgart, 1963.

Heckart, Beverly. *From Bassermann to Bebel: The Grand Bloc's Quest for Reform in the Kaiserreich 1900–1914*. New Haven, 1974.

Heese, Maria. "Der Landschaftswandel im mittleren Ruhrindustriegebiet seit 1820." Dis-sertation, Münster, 1941.

Hehnsen, Heinz-Hugo. "Der Strukturwandel der Landwirtschaft im Ruhrgebiet seit 1880." Dissertation, Cologne, 1955.

Heinen, Ernst. "Zentrumspresse und Kriegszieldiskussion unter besonderer Berücksichti-gung der 'Kölnischen Volkszeitung' und 'Germania.'" Dissertation, Cologne, 1962.

Heinrichs, Werner. "Die Entwicklung der landwirtschaftlichen Betriebsverhältnisse in dem westlichen Teil des Hellweggebietes unter dem Einfluss der Industrie." Disserta-tion, Bonn, 1938.

Heitzer, Horst Walter. *Der Volksverein für das katholische Deutschland im Kaiserreich 1890–1918*. Mainz, 1979.

Helling, Gertrud. "Berechnung eines Index der Agrarproduktion in Deutschland im 19. Jahrhundert." *Jahrbuch für Wirtschaftsgeschichte* 1965/IV: 125–51.

————. "Zur Entwicklung der Produktivität in der deutschen Landwirtschaft im 19. Jahrhundert." *Jahrbuch für Wirtschaftsgeschichte* 1966/I: 129–41.

Hellwig, Karl. "Das landwirtschaftliche Kreditwesen in den Jahren 1913–1923." Disser-tation, Bonn, 1928.

Hendon, David Warren. "The Center Party and the Agrarian Interest in Germany, 1890–1914." Ph.D. dissertation, Emory University, 1976.

————. "German Catholics and the Agrarian League, 1893–1914." *German Studies Re-view* 4 (1981): 427–45.

Henkelmann, Werner. "Fütterung und Tierzucht als Mittel der Produktionskostensen-kung." In *Deutsche Agrarpolitik im Rahmen der inneren und äusseren Wirtschaftspoli-tik*, edited by Fritz Beckmann, Bernhard Harms, Theodor Brinkmann, Hermann Bente, Edgar Salin, and Werner Henkelmann, vol. 1, pp. 667–89. Berlin, 1932.

————. *Zur Frage der optimalen Betriebsgrösse in der Rheinprovinz.* Bonn, 1928.

————. "Der Zusammenhang zwischen Bodennutzung, Bodenerträgen und Viehhaltung." *Landwirtschaftliche Jahrbücher* 74 (1931): 829–923.

Henning, Friedrich-Wilhelm. *Landwirtschaft und ländliche Gesellschaft in Deutschland.* Vol. 2. Paderborn, 1978.

————. "Produktionskosten und Preisbildung für Getreide in den letzten Jahrzehnten des 19. Jahrhunderts." *Zeitschrift für Agrargeschichte und Agrarsoziologie* 25 (1977): 214–36.

Hertzmann, Lewis. *DNVP: Right-Wing Opposition in the Weimar Republic, 1918–1924.* Lincoln, Neb., 1963.

Hesse, A. *Freie Wirtschaft und Zwangswirtschaft im Kriege.* Berlin, 1918.

Hesse, Paul. "Fleischverbrauch und Viehhaltung in der deutschen 'Wirtschaftsgebieten.'" *Landwirtschaftliche Jahrbücher* 69 (1929): 1–104.

Hesselbarth, Helmuth. *Revolutionäre Sozialdemokraten, Opportunisten und die Bauern am Vorabend des Imperialismus.* Berlin, 1968.

Heyermann, Wilhelm. "Die Landarbeiterfrage in Westfalen." Dissertation, Frankfurt, 1925.

Hibbard, Benjamin H. *Effects of the Great War Upon Agriculture in the United States and Great Britain.* New York, 1919.

Hickey, Stephen. "The Shaping of the German Labour Movement: Miners in the Ruhr." In *Society and Politics in Wilhelmine Germany,* edited by Richard J. Evans, pp. 215–40. London, 1978.

Hilferding, Rudolf. "Theoretische Bemerkungen zur Agrarfrage." *Die Gesellschaft* 1927/I: 421–32.

Hobsbawm, E. J. "Peasants and Politics." *Journal of Peasant Studies* 1 (1973): 3–22.

Hömig, Herbert. *Das Preussische Zentrum in der Weimarer Republik.* Mainz, 1979.

Hoener, Erich. "Die Geschichte der christlich-konservativen Partei in Minden-Ravensberg von 1866–1896." Dissertation, Münster, 1923.

Hoffmann, Walther G. *Das Wachstum der deutschen Wirtschaft seit der Mitte des 19. Jahrhunderts.* Berlin, 1965.

Hofmann, Wolfgang. *Die Bielefelder Stadtverordneten: Ein Beitrag zu bürgerlicher Selbstverwaltung und sozialem Wandel 1850 bis 1914.* Lübeck, 1964.

Hohorst, Gerd; Kocka, Jürgen; and Ritter, Gerhard A. *Sozialgeschichtliches Arbeitsbuch: Materialien zur Statistik des Kaiserreichs 1870–1914.* Munich, 1975.

Holländer, Julius Walter. "Der deutsche Zolltarif von 1902: Das wichtigste über seine Entstehungsursachen und Gestaltungsbedingungen." *Schmollers Jahrbuch* 37 (1913): 283–332, 829–57, 1359–1425.

Hollmann, A. H. *Die Landwirtschaft im Kreis Bonn mit besonderer Berücksichtigung der sozialen Verhältnisse der ländlichen Bevölkerung.* Bonn, 1903.

Holmes, Kim R. "The Forsaken Past: Agrarian Conservatism and National Socialism in Germany." *Journal of Contemporary History* 17 (1982): 671–88.

Holt, John Bradshaw. *German Agricultural Policy, 1918–1934: The Development of a National Philosophy Toward Agriculture in Postwar Germany.* Chapel Hill, 1936.

Holtfrerich, Carl-Ludwig. *Die deutsche Inflation 1914–1923: Ursachen und Folgen in internationaler Perspektive.* Berlin, 1980.

Horn, Hannelore. *Der Kampf um den Bau des Mittellandkanals: Eine politologische Un-

tersuchung über die Rolle eines wirtschaftlichen Interessenverbandes in Preussen Wilhelm II. Cologne, 1964.

Howard, W. H. *Die Produktionskosten unserer wichtigsten Feldfrüchte*. Berlin, 1908.

Hughes, Michael. "Economic Interest, Social Attitudes, and Creditor Ideology: Popular Responses to Inflation." In *Die deutsche Inflation: Eine Zwischenbilanz*, edited by Gerald D. Feldman, Carl-Ludwig Holtfrerich, Gerhard A. Ritter, and Peter-Christian Witt, pp. 385–408. Berlin, 1982.

Hunt, James Clark. "The 'Egalitarianism' of the Right: The Agrarian League in Southwest Germany, 1893–1914." *Journal of Contemporary History* 10 (1975): 513–30.

_____. "Peasants, Grain Tariffs and Meat Quotas: Imperial German Protectionism Reexamined." *Central European History* 7 (1974): 311–31.

_____. *The People's Party in Württemberg and Southern Germany, 1890–1914: The Possibilities of Democratic Politics*. Stuttgart, 1975.

Husen, Karl van. *Die Belastung des Kreises Rees mit Schulden, Steuern und Soziallasten im Vergleich zur Vorkriegszeit*. Jena, 1930.

Hussain, Athar, and Tribe, Keith. *Marxism and the Agrarian Question*. Vol. 1. Atlantic Highlands, N.J., 1981.

Imhof, Arthur E. "Women, Family and Death: Excess Mortality of Women in Child-Bearing Age in Four Communities in Nineteenth-Century Germany." In *The German Family: Essays on the Social History of the Family in Nineteenth- and Twentieth-Century Germany*, edited by Richard J. Evans and W. R. Lee, pp. 148–74. London, 1981.

Jackson, George D., Jr. "Peasant Political Movements in Eastern Europe." In *Rural Protest: Peasant Movements and Social Change*, edited by Henry A. Landsberger, pp. 259–315. London, 1974.

Jacobs, Ferdinand. *Deutsche Bauernführer*. Düsseldorf, 1958.

_____. *Von Schorlemer zur Grünen Front: Zur Abwertung des berufsständischen und politischen Denkens*. Düsseldorf, 1957.

Johanns, Karl. "Die Organisation des landwirtschaftlichen Vereinswesens in Westfalen." Dissertation, Münster, 1913.

Jones, Larry Eugene. "Adam Stegerwald und die Krise des deutschen Parteiensystems: Ein Beitrag zur Deutung des 'Essener Programms' vom November 1920." *Vierteljahrshefte für Zeitgeschichte* 27 (1979): 1–29.

_____. "Crisis and Realignment: Agrarian Splinter Parties in the Late Weimar Republic, 1928–1933." In *Peasants and Lords in Modern Germany: Recent Studies in Agricultural History*, edited by Robert G. Moeller, pp. 198–232. Boston, 1986.

_____. "Democracy and Liberalism in the German Inflation: The Crisis of a Political Movement." Forthcoming.

_____. "The Dissolution of the Bourgeois Party System in the Weimar Republic." In *Social Change and Political Development in Weimar Germany*, edited by Richard Bessel and E. J. Feuchtwanger, pp. 268–88. London, 1981.

_____. " 'The Dying Middle': Weimar Germany and the Fragmentation of Bourgeois Politics." *Central European History* 5 (1972): 23–54.

_____. "Inflation, Revaluation, and the Crisis of Middle-Class Politics: A Study in the Dissolution of the German Party System, 1923–1928." *Central European History* 12 (1979): 143–68.

Judt, Tony. *Socialism in Provence: A Study of the Origins of the Modern French Left*. Cambridge, 1979.

Jürgens, Arnulf. "Politischer Konservatismus im ländlichen Bereich: Das bäuerliche Genossenschaftswesen in Westfalen und im Rheinland in der zweiten Hälfte des 19. Jahrhunderts." In *Rheinland-Westfalen im Industriezeitalter: Beiträge zur Landesgeschichte des 19. und 20. Jahrhunderts*, edited by Kurt Düwell and Wolfgang Köllmann, vol. 2, pp. 127–47. Wuppertal, 1984.

Junker, Detlef. *Die deutsche Zentrumspartei und Hitler 1932/33: Ein Beitrag zur Problematik des politischen Katholizismus in Deutschland.* Stuttgart, 1969.

Kaerger, Karl. "Die ländliche Arbeiterverhältnisse in Nordwestdeutschland." In *Die Verhältnisse der Landarbeiter in Deutschland*, Schriften des Vereins für Sozialpolitik, vol. 53, pp. 1–239. Leipzig, 1892.

Kaufmann, Doris. "Vom Vaterland zum Mutterland: Frauen im katholischen Milieu der Weimarer Republik." In *Frauen suchen ihre Geschichte: Historische Studien zum 19. und 20. Jahrhundert*, edited by Karin Hausen, pp. 250–75. Munich, 1983.

Kaufmann, Otto. "Frauenarbeit im 19. Jahrhundert im Homburger Land." *Rheinisch-Westfälische Zeitschrift für Volkskunde* 18 (1972): 76–102.

Kautsky, Karl. *Die Agrarfrage: Eine Übersicht über die Tendenzen der modernen Landwirtschaft und die Agrarpolitik der Sozialdemokratie.* Stuttgart, 1899.

Kellermann, Wilhelm. "Der Westfälische Bauernverein." In *Beiträge zur Geschichte des westfälischen Bauernstandes*, edited by Engelbert Freiherr Kerckerinck zu Borg, pp. 376–477. Berlin, 1912.

Kerckerinck zu Borg, Engelbert Freiherr, ed. *Beiträge zur Geschichte des westfälischen Bauernstandes.* Berlin, 1912.

Kindleberger, Charles P. "Group Behavior and International Trade." In *Economic Response: Comparative Studies in Trade, Finance and Growth*, pp. 19–38. Cambridge, Mass., 1978.

———. *The World in Depression 1929–1939.* Berkeley, 1973.

Kirch, Gerhard. "Person und Individualität." In *Das Dorf als soziales Gebilde*, edited by Leopold von Wiese, pp. 16–26. Munich, 1928.

Kissling, Johannes Baptist. *Geschichte der deutschen Katholikentage.* 2 vols. Münster, 1920–23.

Klaas, Walter. "Der Entwicklungsgang der staatlichen Regelung des Kriegs-Schweinemarktes." In *Das Schwein in der Kriegsernährungswirtschaft*, pp. 27–80. Berlin, 1917.

Klein, Ernst. *Geschichte der deutschen Landwirtschaft im Industriezeitalter.* Wiesbaden, 1973.

Klemm, Volker. "Die Entwicklung der landwirtschaftlichen Produktion während der Agrarkrise von 1927/28 bis 1932/33 in Deutschland." *Wissenschaftliche Zeitschrift der Universität Rostock, Gesellschafts- und sprachwissenschaftliche Reihe* 17 (1968): 187–93.

———. *Ursachen und Verlauf der Krise der deutschen Landwirtschaft von 1927/28 bis 1933.* Habilitationsschrift, Berlin, 1965.

Kluge, Ulrich. *Soldatenräte und Revolution: Studien zur Militärpolitik in Deutschland 1918/19.* Göttingen, 1975.

Koch, Max Jürgen. *Die Bergarbeiterbewegung im Ruhrgebiet zur Zeit Wilhelms II. (1889–1914).* Düsseldorf, 1954.

Kocka, Jürgen. "Class Formation, Interest Articulation and Public Policy: The Origins of the German White-Collar Class in the Late Nineteenth and Early Twentieth Centuries."

In *Organizing Interests in Western Europe: Pluralism, Corporatism and the Transformation of Politics*, edited by Suzanne Berger, pp. 63–81. Cambridge, 1981.

———. "The First World War and the '*Mittelstand*': German Artisans and White Collar Workers." *Journal of Contemporary History* 8 (1973): 101–24.

———. *Klassengesellschaft im Krieg: Deutsche Sozialgeschichte 1914–1918*. Göttingen, 1973.

———. "Vorindustrielle Faktoren in der deutschen Industrialisierung: Industriebürokratie und 'neuer Mittelstand.'" In *Das kaiserliche Deutschland: Politik und Gesellschaft, 1890–1914*, edited by Michael Stürmer, pp. 265–96. Düsseldorf, 1970.

———. "Weltkrieg und Mittelstand: Handwerker und Angestellte in Deutschland, 1914–1918." *Francia* 2 (1974): 431–57.

———. *White Collar Workers in America: A Social-Political History in International Perspective*. Trans. by Maura Kealey. Beverly Hills, 1980.

Köllmann, Wolfgang. *Bevölkerung in der industriellen Revolution: Studien zur Bevölkerungsgeschichte Deutschlands*. Göttingen, 1974.

———. "Die Bevölkerung Rheinland-Westfalens in der Hochindustrialisierungsperiode." In *Bevölkerung in der industriellen Revolution: Studien zur Bevölkerungsgeschichte Deutschlands*, pp. 229–49. Göttingen, 1974.

———. "Rheinland und Westfalen an der Schwelle des Industriezeitalters." In *Bevölkerung in der industriellen Revolution: Studien zur Bevölkerungsgeschichte Deutschlands*, pp. 208–28. Göttingen, 1974.

———. "Rheinland-Westfalen in der deutschen Binnenwanderungsbewegung der Hochindustrialisierungsperiode." In *Bevölkerung in der industriellen Revolution: Studien zur Bevölkerungsgeschichte Deutschlands*, pp. 250–60. Göttingen, 1974.

———. *Sozialgeschichte der Stadt Barmen im 19. Jahrhundert*. Tübingen, 1960.

Köllmann, Wolfgang, and Düwell, Kurt, eds. *Rheinland-Westfalen im Industriezeitalter: Beiträge zur Landesgeschichte des 19. und 20. Jahrhunderts*. Vols 1 and 2. Wuppertal, 1983–84.

Kohler, Eric D. "Inflation and Black Marketeering in the Rhenish Agricultural Economy, 1919–1922." *German Studies Review* 8 (1985): 43–64.

———. "Revolutionary Pomerania, 1919–20: A Study in Majority Socialist Agricultural Policy and Civil-Military Relations." *Central European History* 9 (1976): 250–93.

Koshar, Rudy. "Two 'Nazisms': The Social Context of Nazi Mobilization in Marburg and Tübingen." *Social History* 7 (1982): 27–42.

Kovan, Allen Stanley. "The Reichs-Landbund and the Resurgence of Germany's Agrarian Conservatives, 1919–1923." Ph.D. dissertation, University of California, Berkeley, 1972.

Krebs, Willy. "Die Entwicklung der landwirtschaftlichen Genossenschaften seit der Währungsstabilisierung." *Jahrbücher für Nationalökonomie und Statistik* 130 (1929): 76–97.

———. "Die öffentliche Ernährungswirtschaft und die Organisation der Landwirtschaft unter besonderer Berücksichtigung des Genossenschaftswesens: Dargelegt an der Ergebnissen der Genossenschaftsstatistik." *Jahrbücher für Nationalökonomie und Statistik* 110 (1918): 28–72.

Kretschmar, Hans. *Deutsche Agrarprogramme der Nachkriegszeit: Die agrarpolitischen Forderungen der landwirtschaftlichen Berufsverbände*. Berlin, 1933.

Kroeger, Albert. "Die Entwicklung der landwirtschaftlichen Bodennutzung in der War-
burger Börde und ihren Randzonen." Dissertation, Bonn, 1937.

Krohn, Claus-Dieter. *Stabilisierung und ökonomische Interessen: Die Finanzpolitik des
deutschen Reiches 1923–1927*. Düsseldorf, 1974.

Kuczynski, Robert. *Deutschlands Versorgung mit Nahrungs- und Futtermitteln*. Berlin,
1926.

Kühr, Herbert. *Parteien und Wahlen im Stadt- und Landkreis Essen in der Zeit der Weimarer Republik: Unter besonderer Berücksichtigung des Verhältnisses von Sozialstruktur und politischen Wahlen*. Düsseldorf, 1973.

Küppers, Heinrich. "Zur Entstehung und Entwicklung des Rheinischen Bauernvereins."
Zeitschrift für Agrargeschichte und Agrarsoziologie 28 (1980): 1–31.

Kunz, Andreas. "Stand versus Klasse: Beamtenschaft und Gewerkschaften im Konflikt
um den Personalabbau 1923/24." *Geschichte und Gesellschaft* 9 (1982): 55–86.

————. "Verteilungskampf oder Interessenkonsensus? Einkommensentwicklung und
Sozialverhalten von Arbeitnehmergruppen in der Inflationszeit 1914–1924." In *Die
deutsche Inflation: Eine Zwischenbilanz*, edited by Gerald D. Feldman, Carl-Ludwig
Holtfrerich, Gerhard A. Ritter, and Peter-Christian Witt, pp. 347–84. Berlin, 1982.

Kupperberg, M. "Die Viehhaltung, insbesondere die Schweinehaltung, in den einzelnen
Landesteilen Preussens im Zeitraum 1920 bis 1924 im Vergleich mit dem Stand vor
dem Krieg." *Zeitschrift des preussischen statistischen Landesamts* 65 (1925): 419–50.

Kuske, Bruno. "Der Wirtschaftsraum." In *Der Raum Westfalen*, edited by Hermann Aubin, Ottmar Buhler, Bruno Kuske, and Aloys Schulte, vol. 1, pp. 75–124. Berlin,
1931.

Laer, Wilhelm von. "Die wirtschaftlichen Verhältnisse." In *Beiträge zur Geschichte des
westfälischen Bauernstandes*, edited by Engelbert Freiherr Kerckerinck zu Borg, pp.
164–223. Berlin, 1912.

Landsberger, Henry A., ed. *Latin American Peasant Movements*. Ithaca, 1969.

————, ed. *Rural Protest: Peasant Movements and Social Change*. London, 1974.

Latten, Willy. "Das Dorf als Lebensgemeinschaft." In *Das Dorf als soziales Gebilde*,
edited by Leopold von Wiese, pp. 70–77. Munich, 1928.

Laur, Ernst. *Landwirtschaftliche Betriebslehre für bäuerliche Verhältnisse*. Aarau, 1922.

Laursen, Karsten, and Pedersen, Jørgen. *The German Inflation 1918–1923*. Amsterdam,
1964.

League of Nations. *Agricultural Production in Continental Europe During the 1914–19
War and the Reconstruction Period*. Geneva, 1943.

Lebovics, Hermann. " 'Agrarians' versus 'Industrializers'—Social Conservative Resistance to Industrialism and Capitalism in Late Nineteenth Century Germany." *International Review of Social History* 12 (1967): 31–65.

————. *Social Conservatism and the Middle Classes in Germany 1914–1933*. Princeton, 1969.

Lehmann, Hans Georg. *Die Agrarfrage in der Theorie und Praxis der deutschen und internationalen Sozialdemokratie: Vom Marxismus zum Revisionismus und Bolschewis-
mus*. Tübingen, 1970.

Leonhards, Rudolf. "Die landwirtschaftlichen Betriebsformen des niederbergischen
Landes." Dissertation, Bonn, 1922.

Lepsius, M. Rainer. *Extremer Nationalismus: Strukturbedingungen von der nationalso-

zialistischen Machtergreifung. Stuttgart, 1966.

———. "Parteiensystem und Sozialstruktur: Zum Problem der Demokratisierung der deutschen Gesellschaft." In *Die deutschen Parteien vor 1918*, edited by Gerhard A. Ritter, pp. 56–80. Cologne, 1973.

Lessmann, Wilhelm. "Die deutschen christlichen Bauernvereine als Träger praktischer Agrarpolitik unter besonderer Berücksichtigung der wirtschaftlichen Tätigkeit der westdeutschen Bauernvereine." Dissertation, Kiel, 1928.

Levy, Richard S. *The Downfall of the Anti-Semitic Political Parties in Imperial Germany.* New Haven, 1975.

Lewis, Gavin. "The Peasantry, Rural Change and Conservative Agrarianism: Lower Austria at the Turn of the Century." *Past & Present* No. 81 (1978): 119–43.

Lidtke, Vernon L. *The Alternative Culture: Socialist Labor in Imperial Germany.* New York, 1985.

Liebe, Werner. *Die Deutschnationale Volkspartei 1918–1924.* Düsseldorf, 1956.

Liepmann, Moritz. *Krieg und Kriminalität in Deutschland.* Stuttgart, 1930.

Lindemann, Hugo. *Die deutsche Stadtgemeinde im Kriege.* Tübingen, 1917.

Lindner, Werner. "Die bäuerliche Wohnkultur in der Provinz Westfalen und ihren nördlichen Grenzgebieten." In *Beiträge zur Geschichte des westfälischen Bauernstandes*, edited by Engelbert Freiherr Kerckerinck zu Borg, pp. 635–840. Berlin, 1912.

Linneweber, Gisbert. *Die Landwirtschaft in den Kreisen Dortmund und Hörde unter dem Einfluss der Industrie.* Stuttgart, 1909.

Litman, Simon. *Prices and Price Controls in Great Britain and the United States During the World War.* New York, 1920.

Loë-Bergerhausen, Clemens Freiherr von. *Die Organisation des landwirtschaftlichen Berufsstandes.* Cologne, 1917.

Loomis, Charles P., and Beegle, J. A. "The Spread of German Nazism in Rural Areas." *American Sociological Review* 11 (1946): 724–34.

Lovin, Clifford R. "Agricultural Reorganization in the Third Reich: The Reich Food Corporation (*Reichsnährstand*), 1933–36." *Agricultural History* 43 (1969): 447–61.

———. "Blut und Boden: The Ideological Basis of the Nazi Agricultural Program." *Journal of the History of Ideas* 28 (1967): 279–88.

Lucas, Erhard. *Märzrevolution im Ruhrgebiet: Vom Generalstreik gegen den Militärputsch zum bewaffneten Arbeiteraufstand, März–April 1920.* Vol. 1. Frankfurt, 1970.

———. *Zwei Formen von Radikalismus in der deutschen Arbeiterbewegung.* Frankfurt, 1976.

Ludewig, Hans-Ulrich. *Arbeiterbewegung und Aufstand: Eine Untersuchung zum Verhalten der Arbeiterparteien in den Aufstandsbewegungen der frühen Weimarer Republik 1920–1923.* Husum, 1978.

Lüninck, Hermann Freiherr von. "Die politische Vertretung des deutschen Katholizismus." *Historisch-politische Blätter für das katholische Deutschland* 165 (1920): 555–72.

———. "Das Zentrum am Scheideweg." *Historisch-politische Blätter für das katholische Deutschland* 165 (1920): 53–68, 107–22.

McGuire, Robert A. "Economic Causes of Late-Nineteenth Century Agrarian Unrest: New Evidence." *Journal of Economic History* 41 (1981): 835–52.

McPhee, William N., and Glaser, William A., eds. *Public Opinion and Congressional Elections.* Glencoe, 1962.

Maehl, William Harvey. "German Social Democratic Agrarian Policy, 1890–1895: Reconsidered." *Central European History* 13 (1980): 121–57.

Mahnke, Herbert. "Das Entstehen der Kreditnot in der deutschen Landwirtschaft beim Übergang von der Inflation zur Stabilisierung mit besonderer Berücksichtigung des Kapitalbedarfs." Dissertation, Hamburg, 1926.

Maier, Charles S. *Recasting Bourgeois Europe: Stabilization in France, Germany and Italy in the Decade after World War I.* Princeton, 1975.

Mantzke, Ulrich. "Zur Landarbeiterbewegung im Freistaat Sachsen in den ersten Monaten nach der Novemberrevolution." *Wissenschaftliche Zeitschrift der Universität Rostock, Gesellschafts- und sprachwissenschaftliche Reihe* 17 (1968): 87–96.

Mathews, William Carl. "The Continuity of Social Democratic Economic Policy 1919–20: The Bauer-Schmidt Policy." Forthcoming.

————. "The German Social Democrats and the Inflation: Food, Foreign Trade, and the Politics of Stabilization 1914–1920." Ph.D. dissertation, University of California, Riverside, 1982.

Mattes, Wilhelm. *Die bayerischen Bauernräte: Eine soziologische und historische Untersuchung über bäuerliche Politik.* Stuttgart, 1921.

Matthias, Erich, and Morsey, Rudolf, eds. *Das Ende der Parteien 1933.* Düsseldorf, 1979. (Reprint of 1960 edition.)

Mayer, Arno. "The Lower Middle Class as Historical Problem." *Journal of Modern History* 47 (1975): 409–36.

Meerwarth, Rudolf; Günther, Adolf; and Zimmermann, Waldemar. *Die Einwirkungen des Krieges auf Bevölkerungsbewegung, Einkommen und Lebenshaltung in Deutschland.* Stuttgart, 1932.

Mees, Günther. "Schorlemer-Alst und der westfälische Bauernverein in der deutschen Innenpolitik, vornehmlich der Jahre 1890–1914." Dissertation, Münster, 1956.

Meitzen, August, ed. *Der Boden und die landwirtschaftlichen Verhältnisse des Preussischen Staates.* 8 vols. Berlin, 1868–1908.

Mendershausen, Ralph René. "German Political Catholicism 1912–1919." Ph.D. dissertation, University of California, San Diego, 1973.

Mendras, Henri. *The Vanishing Peasant: Innovation and Change in French Agriculture.* Trans. by Jean Lerner. Cambridge, Mass., 1970.

Methfessel, Werner. "Christlich-Nationale Bauern- und Landvolkpartei (CNBL) 1928–1933." In *Die bürgerlichen Parteien in Deutschland: Handbuch der Geschichte der bürgerlichen Parteien und anderer bürgerlicher Interessenorganisationen vom Vormärz bis zum Jahre 1945*, edited by Dieter Fricke, vol. 1, pp. 241–44. Berlin, 1968.

Meyer, Lothar. *Die deutsche Landwirtschaft während der Inflation und zu Beginn der Deflation.* Tübingen, 1924.

Middleton, Thomas Hudson. *Food Production in War.* Oxford, 1923.

Migdal, Joel S. *Peasants, Politics, and Revolution: Pressures toward Political and Social Change in the Third World.* Princeton, 1974.

Milatz, Alfred. "Reichstagswahlen und Mandatsverteilung 1871 bis 1918." In *Gesellschaft, Parlament und Regierung: Zur Geschichte des Parlamentarismus in Deutschland*, edited by Gerhard A. Ritter, pp. 207–23. Düsseldorf, 1974.

————. *Wähler und Wahlen in der Weimarer Republik.* Neuwied, 1966.

Miller, Susanne. *Die Bürde der Macht: Die deutsche Sozialdemokratie 1918–1920.* Düsseldorf, 1978.

_____. *Burgfrieden und Klassenkampf: Die deutsche Sozialdemokratie im Ersten Weltkrieg*. Düsseldorf, 1974.

Mitchell, Allan. *Revolution in Bavaria 1918–1919: The Eisner Regime and the Soviet Republic*. Princeton, 1965.

Mittmann, Ursula. *Fraktion und Partei: Ein Vergleich von Zentrum und Sozialdemokratie im Kaiserreich*. Düsseldorf, 1976.

Mödder, Joseph. "Handelspolitische Ansichten der rheinischen Landwirtschaft seit der Gründung des Landwirtschaftlichen Vereins für Rheinpreussen." Dissertation, Cologne, 1927.

Moeller, Robert G. "Die Besonderheiten der Deutschen? Neue Beiträge zur Sonderwegsdiskussion." *Internationale Schulbuchforschung* 4 (1982): 71–80.

_____. "Dimensions of Social Conflict in the Great War: The View from the German Countryside." *Central European History* 14 (1981): 142–68.

_____. "The Kaiserreich Recast? Continuity and Change in Modern German Historiography." *Journal of Social History* 17 (1984): 655–83.

_____. "Peasants and Tariffs in the *Kaiserreich*: How Backward were the *Bauern*?" *Agricultural History* 55 (1981): 370–84.

_____. "Winners as Losers in the German Inflation: Peasant Protest over the Controlled Economy 1920–1923." In *Die deutsche Inflation: Eine Zwischenbilanz*, edited by Gerald D. Feldman, Carl-Ludwig Holtfrerich, Gerhard A. Ritter, and Peter-Christian Witt, pp. 255–88. Berlin, 1982.

_____. "Zur Ökonomie des Agrarsektors in den Provinzen Rheinland und Westfalen zwischen 1896 und 1933." In *Rheinland-Westfalen im Industriezeitalter: Beiträge zur Landesgeschichte des 19. und 20. Jahrhunderts*, edited by Kurt Düwell and Wolfgang Köllmann, vol. 2, pp. 290–313. Wuppertal, 1984.

Molt, Peter. *Der Reichstag vor der improvisierten Revolution*. Cologne, 1963.

Mommsen, Hans; Petzina, Dietmar; and Weisbrod, Bernd, eds. *Industrielles System und politische Entwicklung in der Weimarer Republik*. Düsseldorf, 1974.

Mommsen, Wolfgang. "The German Revolution 1918–1920: Political Revolution and Social Protest Movement." In *Social Change and Political Development in Weimar Germany*, edited by Richard Bessel and E. J. Feuchtwanger, pp. 21–54. London, 1981.

Montag, Josef. "Die steuerliche Belastung des landwirtschaftlichen Besitzes in Westfalen." Dissertation, Münster, 1928.

Moore, Barrington, Jr. *Injustice: The Social Bases of Obedience and Revolt*. White Plains, 1978.

_____. *Social Origins of Dictatorship and Democracy: Lord and Peasant in the Making of the Modern World*. Boston, 1966.

Mooser, Josef. "Familien, Heirat und Berufswahl: Zur Verfassung der ländlichen Gesellschaft im 19. Jahrhundert." In *Die Familie in der Geschichte*, edited by Heinz Reif, pp. 137–62. Göttingen, 1982.

_____. "Gleichheit und Ungleichheit in der ländlichen Gemeinde: Sozialstruktur und Kommunalverfassung im östlichen Westfalen vom späten 18. bis in die Mitte des 19. Jahrhunderts." *Archiv für Sozialgeschichte* 19 (1979): 231–62.

_____. *Ländliche Klassengesellschaft 1770–1848: Bauern und Unterschichten, Landwirtschaft und Gewerbe im östlichen Westfalen*. Göttingen, 1984.

————. "Property and Wood Theft: Agrarian Capitalism and Social Conflict in Rural Societies, 1800–1850. A Westphalian Case Study." In *Peasants and Lords in Modern Germany: Recent Studies in Agricultural History*, edited by Robert G. Moeller, pp. 52–80. Boston, 1986.

————. "Soziale Mobilität und familiale Plazierung bei Bauern und Unterschichten: Aspekte der ländlichen Gesellschaft im 19. Jahrhundert am Beispiel des Kirchspiels Quernheim im östlichen Westfalen." In *Familie zwischen Tradition und Moderne: Studien zur Geschichte der Familie in Deutschland und Frankreich vom 16. bis zum 20. Jahrhundert*, edited by Neithard Bulst, Joseph Goy, and Jochen Hoock, pp. 182–201. Göttingen, 1981.

————. "Der Weg vom proto-industriellen zum fabrik-industriellen Gewerbe in Ravensberg, 1830–1914." In *Rheinland-Westfalen im Industriezeitalter: Beiträge zur Landesgeschichte des 19. und 20. Jahrhunderts*, edited by Kurt Düwell and Wolfgang Köllmann, vol. 1, pp. 73–95. Wuppertal, 1983.

Morsey, Rudolf. "Die Deutsche Zentrumspartei." In *Das Ende der Parteien: Darstellungen und Dokumente*, edited by Erich Matthias and Rudolf Morsey, pp. 279–453. Düsseldorf, 1979. (Reprint of 1960 edition.)

————. *Die Deutsche Zentrumspartei 1917–1923*. Düsseldorf, 1966.

————. "Die deutschen Katholiken und der Nationalstaat zwischen Kulturkampf und Erstem Weltkrieg." In *Die deutschen Parteien vor 1918*, edited by Gerhard A. Ritter, pp. 270–98. Cologne, 1973.

————. *Der Untergang des politischen Katholizismus: Die Zentrumspartei zwischen christlichem Selbstverständnis und 'Nationaler Erhebung' 1932/33*. Zürich, 1977.

————. "Die Zentrumspartei in Rheinland und Westfalen." In *Politik und Landschaft*, edited by Walter Först, pp. 9–50. Cologne, 1969.

Müller, Hans. "Der deutsche Katholizismus 1918/19." *Geschichte in Wissenschaft und Unterricht* 17 (1966): 521–36.

Müller, Karl. *Die Frauenarbeit in der Landwirtschaft*. München-Gladbach, 1913.

Müller, Klaus. "Agrarische Interessenverbände in der Weimarer Republik." *Rheinische Vierteljahrsblätter* 38 (1974): 386–405.

————. "Politische Strömungen in den rechtsrheinischen Kreisen des Regierungsbezirks Köln (Sieg, Mühlheim, Wipperfürth, Gummersbach und Waldbröl) von 1879 bis 1900." Dissertation, Bonn, 1963.

————. "Das Rheinland als Gegenstand der historischen Wahlsoziologie." In *Wählerbewegungen in der deutschen Geschichte: Analysen und Berichte zu den Reichstagswahlen 1871–1933*, edited by Otto Büsch, Monika Wölk, and Wolfgang Wölk, pp. 393–408. Berlin, 1978.

————. "Zentrumspartei und agrarische Bewegung im Rheinland 1882–1903." In *Spiegel der Geschichte: Festgabe für Max Braubach*, pp. 828–57. Münster, 1964.

Münch, Friedrich. "Die agitatorische Tätigkeit des Bauernführers Heim: Zur Volksernährungsfrage aus der Sicht des Pressereferates des bayerischen Kriegsministeriums während des Ersten Weltkrieges." In *Bayern im Umbruch: Die Revolution von 1918, ihre Voraussetzungen, ihr Verlauf und ihre Folgen*, edited by Karl Bosl, pp. 301–44. Munich, 1969.

Münchmeyer, G., and Spaetgens, H. "Die Lohnentwicklung in der rheinischen Landwirtschaft." *Landwirtschaftliche Jahrbücher* 57 (1924): 434–537.

Münzberg, Hellmuth. *Deutschlands Verbrauch an Kraftfutter und Versorgung mit tierischen Erzeugnissen.* Berlin, 1928.

Münzinger, Adolf. *Der Arbeitsertrag der bäuerlichen Wirtschaft: Eine bäuerliche Betriebserhebung in Württemberg.* 2 vols. Berlin, 1929.

Muncy, Lysbeth Walker. "The Prussian *Landräte* in the Last Years of the Monarchy: A Case Study of Pomerania and the Rhineland in 1890–1918." *Central European History* 6 (1973): 299–338.

Muth, Heinrich. "Die Entstehung der Bauern- und Landarbeiterräte im November 1918 und die Politik des Bundes der Landwirte." *Vierteljahrshefte für Zeitgeschichte* 21 (1973): 1–38.

_____. "Die Führhungsschichten der Bauernverbände." In *Bauernschaft und Bauernstand 1500–1970*, edited by Günther Franz, pp. 291–321. Limburg/Lahn, 1975.

_____. "Zur Geschichte des Hunsrücker Bauernvereins." *Jahrbuch für Geschichte und Kunst des Mittelrheins und seiner Nachbargebiete* 20/21 (1968/69): 178–220.

Nacken, J. "Fruchtfolgesysteme in der nördlichen Hälfte der niederrheinischen Tieflandsbucht." Dissertation, Bonn, 1926.

Naumann, Friedrich. *Die politischen Parteien.* Berlin, 1910.

Neher, A. *Die wirtschaftliche und soziale Lage der Katholiken im westlichen Deutschland.* Part I. Rottweil, 1927.

Neuhaus, R. "Entwicklungstendenzen der bergischen Landwirtschaft." Dissertation, Bonn, 1932.

Neumann, Sigmund. *Die deutschen Parteien: Wesen und Wandel nach dem Kriege.* Berlin, 1932.

_____. *Modern Political Parties: Approaches to Comparative Politics.* Chicago, 1950.

Nichols, J. Alden. *Germany After Bismarck: The Caprivi Era.* Cambridge, Mass., 1958.

Nichtweiss, Johannes. *Die ausländischen Saisonarbeiter in der Landwirtschaft der östlichen und mittleren Gebiete des Deutschen Reiches: Ein Beitrag zur Geschichte der preussisch-deutschen Politik von 1890–1914.* Berlin, 1959.

Niklas, Wilhelm. "Die Entwicklung der Viehbestände während des Krieges und die hierauf bezüglichen behördlichen Massnahmen." In *Vieh und Fleisch in der deutschen Kriegswirtschaft*, pp. 1–20. Berlin, 1917.

Nipperdey, Thomas. "Interesserverbände und Parteien in Deutschland vor dem ersten Weltkrieg." In *Moderne deutsche Sozialgeschichte*, edited by Hans-Ulrich Wehler, pp. 369–88. Cologne, 1973.

_____. *Die Organisation der deutschen Parteien vor 1918.* Düsseldorf, 1961.

Noakes, Jeremy. *The Nazi Party in Lower Saxony 1921–1933.* Oxford, 1971.

Nocken, Ulrich. "Corporatism and Pluralism in Modern German History." In *Industrielle Gesellschaft und politisches System: Beiträge zur politischen Sozialgeschichte*, edited by Dirk Stegmann, Bernd-Jürgen Wendt, and Peter-Christian Witt, pp. 37–56. Bonn, 1978.

Nolan, Mary. *Social Democracy and Society: Working-Class Radicalism in Düsseldorf 1890–1920.* Cambridge, 1981.

Oberhansberg, Wilhelm. "Die landwirtschaftlichen Betriebsverhältnisse in dem Gebiet zwischen Ruhr- und Wuppertal (Industrie-Randzone)." Dissertation, Bonn, 1923.

Oertzen, Peter von. "Die grossen Streiks der Ruhrbergarbeiterschaft im Frühjahr 1919." *Vierteljahrshefte für Zeitgeschichte* 6 (1958): 231–63.

Osmond, Jonathan. "German Peasant Farmers in War and Inflation, 1914–1924: Stability or Stagnation?" In *Die deutsche Inflation: Eine Zwischenbilanz*, edited by Gerald D. Feldman, Carl-Ludwig Holtfrerich, Gerhard A. Ritter, and Peter-Christian Witt, pp. 289–307. Berlin, 1982.

————. "A Second Agrarian Mobilization? Peasant Associations in South and West Germany, 1918–24." In *Peasants and Lords in Modern Germany: Recent Studies in Agricultural History*, edited by Robert G. Moeller, pp. 168–97. Boston, 1986.

Ostertag, Robert von. "Versorgung mit Fleisch und Milch." In *Deutschlands Gesundheitsverhältnisse unter dem Einfluss des Krieges*, edited by F. Bumm, vol. 1, pp. 43–76. Stuttgart, 1928.

Pabst, Walter. "Der Ruhrkampf." In *Zwischen Ruhrkampf und Wiederaufbau*, edited by Walter Först, pp. 11–50. Cologne, 1972.

Panzer, Arno. "Industrie und Landwirtschaft in Deutschland im Spiegel der Aussenwirtschafts- und Zollpolitik von 1870 bis heute." *Zeitschrift für Agrargeschichte und Agrarsoziologie* 23 (1975): 71–85.

————. "Parteipolitische Ansätze der deutschen Bauernbewegungen bis 1933." In *Europäische Bauernparteien im 20. Jahrhundert*, edited by Heinz Gollwitzer, pp. 524–61. Stuttgart, 1977.

————. *Das Ringen um die deutsche Agrarpolitik von der Währungsstabilisierung bis zur Agrardebatte im Reichstag im Dezember 1928*. Kiel, 1970.

Papen, Franz von. *Der Wahrheit eine Gasse*. Munich, 1952.

Parker, William N. "Agriculture." In *American Economic Growth: An Economist's History of the United States*, edited by Lance E. Davis, Richard A. Easterlin, and William N. Parker, pp. 369–417. New York, 1972.

Patemann, Reinhard. *Der Kampf um die preussische Wahlrechtsreform im Ersten Weltkrieg*. Düsseldorf, 1964.

Perkins, J. A. "The Agricultural Revolution in Germany 1850–1914." *Journal of European Economic History* 10 (1981): 71–129.

Petzina, Dietmar. *Autarkiepolitik im Dritten Reich: Der nationalsozialistische Vierjahresplan*. Stuttgart, 1968.

————. *Die deutsche Wirtschaft in der Zwischenkriegszeit*. Wiesbaden, 1977.

————. "Hauptprobleme der deutschen Wirtschaftspolitik 1932/33." *Vierteljahrshefte für Zeitgeschichte* 15 (1967): 18–55.

Petzina, Dietmar, and Abelshauser, Werner. "Zum Problem der relativen Stagnation der deutschen Wirtschaft in den zwanziger Jahren." In *Industrielles System und politische Entwicklung in der Weimarer Republik*, edited by Hans Mommsen, Dietmar Petzina, and Bernd Weisbrod, pp. 57–76. Düsseldorf, 1974.

Pies, Eberhard. "Sozialpolitik und Zentrum 1924–1928: Zu den Bedingungen sozialpolitischer Theorie und Praxis der Deutschen Zentrumspartei in der Weimarer Republik." In *Industrielles System und politische Entwicklung in der Weimarer Republik*, edited by Hans Mommsen, Dietmar Petzina, and Bernd Weisbrod, pp. 259–70. Düsseldorf, 1974.

Pinot, Pierre. "Food Supply." In *Agriculture and Food Supply in France During the War*, pp. 155–311. New Haven, 1927.

Plachetka, Manfred Günther. "Die Getreide-Autarkiepolitik Bismarcks und seiner Nachfolger im Reichskanzleramt." Dissertation, Bonn, 1969.

Plattmann, Heinrich. "Entwicklung und Stand der Landwirtschaft in den Kreisen Büren und Paderborn während der letzten vier Jahrzehnten." Dissertation, Halle-Wittenberg, 1921.

Plum, Günther. *Gesellschaftsstruktur und politisches Bewusstsein in einer katholischen Region 1928–1933: Untersuchung am Beispiel des Regierungsbezirks Aachen.* Stuttgart, 1972.

Poppinga, Onno. *Bauern und Politik.* Frankfurt, 1975.

Pounds, Norman J. G. *The Ruhr: A Study in Historical and Economic Geography.* London, 1952.

Pridham, Geoffrey. *Hitler's Rise to Power: The Nazi Movement in Bavaria, 1923–1933.* London, 1973.

Priebe, Hermann. "The Modern Family Farm and its Problems: With Particular Reference to the Federal German Republic." In *Economic Problems of Agriculture in Industrial Societies,* edited by Ugo Papi and Charles Nunn, pp. 251–63. New York, 1969.

Pritzel, Ursula. "Wie reagierte die Landwirtschaft auf Preise? Eine Untersuchung an Hand der Preis- und Anbauflächenveränderungen des Getreides in den Jahren 1924/25 bis 1932/33." Dissertation, Jena, 1934.

Pützkaul, Heinrich. *Die landwirtschaftlichen Betriebsverhältnisse in der niederrheinischen Bucht besonders in den Kreisen Euskirchen, Düren, Bergheim und Landkreis Köln.* Berlin, 1912.

Puhle, Hans-Jürgen. *Agrarische Interessenpolitik und preussischer Konservatismus im wilhelminischen Reich (1893–1914): Ein Beitrag zur Analyse des Nationalismus in Deutschland am Beispiel des Bundes der Landwirte und der Deutsch-Konservativen Partei.* 2nd ed. Bonn, 1975.

_____. "Aspekte der Agrarpolitik im 'Organisierten Kapitalismus': Fragen und Probleme vergleichender Forschung." In *Sozialgeschichte heute: Festschrift für Hans Rosenberg,* edited by Hans-Ulrich Wehler, pp. 543–64. Göttingen, 1974.

_____. "Conservatism in Modern German History." *Journal of Contemporary History* 13 (1978): 689–720.

_____. "Lords and Peasants in the Kaiserreich." In *Peasants and Lords in Modern Germany: Recent Studies in Agricultural History,* edited by Robert G. Moeller, pp. 81–109. Boston, 1986.

_____. "Parlament, Parteien und Interessenverbände 1890–1914." In *Das kaiserliche Deutschland: Politik und Gesellschaft 1870–1918,* edited by Michael Stürmer, pp. 340–77. Düsseldorf, 1970.

_____. *Politische Agrarbewegungen in kapitalistischen Industriegesellschaften: Deutschland, USA und Frankreich im 20. Jahrhundert.* Göttingen, 1975.

_____. *Von der Agrarkrise zum Präfaschismus: Thesen zum Stellenwert der agrarischen Interessenverbände in der deutschen Politik am Ende des 19. Jahrhunderts.* Wiesbaden, 1972.

_____. "Warum gibt es in Westeuropa keine Bauernparteien? Zum politischen Potential des Agrarsektors in Frankreich und Spanien." In *Europäische Bauernparteien im 20. Jahrhundert,* edited by Heinz Gollwitzer, pp. 603–67. Stuttgart, 1977.

Quabeck, Anton. *Handbuch für die Spar- und Darlehenskassen-Vereine im Verbande ländlicher Genossenschaften der Provinz Westfalen.* Münster, 1913.

_____. "Das landwirtschaftliche Genossenschaftswesen." In *Beiträge zur Geschichte des westfälischen Bauernstandes*, edited by Engelbert Freiherr Kerckerinck zu Borg, pp. 448–530. Berlin, 1912.

Reekers, Stephanie. *Westfalens Bevölkerung 1818–1955: Die Bevölkerungsentwicklung der Gemeinden und Kreise im Zahlenbild*. Münster, 1956.

Reif, Heinz. "Adel und landwirtschaftliches Vereinswesen im katholischen Westfalen 1819–1862." In *Rheinland-Westfalen im Industriezeitalter: Beiträge zur Landesgeschichte des 19. und 20. Jahrhunderts*, edited by Kurt Düwell and Wolfgang Köllmann, vol. 1, pp. 39–60. Wuppertal, 1983.

———. " 'Erhaltung adligen Stamms und Namens'—Adelsfamilie und Statussicherung im Münsterland 1770 bis 1914." In *Familie zwischen Tradition und Moderne: Studien zur Geschichte der Familie in Deutschland und Frankreich vom 16. bis zum 20. Jahrhundert*, edited by Neithard Bulst, Joseph Goy, and Jochen Hoock, pp. 275–308. Göttingen, 1981.

———. *Westfälischer Adel 1770–1860: Vom Herrschaftsstand zur regionalen Elite*. Göttingen, 1979.

Renborg, Ulf. "Tendencies Towards Concentration and Specialization in Agriculture." In *Economic Problems of Agriculture in Industrial Societies*, edited by Ugo Papi and Charles Nunn, pp. 209–33. New York, 1969.

Reulecke, Jürgen, ed. *Arbeiterbewegung an Rhein und Ruhr: Beiträge zur Geschichte der Arbeiterbewegung in Rheinland-Westfalen*. Wuppertal, 1974.

Reulecke, Jürgen, and Weber, Wolfhard, eds. *Fabrik–Familie–Feierabend: Beiträge zur Sozialgeschichte des Alltags im Industriezeitalter*. Wuppertal, 1978.

Rinteln, Paul. *Das Risiko im landwirtschaftlichen Betriebe: Ein Beitrag zur Frage des Aufbaues und der Führung bodengebundener Intensivbetriebe*. Berlin, 1938.

Rinteln, Paul, and Zimmermann, Edmond. *Die Landwirtschaft in Westfalen und Lippe*. Münster, 1940.

Ritter, Emil. *Die katholisch-soziale Bewegung und der Volksverein für das katholische Deutschland*. Cologne, 1954.

Ritter, Gerhard A. "Kontinuität und Umformung des deutschen Parteiensystems 1918–1920." In *Entstehung und Wandel der modernen Gesellschaft: Festschrift für Hans Rosenberg zum 65. Geburtstag*, edited by Gerhard A. Ritter, pp. 342–84. Berlin, 1970.

———. *Wahlgeschichtliches Arbeitsbuch: Materialien zur Statistik des Kaiserreichs 1871–1918*. Munich, 1980.

———, ed. *Die deutschen Parteien vor 1918*. Cologne, 1973.

———, ed. *Entstehung und Wandel der modernen Gesellschaft: Festschrift für Hans Rosenberg zum 65. Geburtstag*. Berlin, 1970.

Ritter, Kurt. *Die Einwirkungen des weltwirtschaftlichen Verkehrs auf die Entwicklung und den Betrieb der Landwirtschaft insbesondere in Deutschland*. Berlin, 1921.

Roberts, David D. "Petty Bourgeois Fascism in Italy: Form and Content." In *Who Were the Fascists? Social Origins of European Fascism*, edited by Stein Ugelvik Larsen, Bernt Hagtvet, and Jan Petter Myklebust, pp. 337–47. Bergen, 1980.

Rogge, Karl. "Die Betriebskreditorganisation des landwirtschaftlichen Genossenschaftswesens seit der Währungsstabilisierung." Dissertation, Bonn, 1928.

———. "Gegenwartsfragen der Realteilung des ländlichen Grundbesitzes in Westdeutschland." In *Die Vererbung des ländlichen Grundbesitzes in der Nachkriegszeit*,

Schriften des Vereins für Sozialpolitik, vol. 178, pp. 331–84. Munich, 1930.

_____. "Die Gestaltung der geschlossenen Vererbung in Westdeutschland." In *Die Vererbung des ländlichen Grundbesitzes in der Nachkriegszeit*, Schriften des Vereins für Sozialpolitik, vol. 178, pp. 293–330. Munich, 1930.

Rolfes, Max. *Die Bodennutzung in bäuerlichen Betrieben*. Berlin, 1935.

Rolfes, Max, and Zörner, Hans. "Die Umsatzstruktur bäuerlicher Betriebe." *Landwirtschaftliche Jahrbücher* 74 (1931): 945–1003.

Romeyk, Horst. "Die Deutsche Volkspartei in Rheinland und Westfalen 1918–1933." *Rheinische Vierteljahrsblätter* 39 (1975): 189–236.

Rosenberg, Arthur. *Imperial Germany: The Birth of the German Republic 1871–1918*. Trans. by Ian F. D. Morrow. Boston, 1964.

Rosenberg, Hans. *Grosse Depression und Bismarckzeit: Wirtschaftsablauf, Gesellschaft und Politik in Mitteleuropa*. Berlin, 1967.

_____. *Machteliten und Wirtschaftskonjunkturen: Studien zur neueren deutschen Sozial- und Wirtschaftsgeschichte*. Göttingen, 1978.

_____. *Probleme der deutschen Sozialgeschichte*. Frankfurt, 1969.

_____. "Die Pseudodemokratisierung der Rittergutsbesitzerklasse." In *Machteliten und Wirtschaftskonjunkturen: Studien zur neueren deutschen Sozial- und Wirtschaftsgeschichte*, pp. 83–101. Göttingen, 1978.

Ross, Ronald. *Beleaguered Tower: The Dilemma of Political Catholicism in Wilhelmine Germany*. Notre Dame, 1976.

_____. "Enforcing the Kulturkampf in the Bismarckian State and the Limits of Coercion in Imperial Germany." *Journal of Modern History* 56 (1984): 456–82.

Rossberg, Hans. *Der Anteil der Genossenschaften am Neuaufbau des Agrarkredits*. Berlin, 1929.

Rothkegel, Walther. "Die Bewegungen der Kaufpreise für ländliche Besitzungen und die Entwicklung der Getreidepreise 1895–1909." *Schmollers Jahrbuch* 34 (1910): 1689–1747.

_____. *Handbuch der Schätzungslehre für Grundbesitzungen*. Vol. 1. Berlin, 1930.

_____. *Die Kaufpreise für ländliche Besitzungen im Königreich Preussen von 1895 bis 1906*. Leipzig, 1910.

Rürup, Reinhard. "Demokratische Revolution und 'dritter Weg': Die deutsche Revolution von 1918/19 in der neuen wissenschaftlichen Diskussion." *Geschichte und Gesellschaft* 9 (1983): 278–301.

_____. "Problems of the German Revolution 1918–19." *Journal of Contemporary History* 4 (1968): 109–35.

_____, ed. *Arbeiter- und Soldatenräte im rheinisch-westfälischen Industriegebiet: Studien zur Geschichte der Revolution 1918/19*. Wuppertal, 1975.

Sagawe, Berthold. *Krieg und Landwirtschaft: Eine zahlenmässige Darstellung nach Buchführungsergebnissen aus 112 Betrieben der Buchstelle der DLG von 1911/12–1919/20*. Berlin, 1922.

Sauermann, Dietmar. "Hofidee und bäuerliche Familienverträge in Westfalen." *Rheinisch-Westfälische Zeitschrift für Volkskunde* 17 (1970): 58–78.

_____, ed. *Knechte und Mägde um 1900*. Münster, 1972.

Saul, Klaus. "Der Kampf um das Landproletariat: Sozialistische Landagitation, Grossgrundbesitz und preussische Staatsverwaltung." *Archiv für Sozialgeschichte* 15 (1975): 163–208.

————. *Staat, Industrie, Arbeiterbewegung im Kaiserreich: Zur Innen- und Aussenpolitik des Wilhelminischen Deutschland 1903–1914*. Düsseldorf, 1974.

Schaap, Klaus. *Die Endphase der Weimarer Republik im Freistaat Oldenburg: 1928–1933*. Düsseldorf, 1978.

Schauff, Johannes. *Das Wahlverhalten der deutschen Katholiken im Kaiserreich und in der Weimarer Republik*. Edited by Rudolf Morsey. Mainz, 1975.

Schieck, Hans. "Die Behandlung der Sozialisierungsfrage in den Monaten nach dem Umsturz." In *Vom Kaiserreich zur Republik*, edited by Eberhard Kolb, pp. 138–64. Cologne, 1972.

————. "Der Kampf um die deutsche Wirtschaftspolitik nach dem Novemberumsturz 1918." Dissertation, Heidelberg, 1958.

Schindler, A. "Die Standardisierung und die Reform des Abstazes deutscher landwirtschaftlicher Erzeugnisse." In *Deutsche Agrarpolitik im Rahmen der inneren und äusseren Wirtschaftspolitik*, edited by Fritz Beckmann, Bernhard Harms, Theodor Brinkmann, Hermann Bente, Edgar Salin, and Werner Henkelmann, vol. 1, pp. 743–72. Berlin, 1932.

Schissler, Hanna. "The Junkers: Notes on the Social and Historical Significance of the Agrarian Elite in Prussia." In *Peasants and Lords in Modern Germany: Recent Studies in Agricultural History*, edited by Robert G. Moeller, pp. 24–51. Boston, 1986.

Schleh, A. "Die Entwicklung des landwirtschaftlichen Vereinswesens in Westfalen." In *Die Entwicklung der Landeskultur in der Provinz Westfalen im 19. Jahrhundert*, edited by E. Haselhoff and H. Breme, pp. 112–39. Münster, 1900.

Schlotter, Peter. *Die ländliche Arbeiterfrage in der Provinz Westfalen*. Leipzig, 1907.

Schmidt, Gustav. "Parlamentarisierung oder 'Präventive Konterrevolution'? Die deutsche Innenpolitik im Spannungsfeld konservativer Sammlungsbewegung und latenter Reformbestrebungen (1907–1914)." In *Gesellschaft, Parlament und Regierung: Zur Geschichte des Parlamentarismus in Deutschland*, edited by Gerhard A. Ritter, pp. 249–78. Düsseldorf, 1974.

Schmidt, Willy. "Die landwirtschaftlichen Verhältnisse des Siegeskreises." Dissertation, Bonn, 1923.

Schneider, Michael. *Die Christlichen Gewerkschaften 1894–1933*. Bonn, 1982.

————. "Religion and Labour Organisation: The Christian Trade Unions in the Wilhelmine Empire." *European Studies Review* 12 (1982): 345–69.

Schoenbaum, David. *Hitler's Social Revolution: Class and Status in Nazi Germany 1933–1939*. Garden City, 1966.

Schöne, Gerhard. "Die Verflechtung wirtschaftlicher und politischer Motive in der Haltung der Parteien zum Bülowschen Zolltarif (1901/2)." Dissertation, Halle-Wittenberg, 1934.

Schönhoven, Klaus. *Die Bayerische Volkspartei 1924–1932*. Düsseldorf, 1972.

Schramm, Gottfried. "Klassengegensätze im ersten Weltkrieg." *Geschichte und Gesellschaft* 2 (1976): 244–60.

————. "Militarisierung und Demokratisierung: Typen der Massenintegration im ersten Weltkrieg." *Francia* 3 (1975): 376–97.

Schürmann, A. *Die Milchversorgung des Ruhrkohlenbezirks*. Berlin, 1931.

————. *Westdeutschland als Markt für Milch und Milcherzeugnisse*. Berlin, 1933.

Schulte, Eduard. *Kriegschronik der Stadt Münster 1914–1918*. Münster, 1930.

Schulte, Regina. "Bauernmägde in Bayern am Ende des 19. Jahrhunderts." In *Frauen su-*

chen ihre Geschichte: Historische Studien zum 19. und 20. Jahrhundert, edited by Karin Hausen, pp. 110–27. Munich, 1983.

Schulz, Gerhard. "Räte, Wirtschaftsstände und die Transformation des industriellen Verbandswesens am Anfang der Weimarer Republik." In *Gesellschaft, Parlament und Regierung: Zur Geschichte des Parlamentarismus in Deutschland*, edited by Gerhard A. Ritter, pp. 355–66. Düsseldorf, 1974.

_____. "Über Entstehung und Formen von Interessengruppen in Deutschland seit Beginn der Industrialisierung." *Politische Vierteljahresschrift* 2 (1961): 124–54.

Schumacher, Martin. *Land und Politik: Eine Untersuchung über politische Parteien und agrarische Interessen 1914–1923*. Düsseldorf, 1978.

_____. *Mittelstandsfront und Republik: Die Wirtschaftspartei—Reichspartei des deutschen Mittelstandes 1919–1933*. Düsseldorf, 1972.

_____. "Thesen zur Lage und Entwicklung der deutschen Landwirtschaft in der Inflationszeit (1919–1923)." In *Historische Prozesse der deutschen Inflation 1914 bis 1924: Ein Tagungsbericht*, edited by Otto Büsch and Gerald D. Feldman, pp. 215–17. Berlin, 1978.

Schumann, Hans-Gerd. "The Problem of Conservatism: Some Notes on Methodology." *Journal of Contemporary History* 13 (1978): 803–17.

Schwab, Herbert. "Deutscher Bauernbund (DB) 1909–1927." In *Die bürgerlichen Parteien: Handbuch der bürgerlichen Parteien und anderer bürgerlicher Interessenorganisationen vom Vormärz bis zum Jahre 1945*, edited by Dieter Fricke, vol. 1, pp. 415–21. Berlin, 1968.

Seraphim, Hans-Jürgen. *Das Heuerlingswesen in Nordwestdeutschland*. Münster, 1948.

Sering, Max. *Agrarkrisen und Agrarzölle*. Berlin, 1925.

_____. *Internationale Preisbewegung und Lage der Landwirtschaft in den aussertropischen Ländern*. Berlin, 1929.

_____, ed. *Die deutsche Landwirtschaft unter volks- und weltwirtschaftlichen Gesichtspunkten*. Berlin, 1932.

Shanin, Teodor. *The Awkward Class: Political Sociology of the Peasantry in a Developing Society, Russia 1910–1925*. Oxford, 1972.

_____. "The Nature and Logic of the Peasant Economy." *Journal of Peasant Studies* 1 (1973/74): 63–80, 186–206.

Skalweit, August. *Die Deutsche Kriegsernährungswirtschaft*. Stuttgart, 1927.

_____. "Die Familienwirtschaft als Grundlage für ein System der Sozialökonomie." *Weltwirtschaftliches Archiv* 20 (1924): 231–46.

_____. *Das Schwein in der Kriegsernährungswirtschaft*. Berlin, 1917.

_____. *Die Viehhandelsverbände in der deutschen Kriegswirtschaft*. Berlin, 1917.

Skalweit, August, and Krüger, Hans. *Die Nahrungsmittelwirtschaft grosser Städte im Kriege*. Berlin, 1917.

Snowden, Frank M. "From Sharecropper to Proletarian: The Background to Fascism in Rural Tuscany, 1880–1920." In *Gramsci and Italy's Passive Revolution*, edited by John A. Davis, pp. 136–71. London, 1979.

Sogemeier, Martin. *Die Entwicklung und Regelung des Arbeitsmarktes im rheinisch-westfälischen Industriegebiet im Kriege und in der Nachkriegszeit*. Jena, 1922.

Sølta, Jan. *Die Bauern der Lausitz: Eine Untersuchung des Differenzierungsprozesses der Bauernschaft im Kapitalismus*. Bautzen, 1976.

Southern, David B. "The Impact of the Inflation: Inflation, the Courts and Revaluation." In *Social Change and Political Development in Weimar Germany*, edited by Richard Bessel and E. J. Feuchtwanger, pp. 55–76. London, 1981.

Spee, Ferdinand Graf von. "Die landwirtschaftlichen Betriebsverhältnisse in den Gemeinden des Kreises Olpe." Dissertation, Bonn, 1935.

Sperber, Jonathan. *Popular Catholicism in Nineteenth-Century Germany*. Princeton, 1984.

————. "Roman Catholic Religious Identity in Rhineland-Westphalia 1800–70: Quantitative Examples and Some Political Implications." *Social History* 7 (1982): 305–18.

————. "The Shaping of Political Catholicism in the Ruhr Basin, 1848–1881." *Central European History* 16 (1983): 347–67.

————. "The Transformation of Catholic Associations in the Northern Rhineland and Westphalia 1830–1870." *Journal of Social History* 15 (1981): 253–63.

Stadthagen, Hans, and Briefs, Goetz. *Die Preisprüfungsstellen*. Berlin, 1917.

Stegmann, Dirk. "Deutsche Zoll- und Handelspolitik 1924/25–1929 unter besonderer Berücksichtigung agrarischer und industrieller Interessen." In *Industrielles System und politische Entwicklung in der Weimarer Republik*, edited by Hans Mommsen, Dietmar Petzina, and Bernd Weisbrod, pp. 499–513. Düsseldorf, 1974.

————. *Die Erben Bismarcks: Parteien und Verbände in der Spätphase des Wilhelminischen Deutschlands, Sammlungspolitik 1897–1918*. Cologne, 1970.

Stoltenberg, Gerhard. *Politische Strömungen im schleswig-holsteinischen Landvolk 1918–1933: Ein Beitrag zur politischen Meinungsbildung in der Weimarer Republik*. Düsseldorf, 1962.

Studensky, G. A. "Die ökonomische Natur der bäuerlichen Gesellschaft." *Weltwirtschaftliches Archiv* 28 (1928): 318–39.

Stürmer, Michael. *Koalition und Opposition in der Weimarer Republik, 1924–1928*. Düsseldorf, 1967.

————, ed. *Das kaiserliche Deutschland: Politik und Gesellschaft, 1890–1914*. Düsseldorf, 1970.

Stump, Wolfgang. *Geschichte und Organisation der Zentrumspartei in Düsseldorf 1917–1933*. Düsseldorf, 1971.

Tampke, Jürgen. *The Ruhr and Revolution: The Revolutionary Movement in the Rhenish-Westphalian Industrial Region, 1912–1919*. Canberra, 1978.

Teichmann, Ulrich. *Die Politik der Agrarpreisstützung: Marktbeeinflussung als Teil des Agrarinterventionismus in Deutschland*. Cologne-Deutz, 1955.

Tenfelde, Klaus. *Proletarische Provinz: Radikalisierung und Widerstand in Penzberg/ Oberbayern 1900–1945*. Munich, 1982.

————. *Sozialgeschichte der Bergarbeiterschaft an der Ruhr im 19. Jahrhundert*. Bonn–Bad Godesberg, 1977.

Terhalle, Fritz. *Freie oder gebundene Preisbildung? Ein Beitrag zu unserer Preispolitik seit Beginn des Weltkrieges*. Jena, 1920.

Thiess, Karl. *Höchstpreis-Politik*. Berlin, 1916.

Thiess, Karl, and Wiedenfeld, Kurt. *Die Preisbildung im Kriege*. Berlin, 1916.

Tilly, Charles. *The Vendée*. Cambridge, Mass., 1964.

Tilton, Timothy Alan. *Nazism, Neo-Nazism, and the Peasantry*. Bloomington, 1975.

Timoshenko, Vladimir P. *World Agriculture and the Depression*. Ann Arbor, 1933.

Tipton, Frank B. "Farm Labor and Power Politics: Germany 1850–1914." *Journal of Economic History* 34 (1974): 951–79.

———. *Regional Variations in the Economic Development of Germany during the Nineteenth Century.* Middletown, Conn., 1976.

Tirrell, Sarah Rebecca. *German Agrarian Politics After Bismarck's Fall: The Formation of the Farmers' League.* New York, 1951.

Topf, Erwin. *Die grüne Front: Der Kampf um den deutschen Acker.* Berlin, 1933.

Tyszka, Carl von. *Der Konsument in der Kriegswirtschaft.* Tübingen, 1916.

Uhle, Reinhard. "Landwirtschaftlicher Gross- und Kleinbetrieb während der Kriegswirtschaft." *Zeitschrift für die gesamte Staatswissenschaft* 78 (1924): 346–93, 699–744.

Urwin, Derek W. *From Ploughshare to Ballotbox: The Politics of Agrarian Defense in Europe.* Oslo, 1980.

Vasters, J. *Die Landwirtschaft in den Kreisen Erkelenz, Geilenkirchen und Jülich.* Berlin, 1912.

Vergopoulos, Kōstas. "Capitalism and Peasant Productivity." *Journal of Peasant Studies* 5 (1978): 446–65.

Verhandlungen der am 20. und 21. März 1893 in Berlin abgehaltenen Generalversammlung des Vereins für Sozialpolitik über die Bodenbesitzverteilung und die Sicherung des Kleingrundbesitzes. Schriften des Vereins für Sozialpolitik, vol. 58. Leipzig, 1895.

Vierhaus, Rudolf. "Auswirkungen der Krise um 1930 in Deutschland: Beiträge zu einer historisch-psychologischen Analyse." In *Die Staats- und Wirtschaftskrise des Deutschen Reiches 1929–1933*, edited by Werner Conze and Hans Raupach, pp. 155–75. Stuttgart, 1967.

———. "Wahlen und Wählerverhalten in Ostwestfalen und Lippe, untersucht an den Reichstags- und Landtagswahlen von 1867 bis 1912/13." *Westfälische Forschungen* 21 (1968): 54–68.

Vogel, Adolf, and Boehm, Carl. "Einfluss der Preise auf die Produktion in der Landwirtschaft." *Vierteljahrshefte zur Wirtschaftsforschung* New Series 12 (1937/38): 34–53.

Vogelsang, Thilo. *Reichswehr, Staat und NSDAP: Beiträge zur deutschen Geschichte 1930–1932.* Stuttgart, 1962.

Volkov, Shulamit. *The Rise of Popular Antimodernism in Germany: The Urban Master Artisans 1873–1896.* Princeton, 1978.

Walter, A., and Engel, H. *Die Entwicklung der landwirtschaftlichen Zölle seit 1902.* Berlin, 1933.

Warmbold, H. *Futtergetreide im Kriege.* Berlin, 1917.

Warstat, Hans Georg. "Die Preisentwicklung landwirtschaftlicher Produkte und Produktionsmittel vor dem Kriege und nach der Inflation." Dissertation, Bonn, 1933.

Webb, Steven B. "Agricultural Protection in Wilhelminian Germany: Forging an Empire with Pork and Rye." *Journal of Economic History* 42 (1982): 309–26.

———. "Tariff Protection for the Iron Industry, Cotton Textiles and Agriculture in Germany, 1879–1914." *Jahrbücher für Nationalökonomie und Statistik* 192 (1977): 336–57.

Weber, Eugen. *Peasants into Frenchmen: The Modernization of Rural France 1870–1914.* Stanford, 1976.

Weber, Max. *Gesammelte politische Schriften*. Munich, 1921.

Weber-Kellermann, Ingeborg. *Die deutsche Familie: Versuch einer Sozialgeschichte*. Frankfurt, 1974.

Wegmann, Dietrich. *Die leitenden staatlichen Verwaltungsbeamten der Provinz Westfalen 1815–1918*. Münster, 1969.

Wehler, Hans-Ulrich. *Das deutsche Kaiserreich 1871–1918*. Göttingen, 1973.

————. "Die Polen im Ruhrgebiet bis 1918." In *Krisenherde des Kaiserreichs 1871–1918: Studien zur deutschen Sozial- und Verfassungsgeschichte*, pp. 220–37 (2nd ed.). Göttingen, 1979.

Wesemann, Hans-Otto. "Der Westfälische Bauernverein." Dissertation, Halle-Wittenberg, 1927.

White, Dan S. *The Splintered Party: National Liberals in Hessen and the Reich, 1867–1918*. Cambridge, Mass., 1976.

Wieck, Hans Georg. *Die Entstehung der CDU und die Wiedergründung des Zentrums im Jahre 1945*. Düsseldorf, 1953.

Wiedtfeldt, Otto. *Die Bewirtschaftung von Korn, Mehl und Brot im Deutschen Reiche: Ihre Entstehung und ihre Grundzüge*. Berlin, 1919.

Wiegelmann, Günter, ed. *Kultureller Wandel im 19. Jahrhundert: Verhandlungen des 18. Deutschen Volkskunde-Kongresses in Trier vom 13. bis 18. September 1971*. Göttingen, 1973.

Wiese, Leopold von, ed. *Das Dorf als soziales Gebilde*. Munich, 1928.

Wiesemann, Falk. "Arbeitskonflikte in der Landwirtschaft während der NS-Zeit in Bayern 1933–1938." *Vierteljahrshefte für Zeitgeschichte* 25 (1977): 573–90.

————. "Juden auf dem Lande: Die Wirtschaftliche Ausgrenzung der jüdischen Viehhändler in Bayern." In *Die Reihen fast geschlossen: Beiträge zur Geschichte des Alltags unterm Nationalsozialismus*, edited by Detlev Peukert and Jürgen Reulecke, pp. 381–96. Wuppertal, 1981.

Wilken, Folkert. *Volkswirtschaftliche Theorie der landwirtschaftlichen Preissteigerungen in Deutschland von 1895–1913: Eine Studie über die Beziehungen zwischen Agrarwirtschaft und Industriewirtschaft*. Berlin, 1925.

Wilms, Wilhelm. "Grossbauern und Kleingrundbesitz in Minden-Ravensberg." Dissertation, Berlin, 1913.

Winkel, Harald. "Zur Anwendung des technischen Fortschritts in der Landwirtschaft im ausgehenden 19. Jahrhundert." *Zeitschrift für Agrargeschichte und Agrarsoziologie* 27 (1979): 19–31.

Winkelmann. "Die gegenwärtigen bäuerlichen Verhältnisse in der Provinz Westfalen." In *Bäuerliche Zustände in Deutschland*, Schriften des Vereins für Sozialpolitik, vol. 23, pp. 1–24. Leipzig, 1883.

Winkelmann and Jaspers. "Der Personalkredit des ländlichen Kleingrundbesitzes in Westfalen." In *Der Personalkredit des ländlichen Kleingrundbesitzes in Deutschland*, Schriften des Vereins für Sozialpolitik, vol. 74, pp. 135–68. Leipzig, 1896.

Winkler, Heinrich August. "Extremismus der Mitte? Sozialgeschichtliche Aspekte der nationalsozialistischen Machtergreifung." *Vierteljahrshefte für Zeitgeschichte* 20 (1972): 175–91.

————. "From Social Protectionism to National Socialism: The German Small-Business Movement in Comparative Perspective." *Journal of Modern History* 48 (1976): 1–18.

_____. "German Society, Hitler and the Illusion of Restoration 1930–1933." *Journal of Contemporary History* 11 (1976): 1–16.

_____. *Mittelstand, Demokratie und Nationalsozialismus: Die politische Entwicklung von Handwerk und Kleinhandel in der Weimarer Republik.* Cologne, 1972.

_____. *Pluralismus oder Protektionismus? Verfassungspolitische Probleme des Verbandswesens im Deutschen Kaiserreich.* Wiesbaden, 1972.

_____, ed. *Organisierter Kapitalismus: Voraussetzungen und Anfänge.* Göttingen, 1974.

Witt, Peter-Christian. *Die Finanzpolitik des Deutschen Reiches von 1902 bis 1913: Eine Studie zur Innenpolitik des Wilhelminischen Deutschland.* Lübeck, 1970.

_____. "Finanzpolitik und sozialer Wandel in Krieg und Inflation 1918–1924." In *Industrielles System und politische Entwicklung in der Weimarer Republik*, edited by Hans Mommsen, Dietmar Petzina, and Bernd Weisbrod, pp. 395–426. Düsseldorf, 1974.

_____. "Der preussische Landrat als Steuerbeamter 1891–1918: Bemerkungen zur politischen und sozialen Funktion des deutschen Beamtentums." In *Deutschland in der Weltpolitik des 19. und 20. Jahrhunderts: Fritz Fischer zum 65. Geburtstag*, edited by Immanuel Geiss and Bernd-Jürgen Wendt, pp. 205–19. Düsseldorf, 1973.

_____. "Staatliche Wirtschaftspolitik in Deutschland 1918–1923: Entwicklung und Zerstörung einer modernen wirtschaftspolitischen Strategie." In *Die deutsche Inflation: Eine Zwischenbilanz*, edited by Gerald D. Feldman, Carl-Ludwig Holtfrerich, Gerhard A. Ritter, and Peter-Christian Witt, pp. 151–79. Berlin, 1982.

Wolf, Eric R. *Peasant Wars of the Twentieth Century.* New York, 1969.

_____. *Peasants.* Englewood Cliffs, N.J., 1966.

Wrede, Adam. *Eifler Volkskunde.* 3rd ed. Bonn, 1960.

Wunder, Heide. "Zum Stand der Erforschung frühmoderner und moderner bäuerlicher Eliten in Deutschland, Oesterreich und der Schweiz." *Archiv für Sozialgeschichte* 19 (1979): 597–607.

Wunderlich, Frieda. *Farm Labor in Germany 1810–1945: Its Historical Development within the Framework of Agricultural and Social Policy.* Princeton, 1961.

Wurzbacher, Gerhard. "Die berufliche Gliederung in ihrem Wandel und in ihren Auswirkungen auf die gemeindliche Verbundenheit der Bevölkerung." In *Das Dorf im Spannungsfeld industrieller Entwicklung: Untersuchung an den 45 Dörfern und Weilern einer westdeutschen ländlichen Gemeinde*, pp. 29–73. Stuttgart, 1961.

_____, ed. *Das Dorf im Spannungsfeld industrieller Entwicklung: Untersuchung an den 45 Dörfern und Weilern einer westdeutschen ländlichen Gemeinde.* Stuttgart, 1961.

Wygodzinski, Willy, and Müller, August. *Das Genossenschaftswesen in Deutschland.* Leipzig, 1929.

Zeender, John K. "German Catholics and the Concept of an Interconfessional Party, 1917.

_____. "Die rheinische Landwirtschaft." In *Die Rheinprovinz 1815–1915: Hundert Jahre Preussischer Herrschaft am Rhein*, edited by Joseph Hansen, vol. 1, pp. 250–300. Berlin, 1917.

Wygodzinski, Willy, and Müller, August. *Das Genossenschaftswesen in Deutschland.* Leipzig, 1929.

Zeender, John K. "German Catholics and the Concept of an Interconfessional Party, 1900–1922." *Journal of Central European Affairs* 23 (1964): 424–39.

_____. "The German Catholics and the Presidential Election of 1925." *Journal of Modern History* 35 (1963): 366–81.

_____. "The German Center Party during World War I: An Internal Study." *Catholic Historical Review* 42 (1957): 441–68.

_____. *The German Center Party 1890–1906*. Philadelphia, 1976.

Ziche, Joachim. "Kritik der deutschen Bauerntumsideologie." *Sociologia Ruralis* 8 (1968): 105–41.

Zörner, Hans. "Der Einfluss der Betriebsgrösse auf Bodennutzung und Verwertung der Bodenprodukte." In *Deutsche Agrarpolitik im Rahmen der inneren und äusseren Wirtschaftspolitik*, edited by Fritz Beckmann, Bernhard Harms, Theodor Brinkmann, Hermann Bente, Edgar Salin, and Werner Henkelmann, vol. 1, pp. 465–80. Berlin, 1932.

Zofka, Zdenek. *Die Ausbreitung des Nationalsozialismus auf dem Lande: Eine regionale Fallstudie zur politischen Einstellung der Landbevölkerung in der Zeit des Aufstiegs und der Machtergreifung der NSDAP 1928–1936*. Munich, 1979.

Index